An Introduction to Language

An Introduction to Language

FOURTH EDITION

Victoria Fromkin

University of California, Los Angeles

Robert Rodman

North Carolina State University, Raleigh

HOLT, RINEHART AND WINSTON, INC.
New York Chicago San Francisco Philadelphia Montreal
Toronto London Sydney Tokyo

To Disa, Emily, and Zachary

Senior Acquisitions Editor: Charlyce Jones Owen
Senior Project Editor: Lester A. Sheinis
Senior Production Manager: Nancy Myers
Senior Design Supervisor: Louis Scardino
Text Design: Caliber Design Planning
Cover Design: Albert D'Agostino

Library of Congress Cataloging-in-Publication Data

Fromkin, Victoria.
  An introduction to language.

  Includes bibliographies and index.
  1. Language and languages.   2. Linguistics.
I. Rodman, Robert.   II. Title.
P106.F75   1988   410   87–15005

ISBN 0-03-006532-1

Printed in the United States of America

8 9 0 1   118   9 8 7 6 5 4 3 2

Holt, Rinehart and Winston, Inc.
The Dryden Press
Saunders College Publishing

PREFACE

Interest in linguistics—the study of human language—has existed throughout history. Many of the questions this book discusses have been asked for thousands of years. What is language? What do you know when you know a language? Is language unique to the human species? What is the origin of language? Why are there many languages? How and why do languages change? What is the meaning of "meaning"? How do children learn language? Are some languages and dialects simpler than or superior to others? Can machines talk? Can computers understand? What is the biological basis for human language?

In addition to the philosophical interest, practical considerations have also motivated linguists, psychologists, philosophers, educators, sociologists, neurologists, communication engineers, and computer scientists to address these questions. Linguistics provides a theoretical basis for practical applications that include the diagnosis and treatment of language disorders such as aphasia and dyslexia, the planning of "language arts" curricula in schools, the fight against illiteracy in many nations of the world, the development of automatic, computerized speech production and recognition, the learning of foreign languages, and the simplication of legal language.

For these reasons the first three editions of this text were directed toward students of many disciplines. The book has been used in both nonlinguistic and linguistic courses, for majors in computer science and English, in speech pathology and anthropology, in communication studies and philosophy. This fourth edition continues this approach and adds new material to make it suitable for even a wider audience. It also reflects the new developments in linguistic theory and related fields.

Part One sets the framework by discussing the nature of human language and the nature of grammar, linguistic creativity, language universals, and nonhuman communication.

Chapters 2 through 6 in Part Two examine the kinds of linguistic knowledge speakers of Arabic or Zulu, English or Cherokee, or any other human language, possess—the "Grammatical Aspects of Language," which include sounds and sound patterns (phonetics and phonology), words and word formation (morphology), sentence structure (syntax), and meaning (semantics). These chapters have been substantially revised since the third edition; for example, syllable and metrical structures in phonology are discussed, developments in syntactic theory have motivated basic changes in the discussion on syntax, and the sections on semantics and pragmatics are expanded.

Part Three examines "Social Aspects of Language" in its three chapters on language variation, language change, and writing. A new section on Hispanic English has been added.

The final section, Part Four, on "The Biological Aspects of Language," has been greatly expanded. First and second language acquisition are compared, as is human language with the communicative abilities of chimps and other primates. Since the last edition, neurolinguistic research concerned with brain and language has virtually exploded; Chapter 11 discusses some of the new and exciting developments in this area, and, together with the section on sign languages in Chapter 10, examines the neural basis of both spoken and sign language. A new Chapter 12 on language processing by humans and computers has been added, with sections on psycholinguistic production and comprehension models and developments in computer processing—automatic translation, speech synthesis and recognition, and artificial intelligence.

As in the previous editions, the primary concern has been with basic ideas rather than a detailed exposition of formal theory or of the grammar of English or any other language. The text assumes no previous knowledge on the part of the student. A short bibliography at the end of each chapter is included to stimulate the reader to further investigate all aspects of human linguistic ability. Also included are exercises to enhance the student's interest and comprehension of the textual material.

We wish to thank the following reviewers of this edition: Elaine Chaika, Providence College; Richard Veit, University of North Carolina; and Raymond Weitzman, California State University at Fresno. We have also benefited greatly from discussions with and suggestions from friends, colleagues, students, teaching assistants, instructors, and reviewers of the last edition. They are too many to name, but if this text is better than the last, it is because of them. We owe special thanks to Geoffrey Pullum, Paul Schachter, Tim Stowell, and Barbara A. Fennell for their incisive comments on the syntax chapter, and to Walter E. Meyers for his on historical linguistics. The new and edited sections on the brain are due to the meticulous help of Antonio and Hanna Damasio; to Hanna, for her beautifully executed and anatomically correct drawings of the human brain, we are deeply grateful. Our continual gratitude goes to John Rea for his feedback, criticism, and suggestions on every section of the book. The responsibility for errors in fact or judgment is of course ours. Finally, we wish to say "thank you" to the instructors who have used the three earlier editions; without them and their students there would be no fourth edition.

VF
RR

CONTENTS

An Introduction to Language

The Nature of Human Language

Just as birds have wings, man has language. The wings give the bird its peculiar aptitude for aerial locomotion. Language enables man's intelligence and passions to acquire their peculiar characters of intellect and sentiment.

G. H. Lewes, *The Study of Psychology*

Language is not an abstract construction of the learned, or of dictionary-makers, but is something arising out of the work, needs, ties, joys, affections, tastes, of long generations of humanity, and has its bases broad and low, close to the ground.

Walt Whitman

CHAPTER 1

What Is Language?

When we study human language, we are approaching what some might call the "human essence," the distinctive qualities of mind that are, so far as we know, unique to man.

Noam Chomsky, *Language and Mind*

B.C.   **Johnny Hart**

By permission of Johnny Hart and North America Syndicate, Inc.

Whatever else people do when they come together—whether they play, fight, make love, or make automobiles—they talk. We live in a world of language. We talk to our friends, our associates, our wives and husbands, our lovers, our teachers, our parents and in-laws. We talk to bus drivers and total strangers. We talk face to face and over the telephone, and everyone responds with more talk. Television and radio further swell this torrent of words. Hardly a moment of our waking lives is free from

3

words, and even in our dreams we talk and are talked to. We also talk when there is no one to answer. Some of us talk aloud in our sleep. We talk to our pets and sometimes to ourselves. We are the only animals that do so—that talk.

The possession of language, more than any other attribute, distinguishes humans from other animals. To understand our humanity we must understand the language that makes us human. According to the philosophy expressed in the myths and religions of many peoples, it is language that is the source of human life and power. To some people of Africa, a newborn child is a *kuntu,* a ''thing,'' not yet a *muntu,* a ''person.'' Only by the act of learning does the child become a human being. According to this tradition, we all become ''human'' because we all come to know at least one language. But what does it mean to ''know'' a language?

Linguistic Knowledge

When you know a language, you can speak and be understood by others who know that language. This means you have the capacity to produce sounds that signify certain meanings and to understand or interpret the sounds produced by others. We are referring here to normal-hearing individuals. Deaf persons produce and understand sign languages just as hearing persons produce and understand spoken languages.

Everyone knows a language. Why write an entire book on what appears to be so simple a phenomenon? After all, five-year-old children are almost as proficient at speaking and understanding as their parents are. Nevertheless the ability to carry out the simplest conversation requires profound knowledge of which speakers are unaware. This fact is as true for speakers of Japanese as for English speakers, for Eskimos as for Navajos. A speaker of English can produce a sentence with two relative clauses, like

> My goddaughter who was born in Sweden and who now lives in Vermont is named Disa, after a Viking queen.

without knowing what a relative clause is. In a parallel fashion a child can walk without understanding or being able to explain the principles of balance, support, and sequence that permit one to walk. The fact that we know something unconsciously is not unique to language.

What, then, do speakers of English or Quechua or French or Mohawk or Arabic know?

Knowledge of the Sound System

Knowing a language means knowing what sounds are in that language and what sounds are not. This unconscious knowledge is revealed by the way speakers of one language pronounce words from another language. If you speak only English, for example, you may substitute an English sound for a non-English sound when pronouncing "foreign" words. Most English speakers pronounce the name *Bach* with a final *k* sound because the sound represented by the letters *ch* in German is not an English sound. If you pronounce it as the Germans do, you are using a sound outside the English sound system. French people speaking English often pronounce words like *this* and *that* as if they were spelled *zis* and *zat*. The English sound represented by the initial letters *th* is not part of the French sound system, and the French mispronunciation reveals the speakers' unconscious knowledge of this fact.

Even some involuntary cries are constrained by our own language system, and the filled pauses that are sprinkled through conversational speech—like *er* or *uh* or *you know* in English—contain only the sounds found in the language. French speakers, for example, often fill their pauses with the vowel sound that starts their word for egg, *oeuf*—a sound that does not occur in English.

Knowing the sound system of a language includes more than knowing the **inventory** of sounds: it includes knowing which sounds may start a word, end a word, and follow each other. The name of a former president of Ghana was *Nkrumah*, pronounced with an initial sound identical to the sound ending the English word *sing* (for most Americans). Most speakers of English mispronounce it (by Ghanaian standards) by inserting a short vowel before or after the *n* sound. Similarly, the first name of the Australian mystery writer Ngaio Marsh is usually mispronounced in this way. The reason for these "errors" is that no word in English begins with the *ng* sound. Children who learn English discover this fact about our language, just as Ghanaian and Australian children learn that words in their language may begin with the *ng* sound.

We will learn more about sound systems in Chapters 2 and 3.

Knowledge of the Meaning of Words

The minute I set eyes on an animal I know what it is. I don't have to reflect a moment; the right name comes out instantly. . . . I seem to know just by the shape of the creature and the way it acts what animal it is. When the dodo came along he [Adam] thought it was a wildcat. . . . But I saved him. . . . I just spoke up in a quite natural way . . . and said "Well, I do declare if there isn't the dodo!"

Mark Twain, *Eve's Diary*

Knowing the sounds and sound patterns in our language constitutes only one part of our linguistic knowledge. In addition, knowing a language is knowing that certain sound sequences **signify** certain concepts or **meanings.** Speakers of English know what *boy* means and that it means something different from *toy* or *girl* or *pterodactyl*. Knowing a language is therefore knowing how to relate sounds and meanings.

If you do not know a language, the sounds spoken to you will be mainly incomprehensible, because the relationship between speech sounds and the meanings they represent is, for the most part, an **arbitrary** one. You have to learn (when you are acquiring the language) that the sounds represented by the letters *house* (in the written form of the language) signify the concept ; if you know French, this same meaning is represented by *maison;* if you know Twi, it is represented by ɔdaŋ; if you know Russian, by *dom;* if you know Spanish, by *casa.* Similarly, the concept is represented by *hand* in English, *main* in French, *nsa* in Twi, and *ruka* in Russian.

The following are words in some different languages. How many of them can you understand?

a. kyinii	d. asa	g. wartawan
b. doakam	e. toowq	h. inaminatu
c. odun	f. bolna	i. yawwa

Speakers of the languages from which these words are taken know that they have the following meanings:

- a. a large parasol (in a Ghanaian language, Twi)
- b. living creature (in the native American language, Papago)
- c. wood (in Turkish)
- d. morning (in Japanese)
- e. is seeing (in a California Indian language, Luiseño)
- f. to speak (in a Pakistani language, Urdu); ache (in Russian)
- g. reporter (in Indonesian)
- h. teacher (in a Venezuelan Indian language, Warao)
- i. right on! (in a Nigerian language, Hausa)

These examples show that the sounds of words are only given meaning by the language in which they occur. Mark Twain satirizes the idea that something is called X because it looks like X or called Y because it sounds like Y in the quotation at the beginning of this section. Neither the shape nor the other physical attributes of objects determine their pronunciation in any language. As the cartoon on page 7 illustrates, a pterodactyl could have been called a ron.

This arbitrary relationship between the **form** (sounds) and **meaning** (concept) of a word in spoken language is also true of the sign languages used by the deaf. If you see someone using a sign language you do not know, it is doubtful that you will understand the message from the signs alone. A person who knows Chinese Sign Language would find it difficult to understand American Sign Language. Signs that may have originally been **mimetic** (similar to miming) or **iconic** (with a nonarbitrary relationship between form and meaning) change historically as do words, and the iconicity is lost. These signs become **conventional,** so knowing the shape or

HERMAN **Jim Unger**

movement of the hands does not reveal the meaning of the gestures in sign languages.

There is, however, some **"sound symbolism"** in language—that is, words whose pronunciation suggests the meaning. A few words in most languages are **onomatopoeic**—the sounds of the words supposedly imitate the sounds of nature. Even here, the sounds differ from one language to another, reflecting the particular sound system of the language. In English we say *cockadoodledoo* to represent the rooster's crow, but in Russian they say *kukuriku.*

Sometimes particular sound sequences seem to relate to a particular concept. In English many words beginning with *gl* relate to sight, such as *glare, glint, gleam, glitter, glossy, glaze, glance, glimmer, glimpse,* and *glisten.* However, such words are a very small part of any language, and *gl* may have nothing to do with "sight" in another language, or even in other words in English, such as *gladiator, glucose, glory, glycerine, globe,* and so on.

English speakers know the *gl* words that relate to sight and those that do not; they know the onomatopoeic words, and all the words in the basic vocabulary of the language. There are no speakers of English who know all 450,000 words listed in Webster's *Third New International Dictionary;* but even if there were and that were all they knew, they would not know English. Imagine trying to learn a foreign language by buying a dictionary and memorizing words. No matter how many words you learned, you would not be able to form the simplest phrases or sentences in the language or understand a native speaker. No one speaks in isolated words. (Of course, you could search in your traveler's dictionary for individual words to find out how to say something like "car—gas—where?" After many tries, a native might understand this question and then point in the direction of a gas station. If you were answered with a sentence, however, you probably would not understand what was said or be able to look it up, because you would not know where one word ended and another began.) Chapter 4 will further explore word meanings.

The Creativity of Linguistic Knowledge

THE WIZARD OF ID   **Brant Parker and Johnny Hart**

By permission of Johnny Hart and North America Syndicate, Inc.

Knowledge of a language enables you to combine words to form phrases, and phrases to form sentences. You cannot buy a dictionary of any language with all the sentences, because no dictionary can list all the possible sentences. Knowing a language means being able to produce new sentences never spoken before and to understand sentences never heard before. The linguist Noam Chomsky refers to this ability as part of the "creative aspect" of language use. Not every speaker of a language can create great literature, but you, and all persons who know a language, can and do "create" new sentences when you speak and understand new sentences "created" by others.

This creativity shows that language use is not limited to stimulus-response behavior. True, if someone steps on your toe, you will "automatically" respond with a scream or gasp or grunt, but these sounds are really not part of language; they are involuntary reactions to stimuli. After you automatically cry out, you can say, "That was some clumsy act, you big oaf!" or "Thank you very much for stepping on my toe; I was afraid I had elephantiasis and now that I can feel it hurt I know it isn't so," or any one of an infinite number of sentences, because the particular sentence you produce is not controlled by any stimulus.

Knowing a language includes knowing what sentences are appropriate in various situations. Saying "Hamburger costs $2.00 a pound" after someone has just stepped on your toe would hardly be an appropriate response, although it would be possible.

Consider the following sentence:

> Daniel Boone decided to become a pioneer because he dreamed of pigeon-toed giraffes and cross-eyed elephants dancing in pink skirts and green berets on the wind-swept plains of the Midwest.

You may not believe the sentence; you may question its logic; but you can understand it, although you probably never heard or read it before now.

Knowledge of a language, then, makes it possible to understand and produce new sentences. If you counted the number of sentences in this book that you have seen or heard before, the number would be small. Next time you write an essay or a letter, see how many of your sentences are new. Few sentences are stored in your brain, to be "pulled out" to fit some situation or matched with some sentence that you hear. Novel sentences never spoken or heard before cannot be in your memory.

Simple memorization of all the possible sentences in a language is impossible in principle. If for every sentence in the language a longer sentence can be formed, then there is no limit to the length of any sentence and therefore no limit to the number of sentences. In English you can say:

> This is the house.

or

> This is the house that Jack built.

or

> This is the malt that lay in the house that Jack built.

or

> This is the dog that chased the cat that killed the rat that ate the malt that lay in the house that Jack built.

and you need not stop there. How long, then, is the longest sentence? A speaker of English can say:

> The old man came.

or

> The old, old, old, old, old man came.

How many "olds" are too many? Seven? Twenty-three?

It is true that the longer these sentences become, the less likely we would be to hear or to say them. A sentence with 276 occurrences of "old" would be highly unlikely in either speech or writing, even to describe Methuselah; but such a sentence is theoretically possible. That is, if you know English, you have the knowledge to add any number of adjectives as modifiers to a noun.

All human languages permit their speakers to form indefinitely long sentences; "creativity" is a universal property of human language.

To memorize and store an infinite set of sentences would require an infinite storage capacity. However, the brain is finite, and even if it were not, we could not store novel sentences.

Knowledge of Sentences and Nonsentences

When you learn a language you must learn something finite. Your vocabulary is finite (however large it may be), and that can be stored. If sentences in a language were formed by putting one word after another in any order, then knowledge of a language could simply be a set of words. You can see that words are not enough by examining the following strings of words:

(1) a. John kissed the little old lady who owned the shaggy dog.
    b. Who owned the shaggy dog John kissed the little old lady.
    c. John is difficult to love.
    d. It is difficult to love John.
    e. John is anxious to go.
    f. It is anxious to go John.
    g. John, who was a student, flunked his exams.
    h. Exams his flunked student a was who John.

If you were asked to put a star or asterisk before the examples that seemed "funny" or "no good" to you, which ones would you star?[1] Our "intuitive" knowledge about what is or is not an allowable sentence in English convinces us to star b, f, and h. Which ones did you star?

Would you agree with the following judgments?

(2) a. What he did was climb a tree.
    b. *What he thought was want a sports car.
    c. Drink your beer and go home!
    d. *What are drinking and go home?
    e. I expect them to arrive a week from next Thursday.
    f. *I expect a week from next Thursday to arrive them.
    g. Linus lost his security blanket.
    h. *Lost Linus security blanket his.

---

[1]The asterisk is used before examples that speakers reject for any reason. This notation will be used throughout the book.

If you starred the same ones we did, then you agree that not all strings of words constitute sentences in a language, and knowledge of a language determines which are and which are not. Therefore, in addition to knowing the words of the language, linguistic knowledge must include "rules" for forming sentences and making judgments like those you made about the examples in (1) and (2). These rules must be finite in length and finite in number so that they can be stored in our finite brains; yet they must permit us to form and understand an infinite set of new sentences, as we discussed above. The nature of these rules will be discussed in Chapter 5.

A language, then, consists of all the sounds, words, and possible sentences. When you know a language, you know the sounds, the words, and the rules for their combination.

Linguistic Knowledge and Performance

"What's one and one and one and one and one and one and one and one and one and one?"
"I don't know," said Alice. "I lost count."
"She can't do Addition," the Red Queen interrupted.

Lewis Carroll, *Through the Looking-Glass*

PEANUTS   **Charles Schulz**

Reprinted by permission: © 1964 United Feature Syndicate, Inc.

Speakers' linguistic knowledge permits them to form longer and longer sentences by joining sentences and phrases together or adding modifiers to a noun. Whether you stop at three, five, or eighteen adjectives, it is impossible to limit the number you could add if desired. Very long sentences are theoretically possible, but they are highly improbable. Evidently there is a difference between having the knowledge necessary to produce sentences of a language and applying this knowledge. It is a difference between what you *know,* which is your linguistic **competence,** and how you *use* this knowledge in actual speech production and comprehension, which is your linguistic **performance.**

Speakers of all languages have the knowledge to understand or produce sentences of any length. When they attempt to use that knowledge, though—when they perform linguistically—there are physiological and psychological reasons that limit the number of adjectives, adverbs, clauses, and so on. They may run out of breath;

their audience may leave; they may lose track of what they have said; and, of course, no one lives forever.

When we speak we usually have a certain message to convey. At some stage in the act of producing speech we must organize our thoughts into strings of words. Errors occur, though, and everyone produces speech errors or "slips of the tongue" such as the one in the "Wizard of Id" cartoon.

THE WIZARD OF ID   **Brant Parker and Johnny Hart**

By permission of Johnny Hart and North America Syndicate, Inc.

Our errors, however, are involuntary deviations from what we wish to say. Dr. Spooner (after whom the word "spoonerism" was coined) once said to his class, "You have hissed my mystery lecture and have tasted the whole worm," instead of his intended "You have missed my history lecture and have wasted the whole term." His slip illustrates the difference between linguistic knowledge and the way we use that knowledge in performance.

Linguistic knowledge, for the most part, is *not* conscious knowledge. The linguistic system—the sounds, structures, meanings, words, and rules for putting them all together—is learned subconsciously, with no awareness that rules are being learned. Just as we are unconscious of the physical rules that allow us to stand, walk, or crawl on all fours, to jump, catch a baseball, or ride a bicycle, so we are unconscious of the linguistic rules that enable us to speak, understand, and make judgments about sentences. Knowledge of these rules represents a complex cognitive system. The nature of this system is what this book is all about.

What Is Grammar?

We use the term "grammar" with a systematic ambiguity. On the one hand, the term refers to the explicit theory constructed by the linguist and proposed as a description of the speaker's competence. On the other hand, [it refers] to this competence itself.

N. Chomsky and M. Halle, *The Sound Pattern of English*

Descriptive Grammars

The sounds and sound patterns, the basic units of meaning, such as words, and the rules to combine them to form new sentences constitute the **grammar** of a language. The grammar, then, is what we know; it represents our linguistic competence. To understand the nature of language we must understand the nature of this internalized, unconscious set of rules, which is part of every grammar of every language.

Every human being who speaks a language knows its grammar. When linguists wish to describe a language, they attempt to describe the grammar of the language that exists in the minds of its speakers. There may be some differences among speakers' knowledge, but there must be shared knowledge, because it is this grammar that makes it possible to communicate through language. To the extent that the linguist's description is a true model of the speakers' linguistic capacity, it will be a good or bad description of the grammar and of the language itself. Such a model is called a **descriptive grammar.** It does not tell you how you *should* speak; it describes your basic linguistic knowledge. It explains how it is possible for you to speak and understand, and it tells what you know about the sounds, words, phrases, and sentences of your language.

We have used the word *grammar* in two ways: the first in reference to the grammar speakers have in their brains; the second as the model or description of this internalized grammar. Almost 2000 years ago the Greek grammarian Dionysius Thrax defined grammar as that which permits us either to speak a language or to speak about a language. From now on we will not differentiate these two meanings, because the linguist's descriptive grammar is an attempt at a formal statement (or theory) of the speakers' grammar.

When we say in later chapters that there is a rule in the grammar—such as "Every sentence has a noun phrase subject and a verb phrase predicate"—we posit the rule in both the "mental" grammar and the model of it, the linguist's grammar. When we say that a sentence is **grammatical,** we mean that it conforms to the rules of both grammars; conversely, an **ungrammatical** (starred) sentence deviates in some way from these rules. If, however, we posit a rule for English that does not agree with your intuitions as a speaker, then the grammar we are describing is in some way different from the grammar that represents your linguistic competence; that is, your language is not the one we are describing. No language or variety of a language (called a dialect) is superior to any other in a linguistic sense. Every grammar is equally complex and logical and capable of producing an infinite set of sentences to express any thought. If something can be expressed in one language or one dialect, it can be expressed in any other language or dialect. It might involve different means and different words, but it can be expressed.

No grammar, therefore no language, is either superior or inferior to any other. Languages of technologically undeveloped cultures are not primitive or ill-formed in any way.

Prescriptive Grammars

I don't want to talk grammar. I want to talk like a lady.
G. B. Shaw, *Pygmalion*

By permission of Frank Interlandi; © 1978 Los Angeles Times.

The views expressed in the section above are not those of all grammarians now or in the past. From ancient times until the present ''purists'' have believed that language change is corruption and that there are certain ''correct'' forms that all educated people should use in speaking and writing. The Greek Alexandrians in the first century, the Arabic scholars at Basra in the eighth century, and numerous English grammarians of the eighteenth and nineteenth centuries held this view. They wished to *prescribe* rather than describe the rules of grammar, which gave rise to the writing of **prescriptive grammars.**

With the rise of capitalism, a new middle class emerged who wanted their children to speak the dialect of the ''upper'' classes. This desire led to the publication of many prescriptive grammars. In 1762 an influential grammar, *A Short Introduction to English Grammar with Critical Notes,* was written by Bishop Robert Lowth. Lowth, influenced by Latin grammar and by personal preference, prescribed a number of new rules for English. Before the publication of his grammar, practically everyone—upper-class, middle-class, and lower-class speakers of English—said *I don't have none, You was wrong about that,* and *Mathilda is fatter than me.* Lowth, however, decided that ''two negatives make a positive'' and therefore one should say *I don't have any;* that even when *you* is singular it should be followed by the plural *were;* and that *I* not *me, he* not *him, they* not *them,* and so forth should follow *than* in comparative constructions. Many of these ''rules'' were based on Latin grammar, which had already given way to different rules in the languages that developed from Latin. Because Lowth was influential and because the rising new class wanted to speak ''properly,'' many of these new rules were legislated into English grammar, at least for the ''prestige'' dialect. Grammars such as Lowth wrote are quite different from the descriptive grammars we have been discussing. Their goal is not to describe the rules people know, but to tell them what rules they should know.

In 1908, a grammarian, Thomas R. Lounsbury, wrote: ''There seems to have been in every period in the past, as there is now, a distinct apprehension in the minds of very many worthy persons that the English tongue is always in the condition approaching collapse and that arduous efforts must be put forth persistently to save it from destruction.''

Today our bookstores are filled with books by language ''purists'' attempting to do just that. Edwin Newman, for example, in his books *Strictly Speaking,* and *A Civil Tongue* rails against those who use the word *hopefully* to mean ''I hope,'' as in ''Hopefully, it will not rain tomorrow,'' instead of using it ''properly'' to mean ''with hope.'' What Newman fails to recognize is that language changes in the course of time and words change meaning, and the meaning of *hopefully* has been broadened for most English speakers to include both usages. Other ''saviors'' of the English language blame television, the schools, and even the National Council of Teachers of English for failing to preserve the standard language, and they mount attacks against those college and university professors who suggest that Black English and other dialects are viable, living, complete languages. Although not mentioned by name, the authors of this textbook would clearly be among those who would be criticized by these new prescriptivists.

There is even a literary organization dedicated to the proper use of the English language, called the Unicorn Society of Lake Superior State College, which issues an annual ''dishonor list'' of words and phrases of which they do not approve, including the word ''medication,'' which they say ''We can no longer afford. It's too expensive. We've got to get back to the cheaper 'medicine.'"[2] At least these guardians of the English language have a sense of humor; but they as well as the other prescriptivists are bound to fail. Language is vigorous and dynamic and constantly changing. All languages and dialects are expressive, complete, and logical, as much so as they were 200 or 2000 years ago. If sentences are muddled, it is not because of the language but because of the speakers. Prescriptivists should be more concerned about the thinking of the speakers than about the language they use. "Hopefully" this book will convince you of this idea.

Teaching Grammars

B.C.   **Johnny Hart**

By permission of Johnny Hart and North America Syndicate, Inc.

The grammar of a language is different from a **teaching grammar,** which is used to learn another language or dialect. In countries where it is advantageous to speak a "prestige" dialect, people who do not speak it natively may wish to learn it. Teaching grammars state explicitly the rules of the language, list the words and their pronunciations, and aid in learning a new language or dialect. As an adult, it is difficult to learn a second language without being instructed. Teaching grammars assume that the student already knows one language and compares the grammar of the target language with the grammar of the native language. The meaning of a word is given by providing a **gloss**—the parallel word in the student's native language, such as *maison* "house." It is assumed that the student knows the meaning of the gloss "house," and so the meaning of the French word *maison*.

Sounds of the target language that do not occur in the native language are often described by reference to known sounds. Thus the student might be aided in producing the French sound *u* in the word *tu* by instructions such as "Round your lips while producing the vowel sound in *tea*."

The rules on how to put words together to form the grammatical sentences also refer to the learners' knowledge of their native language. Thus the teaching grammar *Learn Zulu* by Sibusiso Nyembezi states that "The difference between

[2]Los Angeles *Times*, Jan. 2, 1978, Part 1, p. 21.

singular and plural is not at the end of the word but at the beginning of it," and warns that "Zulu does not have the indefinite and definite articles 'a' and 'the.'" Such statements assume students know the rules of their own grammar. Although they might be prescriptive in the sense that they attempt to teach the student what is or is not a grammatical construction in the new language, their aim is different from grammars that attempt to change the rules or usage of a language already learned.

This book is not primarily concerned with either prescriptive or teaching grammars. The matter, however, is considered in Chapter 7 in the discussion of standard and nonstandard dialects.

Language Universals

In a grammar there are parts which pertain to all languages; these components form what is called the general grammar. In addition to these general (universal) parts, there are those which belong only to one particular language; and these constitute the particular grammars of each language.

Du Marsais, c. 1750

The way we are using the word *grammar* differs in another way from its most common meaning. In our sense, the grammar includes everything speakers know about their language—the sound system, called **phonology;** the system of meanings, called **semantics;** the rules of word formation, called **morphology;** and the rules of sentence formation, called **syntax.** It also, of course, includes the vocabulary of words—the dictionary or **lexicon.** Many people think of the grammar of a language as referring solely to the syntactic rules. This latter sense is what students usually mean when they talk about their class in "English grammar."

Our aim is more in keeping with that stated in 1784 by the grammarian John Fell in "Essay Towards an English Grammar": "It is certainly the business of a grammarian to find out, and not to make, the laws of a language." This business is just what the linguist attempts—to find out the laws of a language, and the laws that pertain to all languages. Those laws that pertain to all human languages, representing the universal properties of language, constitute a **universal grammar.**

Throughout the ages, philosophers and linguists have been divided on the question of whether there are universal properties that hold for all human languages and are unique to them. Most modern linguists are on the side of the "universalists," finding common, universal properties in the grammars of all languages. Such properties may be said to constitute a "universal" grammar of human language.

About 1630, the German philosopher Alsted first used the term *general grammar* as distinct from special grammar. He believed that the function of a general grammar was to reveal those features "which relate to the method and etiology of grammatical concepts. They are common to all languages." Pointing out that "general grammar is the pattern 'norma' of every particular grammar whatsoever,'' he implored ''eminent linguists to employ their insight in this matter.''[3]

Three and a half centuries before Alsted, the scholar Robert Kilwardby held that linguists should be concerned with discovering the nature of language in general. So concerned was Kilwardby with universal grammar that he excluded considerations of the characteristics of particular languages, which he believed to be as ''irrelevant to a science of grammar as the material of the measuring rod or the physical characteristics of objects were to geometry.''[4] Kilwardby was perhaps too much of a universalist; the particular properties of individual languages are relevant to the discovery of language universals, and they are of interest for their own sake.

Someone attempting to study Latin, Greek, French, or Swahili as a second language may assert, in frustration, that those ancient scholars were so hidden in their ivory towers that they confused reality with idle speculation; yet the more we investigate this question, the more evidence accumulates to support Chomsky's view that there is a universal grammar, which is part of the human biologically endowed language faculty. It may be thought of ''as a system of principles which characterizes the class of possible grammars by specifying how particular grammars are organized (what are the components and their relations), how the different rules of these components are constructed, how they interact, and so on.''[5]

To discover the nature of this Universal Grammar whose principles characterize all human languages is the major aim of **linguistic theory.** The linguist's goal is to discover the ''laws of human language'' as the physicist's goal is to discover the ''laws of the physical universe.'' The complexity of language, a product of the human brain, undoubtedly means this goal will never be fully achieved. Just as Newtonian physics was enlarged by Einsteinian physics, so the linguistic theory of Universal Grammar develops, and each new discovery, some of which are discussed in this book, sheds new light on what human language is.

We can state a number of facts pertaining to all languages:

1. Wherever humans exist, language exists.
2. There are no ''primitive'' languages—all languages are equally complex and equally capable of expressing any idea in the universe. The vocabulary of any language can be expanded to include new words for new concepts.
3. All languages change through time.
4. The relationships between the sounds and meanings of spoken languages and between the gestures (signs) and meanings of sign languages are for the most part arbitrary.
5. All human languages utilize a finite set of discrete sounds (or gestures) that are combined to form meaningful elements or words, which themselves form an infinite set of possible sentences.

[3]V. Salmon. 1969. ''Review of *Cartesian Linguistics* by N. Chomsky.'' *Journal of Linguistics* 5: 165–187.

[4]V. Salmon, op. cit.

[5]Noam Chomsky. 1979. *Language and Responsibility.* (Based on conversations with Misou Ronat.) Pantheon Books. New York. P. 180.

6. All grammars contain rules for the formation of words and sentences of a similar kind.

7. Every spoken language includes discrete sound segments like *p*, *n*, or *a*, which can all be defined by a finite set of sound properties or features. Every spoken language has a class of vowels and a class of consonants.

8. Similar grammatical categories (for example, noun, verb) are found in all languages.

9. There are semantic universals, such as "male" or "female," "animate" or "human," found in every language in the world.

10. Every language has a way of referring to past time, negating, forming questions, issuing commands, and so on.

11. Speakers of all languages are capable of producing and comprehending an infinite set of sentences. Syntactic universals reveal that every language has a way of forming sentences such as:

> Linguistics is an interesting subject.
> I know that linguistics is an interesting subject.
> You know that I know that linguistics is an interesting subject.
> Cecilia knows that you know that I know that linguistics is an interesting subject.
> Is it a fact that Cecilia knows that you know that I know that linguistics is an interesting subject?

12. Any normal child, born anywhere in the world, of any racial, geographical, social, or economic heritage, is capable of learning any language to which he or she is exposed. The differences we find among languages cannot be due to biological reasons.

It seems that Alsted and Du Marsais (and we could add many other "universalists" from all ages) were not spinning idle thoughts. We all speak "human language."

Animal "Languages"

No matter how eloquently a dog may bark, he cannot tell you that his parents were poor but honest.

Bertrand Russell

Whether language is the exclusive property of the human species is an interesting question. The idea of talking animals probably is as old and as widespread among human societies as language is itself. No culture lacks a legend in which some animal plays a speaking role. All over West Africa, children listen to folk tales in which a "spider-man" is the hero. "Coyote" is a favorite figure in many native American tales, and there is hardly an animal who does not figure in Aesop's famous fables. Hugh Lofting's fictional Doctor Doolittle's major accomplishment was his ability to communicate with animals.

The Far Side. By Gary Larson. © 1983, 1984 Chronicle Features, San Francisco.

If language is viewed only as a system of communication, then many species communicate. Humans also use systems other than their language to relate to each other and to send "messages." Above we mentioned specific properties as defining human language. The question is whether they, or any subset of them, are unique to the human animal.

"Talking" Parrots

Most humans who acquire language utilize speech sounds to express meanings, but such sounds are not a necessary aspect of language, as evidenced by the sign languages of the deaf. The use of speech sounds is therefore not a basic part of what we have been calling language. The chirping of birds, the squeaking of dolphins, and the dancing of bees may potentially represent systems similar to human languages. If animal communication systems are not like human language, it will not be due to a lack of speech.

Conversely, when animals vocally imitate human utterances, it does not mean they possess language. Language is a system that relates sounds (or gestures) to meanings. "Talking" birds such as parrots and mynah birds are capable of faithfully reproducing words and phrases of human language that they have heard; but when a parrot says "Polly wants a cracker," she may really want a ham sandwich or a drink of water or nothing at all. A bird that has learned to say "hello" or "goodbye" is as likely to use one as the other, regardless of whether people are arriving or departing. The bird's utterances carry no meaning. They are speaking neither English nor their own language when they sound like us.

Talking birds do not dissect the sounds of their imitations into discrete units. *Polly* and *Molly* do not rhyme for a parrot. They are as different as *hello* and *goodbye* (or as similar). One property of all human languages (which will be discussed further in Chapter 2) is the "discreteness" of the speech or gestural units, which are ordered and reordered, combined and split apart. A parrot says what it is taught, or what it hears, and no more. If Polly learns "Polly wants a cracker" and "Polly wants a doughnut" and also learns to imitate the single words *whiskey* and *bagel,* she will not spontaneously produce, as children do, "Polly wants whiskey" or "Polly wants a bagel" or "Polly wants whiskey and a bagel." If she learns *cat* and *cats* and *dog* and *dogs* and then learns the word *parrot,* she will be unable to form the plural *parrots;* nor can a parrot form an unlimited set of utterances from a finite set of units. Therefore, the ability to produce sounds similar to those used in human language cannot be equated with the ability to learn a human language.

The Birds and the Bees

The birds and animals are all friendly to each other, and there are no disputes about anything. They all talk, and they all talk to me, but it must be a foreign language for I cannot make out a word they say.

Mark Twain, *Eve's Diary*

Most animals possess some kind of "signaling" communication system. Among the spiders there is a complex system for courtship. The male spider, before he approaches his lady love, goes through an elaborate series of gestures to inform her that he is indeed a spider and not a crumb or a fly to be eaten. These gestures are invariant. One never finds a "creative" spider changing or adding to the particular courtship ritual of his species.

A similar kind of "gesture" language is found among the fiddler crabs. There are forty different varieties, and each variety uses its own particular claw-waving movement to signal to another member of its "clan." The timing, movement, and posture of the body never change from one time to another or from one crab to another within the particular variety. Whatever the signal means, it is fixed. Only one meaning can be conveyed. There is not an infinite set of fiddler crab "sentences."

The imitative sounds of talking birds have little in common with human language, but the calls and songs of many species of birds do have a communicative function, and they resemble human languages in that there may be "dialects" within the same species. Bird **calls** (consisting of one or more short notes) convey messages associated with the immediate environment, such as danger, feeding, nesting, flocking, and so on. Bird **songs** (more complex patterns of notes) are used to "stake out" territory and to attract mates. There is no evidence of any internal structure to these songs, nor can they be segmented into independently meaningful parts as words of human language can be. In a study of the territorial song of the European robin,[6] it was discovered that the rival robins paid attention only to the alternation between high-pitched and low-pitched notes, and which came first did not matter. The message varies only to the extent of how strongly the robin feels about his possession and to what extent he is prepared to defend it and start a family in that territory. The different alternations therefore express "intensity" and nothing more. The robin is creative in his ability to sing the same thing in many different ways, but not creative in his ability to use the same "units" of the system to express many different messages with different meanings.

To what degree human language is biologically conditioned (or **innate**) and to what degree it is learned is one of the fundamental questions of linguistics. The songs of some species of birds appear to be innate. This question will be discussed in Chapter 11, which deals with language and the brain.

Despite certain superficial similarities to human language, bird calls and songs are fundamentally different kinds of communicative systems. The number of messages that can be conveyed is finite, and messages are stimulus-controlled.

This distinction is also true of the system of communication used by honeybees. A forager bee is able to return to the hive and tell other bees where a source of food is located. It does so by forming a dance on a wall of the hive that reveals the location and quality of the food source. For one species of Italian honeybee, the dancing behavior may assume one of three possible patterns: *round* (which indicates locations near the hive, within twenty feet or so), *sickle* (which indicates locations at twenty to sixty feet distance from the hive), and *tail-wagging* (for distances that exceed sixty feet). The number of repetitions per minute of the basic pattern in the

---

[6]R. G. Busnel and J. Bremond. 1962. "Recherche du Support de l'Information dans le Signal Acoustique de Défense Territoriale du Rougegorge." *C. R. Acad. Sci. Paris* 254: 2236–2238.

tail-wagging dance indicates the precise distance; the slower the repetition rate, the longer the distance.

The bees' dance is an effective system of communication for bees. It is capable, in principle, of infinitely many different messages, like human language; but unlike human language, the system is confined to a single subject—distance from the hive. The inflexibility was shown by an experimenter who forced a bee to walk to the food source. When the bee returned to the hive, it indicated a distance twenty-five times farther away than the food source actually was. The bee had no way of communicating the special circumstances in its message. This absence of creativity makes the bees' dance qualitatively different from human language.

In the seventeenth century, the philosopher and mathematician René Descartes pointed out that the communication systems of animals are qualitatively different from the language used by humans:

> It is a very remarkable fact that there are none so depraved and stupid, without even excepting idiots, that they cannot arrange different words together, forming of them a statement by which they make known their thoughts; while, on the other hand, there is no other animal, however perfect and fortunately circumstanced it may be, which can do the same.[7]

Descartes goes on to state that one of the major differences between humans and animals is that human use of language is not just a response to external, or even internal, emotional stimuli, as are the sounds and gestures of animals. He warns against confusing human use of language with "natural movements which betray passions and may be . . . manifested by animals."

To hold that animals communicate by systems qualitatively different from human language systems is not to claim human superiority. Humans are not inferior to the one-celled amoeba because they cannot reproduce by splitting in two; they are just different sexually. All the studies of animal communication systems, including those of chimpanzees (discussed in Chapter 10), provide evidence for Descartes' distinction between other animal communication systems and the linguistic creative ability possessed by the human animal.

Summary

We are all intimately familiar with at least one language, our own; yet few of us ever stop to consider what we know about it. There is no book that contains the English or Russian or Zulu language. The words of a language can be listed in a dictionary, but not all the sentences, and a language consists of these sentences as well as words. Speakers use a finite set of rules to produce and understand an infinite set of possible sentences.

---

[7]René Descartes, "Discourse on Method," V. In *The Philosophical Works of Descartes,* trans. by E. S. Haldane and G. R. T. Ross. Vol. I, p. 116.

These rules comprise the **grammar** of a language, which is learned when you "acquire" the language and includes the sound system (the **phonology**), how words may be combined into phrases and sentences (the **syntax**), the ways in which sounds and meanings are related (the **semantics**), and the words or **lexicon.** The sounds and meanings of these words are related in an **arbitrary** fashion. If you had never heard the word *syntax* you would not, by its sounds, know what it meant. Language, then, is a system that relates sounds with meanings, and when you know a language you know this system.

This knowledge (linguistic **competence**) is different from behavior (linguistic **performance**). If you woke up one morning and decided to stop talking (as the Trappist monks do after they take a "vow of silence"), you would still have knowledge of your language. This ability or competence underlies linguistic behavior. If you do not know the language, you cannot speak it; but if you know the language, you may choose not to speak.

Grammars are of three kinds. The **descriptive grammar** of a language represents the unconscious linguistic knowledge or capacity of its speakers. Such a grammar is a model of the "mental grammar" every speaker of the language knows. It does not teach the rules of the language; it describes the rules that are already known. A grammar that attempts to legislate what your grammar should be is called a **prescriptive grammar.** It prescribes; it does not describe, except incidentally. **Teaching grammars** are written to help people learn a foreign language or a dialect of their own language.

The more linguists investigate the thousands of languages of the world and describe the ways in which they differ from each other, the more they discover that these differences are limited. There are linguistic universals that pertain to all parts of grammars, the ways in which these parts are related, and the forms of rules. These principles comprise the **universal grammar,** which forms the basis of the specific grammars of all possible human languages.

If language is defined merely as a system of communication, then language is not unique to humans. There are, however, certain characteristics of human language not found in the communication systems of any other species. A basic property of human language is its **creative aspect**—a speaker's ability to combine the basic linguistic units to form an *infinite* set of "well-formed" grammatical sentences, most of which are novel, never before produced or heard.

The fact that deaf children learn language shows that the ability to hear or produce sounds is not a necessary prerequisite for language learning. Further, the ability to imitate the sounds of human language is not a sufficient basis for learning language; "talking" birds imitate sounds but can neither segment these sounds into smaller units, nor understand what they are imitating, nor produce new utterances to convey their thoughts.

Birds, bees, crabs, spiders, and most other creatures communicate in some way, but the information imparted is severely limited and stimulus-bound, confined to a small set of messages. The system of language represented by intricate mental grammars, which are not stimulus-bound and which generate infinite messages, is unique to the human species.

References

Chomsky, Noam. 1975. *Reflections on Language*. Pantheon Books. New York.

Chomsky, Noam. 1972. *Language and Mind*, enlarged ed. Harcourt Brace Jovanovich. New York.

Gould, J. L., and C. G. Gould. 1983. "Can a Bee Behave Intelligently?" *New Scientist* 98:84–87.

Lieber, Justin. 1975. *Noam Chomsky: A Philosophic Overview*. St. Martin's Press. New York.

Lyons, John. 1970. *Noam Chomsky*. Viking. New York.

Newmeyer, Frederick J. 1983. *Grammatical Theory: Its Limits and Possibilities*. University of Chicago Press. Chicago, Ill.

Sebeok, T. A., ed. 1977. *How Animals Communicate*. Indiana University Press. Bloomington, Ind.

Von Frisch, K. 1967. *The Dance Language and Orientation of Bees*, trans. by L. E. Chadwick. Belknap Press of Harvard University Press. Cambridge, Mass.

Exercises

1. An English speaker's knowledge includes the sound sequences of the language. When new products are put on the market, the manufacturers have to think up new names for them that conform to the allowable sound patterns. Suppose you were hired by a manufacturer of soap products to name five new products. What names might you come up with? List them.

    We are interested not in the spelling of the words but in how they are pronounced. Therefore, describe in any way you can how the words you list should be pronounced. Suppose, for example, you named one soap powder *Blick*. You could describe the sounds in any of the following ways:

    > *bl* as in *blood, i* as in *pit, ck* as in *stick*
    > *bli* as in *bliss, ck* as in *tick*
    > *b* as in *boy, lick* as in *lick*

2. Consider the following sentences. Put a star (*) after those that do not seem to conform to the rules of your grammar, that are ungrammatical for you. State, if you can, why you think the sentence is ungrammatical.

    a. Robin forced the sheriff go.
    b. Napoleon forced Josephine to go.
    c. The Devil made Faust go.
    d. He passed by a large sum of money.
    e. He came by a large sum of money.
    f. He came a large sum of money by.
    g. Did in a corner little Jack Horner sit?
    h. Elizabeth is resembled by Charles.
    i. Nancy is eager to please.
    j. It is easy to frighten Emily.
    k. It is eager to love a kitten.
    l. That birds can fly amazes.
    m. The fact that you are late to class is surprising.
    n. Has the nurse slept the baby yet?
    o. I was surprised for you to get married.
    p. I wonder who and Mary went swimming.
    q. Myself bit John.

3. It was pointed out in this chapter that a small set of words in languages may be onomatopoeic; that is, their sounds "imitate" what they refer to. *Ding-dong, tick-tock, bang, zing, swish,* and *plop* are such words in English. Construct a list of ten new words. Test them on at least five friends to see if they are truly "nonarbitrary" as to sound and meaning.

    (1)   (6)
    (2)   (7)
    (3)   (8)
    (4)   (9)
    (5)   (10)

4. Although sounds and meanings of most words in all languages are arbitrarily related, there are some communication systems in which the ''signs'' unambiguously reveal their ''meaning.''

    a. Describe (or draw) five different signs that directly show what they mean. Example: a road sign indicating an S curve.

    b. Describe any other communication system that, like language, consists of arbitrary symbols. Example: traffic signals, where red means stop and green means go.

5. Consider these two statements:

    > I learned a new word today.
    > I learned a new sentence today.

    Do you think the two statements are equally probable, and if not, why not?

6. What do the barking of dogs, the meowing of cats, and the singing of birds have in common with human language? What are some of the basic differences?

7. A wolf is able to express subtle gradations of emotion by different positions of the ears, the lips, and the tail. There are eleven postures of the tail that express such emotions as self-confidence, confident threat, lack of tension, uncertain threat, depression, defensiveness, active submission, and complete submission. This system seems to be complex. Suppose there were a thousand different emotions that the wolf could express in this way. Would you then say a wolf had a language similar to a human's? If not, why not?

8. Suppose you taught a dog to *heel, sit up, beg, roll over, play dead, stay, jump,* and *bark* on command, using the italicized words as cues. Would you be teaching it language? Why or why not?

9. State some ''rule of grammar'' that you have learned is the ''correct'' way to say something, but that you do not generally use in speaking. For example, you may have heard that *It's me* is incorrect and that the correct form is *It's I.* Nevertheless you always use *me* in such sentences, your friends do also, and in fact, *It's I* sounds odd to you.

    Write a short essay presenting arguments against someone who tells you that you are wrong. Discuss how this disagreement demonstrates the difference between descriptive and prescriptive grammars.

Grammatical Aspects of Language

We may think of a grammar, represented somehow in the mind, as a system that specifies the phonetic, syntactic, and semantic properties of an infinite class of potential sentences. The child knows the language so determined by the grammar that [has been] acquired. This grammar is a representation of . . . "intrinsic competence."

N. Chomsky, "On Cognitive Structures and Their Development: A Reply to Piaget"

C H A P T E R

2

Phonetics: The Sounds of Language

The voice is articulated by the lips and the tongue. . . . Man speaks by means of the air which he inhales into his entire body and particularly into the body cavities. When the air is expelled through the empty space it produces a sound, because of the resonances in the skull. The tongue articulates by its strokes; it gathers the air in the throat and pushes it against the palate and the teeth, thereby giving the sound a definite shape. If the tongue would not articulate each time, by means of its strokes, man would not speak clearly and would only be able to produce a few simple sounds.

Hippocrates, *De Carnibus*, VIII (c. 400 B.C.E.)

When we speak or understand someone speaking a language we know, we use the language system to relate the sounds produced or heard to specific meanings. When we hear a language we do not know, it sounds like gibberish. We do not know where one word ends and another begins. Even if we did, we would not understand the meaning.

Knowing a language means knowing what sounds are in the language, how they are ''strung'' together, and what these different sound sequences mean. Although the sounds of French or Xhosa or Quechua are uninterpretable by someone who does not speak those languages, and although some sounds in one language are not in another, the sounds of all the languages of the world together constitute a limited set.

Sound Segments

The study of the speech sounds that are utilized by all human languages to represent meanings is called **phonetics.** To describe these sounds it is necessary to decide what an ''individual sound'' is and how each sound differs from all others. This task is not as easy as it seems.

HERMAN   **BY UNGER**

"Keep out! Keep out! K-E-E-P O-U-T."

Individual Sounds

A speaker of English "knows" that there are three sounds in the word *cat*, the initial sound represented by the letter *c*, the second by *a*, and the final sound by *t;* yet physically the word is just one continuous sound. You can **segment** the one sound into parts because you know English. The ability to analyze a word into its individual sound segments does not depend on knowledge of how the word is spelled. Both *not* and *knot* have three sounds, even though the first sound in *knot* is represented by the two letters *kn*. Similarly, the printed word *psycho* has six letters that represent only four sounds—*ps, y, ch, o*.

If you hear a man clearing his throat, you would be unable to segment the sound into a sequence of discrete units because the sounds produced are not sounds in the language. The difficulty is not that it is a single continuous sound; you do not produce one sound, then another, then another when you say the word *cat*. You move your organs of speech continuously to produce a continuous signal.

Although the sounds we produce and hear and comprehend during speech are continuous, everyone throughout history who has attempted to analyze language has recognized that speech utterances can be segmented into individual units. According to an ancient Hindu myth, the god Indra, in response to an appeal by the other gods, attempted for the first time to segment speech into its separate elements. After he accomplished this feat, according to the myth, the sounds could be regarded as language. Indra therefore may be the first phonetician.

In this sense, speech is similar to music. A person who has not studied music cannot write the sequence of individual notes combined by a violinist into one changing continuous sound. A trained musician, however, finds it a simple task. Every human speaker, without special training, can segment a speech signal.

Just as we cannot analyze a musical passage without musical knowledge, so we need linguistic knowledge to segment speech into pieces. Neither the acoustic speech signal alone nor the movements of the vocal organs used to produce speech provides enough information for phonetic analysis; neither shows the breaks between the sounds or even between the words.

Identity of Speech Sounds

The task is even more complicated because no two speakers ever say the "same thing" identically. The speech signal produced when one speaker says *cat* will not be identical to the signal produced when another says *cat* or even when the first speaker repeats the word. Nevertheless speakers understand each other, because they know the same language.

Our knowledge of a language determines when we judge physically different sounds to be the same; we know which aspects or properties of the signal are important and which are not. For example, if someone coughs in the middle of saying "How (cough) are you?" a listener will interpret this signal simply as "How are you?" If you looked at a picture of the physical signal produced, called a sound spectrogram, the two utterances would be very different. Despite acoustic differences, the phonetic properties that distinguish one sound from another, such as *b* from *d* in English, remain fairly constant across all English speakers and times. In Chapter 1, language and speech were distinguished. Our linguistic knowledge, our mental grammar, makes it possible to ignore nonlinguistic differences in speech.

Furthermore, we are capable of making many sounds that we know intuitively are not speech sounds in our language. Many English speakers can make a clicking sound, which writers sometimes represent as *tsk tsk tsk,* but these sounds are not part of the English sound system. They never occur as part of the words of the sentences we produce. It is, in fact, difficult for many English speakers to combine this clicking sound with other sounds; yet clicks are speech sounds in Xhosa, Zulu, Sotho, and Khoikhoi, languages spoken in southern Africa, just like the *k* or *t* in English. Speakers of those languages have no difficulty producing them as parts of words. The language Xhosa begins with one of these clicks. Thus *tsk* is a speech sound in Xhosa but not in English; *th* is a speech sound in English but not in French. The sound produced with a closed mouth when we are trying to clear a tickle in our throats is not a speech sound in any language, nor is the sound produced when we sneeze.

The science of phonetics attempts to describe all the sounds used in human language—sounds that constitute an important subset of the totality of sounds that humans are capable of producing.

The process by which we use our linguistic knowledge to produce a meaningful utterance is complicated. It can be viewed as a chain of events starting with an idea or message in the brain or mind of the speaker and ending with a similar message in the brain of the hearer. The message is put into a form that is dictated by the language we are speaking. It must then be transmitted by nerve signals to the organs of speech articulation, which produce different physical sounds.

Speech sounds can be described at any stage in this chain of events. The study of the physical properties of the sounds themselves is called **acoustic phonetics,** and the study of the way listeners perceive these sounds is called **auditory phonetics,** both of which will be discussed in Chapter 12. **Articulatory phonetics** is the study of how the vocal tract produces the sounds of language, which will be the primary concern in this chapter.

Articulatory Phonetics

The principles of pronunciation are those general laws of articulation which determine the character, and fix the boundaries of every language; as in every system of speaking, however irregular, the organs must necessarily fall into some common mode of enunciation or the purpose of Providence in the gift of speech would be absolutely defeated. These laws, like every other object of philosophical inquiry, are only to be traced by an attentive observation and enumeration of particulars. . . .

John Walker, 1823[1]

All normal languages involve sounds produced by the upper respiratory tract. To understand the nature of language it is necessary to understand the nature of these sounds and how they are produced. Articulatory phonetics attempts to provide a framework to do so.

Airstream Mechanisms

The production of any speech sound (or any sound at all) involves the movement of an airstream. Most speech sounds are produced by pushing air from the lungs out of the body through the mouth and sometimes through the nose. Because lung air is used, these sounds are called *pulmonic* sounds; because the air is pushed *out,* they are called *egressive.* The majority of sounds used in languages of the world are produced by a **pulmonic egressive airstream mechanism.** All the sounds in English are produced in this manner.

Other airstream mechanisms are used in other languages to produce sounds called *ejectives, implosives,* and *clicks.* Instead of lung air, the body of air in the mouth can be moved. When this air is sucked in instead of flowing out, *ingressive* sounds, like implosives and clicks, are produced. When the air in the mouth is

[1]John Walker. 1823. *A Critical Pronouncing Dictionary and Expositor of the English Language,* 26th edition. London: A. Wilson. P. 11.

pushed out, ejectives are produced; they are therefore also egressive sounds. Implosives and ejectives are produced by a **glottalic airstream mechanism,** whereas clicks are produced by a **velaric airstream mechanism.** Ejectives are found in many native American, African, and Caucasian languages. Implosives also occur in the languages of the Americas and throughout Africa, India, and Pakistan. Clicks occur in the Southern Bantu languages such as Xhosa and Zulu, and in the languages spoken by the Bushmen and Khoikhoi. A detailed description of these different airstream mechanisms goes beyond the requirements of an introductory text. They are mentioned to show that sounds can be classified according to the airstream mechanism used to produce them. In the rest of this chapter we will be discussing only sounds produced by a pulmonic egressive airstream mechanism.

Voiced and Voiceless Sounds

The airstream from the lungs moves up through the trachea, or windpipe, and through the opening between the vocal cords, which is called the **glottis.** (See Figure 2–1.)

If the vocal cords are apart, the airstream is not obstructed at the glottis, and it passes freely into the **supraglottal** cavities (the parts of the vocal tract above the glottis). The sounds produced in this way are **voiceless** sounds. The sounds represented by *p, t, k,* and *s* in the English words *pit, tip, kit, sip,* and *kiss* are voiceless sounds.

If the vocal cords are together, the airstream forces its way through and causes them to *vibrate.* Such sounds are called **voiced** sounds and are illustrated by the sounds spelled *b, d, g,* and **z** in the words *bad, god, dog, zebra,* and *buzz.* If you put a finger in each ear and say ''z-z-z-z-z'' you can feel the vibrations of the vocal cords. If you now say ''s-s-s-s'' you will not feel these vibrations (although you hear a hissing sound in your mouth). When you whisper, you are making all the speech sounds voiceless. The voiced/voiceless distinction is important in English. It is this phonetic feature or property that distinguishes between word pairs like the following:

pit/bit, fine/vine, tin/din, seal/zeal

The first word of each pair begins with a voiceless sound and the second word with a voiced sound. All other aspects of the sounds of these words are identical; the position of the lips and tongue is the same in each of the paired words.

The state of the vocal cords during speech thus permits us to classify speech sounds into two large classes—**voiced** and **voiceless.** We can specify each voiced sound as [+voiced] and each voiceless sound as [−voiced], a descriptive term equivalent to voiceless. Thus one feature with two values [±voiced] divides the set of all sounds into two classes.

Words may also be distinguished if their final sounds differ as to vocal cord position, as in *nap* and *nab, writ* and *rid, rack* and *rag, wreath* and *wreathe, rich* and *ridge.* You will notice that the English spelling system does not represent these

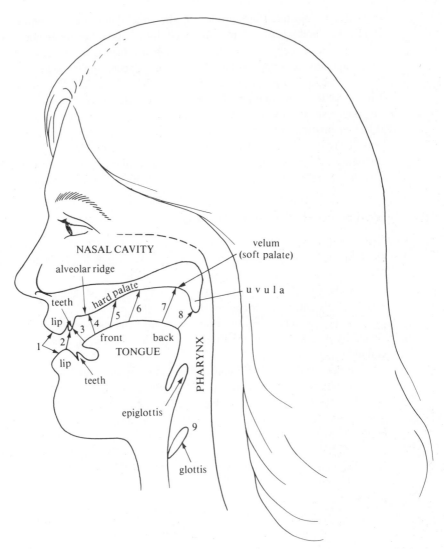

FIGURE 2–1 The vocal tract. Places of articulation: 1, bilabial; 2, labiodental; 3, dental or interdental; 4, alveolar; 5, palatoalveolar; 6, palatal; 7, velar; 8, uvular; 9, glottal.

differences perfectly; for example, the *ck* that ends *rack* represents a simple [−voiced] *k* sound. We will discuss sounds and spelling in a later section. In these pairs of words the first word ends in a voiceless or [−voiced] sound and the second word ends in a voiced or [+voiced] sound.

Sounds must differ from each other in ways other than voicing, because although *p, t, k* are all voiceless and *b, d, g* are all voiced, each sound is distinct from all the others. What other phonetic properties distinguish sounds?

Nasal and Oral Sounds

If you say *pad, bad,* and *mad,* you will notice that the initial sounds are similar. The *p, b,* and *m* are all produced by closing the lips. *p* differs from *b* because in producing the voiceless *p* the vocal cords are apart; the glottis is open. *b* is voiced because the vocal cords are together and vibrating. If you put your hands over your ears and keep your lips together prolonging the pronunciation of the *b* in *bad* you will feel the hum of the vibrations while your lips are closed. If you do the same in producing a prolonged "m-m-m-m" in *mad,* you will see that *m* is also a voiced sound. What, then, distinguishes the *m* from the *b?*

  m is a **nasal** sound. When you produce *m,* air escapes not only through the mouth (when you open your lips) but also through the nose.

  In Figure 2–1 notice that the roof of the mouth is divided into the **hard palate** and the **soft palate** or **velum.** The hard palate is the bony structure at the front of the mouth. You can feel this hard palate with your finger. As you move your finger back you can feel the section of the palate where the flesh becomes soft and movable. This soft, movable part is the velum. Hanging down from the end of the soft palate or velum is the **uvula,** which you can see in a mirror if you open your mouth wide and say "aaah." When the velum is raised all the way to touch the back of the throat, the passage through the nose is cut off. When the nasal passage is blocked in this way, the air can escape only through the mouth. Sounds produced this way are called **oral** sounds. *p* and *b* are oral sounds. When the velum is lowered, air escapes through the nose as well as the mouth. Sounds produced this way are called **nasal** sounds. *m, n,* and *ng* are the nasal consonants of English. The diagrams in Figure 2–2 show the position of the lips and the velum when *m* and *p* or *b* are articulated.

  The difference between *bad* and *mad, dot* and *not,* is due only to the position of the velum in the first sounds of the words. In *bad* and *dot* the velum is raised, preventing air from entering the nasal cavity. *b* and *d* are therefore **oral** sounds. In *mad* and *not* the velum is lowered and air travels through the nose as well as the mouth. *m* and *n* are therefore **nasal** sounds. Note that *b, d, m,* and *n* are all voiced.

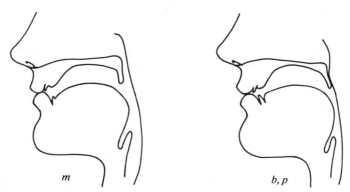

m   *b, p*

FIGURE 2–2 Position of lips and velum for *m* (lips together, velum down) and *b* or *p* (lips together, velum up).

Words with final consonants alike in all other respects may differ with respect to the oral–nasal distinction. The final sounds of *rib* and *rim, mad* and *man, dig* and *ding* (the *ng* represents one sound)[2] are identical except that the first of each pair is oral, the second is nasal.

These **phonetic features** or properties permit the classification of speech sounds into four classes: voiced, voiceless, nasal, oral. One sound may belong to more than one class, as shown in Table 2–1.

TABLE 2–1 Classes of Speech Sounds

	Oral (−nasal)	Nasal (+nasal)
Voiced [+voiced]	b d g	m n ng
Voiceless [−voiced]	p t k	*

*Nasal consonants in English are usually voiced. Both voiced and voiceless nasals occur in other languages, as will be discussed below.

These sounds can also be classified by specifying them as + or − for each phonetic property we have discussed, as shown in Table 2–2.

It is easy by this method to determine the different classes of speech sounds. All sounds marked [+voiced] are in the class of voiced sounds, and all sounds marked [−voiced] are in the class of voiceless sounds; all sounds marked [+nasal] are in the class of nasal sounds, and those marked [−nasal] are in the class of oral sounds. Thus, the two features—[±voiced] and [±nasal]—classify all speech sounds into four sets: $\begin{bmatrix} +\text{voiced} \\ +\text{nasal} \end{bmatrix} \begin{bmatrix} +\text{voiced} \\ -\text{nasal} \end{bmatrix} \begin{bmatrix} -\text{voiced} \\ +\text{nasal} \end{bmatrix} \begin{bmatrix} -\text{voiced} \\ -\text{nasal} \end{bmatrix}$[3].

TABLE 2–2 Feature Values of Oral, Nasal, Voiced, and Voiceless Sounds

	p	t	k	b	d	g	m	n	ng (ŋ)
Voiced	−	−	−	+	+	+	+	+	+
Nasal	−	−	−	−	−	−	+	+	+

[2]The single sound usually represented by *ng* in the English spelling system can also be symbolized by ŋ. Phonetic symbols for all the sounds will be discussed below.

[3]When the value of more than one feature of a phonetic segment is specified, the features may be given sequentially, by writing [+voiced, −nasal], or in a column, as $\begin{bmatrix} +\text{voiced} \\ -\text{nasal} \end{bmatrix}$. These notations are equivalent.

Places of Articulation

b, d, and *g* are all voiced nonnasal (oral) sounds, which we have designated as $\begin{bmatrix} +\text{voiced} \\ -\text{nasal} \end{bmatrix}$. What, then, distinguishes them? We know they are distinct because we recognize *brew, drew,* and *grew,* and *bash, dash,* and *gash* as different words with different meanings. There must be other phonetic features that distinguish them besides those already discussed.

Labials By moving the tongue and lips we are able to change the shape of the oral cavity and produce different sounds. When we produce a *p, b,* or *m* we **articulate** by bringing both lips together. These sounds are therefore called **bilabials.**

We also use our lips to form *f* and *v* as in *fine* and *vine.* To produce these sounds we articulate by touching the bottom lip to the upper teeth, which is why these sounds are called **labiodental,** *labio-* referring to lips and *dental* to teeth.

The class of **labial** sounds in English consists of the three bilabials *b, p,* and *m* and the two labiodentals *f* and *v.* Using the feature [±labial], all these sounds can be specified as [+labial] and all other sounds as [−labial].

Interdentals To produce the sounds represented by the *th* beginning the words *thin* and *then,* the tip of the tongue is inserted between the upper and lower teeth. These sounds are **interdental** ("between the teeth"). In the English spelling system, the same sequence of letters, *th,* is used to represent the voiceless interdental in *thin* and *ether* and the voiced interdental in *then* and *either.*

Labial and interdental sounds are all articulated at the front of the oral cavity. Together they form a class of sounds which can be specified as [+front]. The technical term for the phonetic feature to distinguish this class is [±anterior]. Labial sounds are therefore $\begin{bmatrix} +\text{anterior} \\ +\text{labial} \end{bmatrix}$ and interdental sounds are $\begin{bmatrix} +\text{anterior} \\ -\text{labial} \end{bmatrix}$.

We will see below that there are other sounds that are [+anterior].

Alveolars To articulate *d, n, t, s,* or *z,* the tip of the tongue is raised to the bony tooth ridge, called the **alveolar ridge** (see Figure 2–1). Sounds produced by raising the front part of the tongue to the alveolar ridge are thus called **alveolar** sounds. If you say *do, new, two, Sue, zoo,* you will notice that the first sounds in all these words are alveolar sounds. The *t* and *s* are voiceless alveolar sounds, and the *d, z,* and *n* are voiced. Only *n* is nasal.

Alveolar sounds, like labials and interdentals, are articulated at or in front of the alveolar ridge, that is, in the anterior section of the mouth, and are therefore also specified as [+anterior], to distinguish them from the class of **posterior** sounds.

Velars Another class of sounds is produced by raising the back of the tongue to the soft palate or velum. The initial and final sounds of the words *kick, gig* and the final sounds of the words *back, bag,* and *bang* are produced in this way and are called **velar** sounds. The *k* is a voiceless, oral velar; the *g* is a voiced oral velar, and the *ng* (which never occurs at the beginning of words in English) is a voiced nasal velar. Because the back of the tongue is the articulator, these sounds are obviously [−anterior]. Velars are also [+back] or [+posterior], because they are articulated by raising the back part of the tongue to the velum, which is the back part of the roof of the mouth.

Palatals (or Alveopalatals)   To produce the sounds in the middle of the words *mesher* and *measure,* the front part of the tongue is raised to a point on the hard palate just behind the alveolar ridge. The voiceless sound in *mesher* (spelled *sh*) and the voiced sound in *measure* (spelled *s*) are **palatal** sounds (sometimes also called **alveopalatal** or **postalveolar**). In English the voiced palatal never begins words (except in words borrowed from French, like *genre* or *gendarme,* which some English speakers produce with a French pronunciation). The voiceless palatal sound begins the words *shoe, sure, shut,* and *sugar* and ends the words *rush, push,* and *lush.* Notice that these sounds are articulated neither at the front nor at the back of the mouth and are therefore in the class of sounds specified as $\begin{bmatrix} -\text{anterior} \\ -\text{back} \end{bmatrix}$.

Coronals   Each phonetic feature we have discussed above designates a different class of speech sounds. Each sound groups with the other sounds specified by the same value of each feature. As we shall see in Chapter 3, sounds that share feature values function *as a class* in the languages of the world. Some classes are designated by a single feature, such as [+voiced] or [+nasal]. Other classes require two feature specifications, such as $\begin{bmatrix} -\text{voiced} \\ -\text{nasal} \end{bmatrix}$, the class of voiceless oral sounds. Each feature reflects a particular aspect of the sound produced, and sounds cluster according to that property. Alveolar and palatal sounds share such a property; they are articulated by raising the tongue blade toward the hard palate. The feature [±coronal] is used to distinguish between this class of sounds, which are [+coronal], and all other sounds, which are [−coronal].

Manners of Articulation

We have already described a number of phonetic properties that permit us to describe many overlapping classes of speech sounds; yet we are still unable to distinguish *t* from *s.* Both are voiceless oral alveolar, that is, $\begin{bmatrix} -\text{voiced} \\ -\text{nasal} \\ +\text{anterior} \\ -\text{labial} \\ +\text{coronal} \end{bmatrix}$ sounds.

What, then, distinguishes these sounds? Some of the features discussed do not reflect the movements of the tongue, teeth, or lips, which are the main **articulators** changing the shape or geometry of the vocal tract. Rather they reflect the way the airstream is affected as it travels from the lungs up and out of the mouth and nose. Such features or phonetic properties have traditionally been referred to as **manners of articulation.**

Stops and Continuants   Once the airstream enters the oral cavity, it may be stopped, it may be partially obstructed, or it may flow freely out of the mouth. Sounds that are *stopped completely in the oral cavity* for a brief period are, not surprisingly, called **stops.** They can be distinguished from all other speech sounds, which are called **continuants** because the stream of air continues without complete interruption through the mouth opening.

p, b, m, t, d, n, k, g, and *ng* sounds in words like *tap, tab, tam, tat, tad, tan, tack, tag,* and *tang* are stops that occur in English.

In the production of the nasal stops *n, m,* and *ng,* the air does continue to "escape" through the nose during the blockage of the airflow in the mouth; nevertheless they are classified as noncontinuant stops because the feature [±continuant] refers to the passage of air through the mouth.

The nonnasal or oral stops are also called **plosives,** because the air that is blocked in the mouth "explodes" when the closure is released. This explosion does not occur during the production of the nasal stops, because the air has an "escape route" through the nose.

p, b, and *m* are bilabial stops, with the airstream stopped at the mouth by the complete closure of the lips.

t, d, and *n* are alveolar stops; the airstream is stopped by the tongue making a complete closure at the alveolar ridge.

k, g, and *ng* are velar stops, with the complete closure at the velum.

In Quechua, a major language spoken in Bolivia and Peru, one also finds **uvular stops** which are produced when the back of the tongue is raised and moved backward to form a complete closure with the uvula. The letter *q* in words in this language, as in the language name, usually represents a uvular stop, which may occur voiced or voiceless.

All sounds fall into one of the two classes (which of course intersect with other classes) distinguished by the feature [±continuant]. Stops belong to the class of [−continuant] sounds, and nonstops to the class of [+continuant] sounds.

Aspirated and Unaspirated Sounds   During the production of voiceless sounds the glottis is open, and the air passes freely through the opening between the vocal cords. When a voiceless sound is followed by a voiced sound, as it often is, the vocal cords must close.

Voiceless sounds fall into two classes depending on the timing of the vocal cord closure. In English when we pronounce the word *pit* there is a brief period of voicelessness immediately after the *p* sound is released. That is, after the lips come apart the vocal cords remain open for a short time. Such sounds are called **aspirated** or [+aspirated] because an extra puff of air is produced.

When we pronounce the *p* in *spit,* however, the vocal cords start vibrating as soon as the lips are opened. Such sounds are called **unaspirated** or [−aspirated].

The *t* in *tick* and the *k* in *kin* are also aspirated voiceless stops, whereas the *t* in *stick* and the *k* in *skin* are unaspirated. If you hold a strip of paper in front of your lips and say *pit*, a puff of air (the aspiration) will push the paper. The paper will not move when you say *spit*.

Figure 2–3 shows in a diagrammatic form the timing of the articulators (in this case the lips) in relation to the state of the vocal cords. Notice that in the production of the voiced *b*, the vocal cords are vibrating throughout the closure of the lips and continue to vibrate for the vowel production after the lips are opened. In the [−aspirated] or unaspirated *p* in *spin*, the vocal cords are open during the lip closure and come together and start vibrating as soon as the lips open. In the production of the [+aspirated] *p* in *pin*, the vocal cords remain apart for a brief period after the lip closure is released.

Although you might not have noticed that the *p*'s in *pin* and *spin* or *pit* and *spit* are different sounds, in English all the voiceless stops that occur at the beginning of a word are aspirated, whereas those that occur after an *s* are unaspirated. This difference is important in the phonological description of the sounds, which we will discuss in greater detail in Chapter 3.

Fricatives   In the production of some sounds, the airstream is not completely stopped but is obstructed from flowing freely. If you put your hand in front of your

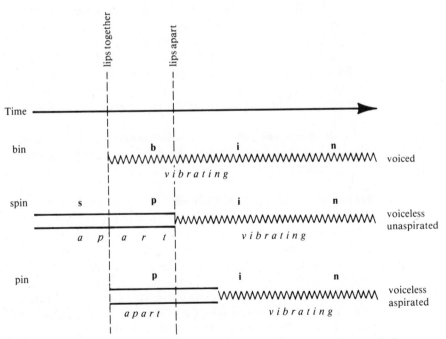

FIGURE 2–3 Timing of articulators and vocal cord vibration for voiced, voiceless unaspirated, and voiceless aspirated stops.

mouth and produce an *s, z, f, v, th,* or *sh* sound, you will feel the air coming out of your mouth. The passage in the mouth through which the air must pass, however, is narrow, causing **friction** or turbulence. The air particles are pushed against one another, producing noise because of the friction. Such sounds are called **fricatives.** (They are also sometimes referred to as **spirants,** from the Latin word *spirare,* "to blow.")

In the production of the labiodental fricatives *f* and *v,* the friction is created at the lips, where a narrow passage permits the air to escape.

s and *z* are alveolar fricatives, with the friction created at the alveolar ridge.

Palatal or alveopalatal fricatives, such as those in *mesher* and *measure,* are produced with friction created as the air passes through the narrow opening behind the alveolar ridge.

In the production of the interdental fricatives, represented by ***th*** in *thin* and *then,* the friction occurs at the opening between the tongue and teeth.

Most dialects of modern English do not include velar fricatives, although they occurred in an earlier stage of English in such words as *right, knight, enough,* and *through,* where ***gh*** occurs in the spelling. If you raise the back of the tongue as if you were about to produce a *g* or *k,* but stop just short of touching the velum, you will produce a velar fricative. The ***ch*** ending in the German pronunciation of the composer *Bach* is a velar fricative. Some speakers of modern English substitute a voiceless velar fricative in words like *bucket* and a voiced velar fricative in such words as *wagon* for the velar stops that occur for other speakers in those words.

In some languages of the world, such as French, *uvular fricatives* occur as the production of the sound represented by *r* in words such as *rouge* "red" or *rose* "pink." In Arabic *pharyngeal fricatives* are produced by pulling the tongue root toward the back wall of the pharynx. It is difficult to pull the tongue far enough to make a complete pharyngeal stop closure, but both voiced and voiceless pharyngeal fricatives can be produced and can be distinguished from velar fricatives.

All fricatives are [+continuant] sounds; although the airstream is obstructed as it passes through the oral cavity, it is not completedly stopped.

Affricates   Some sounds are produced by a stop closure followed immediately by a slow release of the closure characteristic of a fricative. These sounds are called **affricates.** The sounds that begin and end the words *church* and *judge* are voiceless and voiced affricates, respectively. Phonetically, an affricate is a sequence of a stop plus a fricative. Thus, the ***ch*** in *church* is the same as the sound combination ***t*** + ***sh,*** as is revealed by observing that in fast speech *white shoes* and *why choose* may be pronounced identically. Because the air is stopped completely during the initial articulation of an affricate, these sounds are [−continuant]s.

Sibilants   The friction created in the production of the fricatives in the words *sit, zip, shoe, leisure,* and *measure* and the affricates in the words *church* and *judge* cause a "hissing" sound. These sounds are often classed as **sibilants.** In the production of sibilants and also labiodentals, the airstream coming against the teeth or the hard alveolar ridge produces even more noise or stridency than is produced during the articulation of the interdental fricatives. Therefore sibilants and labiodental fricatives are specified as [+strident] fricatives, to distinguish them from the "less noisy" sounds.

Obstruents and Sonorants

The nonnasal stops, the fricatives, and the affricates form a major class of sounds. Because the airstream cannot escape through the nose, it is either fully obstructed in its passage through the vocal tract as in nonnasal stops and affricates, or partially obstructed in the production of fricatives. These sounds are called **obstruents** and are distinguished from the other major class of sounds, which are called **sonorants.**

Nasal stops are sonorant because although the air is blocked in the mouth it continues to resonate and move through the nose.

Fricatives are continuant obstruents because although the air is not completely stopped in its passage through the oral cavity, it is obstructed, causing the friction noted above.

Nonnasal stops and affricates are noncontinuant obstruents; there is complete blockage of the air during the production of these sounds. The closure of a stop is released abruptly, as opposed to the closure of an affricate, which is released gradually, causing friction.

This one **binary** or "two-valued" (+ or −) feature, [±sonorant], provides a way to contrast these two classes in all languages in the world. Obstruents, then, are [−sonorant].

[+consonantal] Sounds   Nasals, for the reasons given above, are [+sonorant] sounds; yet they resemble the obstruents, in that the oral cavity is constricted during their articulation. Obstruents and nasals form a class of [+consonantal] sounds. We shall discuss the [−consonantal] class of sounds below.

Four major subclasses of [+consonantal] sounds may be specified by the features [±sonorant], [±continuant], and [±strident]. Because some fricatives are [+strident] and others are [−strident], the value for this feature is left blank in Table 2–3. Notice, however, that each class of sounds differs by at least one feature value from the other three classes.

The sounds *l* and *r* are nonnasal sonorants, specified as $\begin{bmatrix} +\text{consonantal} \\ +\text{sonorant} \\ -\text{nasal} \end{bmatrix}$.

TABLE 2–3 Feature Specification of Four Classes of [+consonantal] Sounds

	Oral Stops	Nasal Stops	Fricatives	Affricatives
FEATURES				
Sonorant	−	+	−	−
Continuant	−	−	+	−
Strident	−	−		+

SARGE

Reprinted with special permission of King Features Syndicate, Inc.

There is some obstruction of the airstream in the mouth, but not enough to cause any real constriction or friction. These sounds are called **liquids.**

l is a **lateral** sound. The tongue is raised to the alveolar ridge, but the sides of the tongue are down, permitting the air to escape laterally over the sides of the tongue.

The sound *r* is produced in a variety of ways. Many English speakers produce *r* by curling the tip of the tongue back behind the alveolar ridge. Such sounds are called **retroflex** sounds.

In some languages, the *r* may be a **trill,** which is produced by the tip of the tongue vibrating against the roof of the mouth. A trilled *r* occurs in many contemporary languages, such as Spanish. In addition to the alveolar trill, uvular trills occur, as in French. A uvular trill is produced by vibrating the uvula.

In other languages the *r* is produced by a single **tap** instead of a series of vibrating taps. In Spanish both the trilled and tapped *r* occur.

One may also produce an *r* by making the tongue **flap** against the alveolar ridge. Some speakers of British English pronounce the *r* in the word *very* with a flap. It sounds like a "very fast" *d*. Most American English speakers produce a flap instead of a *t* or *d* in words like *writer* or *rider,* or *latter* or *ladder.*

In English, *l* and *r* are regularly voiced. When they follow voiceless sounds, as in *please* and *price,* they may be automatically "devoiced." Many languages of the world have a voiceless *l*. Welsh is such a language; the name *Lloyd* in Welsh starts with a voiceless *l*. English speakers find it difficult to produce a voiceless *l* when it occurs initially and usually substitute the voiced *l*.

Some languages lack liquids entirely, or have only a single one. The Cantonese dialect of Chinese has the single liquid *l*. Some English words are difficult for Cantonese speakers to pronounce, and they may substitute an *l*-sound for an *r*-sound.

The reason why speakers in languages with only one liquid tend to use that sound as a substitute for the sound that does not occur in their language is because of the acoustic similarity of these sounds. This likeness is why they are grouped together in one class and why they function as a single class of sounds in certain circumstances. For example, in English, the only two consonants that occur after an initial *k, g, p,* or *b* are the liquids *l* and *r*. We have *crate, clock* (the "c" represents the *k* sound), *plate, prate, bland,* and *brand* but no word starting with *ps, bt, pk,* and so on. (Notice that in words like *psychology* or *pterodactyl* the "p" is not pronounced. Similarly in *knight* or *knot* the "k" is not pronounced, although at an earlier stage of English, it was.)

Glides   The sounds *y* and *w* are produced with little or no obstruction of the airstream in the mouth. When occurring in a word, they must always be either preceded or followed directly by a vowel. In articulating *y* or *w* the tongue moves rapidly in gliding fashion either toward or away from a neighboring vowel; hence the term **glide.** Glides are transition sounds that are sometimes called **semivowels.** They may be specified by the features $\begin{bmatrix} -\text{consonantal} \\ +\text{sonorant} \end{bmatrix}$. They differ from vowels in that they do not form the peak of a syllable. We shall discuss this point further below.

   y is a **palatal glide;** the blade of the tongue is raised toward the hard palate in a position almost identical to that in producing the vowel sound in the word *beat.* In pronouncing *you,* the tongue moves rapidly from the *y* to the *ou* vowel.

   The glide *w* is produced by both raising the back of the tongue toward the velum and simultaneously rounding the lips. It is therefore a **labiovelar glide,** or a rounded velar glide. In the dialect of English whose speakers have different pronunciations for the words *which* and *witch,* the velar glide in the first word is voiceless, and in the second word it is voiced. The position of the tongue and the lips for *w* is similar to that for producing the vowel sound in *lute,* but the *w* is a glide because the tongue moves quickly to the vowel that follows.

   The *h* sound that starts words such as *house, who,* and *hair* is also a glide. The glottis is open as in the production of voiceless sounds. No other modification of the airstream mechanisms occurs in the mouth. In fact, the tongue and lips are usually in the position for the production of the following vowel as the airstream passes through the open glottis. The air or noise produced at the glottis is heard as *h,* and for this reason, it is sometimes classified as a **voiceless glottal fricative.** However, the *h* differs from "true" consonants in that there is no obstruction in the oral cavity. It also differs from vowels, which are articulated by moving the tongue. When it is both preceded and followed by a vowel in English it is often voiced, as in *ahead* and *cohabit.*

   If the air is stopped completely at the glottis by tightly closed vocal cords, the sound produced is a **glottal stop.** This sound is sometimes used instead of a *t* in *button* and *Latin.* It also may occur in colloquial speech at the end of words like *don't, won't,* or *can't.* In one American dialect it regularly replaces the "tt" sound in words like *bottle* or *glottal.* If you say "ah-ah-ah-ah" with one "ah" right after another but do not sustain the vowel sound, you will be producing glottal stops between the vowels. Like the *h,* it differs from both consonants and vowels and therefore may be classified as a glide. Because the air is completely blocked at the glottis, some linguists classify it as a stop.

Syllabic Sounds

HIGGINS: *Tired of listening to sounds?*
PICKERING: *Yes. It's a fearful strain. I rather fancied myself because I can pronounce twenty-four distinct vowel sounds, but your hundred and thirty beat me. I can't hear a bit of difference between most of them.*
HIGGINS: *Oh, that comes with practice. You hear no difference at first, but you keep on listening and presently you find they're all as different as A from B.*

G. B. Shaw, *Pygmalion*

Every language of the world contains the two basic classes of speech sounds often referred to by the cover terms **consonants** and **vowels.** In the production of consonants the flow of air is obstructed as it travels through the mouth. Vowels are produced with no oral obstruction whatsoever. Oral and nasal stops, fricatives, affricates, liquids, and glides all have some degree of obstruction and are therefore consonants. Consonants do not correspond exactly to the sounds specified as [+consonantal], because glides are [−consonantal], forming a subclass with vowels (which is why they often occur as part of a vocalic diphthong). However, unlike vowels, glides are produced with some small oral obstruction and therefore do not constitute syllable peaks, as do vowels. Vowels usually constitute the "main core" or the **nucleus** of syllables. Vowels, like glides, are [−consonantal] and [+sonorant]. They differ from glides because they constitute syllable peaks; so vowels are [+syllabic], whereas glides are [−syllabic].

Liquids and nasals can be syllabic—that is, they may constitute separate syllables, as in the words *medal, feather, mutton,* or *rhythm;* or they may be nonsyllabic, as in the words *lead, read, deal, dear, name,* or *mean.* For this reason in the class of liquids in Table 2–4 below, they are specified as either [+syllabic] or [−syllabic]. (The syllabicity of liquids and nasal consonants may also be shown by describing the words in which they function as syllables as having short vowels before the liquids.)

Table 2–4 shows how four different classes of speech sounds may be distinguished by the features [±consonantal], [±syllabic], and [±sonorant].

TABLE 2–4 Specifications of Four Major Classes of Sounds

	Classes			
	Obstruents	Vowels	Glides	Nasals and Liquids
Features				
Consonantal	+	−	−	+
Syllabic	−	+	−	−/+
Sonorant	−	+	+	+

By the system shown in Table 2–4, obstruents and vowels are distinct classes; they do not share any feature. Glides are like consonants in that they are in the class of [−syllabic] sounds, but they are like vowels in that they are [−consonantal] and [+sonorant]. Similarly, liquids and nasals are in the [+consonantal] class with obstruents, but share the feature [+sonorant] with vowels (and sometimes are [+syllabic]). Nonsyllabic liquids, nasals, and glides are in the class of [+sonorant, −syllabic] sounds.

Vowels

FRANK AND ERNEST   **Bob Thaves**

© 1980 Newspaper Enterprise Association, Inc.

The quality of vowels is determined by the particular configuration of the vocal tract. Different parts of the tongue may be raised or lowered. The lips may be spread or pursed. The passage through which the air travels, however, is never so narrow as to obstruct the free flow of the airstream.

Vowel sounds carry pitch and loudness; you can sing vowels. They may be long or short. Vowels can "stand alone"—they can be produced without any consonants before or after them. You can say the vowels of *beat, bit,* or *boot,* for example, without the initial *b* or the final *t*. It is more difficult to produce a consonant without some kind of vowel attached.

There have been many different schemes for describing vowel sounds. They may be described by articulatory features, as in classifying consonants. Many beginning students of phonetics find this method more difficult to apply to vowel articulations than to consonant articulations. In producing a *t*, you can feel your tongue touch the alveolar ridge. When you make a *p*, you can feel your two lips come together, or you can watch the lips move in a mirror. Because vowels are produced without any articulators touching or even coming close together it is often difficult to figure out just what is happening. One of the authors of this book, at the beginning of her graduate work, almost gave up the idea of becoming a linguist because she could not understand what was meant by "front," "back," "high," and "low" vowels.

These terms do have meaning, though. If you watch an X-ray movie of someone talking, you can see why vowels have traditionally been classified according to three questions:

1. How high is the tongue?
2. What part of the tongue is involved; that is, what part is raised or lowered?
3. What is the position of the lips?

There are other distinguishing features, such as length, nasalization, and tenseness, which we will discuss below.

Tongue Position   The three diagrams in Figure 2–4 show that the tongue in the production of the vowels in the words *heat* and *hoot* is very high in the mouth; but in *heat* it is the front part of the tongue that is raised, and in *hoot* it is the back part of the tongue. (Prolong the vowels of these words and try to feel your tongue rise.) Both of these vowels can thus be specified as [+high], with the back vowel in *hoot* also specified as [+back] to distinguish it from the [−back] vowel in *heat*.

The vowels in the words *bit* and *put* are similar to those in *beat* and *boot*, but the tongue is a little lower in the mouth.

To produce the vowel sound of *hot* or *bar* or *ah*, the back of the tongue is lowered. (The reason a doctor examining your throat may ask you to say ''ah'' is

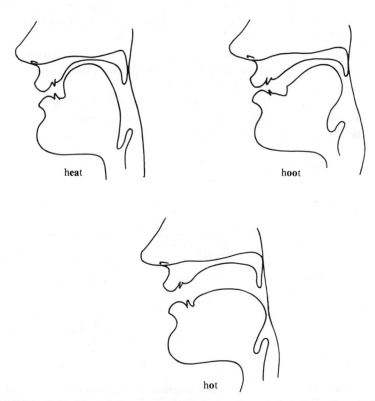

heat

hoot

hot

FIGURE 2–4 Position of the tongue in producing the vowels in *heat, hoot,* and *hot.*

that the tongue is low and easy to see over.) This vowel is therefore [+low] and [+back].

The vowel in *hat* is produced with the front part of the tongue lowered. It is [+low] like the vowel in *hot,* but distinguished from it by being [−back].

To produce the vowels in *bait* and *boat,* the tongue is raised to a mid-position between the high and low vowels discussed above. They are thus **mid vowels,** or [−high] and [−low], with the vowel in *bait* being [−back] and the vowel in *boat* being [+back]. The tongue positions in the vowels in *bet* and *bore* are slightly lower than in *bait* and *boat,* respectively.

To produce the vowel in the word *butt,* the tongue is neither high nor low, front nor back. This vowel and the slightly different final vowel in the word *Rosa* are mid, central vowels, which can be specified as [−high, −low, +back].

Lip Rounding Vowels also differ as to whether the lips are rounded. The vowels in *boot, put, boat,* and *bought* (or *bore*) are produced with the back of the tongue at decreasing heights, just like the front vowels in *beet, bit, bait, bet,* and *bat.* However, these back vowels are all pronounced with the lips pursed or **rounded.** The low vowel in *hot* is the only English back vowel that occurs without lip rounding. The mid, central vowel is also unrounded.

Using the phonetic properties or dimensions of the tongue—front to back, high to low, lip rounding vs. nonrounding—we can classify these English vowels as in Figure 2–5.

As Figure 2–5 shows, there are no words with front-rounded vowels in English. This situation is not true of all languages. French and Swedish, for example, have both front and back rounded vowels.

In English, a high back unrounded vowel does not occur, but in Mandarin Chinese, in Japanese, in the Cameroonian language Fe?Fe?, and in many other languages, this vowel is part of the phonetic inventory of sounds. There is, for

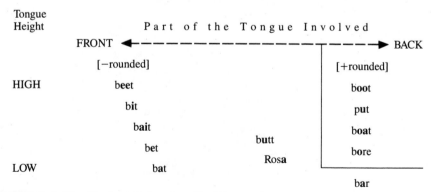

FIGURE 2–5 Classification of American English vowels.

example, a Chinese word meaning "four" that is pronounced with an initial *s* followed by a vowel similar to the one in *boot* but with nonrounded spread lips. This word is distinguished from the word meaning "speed," which we could represent as *soo*.

Diphthongs Many languages, including English, have vowels called **diphthongs,** which could also be described as a sequence of two sounds, vowel + glide. The vowels we have studied so far are all simple vowels called **monophthongs.** The vowel sounds in the words *bite* and *rite* are produced with the *a* vowel sound of *father* followed by the *y* glide. The vowels in *bout, brown,* and *hour* are produced by some speakers of English with a similar *a* sound followed by the glide *w.* The third diphthong that occurs in English is the vowel sound in *boy and soil,* which may be described as the vowel that occurs in *bore* (without the *r*) followed by the *y* glide.

Tense and Lax Vowels The vowels in the following pairs of words may be distinguished by the feature [±tense], with the vowel in the first word of the pair **tense** or [+tense] and the second word [−tense] or **lax**:

Tense [+tense]	Lax [−tense]
beat	bit
bait	bet
boot	put
boat	bought

The lax vowels are produced with a slightly lower tongue position than in their tense counterparts. Tense vowels are sometimes also slightly diphthongized for some speakers of English. For such speakers the tense front vowels are followed by a short *y* glide, and the tense back vowels by a short *w* glide.

Nasalization Vowels, like consonants, can be produced with a raised velum that prevents the air from escaping through the nose, or with a lowered velum that permits air to pass through the nasal passage. When the nasal passage is blocked, **oral** vowels, shown as [−nasal], are produced; when the nasal passage is open, **nasal** or **nasalized** vowels, shown as [+nasal], are produced. In English, nasal vowels occur only before nasal consonants, and oral vowels occur only before oral consonants.[4] The words *bean, bin, bane, Ben, ban, boon, bun, bone, beam, bam, boom, bing, bang,* and *bong* are examples of words that contain nasalized vowels.

In languages like French, Polish, and Portuguese, nasalized vowels may occur when no nasal consonant is adjacent.

---

[4]In fast colloquial speech, some speakers "drop" the nasal consonant when it occurs before voiceless stops such as *hint* or *camp,* leaving just the nasal vowel; but the word originates with a nasal consonant.

Prosodic Features

Some speech sounds are differentiated in ways not yet described. For example, there are languages in which two words are distinguished in meaning depending on whether the vowel is long or short in **duration.**[5] A vowel can be lengthened by prolonging it. A consonant is made long by maintaining the closure or obstruction for a longer period of time.

When we speak we also change the **pitch** of our voice. The pitch produced depends upon how fast the vocal cords vibrate; the faster they vibrate, the higher the pitch. In physical or acoustic terms, pitch is referred to as the **fundamental frequency** of the sound signal.

We are also able to change the loudness of the sounds and sound sequences. In many languages, some syllables or vowels are produced with a change in pitch (usually higher), more loudly, and longer than other vowels in the word or sentence. They are referred to as **stressed** vowels or syllables.

In Chapter 3, we will discuss the ways in which **prosodic features**—*length, pitch,* and the complex feature *stress*—are used to distinguish words and the meanings of sentences in different ways in different languages.

The phonetic properties and features we have discussed are broad terms covering many even finer distinctions. In this chapter we are merely attempting to present a general view of how such phonetic properties differentiate the sounds found in human languages, and how they are produced.

The Phonetic Alphabet

Once a Frenchman who'd promptly said "Oui"
To some ladies who'd asked him if houi
    Cared to drink, threw a fit
    Upon finding that it
Was a tipple no stronger than toui.

Anonymous

The one-l lama,
He's a priest.
The two-l llama,
He's a beast.

And I will bet
A silk pajama
There isn't any
Three-l lllama.

Ogden Nash[6]

---

[5]"Long" and "short" are *not* used by linguists to distinguish the *i* sound in *bite* from the *i* sound in *bit*, and so on, as they are in dictionaries and "grammar" books.
[6]"The Lama" from *Verses from 1929 On* by Ogden Nash. Reprinted by permission of Curtis Brown Ltd., London, on behalf of the Estate of Ogden Nash.

By permission of Johnny Hart and North America Syndicate, Inc.

In the discussion of the phonetic properties or features that are used to distinguish and define speech sounds, we were faced with certain problems. We noted, for example, that in English the letter *p* is used to represent both the aspirated voiceless stop in *pit* and the unaspirated voiceless stop in *spit*. Alphabetic spelling represents the pronunciations of words; but it is often the case that the sounds of the words in a language are rather unsystematically represented by **orthography**—that is, by spelling.

Suppose all Earthlings were destroyed by some horrible catastrophe, and years later Martian astronauts exploring Earth discovered some fragments of English writing that included the following sentence:

Did **he** bel**ie**ve that C**ae**sar could s**ee** the p**eo**ple s**ei**ze the s**ea**s?

How would a Martian linguist decide that **e, ie, ae, ee, eo, ei,** and **ea** all represented the same sound? To add to the confusion, later this sentence might crop up:

The sill**y** am**oe**ba stole the k**ey** to the mach**i**ne.

English speakers learn how to pronounce these words when learning to read and write and know that *y, oe, ey,* and *i* also represent the same sound as the bold-face letters in the first sentence.

This inconsistent spelling system prompted Ambrose Bierce to define **orthography** as "the science of spelling by the eye instead of the ear."[7] Mark Twain wrote: "They spell it Vinci and pronounce it Vinchy; foreigners always spell better than they pronounce." He was fully aware that it is not only "foreigners" whose spelling differs from pronunciation.[8]

Spelling Reformers

The English have no respect for their language, and will not teach their children to speak it. They cannot spell it because they have nothing to spell it with but an old foreign alphabet of which only the consonants—and not all of them—have any agreed speech value.

G. B. Shaw, Preface to *Pygmalion*

B.C.   **Johnny Hart**

By permission of Johnny Hart and North America Syndicate, Inc.

The discrepancy between spelling and sounds gave rise to a movement of "spelling reformers." They wanted to revise the alphabet so that one letter would correspond to one sound, and one sound to one letter, thus simplifying spelling. This alphabet would be a **phonetic alphabet.**

[7]Ambrose Bierce. *The Devil's Dictionary.* Dolphin Books, Doubleday & Co., Inc. Garden City, N.Y. P. 150.
[8]Mark Twain. 1869. *The Innocents Abroad.* Harper & Row. New York. Ch. 19.

George Bernard Shaw followed in the footsteps of three centuries of spelling reformers in England. In typical Shavian manner he pointed out that we could use the English spelling system to spell *fish* as *ghoti*—the *gh* like the sound in *enough,* the *o* like the sound in *women,* and the *ti* like the sound in *nation.* Shaw was so concerned about English spelling that he included in his will a provision for a new "Proposed English Alphabet" to be administered by a "Public Trustee" who would have the duty of seeking and publishing a more efficient alphabet. This alphabet was to have at least forty letters to enable "the said language to be written without indicating single sounds by groups of letters or by diacritical marks." After Shaw's death in 1950, 450 designs for such an alphabet were submitted from all parts of the globe. Four alphabets were judged to be equally good, and the £500 sterling prize was divided among their designers. An "expert" collaborated with these four to produce the alphabet designated in Shaw's will. Shaw also stipulated in his will that his play *Androcles and the Lion* be published in the new alphabet, with "the original Doctor Johnson's lettering opposite the transliteration page by page and a glossary of the two alphabets." This version of the play was published in 1962.

If we look at English spelling, it is easy to understand why there is a need for a phonetic alphabet. Different letters may represent a single sound, as shown in the following instances:

> *to*   *too*   *two*   thr*ough*   thr*ew*   cl*ue*   sh*oe*

A single letter may represent different sounds:

> d*a*me   d*a*d   f*a*ther   c*a*ll   vill*a*ge   m*a*ny
>
> *p*in/s*p*in   *k*in/s*k*in   *t*ick/s*t*ick

A combination of letters may represent a single sound:

> *sh*oot   *ch*aracter   *Th*omas   *ph*ysics
> ei*th*er   d*ea*l   rou*gh*   na*ti*on
> c*oa*t   gla*ci*al   *th*eater   pl*ai*n

Some letter have no sound at all in certain words:

> *m*nemonic   *w*hole   resi*g*n   g*h*ost
> *p*terodactyl   *w*rite   hole   cor*p*s
> *p*sychology   s*w*ord   de*b*t   *g*naw
> bou*gh*   lam*b*   is*l*and   *k*not

Some sounds are not represented in the spelling. In many words the letter *u* represents a *y* sound followed by a *u* sound:

> c*u*te   (compare: c*oo*t)
> f*u*tile   (compare: r*u*le)
> *u*tility   (compare: *U*zbek)

One letter may represent two sounds; the final *x* in *Xerox* represents a *k* followed by an *s*.

Because of this lack of correspondence between spelling and sounds, new alphabets continue to be developed in the attempt to solve the problem. An alphabet called UNIFON was invented in 1959 by a Chicago economist, John Malone. It includes 40 letters, all based on Roman capital letters with some alterations; for example ∮ is used for the palatal fricative initial sound in *sure;* ¢ represents the voiced affricate sound in *chair*. According to its inventor, UNIFON will be adopted by Congress as the official alphabet by the year 2020. Unfortunately, the problems faced by earlier spelling reformers and inventors of new alphabets still remain, and it is not clear why this alphabet is any better than others that have been proposed during the last 400 years. (This matter is further discussed in Chapter 9 on Writing Systems.)

From "Universal Characters" to the IPA

Whether we support or oppose spelling reform in English, it is clear that to describe the sounds of English, or any other language, we cannot depend on the spelling of words. Shaw was not totally wrong. The alphabets designed to fulfill Shaw's will, however, were not the first phonetic alphabets. In 1617, Robert Robinson produced an alphabet that attempted to provide a relationship between "articulation" and the shapes of the letters. In 1657, Cave Beck produced *A Universal Character,* a publication described on its title page as "The Universal Character by which all the Nations in the World may understand one another's Conceptions, Reading out of one Common Writing their own Mother Tongues." In 1668, Bishop John Wilkins proposed a similar universal alphabet; and in 1686, Francis Lodwick published "An Essay Towards an Universal Alphabet," which he had worked out and circulated many years before. Lodwick's aim was to provide an alphabet "which should contain an Enumeration of all such Single Sounds or Letters as are used in any Language. . . . All single sounds ought to have single and distinct characters" and no one character shall "have more than one Sound, nor any one Sound be expressed by more than one Character." Lodwick, like Cave Beck before him and others who followed him, did not use Roman letters. He designed his own "letters" in such a way that similar sounds were represented by similar symbols. The concept of "similarity" refers to the classes of sounds discussed above, which share articulatory features. In Shaw's lifetime, the phonetician Henry Sweet, the prototype for Shaw's own Henry Higgins in the play *Pygmalion* (which many people know as *My Fair Lady*), produced a phonetic alphabet.

These alphabets were not developed by "spelling reformers" but by scholars interested in methods by which speech sounds could be described and symbolized. This interest led the International Phonetics Association (IPA) to develop a phonetic alphabet in 1888 that could be used to symbolize the sounds found in all languages. Because many languages use a Roman alphabet like that used in the English writing system, the IPA phonetic symbols are based on the Roman letters. These phonetic symbols have a consistent value, unlike ordinary letters, which may or may not represent the same sounds in the same or different languages. The IPA phonetic alphabet is still the primary one used all over the world today by phoneticians, language teachers, speech pathologists, linguists, and anyone wishing to symbolize the spoken word.

It is of course impossible to construct any set of symbols that will specify all the minute differences between sounds. Even Shaw recognized this limitation when in his will he directed his Trustee

> to bear in mind that the proposed British Alphabet does not pretend to be exhaustive as it contains only sixteen vowels whereas by infinitesimal movements of the tongue countless different vowels can be produced all of them in use among speakers of English who utter the same vowels no oftener than they make the same fingerprints.

Even if we could specify all the details of different pronunciations, we would not want to. A basic fact about speech is that no two utterances are ever physically the same. If a speaker says "Good morning" on Monday and again on Tuesday, there will be some slight differences in the sounds on the two days. In fact, if the same person says "Good morning" twice in succession on the same day, the two utterances will not be physically identical. If another speaker says "Good morning," the physical sounds (that is, the acoustic signal) produced will also differ from those produced by the first speaker; yet all the "Good mornings" are considered to be repetitions of the same utterance.

This fact about language is interesting. Some differences in the sounds of an utterance are important in trying to comprehend it, and other differences can be ignored. Even though we never produce or hear exactly the same utterance twice, speakers know when two utterances are linguistically the same or different. Some properties of the sounds are therefore more important linguistically than others.

A phonetic alphabet should include enough symbols to represent the "crucial" differences. At the same time it should not, and cannot, include all noncrucial differences, because such differences are infinitely varied.

A list of phonetic symbols that can be used to represent all the basic speech sounds of English is given in Table 2–5. The symbols omit many details about the

TABLE 2–5 A Phonetic Alphabet for American English Pronunciation

Consonants							Vowels			
p^h	pill	t^h	till	k^h	kill		i	beet	ɪ	bit
p	spill	t	still	k	skill		e	bait	ɛ	bet
b	bill	d	dill	g	gill		u	boot	ʊ	foot
m	mill	n	nil	ŋ	ring		o	boat	ɔ	bought
f	feel	D	rider	h	high		æ	bat	a	pot
v	veal	s	seal	ʔ	bottle		ʌ	but	ə	sofa
θ	thigh	z	zeal	l	leaf		aj	bite	aw	bout
ð	thy	č	chill	r	reef		ɔj	boy		
š	shill	ǰ	Jill	j	you					
ž	azure	ʍ	which	w	witch					

sounds and how they are produced in different words, and in different places in words. These symbols are meant to be used by persons knowing English.

The symbol [ə] is called a **schwa.** It will be used in this book only to represent unstressed vowels, as illustrated in Table 2–6. (Note that there is great variation in the way speakers of English produce this vowel, but it is phonetically similar to the wedge symbol [ʌ], which will be used only in stressed syllables.)

To differentiate between the spelling of a word and the pronunciation, we will sometimes enclose the phonetic symbols in brackets [ ]. Thus the word spelled *boat* would be **transcribed phonetically** as [bot].

TABLE 2–6 Phonetic Symbol/English Spelling Correspondences

Consonants

Symbol	Examples
p	s*p*it ti*p* a*p*ple am*p*le hiccou*gh*
pʰ	*p*it *p*rick *p*laque ap*p*ear
b	*b*it ta*b* *b*rat bu*bb*le
m	*m*itt ta*m* s*m*ack E*mm*y ca*m*p co*mb*
t	s*t*ick pi*t* kiss*ed* wri*te*
tʰ	*t*ick in*t*end *pt*erodactyl a*tt*ack
d	*D*ick ca*d* *d*rip lov*ed* ri*de*
n	*n*ick ki*n* s*n*ow *mn*emonic desig*n* *gn*ostic *pn*eumatic k*n*ow
k	s*k*in sti*ck* s*c*at criti*qu*e o*ch*er ex*c*eed
kʰ	*c*url *k*in *ch*arisma *c*ritic me*ch*anic *c*lose
g	*g*irl *g*uard bur*g* o*g*re lon*g*er Pittsbur*gh*
ŋ	si*ng* thi*n*k fi*n*ger si*ng*er a*n*kle
f	*f*at *ph*iloso*ph*y *f*lat *ph*logiston co*ff*ee ree*f* cou*gh*
v	*v*at do*v*e gra*v*el ra*v*age
s	*s*ip *s*kip *p*sychology pa*ss* pat*s* democra*c*y *s*cissors fa*s*ten de*c*eive de*s*cent *ps*eudo pea*ce*
z	*z*ip ja*zz* ra*z*or pad*s* ki*ss*es *X*erox lie*s* pea*s* *x*ylophone de*s*ign la*z*y *s*cissor*s* mai*ze*
θ	*th*igh *th*rough wra*th* e*th*er wrea*th* Ma*tth*ew
ð	*th*y *th*eir wea*th*er la*the* mo*th*er ei*th*er
š	*sh*oe mu*sh* mi*ss*ion na*ti*on fi*sh* gla*ci*al *s*ure Ru*ss*ian
ž	mea*s*ure vi*s*ion a*z*ure ca*s*ual deci*s*ion rou*ge* (for those who do not pronounce this word with the final sound of *judge*)
č	*ch*oke ma*tch* fea*t*ure ri*ch* righ*t*eous
ǰ	*j*udge mid*g*et *G*eorge ma*g*istrate re*g*ion resi*d*ual
l	*l*eaf fee*l* ca*ll* sing*l*e
r	*r*eef fea*r* Pa*r*is singe*r*
j	*y*ou *y*es pla*y*ing feu*d* *u*se
w	*w*itch s*w*im mo*w*ing q*u*een
ʍ	*wh*ich *wh*ere *wh*ale (for speakers who pronounce *which* differently than *witch*)
h	*h*at *wh*o *wh*ole re*h*ash
ʔ	bo*tt*le bu*tt*on glo*tt*al (for some speakers)

TABLE 2–6 Phonetic Symbol/English Spelling Correspondences (continued)

Vowels	
i	b*ee*t b*ea*t b*e* rec*ei*ve k*ey* bel*ie*ve am*oe*ba p*eo*ple C*ae*sar Vasel*i*ne ser*e*ne lil*y*
I	b*i*t cons*i*st *i*njury b*i*n b*ee*n
e	b*a*te b*ai*t r*ay* gr*ea*t *ei*ght g*au*ge r*ei*gn th*ey*
ɛ	b*e*t ser*e*nity s*ay*s g*ue*st d*ea*d s*ai*d
æ	p*a*n *a*ct l*au*gh comr*a*de r*a*lly
u	b*oo*t l*u*te wh*o* s*e*wer d*u*ty thr*ough* t*o* t*oo* tw*o* m*o*ve L*ou*
U	p*u*t f*oo*t b*u*tcher c*ou*ld
ʌ	c*u*t t*ou*gh am*o*ng *o*ven d*oe*s c*o*ver fl*oo*d b*i*rd h*e*rd w*o*rd f*u*r
o	c*oa*t g*o* b*eau* gr*ow* th*ough* t*oe* *ow*n *o*ver mel*o*dious
ɔ	c*augh*t wr*o*ng st*a*lk c*o*re s*aw* b*a*ll *awe*
a	c*o*t f*a*ther p*a*lm serge*a*nt h*o*nor h*o*spital mel*o*dic
ə	sof*a* *a*lone princip*a*l symph*o*ny ros*e*s diffic*u*lt s*u*ppose mel*o*dy tedi*ou*s w*a*nted th*e* *A*merica
aj	b*i*te s*igh*t b*y* d*ie* d*ye* St*ei*n *ai*sle ch*oi*r l*i*ar *i*sland h*eigh*t s*i*gn
aw, æw	ab*ou*t br*ow*n d*ou*bt c*ow*ard
ɔj	b*oy* d*oi*ly

Table 2–6 illustrates the different spellings of the sounds these symbols represent. Some of these pronunciations may differ from yours, so some of the examples may be confusing. For example, some speakers of American English pronounce the words *cot* and *caught* identically. In the dialect described here, *cot* and *caught* are pronounced differently, so *caught* is given as an example for the symbol [ɔ]. Many speakers who pronounce *cot* and *caught* identically pronounce *car* and *core* with different vowels. If you use the vowel of *car* to say *cot* and the vowel of *core* to say *caught,* you will be approximating the dialect that distinguishes the two words. There are also a number of English dialects in which the *r* sound is not pronounced unless it occurs before a vowel. Speakers of this dialect would pronounce the word *bird* with a vowel not symbolized in the chart; that is, [ɚ]. The selection of the dialect in this book is of necessity arbitrary; we draw upon a number of dialects so as to provide the major symbols that can describe dialects of American English. Do not dwell on confusing particulars, but let them impress upon you the complexity of the problem.

Some of the symbols in Table 2–6 are those traditionally used by linguists in the United States in place of IPA symbols:

U.S.		IPA		U.S.		IPA
š	=	ʃ		I	=	ι
ž	=	ʒ		U	=	ω
č	=	tʃ				
ǰ	=	dʒ				
D	=	ɹ				

The symbol [y] is often substituted in the United States for the IPA symbol [j] to represent the palatal glide. For reasons given below we are using the IPA symbol. You may use the two versions interchangeably in the exercises at the end of this chapter, but you should try to be consistent.

Using these symbols, we can now unambiguously represent the pronunciation of words. For example, words spelled with *ou* may have different pronunciations. To distinguish between the symbols representing sounds and the alphabet letters, we put the phonetic symbols between brackets:

Spelling	Pronunciation
though	[ðo]
thought	[θɔt]
rough	[rʌf]
bough	[baw]
through	[θru]
would	[wʊd]

Notice that only in *rough* do the letters *gh* represent any sound; that is, the sound [f]. Notice also that *ou* represents six different sounds, and *th* two different sounds. The *l* in *would,* like the *gh* in all but one of the words above, is not pronounced at all.

The symbols given in the list are not sufficient to represent the pronunciation of words in all languages. We would need another symbol for the voiceless velar fricative in the German word *Bach,* [x], for the French uvular trill, [ʀ], and for the French rounded high front vowel in *tu* ''you'' (singular), which is represented by the IPA symbol [y]. (The American use of [y] as the symbol for the palatal glide instead of the IPA [j] can create difficulties, which is one reason we have used the IPA symbol for this sound.) The French rounded vowels can be symbolized as follows:

[y] as in *tu* [ty] ''you'' (singular)	The tongue position as for [i] but the lips are rounded
[ø] as in *bleu* [blø] ''blue''	The tongue position as for [e] but the lips are rounded
[œ] as in *heure* ''hour''	The tongue position as in [ɛ] but the lips are rounded

Diacritics

We noted above in the discussion of nasalization that in French, vowels may be oral or nasal. To designate nasality the **diacritic** mark [˜] is placed over the vowel, as in these English words:

bomb [bãm]   *boon* [bũn]   *bean* [bĩn]

The French nasalized vowels that are not followed by an adjacent consonant may also be symbolized in this way. Notice that in the French spelling system an *n* (which is silent in the words below) is included to indicate that the preceding vowel is nasalized.

[ɛ̃]	as in *vin* [vɛ̃]	"wine"
[ã]	as in *an* [ã]	"year"
[õ]	as in *son* [sõ]	"sound"
[œ̃]	as in *brun* [brœ̃]	"brown"

Other diacritics added to symbols are used to distinguish between sounds. A long segment may be indicated by a colon [:] placed after the lengthened symbol or by a doubled symbol. Long vowels or consonants are sometimes called **geminates.** In Italian, for example, both long or geminate and short consonants occur:

[papa] "Pope"   [pap:a] "porridge"

In Korean long vowels contrast with short vowels:

[kul] "oyster"   [kuul] "tunnel"

To differentiate a voiceless lateral liquid like the *ll* in *Lloyd* the symbol [̥] is placed under the segment; thus *Lloyd* in Welsh would be phonetically transcribed as [l̥ɔjd], whereas in English it would be [lɔjd].

A capital C is often used to represent the class of consonants (all nonvowels), V for the class of vowels, G for glides, and L for liquids. A syllabic consonant may also be specified as Ç, and a rounded consonant that often occurs before a rounded vowel by a superscript ^{w}.

We can summarize these diacritics and additional symbols as follows:

C = Consonant	C: = long C	C^w = rounded C
V = Vowel	V: = long V	V̄ = nasalized V
L = Liquid	C̥ = voiceless C	C̩ = syllabic C
G = Glide	V́ = stressed V	

Phonetic Features

Now that we have a phonetic alphabet—a set of symbols which can be used to differentiate all the phonetic sound segments in a one symbol–one sound fashion—we can classify the sounds of American English according to their phonetic features, as shown in Table 2–7.

The classes that are specified in Table 2–7 play an important role in the phonological and phonetic rules of languages we will discuss in Chapter 3 and throughout the book.

Such a classification is helpful, but the binary feature specifications we discussed earlier provide a simpler and more explanatory description of why sounds are grouped into intersecting sets. This classification is shown in Table 2–8, Table 2–9, and Table 2–10.

TABLE 2–7 Classification of Phonetic Symbols for American English Nonvowel Sounds

	Bilabial	Labiodental	Interdental	Alveolar	Palatal	Velar	Glottal
Stop (oral)							
voiceless unaspirated	p			t		k	
voiceless aspirated	pʰ			tʰ		kʰ	
voiced	b			d		g	
Nasal (stop)	m			n		ŋ	
Fricative							
voiceless		f	θ	s	š		
voiced		v	ð	z	ž		
Affricate							
voiceless					č		
voiced					ǰ		
Glide							
voiceless						ʍ	h ?
voiced					j	w	
Liquid				l r			

TABLE 2–8 Phonetic Features of American English Obstruents

	p	pʰ	b	t	tʰ	d	k	kʰ	g	f	v	θ	ð	s	z	š	ž	č	ǰ
sonorant	−	−	−	−	−	−	−	−	−	−	−	−	−	−	−	−	−	−	−
consonantal	+	+	+	+	+	+	+	+	+	+	+	+	+	+	+	+	+	+	+
syllabic	−	−	−	−	−	−	−	−	−	−	−	−	−	−	−	−	−	−	−
continuant	−	−	−	−	−	−	−	−	−	+	+	+	+	+	+	+	+	−	−
aspirated*	−	+		−	+		−	+											
voiced	−	−	+	−	−	+	−	−	+	−	+	−	+	−	+	−	+	−	+
labial	+	+	+	−	−	−	−	−	−	+	+	−	−	−	−	−	−	−	−
anterior	+	+	+	+	+	+	−	−	−	+	+	+	+	+	+	−	−	−	−
coronal	−	−	−	+	+	+	−	−	−	−	−	+	+	+	+	+	+	+	+
back	−	−	−	−	−	−	+	+	+	−	−	−	−	−	−	−	−	−	−
strident	−	−	−	−	−	−	−	−	−	+	+	−	−	+	+	+	+	+	+
nasal**	−	−	−	−	−	−	−	−	−	−	−	−	−	−	−	−	−	−	−

*We have only marked the values of the feature "aspirated" for voiceless stops; the other sounds are not distinguished by this feature.
**Because all obstruents are [−sonorant], the [−nasal] specification is redundant as it is predictable; we have included it for comparison with Table 2–9.

In these tables, all sounds marked + for a certain feature belong in one class and those marked − in another class; for example, the class of nasals includes all the sounds marked [+nasal]; the class of oral stops and affricates is specified as [−continuant].

It is not necessary to include as features all the terms we have used to describe the sounds. For example, alveolar sounds are [+anterior, +coronal]; we do not need a feature [±alveolar]. Similarly, "liquids" are unambiguously specified as the only sounds that are [+consonantal], [+sonorant], and [−nasal].

We will refer to the classes of sounds shown in these tables in Chapter 3.

TABLE 2–9 Phonetic Features of American English Sonorant Consonants and Glides

	m	n	ŋ	l	r	w	j	h	ʔ
sonorant*	+	+	+	+	+	+	+	+	+
consonantal	+	+	+	+	+	−	−	−	−
syllabic	+/−	+/−	+/−	+/−	+/−	−	−	−	−
continuant	−	−	−	+	+	+	+	+	−
voiced	+	+	+	+	+	+	+	−	−
labial	+	−	−	−	−	+	−	−	−
anterior	+	+	−	+	+	−	−	−	−
coronal	−	+	−	+	+	−	+	−	−
back	−	−	+	−	−	+	−	+	+
nasal	+	+	+	−	−	−	−	−	−
lateral	−	−	−	+	−	−	−	−	−

*[+sonorant] segments are redundantly [−strident].

TABLE 2–10 Phonetic Features of American English Stressed Vowels*

	i	I	e	ɛ	æ	u	U	o	ɔ	a	ʌ
high	+	+	−	−	−	+	+	−	−	−	−
low	−	−	−	−	+	−	−	−	−	+	−
back	−	−	−	−	−	+	+	+	+	+	+
rounded	−	−	−	−	−	+	+	+	+	−	−
tense	+	−	+	−	−	+	−	+	−	−	−

*All these vowels are [+sonorant, −consonantal, +syllabic, +voiced]. The diphthongs [aj, aw, and ɔj] would be represented by a two-column feature matrix of the vowel followed by the glide.

Summary

The science of speech sounds is called **phonetics.** It aims to provide the set of **features,** or properties, that can describe all the sounds used in human language.

When we speak, the physical sounds we produce are continuous stretches of sound, which are the physical representations of strings of **discrete linguistic segments.**

All human speech sounds fall into classes according to their phonetic properties or features—that is, according to how they are produced. Sounds may be either **voiced** or **voiceless; oral** or **nasal; labial, alveolar, palatal, velar, uvular,** or **glottal.** They may also be **fricatives** or **stops** and either **consonants, vowels, glides,** or **liquids.**

Vowels differ according to the position of the tongue and lips: **high, mid,** or **low** tongue; **front** or **back** of the tongue; **rounded** or **unrounded** lips. There are general and regular processes (rules) in all languages that utilize these classes of sounds.

To describe these speech sounds we cannot depend on the way words are spelled. Conventional spellings represent only partially the pronunciation of words. For this reason, a **phonetic alphabet** such as that devised in 1888 by the International Phonetics Association (IPA) is used, in which each phonetic symbol stands for one and only one sound. The phonetic symbols that can be used to represent the sounds of English are presented in this chapter.

Because each phonetic segment is composed of a **bundle** of features, it may be more adequately represented as a **matrix** of binary phonetic features, each marked + or −. All sounds marked by the same value for a feature belong to that class. For example, a sound marked [+voiced] belongs to the class containing all voiced segments; a sound marked [−nasal] belongs to the class of all oral segments.

Diacritics to specify such properties as **nasalization, length, voicelessness, syllabicity, stress,** and **rounding** may be combined with the phonetic symbols for more detailed phonetic transcriptions.

By means of these phonetic features we can describe all speech sounds.

References

Abercrombie, David. 1967. *Elements of General Phonetics*. Aldine. Chicago.

Chomsky, N., and M. Halle. 1968. *The Sound Pattern of English*. Ch. 8. Harper & Row. New York.

International Phonetic Association. 1949. *Principles of the International Phonetics Association*. Rev. ed. IPA. London.

Ladefoged, Peter. 1982. *A Course in Phonetics*. 2d ed. Harcourt Brace Jovanovich. New York.

Ladefoged, Peter. 1971. *Preliminaries to Linguistic Phonetics*. University of Chicago Press. Chicago.

Exercises

1. Write the phonetic symbol for the first sound in each of the following words, according to the way you pronounce it.

    Examples: ooze   [u]   psycho   [s]

    a. judge   [ ]   f. thought   [ ]
    b. Thomas   [ ]   g. contact   [ ]
    c. though   [ ]   h. phone   [ ]
    d. easy   [ ]   i. civic   [ ]
    e. pneumonia   [ ]   j. usury   [ ]

2. Write the phonetic symbol for the *last* sound in each of the following words:

    a. fleece   [ ]   f. cow   [ ]
    b. neigh   [ ]   g. rough   [ ]
    c. long   [ ]   h. cheese   [ ]
    d. health   [ ]   i. bleached   [ ]
    e. watch   [ ]   j. rags   [ ]

3. Write the following words in phonetic transcription, according to your pronunciation.

    Example: gnome   [nõm]

    a. physics   f. marry
    b. merry   g. tease
    c. weather   h. heath
    d. coat   i. Mary
    e. yellow   j. "your name"

4. Below is a phonetic transcription of one of the verses in the poem *The Walrus and the Carpenter* by Lewis Carroll. The speaker who transcribed it may not have exactly the same pronunciation as you; there are many alternate correct versions. However, there is *one* major error in each line that is an impossible pronunciation for any American English speaker. The error may consist of an extra symbol, a missing symbol, or a wrong symbol in the word.

    Write the word in which the error occurs in the *correct* phonetic transcription.

    Corrected Word

    a. ðə tʰãjm hæz cʌm   [Kʰʌm   ]
    b. ðə wɔlrʌs sed
    c. tʰu tʰɔlk əv mẽni θĩŋz
    d. əv šuz ãnd šɪps
    e. ænd silĩŋ wæx
    f. əv kʰæbəgəz ænd kʰĩŋz   (Exercise 4 continued on p. 66.)

Corrected Word

g. ænd waj ðə si ɪs bɔjlĩŋ hat   [   ]

h. æ̃nd wɛθər pʰɪgz hæv wĩŋz

5. Write the symbol that corresponds to each of the following phonetic descriptions; then give an English word that contains this sound.

Example: voiced alveolar stop   [d] *dog*

a. voiceless bilabial unaspirated stop
b. low front vowel
c. lateral liquid
d. velar nasal
e. voiced interdental fricative
f. voiceless affricate
g. palatal glide
h. mid lax front vowel
i. high back tense vowel

6. In each of the following pairs of words, the bold italicized sounds differ by one or more phonetic properties (features). State the differences and, in addition, state what properties they have in common.

Example: phone–phonic   The *o* in *phone* is mid, tense, round.
                            The *o* in *phonic* is low, unround.
                            Both are back vowels.

a. ba*th*–ba*th*e
b. redu*c*e–redu*c*tion
c. *c*ool–*c*old
d. wi*f*e–wi*v*es
e. cat*s*–dog*s*
f. i*m*polite–i*n*decent

7. Match the sounds under column A with *one or more* features from column B, as illustrated in the first one.

A		B	
[ð]	1.	1.	[+voiced]
[u]		2.	[−anterior]
[t]		3.	[+nasal]
[z]		4.	[+back]
[ŋ]		5.	[+sonorant]
[l]		6.	[+coronal]
[θ]		7.	[+lateral]
[a]		8.	[+rounded]
		9.	[−continuant]

8. A phonetic symbol is a "cover term" for a composite of distinctive phonetic properties or features. Define each of the symbols below by marking + or −

(Exercise 8 continued on p. 67.)

for each given feature, depending on whether the property is present or absent.

a.

	m	l	θ	s	č	g	w
sonorant							
consonantal							
continuant							
voiced							
labial							
anterior							
coronal							
back							
nasal							
lateral							
strident							

b.

	a	o	I	u	i	ɛ	ʌ
high							
low							
back							
tense							
round							

9. A natural class is a group of sounds sharing one or more features in common. For each group of sounds listed below, there is one sound that does not share any phonetic features with all the others in the set. Indicate which sound is not a member of the natural class, and the phonetic features the other sounds in the class share.

Example: [p] [b] [s] [m] [v] [f]   1) [s]
2) The other sounds are all labial.

a. [g] [p] [b] [d] [z] [v]
b. [u] [i] [ɛ] [o] [e]
c. [g] [k] [b] [d] [p] [v] [t]
d. [a] [u] [e] [w] [i] [o]

(Exercise 9 continued on p. 68.)

e. [z] [v] [s] [ž] [g]
f. [m] [n] [b] [ŋ]
g. [t] [z] [d] [n] [f] [s] [ž]
h. [æ] [u] [i] [e] [ɛ] [a]

10. Write the following sentences in regular English spelling.
a. nõm čãmski ɪz ə lĩŋgwɪst hu tʰičəz æt ẽm aj tʰi

b. fõnɛtɪks ɪz ðə stʌdi ʌv spič sãw̃ndz

c. ɔl læ̃ŋgwɪǰəz juz sãw̃ndz pʰrodust baj ðə ʌpər rɛspərətɔri sɪstẽm

d. ĩn wʌ̃n dajəlɛkt ʌv ɪŋglɪš kʰat ðə nãw̃n æ̃nd kʰɔt ðə vʌrb ar pʰronãw̃nst
ðə sẽm

e. sʌ̃m pʰipəl θĩŋk fõnɛtɪks ɪz vɛri ĩntərɛstĩŋ

f. vɪktɔrijə frãmkĩn æ̃nd rabərt radmẽn ar ðə ɔθərz ʌv ðɪs tɛkstbʊk

Phonology: The Sound Patterns of Language

Speech is human, silence is divine, yet also brutish and dead; therefore we must learn both arts.

Thomas Carlyle, 1795–1881

Phonology is the study of telephone etiquette.

A high school student[1]

I believe that phonology is superior to music. It is more variable and its pecuniary possibilities are far greater.

Erik Satie (from the cover of a record album)

Phonology is not the study of telephone etiquette, nor the study of telephones. Phonology is the study of the sound patterns of human language; it is also the kind of knowledge that speakers have about the sound patterns of their particular language. We are not sure what Satie had in mind regarding "its pecuniary possibilities" (not knowing any rich phonologists) nor why he believed it superior to music. It might be because every speaker of a language knows its phonology, whereas knowledge of music is far from universal. It is true that the phonologies of the world's languages are variable, but their similarities are greater than their differences. Speech sounds as physical entities may be infinitely varied, but when they function as elements in a language, as phonological units, they are highly constrained. This fact is one of the reasons why the study of language sound systems is a fascinating one, for it reveals how linguistic ability enables people to extract regularities from constantly varying physical sounds. Despite the infinite variations that occur when we speak, all speakers of a language agree that certain utterances are "the same" and others are "different." Phonology explains why.

Linguists are interested in how sound systems may vary and in how they are similar, in the phonetic and phonological universals found in all languages. The

[1]As reported in Amsel Greene. 1969. *Pullet Surprises*. Scott, Foresman & Co. Glenview, Ill.

same relatively small set of phonetic properties or features characterizes all human speech sounds; the same classes of these sounds are utilized in languages spoken from the Arctic Circle to the Cape of Good Hope; and the same kinds of regular patterns of speech sounds occur all over the world. When you learn a language, you learn which speech sounds occur in your language and how they pattern according to regular rules.

Phonology is concerned with this kind of linguistic knowledge. Phonetics, as discussed in the previous chapter, provides the means for describing speech sounds; phonology studies the ways in which speech sounds form systems and patterns in human language. The phonology of a language, then, is the system and pattern of the speech sounds. We see that the word *phonology* is used in two ways: as the *study* of sound patterns in language and as the *sound pattern* of a given language.

Phonological knowledge permits a speaker to produce sounds that form meaningful utterances, to recognize a foreign accent, to make up new words, to add the appropriate phonetic segments to form plurals and past tenses, to produce aspirated and unaspirated voiceless stops in the appropriate context, to recognize what is or is not a sound in the language, and to know that different phonetic strings may represent the same "meaningful unit." The grammar of the language represents the totality of speakers' linguistic knowledge, so knowledge of the sound patterns—the phonology—must be part of this grammar. In this chapter we shall discuss the kinds of things that speakers know about the sound system of their language—their phonological knowledge.

Phonemes: The Phonological Units of Language

In the physical world the naive speaker and hearer actualize and are sensitive to sounds, but what they feel themselves to be pronouncing and hearing are "phonemes."
Edward Sapir, 1933

Phonological knowledge goes beyond the ability to produce all the phonetically different sounds of a language. It includes this ability, of course. A speaker of English can produce the sound [θ] and knows that this sound occurs in English, in words like *thin* [θĭn], *ether* [iθər], or *bath* [bæθ]. English speakers may or may not be able to produce a "click" or a velar fricative, but even if they can, they know that such sounds are not part of the phonetic inventory of English. Many speakers are unable to produce such "foreign" sounds. French speakers similarly know that [θ] is not part of the phonetic inventory of French and often find it difficult to pronounce a word like *thin* [θĭn], pronouncing it [sĭn].

An English speaker also knows that [ð], the voiced counterpart of [θ], is a sound of English, occurring in words like *either* [iðər], *then* [ðɛ̃n], and *bathe* [beð].

Knowing the sounds (the phonetic units) of a language is only a small part of phonological knowledge.

In Chapter 1, we discussed the fact that knowing a language implies knowing the set of words that comprise the vocabulary, or lexicon, of that language. You might know fewer or more words than your next-door neighbor, but each word you have learned is stored in your memory as part of the grammar of the language. When you know a word, you know both its **form** (the sounds that represent it) and its **meaning.** We have already seen that the relationship between the form and the meaning of a word is *arbitrary*. You must learn both: knowing the meaning does not tell you its pronunciation, and knowing how to say it does not tell you what it means (if you did not know already).

Consider the forms and meanings of the following English words:

sip	fine	chunk
zip	vine	junk

Each word differs from the other words in both form and meaning. The difference between *sip* and *zip* is "signaled" by the fact that the initial sound of the first word is *s* [s] and the initial sound of the second word is *z* [z]. The forms of the two words—that is, their sounds—are identical except for the initial consonants. [s] and [z] can therefore distinguish or *contrast* words. They are *distinctive* sounds in English. Such distinctive sounds are called **phonemes.**

We see from the contrast between *fine* and *vine* and between *chunk* and *junk* that [f], [v], [č], and [ǰ] must also be phonemes in English for the same reason—because substituting a [v] for [f] or a [č] for [ǰ] produces a different word.

Even if we did not know what phonetic properties or features distinguish these sounds, we would know that these sound segments represent phonemes in the English phonological system. Phonetics provides the means to describe the sounds, showing how they differ; phonology tells us that they function as phonemes, acting to contrast words.

Minimal Pairs

B.C.   **Johnny Hart**

By permission of Johnny Hart and North America Syndicate, Inc.

A first rule of thumb to determine the phonemes of any language is to see whether substituting one sound for another results in a different word. If it does, the two sounds represent different phonemes. When two different forms are identical in every way except for one sound segment that occurs in the same place in the string, the two words are called **minimal pairs.** *Sip* and *zip* are minimal pairs, as are *fine* and *vine,* and *chunk* and *junk.* Note that *seed* [sid] and *soup* [sup] are not minimal pairs because they differ in two sounds, the vowels and the final consonants. Similarly, *bar* [bar] and *rod* [rad] are not minimal pairs because although only one sound differs in the two words, the [b] occurs initially and the [d] occurs finally. Of course, we can find a minimal pair which shows that [b] and [d] are phonemes in English: *bean* and *dean, bark* and *dark, bill* and *dill, rib* and *rid.* Substituting a [d] for a [b] changes both the phonetic form and its meaning.

[b] and [d] also contrast with [g], as the following words show:

>   bill/dill/gill   rib/rid/rig

Therefore [b], [d], and [g] are all phonemes in English and constitute a **minimal set.** We have many minimal sets in English, which makes it relatively ''easy'' to determine what the English phonemes are. All the following words are identical except for the vowels; therefore each vowel represents a phoneme.

beat	[bit]	[i]	boot	[but]	[u]
bit	[bɪt]	[ɪ]	but	[bʌt]	[ʌ]
bait	[bet]	[e]	boat	[bot]	[o]
bet	[bɛt]	[ɛ]	bought	[bɔt]	[ɔ]
bat	[bæt]	[æ]	bout	[bawt]	[aw]
bite	[bajt]	[aj]	bot[2]	[bat]	[a]

It can also be demonstrated that [ʊ] and [ɔj], which are not part of the minimal set listed above, are phonemes of English by other minimal pairs in which these vowels contrast meanings, such as *book* [bʊk] and *beak* [bik], *look* [lʊk] and *leak* [lik], *boy* [bɔj] and *buy* [baj], or *soil* [sɔjl] and *sail* [sel].

As the B.C. cartoon shows, the contrasts among

> *crick* [ɪ]   *creek* [i]   *crook* [ʊ]   *croak* [o]

illustrate that there are other minimal sets in English. *Crack* [æ], *crock* [a], and *crake* [e] (a short-billed bird) are also members of this contrasting set.

For some speakers, *crick* and *creek* are pronounced identically, another example of regional dialect differences; but most speakers of this dialect still contrast the vowels in *beat* and *bit,* so these high front vowels are phonemes in their dialect. Although [bat], for some speakers, and [bʊt] are not actual words in English, they are sequences or strings of sounds, all of which represent phonemes, and the sequences of these phonemes are permissible in English. (We will discuss permissible sequences below.) We might then say that they are **nonsense words** (permissible forms with no meanings) or **possible words.** Similarly, *creck* [krɛk], *cruke* [kruk], *cruk* [krʌk], and *crike* [krajk] are nonexistent but possible words in English.

---

[2]A *bot* is the larva of a botfly.

Madison Avenue advertisers constantly take advantage of the fact that they can use possible but nonoccurring words for the names of new products. We would hardly expect a new product to come on the market with the name [xik], because [x] (the voiceless velar fricative) is not a phoneme in English. Nor would a new soap be called *Zhleet* [žlit], because in English, the voiced palatal fricative [ž] can not occur initially before a liquid. Possible but nonoccurring words such as *Bic* [bɪk] before it was coined as a brand name are **accidental gaps** in the vocabulary. An accidental gap is a form that "obeys" all the phonological rules of the language—it includes native phonemes in a permitted order—but has no meaning. An actual, occurring word is a combination of both a permitted form and a meaning.

Further examples of minimal pairs in English provide evidence for other phonemes. Change in the phonetic form produces a different word. When such a change is the result of the substitution of just one sound segment, the two different segments must represent different phonemes. There is no other way to account for these particular meaning contrasts.

Distinctive Features

In order for two phonetic forms to differ and to contrast meanings, there must be some phonetic difference between the substituted sounds. The minimal pairs *seal* and *zeal* show that [s] and [z] represent two contrasting phonemes in English. From the discussion of phonetics in Chapter 2 we know that the only difference between [s] and [z] is a voicing difference; [s] is voiceless or [−voiced] and [z] is voiced or [+voiced]. It is this phonetic feature that distinguishes the two words. Voicing therefore plays a special role in English (and in many other languages). It also distinguishes *feel* from *veal* [f]/[v] and *ether* from *either* [θ]/[ð]. When a feature distinguishes one phoneme from another, it is a **distinctive feature** (or a phonemic feature). When two words are exactly alike phonetically except for one feature, the phonetic difference is **distinctive,** since this difference alone accounts for the contrast or difference in meaning. As discussed in Chapter 2, a single feature has two values, + and −: [±nasal], [±voiced], [±consonantal], and so forth. A phonetic feature is distinctive when the + value of that feature found in certain words contrasts with the − value of that feature in other words.

The minimal pairs given below illustrate some of the distinctive features in the phonological system of English.

bat [bæt]	mat [mæt]	The difference between *bat* and *mat* is due only to the difference in nasality between [b] and [m]. [b] and [m] are identical in all features except for the fact that [b] is oral or [−nasal] and [m] is nasal or [+nasal]. Therefore nasality or [±nasal] is a distinctive feature of English consonants.
rack [ræk]	rock [rak]	The two words are distinguished only because [æ] is a front vowel and [a] is a back vowel. They

| | | | | are both low, unrounded vowels. [±back] is therefore a distinctive feature of English vowels. |
| see | [si] | zee | [zi] | The difference is due to the voicelessness of the [s] in contrast to the voicing of the [z]. Therefore voicing ([±voiced]) is a distinctive feature of English consonants. |

Sounds That Are Not Phonemes: Features That Do Not Contrast   The method of substituting one sound for another to determine whether a new word is created may also be used to show that not all sounds that occur phonetically in a language represent separate phonemes. Again, this ''tool'' may be helpful in analysis, but remember that it is the **presence of contrast,** not the lack of contrast, that shows the phonemic distinctions.

In Chapter 2 it was shown that *phonetically* both oral and nasalized vowels occur in English. The following examples show them:

bean	[bĩn]	bead	[bid]
roam	[rõm]	robe	[rob]

Nasalized vowels only occur in English syllables before nasal consonants. If an oral vowel is substituted for the nasal vowels in *bean* and *roam,* the meanings of the two words would not be changed. Try to say these words keeping your velum up until your tongue makes the stop closure of the [n] or your lips come together for the [m]. It will not be easy for you, because in English we automatically lower the velum when producing vowels before nasals in the same syllable. (If a vowel is syllable final in a two-syllable word, and the second syllable begins with a nasal, the preceding vowel is not necessarily nasalized, as, for example, the [o] in *phoneme* [fo-nĩm].)

Now try to produce a nasal vowel (lower your velum immediately after you articulate the consonant) in the words *by, see,* or *go* to produce [bãy], [sĩ], and [gõ]. If you spoke like this, people would probably say you have a ''nasal twang,'' but they would understand you to be saying *by, see,* and *go.* Changing the forms of the words by substituting nasalized vowels does not change the meanings.

A substitution of [i] for [ɛ] in *economics* does not change the meaning of the word, either. However, if the substitution of one sound for another in one or two words does not change the meaning, the two sounds may still be two phonemes. There is a difference between the substitution of [i] for [ɛ] in *economics* and the substitutions we have observed between oral and nasalized vowels. [i] and [ɛ] were shown by a number of other examples to represent different phonemes. We can find no such cases to demonstrate that [o] and [õ], for example, represent different phonemes. That is, there are no two words, different in meaning, in which the only difference phonetically is that in one word a vowel is oral and in the other the vowel—identical in all other respects—is nasal.

A further, more important difference between [i] and [ɛ], on the one hand, and [i] and [ĩ] (or [u] and [ũ], [o] and [õ], [a] and [ã], and so on) is that there are general principles in the phonology of English that tell us when nasalized vowels occur—always before nasal consonants—but there are no such principles or rules to predict when [i] occurs instead of [ɛ] or [ɪ] or [u] or [a] or any of the other vowel phonemes. We must learn, when learning the words, that [i] occurs in *beat* and [ɛ] occurs in *bet*.

The rule, or general principle, that predicts when a vowel will be oral and when the same vowel phoneme will be nasalized is exemplified in the following sets of words and nonwords:

	Words						**Nonwords**		
bee	[bi]	bead	[bid]	bean	[bĩn]		*[bĩ]	*[bĩd]	*[bin]
lay	[le]	lace	[les]	lame	[lẽm]		*[lẽ]	*[lẽs]	*[lem]
baa	[bæ]	bad	[bæd]	bang	[bæ̃ŋ]		*[bæ̃]	*[bæ̃d]	*[bæŋ]

As these words illustrate, in English, oral vowels occur in final position and before nonnasal consonants; nasalized vowels occur only before nasal consonants. The "nonwords" show us that nasalized vowels do not occur finally or before nonnasal consonants. Therefore oral vowels and their nasalized counterparts never contrast. Nasalization of vowels in English is predictable by a rule, which can be stated as:

> (1) Nasalize a vowel or diphthong (vowel + glide) when it occurs before a word-final or syllable-final nasal consonant.

The value (+ or −) of the feature [±nasal] is predictable for the class of vowel segments in English. When a feature value is predictable by a general principle or rule, it is not a distinctive or phonemic feature for that class of segments. Therefore, the feature [±nasal] is not a distinctive feature for English vowels, although it is distinctive for English consonants.

We have seen that nasalized vowels do occur phonetically. We can conclude, then, that there is no one-to-one correspondence between phonetic segments and phonemes in a language. From the examples given above we see that one phoneme may be realized phonetically (that is, pronounced) as more than one phonetic segment. Each vowel phoneme in English is realized as either an oral vowel or a nasal vowel, depending on its context.

Phonemes, Phones, and Allophones   Some new terminology may help to clarify the situation. A phonetic unit or segment is called a **phone**. A **phoneme** is a more abstract unit. We must know the phonological rules of the language to know how to pronounce a phoneme, because in one context it may be realized as one phone (for example, [i]) and in another context as a different phone (for example, [ĩ]). To distinguish between phonemes and phones we will use slashes / / to enclose phonemic segments or phonemic transcriptions of words and will continue to use the square brackets [ ] for phonetic segments or phonetic transcriptions. Thus we will represent the vowel phoneme in *bead* and *bean* as /i/ in both words. This phoneme is pronounced (or realized) as [i] in *bead* [bid] and [ĩ] in *bean* [bĩn].

We have seen that a single phoneme may be phonetically realized or pronounced as two or more phones. The different phones that "represent" or are *derived* from one phoneme are called the **allophones** of that phoneme. An **allophone** is therefore a **predictable phonetic variant** of a phoneme. In English, each vowel phoneme has both an oral and a nasalized allophone. The choice of the allophone is not random or haphazard; it is **rule-governed,** as illustrated by the general principle determining the occurrence of oral and nasalized vowels in English. No one is explicitly taught these rules. They are "constructed" by the learner; language acquisition, to a certain extent, is rule construction. Speakers probably do not know that they know these rules; yet they produce the nasalized allophones of the vowel phonemes automatically whenever they occur before nasal consonants. Much knowledge is unconscious knowledge and requires scientific investigation to understand it.

When two or more sounds never occur in the same phonemic context or environment they are said to be in **complementary distribution.** The examples of the words and nonwords given on page (75) illustrate the complementary distribution of the oral and nasalized allophones of English phonemes. This distribution is shown in Table 3–1.

TABLE 3–1 Distribution of Oral and Nasal Vowels in English Syllables

	In Final Position	Before Nasal Consonants	Before Oral Consonants
Oral vowels	Yes	No	Yes
Nasal vowels	No	Yes	No

When oral vowels occur, nasal vowels do not occur, and vice versa. It is in this sense that the phones are said to complement each other or to be in complementary distribution.

Predictability of Redundant Features Nasality is a predictable or **redundant** feature for vowels in English. Whether a vowel is [−nasal] or [+nasal] is said to be redundant because the value of this feature depends on other segments of the word. If the vowel occurs before a nasal consonant in the same syllable, the vowel is predictably [+nasal]; the value of this feature is therefore redundant. It is not specific to any particular word but determined by a general rule.

The nasality feature, however, is not redundant for consonants in English; whether or not a consonant is [+nasal] cannot be predicted by a general rule but must be specified for each word. There is no rule that can predict that the word *bean* will have a final /n/ rather than a /d/; in learning the word we must learn this fact. Similarly, the fact that *meat* begins with the bilabial nasal [m] is an arbitrary, nonpredictable fact about this particular word. The first consonant must therefore be specified as [+nasal] to distinguish it from the /b/ of the first consonant in the word *beat,* which is [−nasal].

The fact that the vowel in *bean* is nasalized is not a fact about only this word but about all the words in which the vowel is followed by a nasal consonant. If you had not learned the "vowel nasalization" rule, you would not pronounce the words according to the normal English pronunciation.

The rule stated above is found in many languages of the world. This fact is not surprising; it is a plausible or "natural" rule, because it is more difficult to prevent nasalizing a vowel before a nasal consonant than it is to nasalize it in this context. To prevent nasalization, timing of the velic closure must be very precise.

This difficulty does not mean, however, that nasality cannot be distinctive for vowels in other languages. We have already seen some examples of nasalized vowels in French in Chapter 2. In the Ghanaian language Akan (or Twi), nasalized and oral vowels occur both phonetically and phonemically; nasalization is a distinctive feature for vowels in Akan, as the following examples illustrate:

[ka]	"bite"	[kã]	"speak"
[fi]	"come from"	[fĩ]	"dirty"
[tu]	"pull"	[tũ]	"hole/den"
[nsa]	"hand"	[nsã]	"liquor"
[či]	"hate"	[čĩ]	"squeeze"
[pam]	"sew"	[pãm]	"confederate"

These examples show that vowel nasalization is not predictable in Akan. As shown by the last minimal pair—[pam] / [pãm]—there is no rule that nasalizes vowels before nasal consonants. We also find word-final oral vowels contrasting with word-final nasalized vowels (after identical initial consonants). The change of form—the substitution of nasalized for oral vowels, or vice versa—does change the meaning. Both oral and nasal vowel phonemes must therefore exist in Akan.

Notice that two languages may have the same phonetic segments (phones) but have two different phonemic systems. Both oral and nasalized vowels exist in English and Akan phonetically; English has no nasalized vowel phonemes, but Akan does. The same phonetic segments function differently in the two languages. Nasalization of vowels in English is *redundant and nondistinctive;* nasalization of vowels in Akan is *nonredundant and distinctive.*

We can further illustrate the fact that two languages can have the same set of phonetic segments with different phonemic systems by examining the voiceless stops. In the previous chapter we pointed out that in English both aspirated and unaspirated voiceless stops occur. The voiceless aspirated stops [pʰ] [tʰ] [kʰ] and the voiceless unaspirated stops [p] [t] [k] are in complementary distribution in English, as is shown by stating the environments or contexts in which they occur:

Word (or Syllable) Initially Before a Stressed Vowel			**After a Word (or Syllable) Initial /S/**		
[pʰ]	**[tʰ]**	**[kʰ]**	**[p]**	**[t]**	**[k]**
pill	till	kill	spill	still	skill
[pʰɪl]	[tʰɪl]	[kʰɪl]	[spɪl]	[stɪl]	[skɪl]
par	tar	car	spar	star	scar
[pʰar]	[tʰar]	[kʰar]	[spar]	[star]	[skar]

Despite the phonetic difference between the unaspirated and aspirated phones, speakers of English (if they are not analyzing the sounds as linguists or phoneticians) usually consider the [pʰ] in *pill* and the [p] in *spill* to be the ''same'' sound, just as they consider the [i] and [ĩ] that represent the phoneme /i/ in *bead* and *bean* to be the ''same.'' They do so because the difference between them, in this case the feature *aspiration,* is **predictable, redundant, nondistinctive,** and **nonphonemic** (all equivalent terms). The aspirated and the nonaspirated phones are in complementary distribution. Voiceless stops are always aspirated when they occur at the beginning of a word before stressed vowels, and they are always unaspirated after an initial /s/. This distribution is a fact about English phonology. There are two *p* sounds (or phones) in English, but only one *p* phoneme. (This arrangement is also true of *t* and *k*.) A phoneme is an **abstract unit.** We do not utter phonemes; we produce phones. /p/ is a phoneme in English that is realized phonetically (pronounced) as either [p] or [pʰ]. [p] and [pʰ] are allophones of the phoneme /p/. Another way of stating this fact is to say that the [p] and [pʰ] are **derived** from /p/ by a rule:

> (2) Aspirate a voiceless stop—/p/, /t/, or /k/—when it occurs word initially or syllable initially before a stressed vowel.

The discussion on oral and nasalized vowels above pointed out that the same phones (phonetic segments) can occur in two languages but pattern differently because the phonemic system is different. Aspiration of voiceless stops further illustrates this fact. Both aspirated and unaspirated voiceless stops occur in English and Thai (the major language spoken in Thailand), but they function differently in the two languages. Aspiration in English is not a phonemic or distinctive feature, because its presence or absence is predictable. In Thai, however, it is not predictable, as the following examples show:

Voiceless Unaspirated		**Voiceless Aspirated**	
[paa]	*forest*	[pʰaa]	*to split*
[tam]	*to pound*	[tʰam]	*to do*
[kat]	*to bite*	[kʰat]	*to interrupt*

The voiceless unaspirated and the voiceless aspirated stops in Thai are not in complementary distribution. They occur in the same positions in the minimal pairs above; they contrast and are therefore phonemes in Thai. Both English and Thai have the phones [p] [pʰ] [t] [tʰ] [k] and [kʰ]; in English they represent the three phonemes /p/ /t/ /k/; in Thai each phone represents a separate phoneme—/p/ /pʰ/ /t/ /tʰ/ /k/ /kʰ/. [±aspiration] is a distinctive feature in Thai; it is a nondistinctive phonetic feature in English.

The minimal pairs *seal/zeal, fine/vine,* and *thigh/thy* show that voicing is a distinctive feature in English. The initial sounds of the first words of the pair are all [−voiced], and the initial sounds of the second words are [+voiced]. They differ in no other way.

Pill/bill, till/dill, and *kill/gill* also contrast in the same way; but the voiceless stops are also aspirated. They differ in both voicing and aspiration. Is it the aspiration or the voicing difference that signals the phonemic difference in these pairs? We have already seen that voicing must be a distinctive feature from the minimal pairs in which it is the only difference. As we cannot predict when voicing will occur but can predict when aspiration will occur (as stated in Rule 2 and as shown in the table below), the phonemic or distinctive feature that distinguishes the *pill/bill* pairs must be voicing rather than aspiration.

Voiceless Unaspirated $\begin{bmatrix} -\text{voiced} \\ -\text{aspirated} \end{bmatrix}$			Voiceless Aspirated $\begin{bmatrix} -\text{voiced} \\ +\text{aspirated} \end{bmatrix}$			Voiced* [+voiced]		
/spɪl/	[spɪl]	*spill*	/pɪl/	[pʰɪl]	*pill*	/bɪl/	[bɪl]	*bill*
/stɪl/	[stɪl]	*still*	/tɪl/	[tʰɪl]	*till*	/dɪl/	[dɪl]	*dill*
/skɪl/	[skɪl]	*skill*	/kɪl/	[kʰɪl]	*kill*	/gɪl/	[gɪl]	*gill*

(*Note that voiced segments are not marked either [−aspirated] or [+aspirated] for the reasons given in Chapter 2.)

In Thai, voiced stops also occur. Just as in English, voiceless unaspirated, voiceless aspirated, and voiced phones occur; but in Thai these phones represent phonemes. [±voicing] and [±aspiration] are *both* distinctive phonemic features in Thai, as is shown by these three-way minimal contrastive sets:

Voiceless Unaspirated $\begin{bmatrix} -\text{voiced} \\ -\text{aspirated} \end{bmatrix}$			Voiceless Aspirated $\begin{bmatrix} -\text{voiced} \\ +\text{aspirated} \end{bmatrix}$			Voiced [+voiced]		
/paa/	[paa]	*forest*	/pʰaa/	[pʰaa]	*to split*	/baa/	[baa]	*shoulder*
/tam/	[tam]	*to pound*	/tʰam/	[tʰam]	*to do*	/dam/	[dam]	*black*

The phonetic feature matrices for the labial stops in the three Thai words would be identical to the phonetic specifications of the labials in *spit, pit,* and *bit* in English; but the Thai phonemic specifications would differ. The /p/ in "forest" would have to be marked [−aspirated] and the /pʰ/ in "split" would have to be marked [+aspirated], as aspiration is contrastive.

Once more we see that the same phonetic segments can form different phonemic patterns in different languages. We can illustrate this fact graphically:

Thai Phonemes   Phonetic Segments   English Phonemes

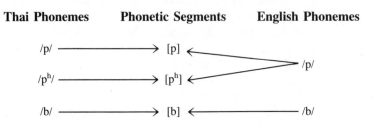

The phonetic facts alone do not reveal what is distinctive or phonemic. **The phonetic representation of utterances shows what speakers know about the pronunciation of utterances; the phonemic representation of utterances shows what the speakers know about the abstract underlying phonology.** That pot /pat/ and spot /spat/ are transcribed with an identical /p/ reveals the fact that English speakers consider the [pʰ] in pot [pʰat] and the [p] in spot [spat] to be phonetic manifestations of the same phoneme /p/.

Children learn which features are distinctive in their language and which are not. One phonetic feature may be distinctive for one class of sounds but predictable or nondistinctive for another class of sounds—for example, the feature nasality in English. [+nasal] is a distinctive feature for English consonants but a nondistinctive, predictable phonetic feature for English vowels. In French, it is distinctive for both consonants and vowels. Aspiration in English is totally predictable. It is nondistinctive for any class of sounds.

The + or − values of some features are predictable because of the segments that precede or follow; the phonological context determines the value of the feature. Aspiration cannot be predicted in isolation but only when a voiceless stop occurs in a word, because the presence or absence of the feature depends on where the voiceless stop occurs and what precedes or follows it. It is determined by its phonemic environment. Similarly, the oral or nasal quality of a vowel depends on its environment. If it is followed by a nasal consonant it is predictably [+nasal].

Some features, however, are predictable or redundant due to the specification of the other features of that segment. That is, given the presence of certain features, we can predict the value of other features without any reference to the surrounding segments.

In English, as pointed out in the preceding chapter, all front vowels are predictably nonround. Unlike French, there are no rounded front vowels in English. We can say that if a vowel in English is specified as [−back] it is also redundantly, predictably [−round]. In marking the feature values for [−back] vowels in English, we can, then, omit the [−round] marking. A blank would indicate that the value of that feature is predictable by a phonological rule of the language.

For certain classes of sounds, the values of some features are **universally implied** for all languages. Thus, all stops—[−continuant] segments—are universally and predictably [−syllabic].

Form and Meaning

We have said above that when the substitution of one sound segment for another results in a different word, we have sufficient evidence that the two sounds represent two different phonemes. Note, however, that two different forms may be identical in meaning, as shown by the fact that some speakers pronounce the first sound of the word *economics* as [ε] and others as [i]. These two strings of sounds are not minimal pairs; the substitution of [ε] for [i] or vice versa does produce another word. Similarly, some speakers pronounce *ration* as [rešǝn] and others as [ræšǝn]. Such pairs do not tell us whether [i] and [e] and [æ] represent phonemes in the language. We know, however, that these sounds are contrastive from such pairs as *beat/bet* [i]/[ε] and *bait/bat* [e]/[æ]. The different pronunciations of *economics* or *ration* are **free variations;** one meaning of each word is represented by two different phonemic forms.

Homonyms or homophones also show that two words of different meanings may have identical forms; that is, they may be pronounced exactly alike. Thus [sol] can mean ''sole'' or ''soul.'' ''Sole'' itself has three meanings—''shoe bottom,'' ''fish,'' and ''only''—thus giving [sol] at least *four* meanings to one form. The sentence ''Greta Garbo ate her cottage cheese with relish [rɛliš]'' could mean she ate with ''gusto'' or with a particular kind of sauce.

The determining fact is whether there is both a change in form (pronunciation) and a change in meaning. When both changes occur, we know that the substituted sound segments represent different phonemes.

Minimal pairs and complementary distribution of phonetic units are helpful clues in the attempt to discover the inventory of phonemes in a language. By themselves, however, they do not determine the phonemic representation of utterances, as will be shown below in the discussion of phonological rules.

Vowel and Consonant Length

In Chapter 2 we mentioned in the discussion of prosodic features that the length of a segment (whether a consonant or vowel is long or short) may be linguistically important.

In English, if you pronounce a word by sustaining the vowel—that is, by making it longer—the meaning of the word does not change. Vowel length is **noncontrastive** in English. Phonetically, both tense and lax vowels are slightly longer before voiced consonants than before voiceless ones, and also at the end of words, as the following examples show:

"beat"	/bit/	[bit]
"bead"	/bid/	[bi:d]
"bee"	/bi/	[bi:]
"bit"	/bɪt/	[bɪt]
"bid"	/bɪd/	[bɪːd]
"loot"	/lut/	[lut]
"lewd"	/lud/	[lu:d]
"Lou"	/lu/	[lu:]
"rote"	/rot/	[rot]
"road"	/rod/	[ro:d]
"row"	/ro/	[ro:]

Because the vowels with longer duration are predictable, vowel length in English is nonphonemic. You could, if you wanted, prolong the pronunciation of the vowel in a word before a voiceless consonant and it would not make any difference in meaning. Suppose you said:

"I feel beeeaaat" instead of "I feel beat"

pronouncing the /i/ vowel really long, as if it were phonetically transcribed as [bi::::t]. Someone listening might think you were extremely tired but would not have difficulty knowing that the word had the same meaning as [bit].

In other languages, however, vowel length is nonpredictable, and whether a vowel is long or short in duration can distinguish meanings. Vowel length is phonemic in Danish, Finnish, Arabic, and Korean. Consider the following "minimal pairs" in Korean:

il	"day"	i:l	"word"
seda	"to count"	se:da	"strong"
kul	"oyster"	ku:l	"tunnel"

Vowel length is also phonemic in Japanese, as shown by the following pairs:

| biru | "building" | bi:ru | "beer" |
| tsuji | "a proper name" | tsu:ji | "moving the bowels" |

When teaching at a university in Japan, one of the authors of this book inadvertently pronounced Ms. Tsuji's name as Tsu:ji-san. (The -san is a suffix used to show respect.) The effect of this error quickly taught him to understand the phonemic nature of vowel length in Japanese.

Consonant length also is contrastive in Japanese. A consonant may be lengthened by prolonging the closure: a long t [t:] or [tt] can be produced by holding the tongue against the alveolar ridge twice as long as for a short t [t]. The following minimal pairs illustrate that length is a phonemic feature for Japanese consonants:

| shite | "doing" | shitte | "knowing" |
| saki | "ahead" | sakki | "before" |

Luganda, an African language, also contrasts long and short consonants; /kkula/ means "treasure" and /kula/ means "grow up." (In both these words the first vowel is produced with a high pitch and the second with a low pitch. We will discuss pitch as a phonemic feature below.) Likewise the Italian word for "grand-father" is *nonno* /nonnɔ/, contrasting with the word for "ninth," which is *nono* /nonɔ/.

In English consonants may be pronounced long if they occur across word boundaries. Many English speakers will produce a longer closure of the /t/ in *white tie* than in *why tie?*. In such cases the [t:] is in free variation with a short [t].

The lengthened duration of two identical consonants or vowels can be symbolized by the colon, as in /t:/ or /a:/, or by doubling the segment, as in /tt/ or /aa/. Such long segments, called **geminates,** may occur phonetically as in English or phonemically as in Japanese.

The grammar of a language includes all the kinds of information we have been discussing: what the distinctive phonemic units of the language are; which phonetic features are phonemic or distinctive; and which are nonphonemic or predictable. A grammar of French would not include a /θ/ as part of the phonemic representation of any word, just as a grammar of English would not include a /x/. English would have one voiceless labial stop phoneme, /p/, but Thai would have two, /p/ and /pʰ/. Both would include /b/. In English length is not a distinctive feature for either vowels or consonants; for Japanese it is phonemic for both classes of phonemes. These examples show that two languages may have the same phonetic segments but a different set of phonemes. The grammar must account for both the phonemes in the language and the way they are pronounced.

Sequences of Phonemes

If you were to receive the following telegram, you would have no difficulty in correcting the "obvious" mistakes:

    BEST WISHES FOR VERY HAPPP BIRTFDAY

because sequences such as BIRTFDAY do not occur in the language.

Colin Cherry, *On Human Communication*

Speakers know more about the phonological system of their language than the inventories of phonemic and phonetic units. They also know that the phonemes of the language cannot be strung together in any random order to form words. The phonological system determines which phonemes can begin a word, end a word, and follow each other.

Sequential Constraints

Your knowledge of such sequential rules is easy to demonstrate. Suppose you were given four cards, each of which had a different phoneme of English printed on it:

Drawing by Ziegler; © 1986 The New Yorker Magazine, Inc.

k	b	l	ɪ

If you were asked to arrange these cards to form all the ''possible'' words that these four phonemes could form, you might order them as follows:

b	l	ɪ	k
k	l	ɪ	b
b	ɪ	l	k
k	ɪ	l	b

These arrangements are the only permissible ones for these phonemes in English. */lbkɪ/, */ɪlbk/, */bkɪl/, and */ɪlkb/ are not possible words in the language. Although /blɪk/ and /klɪb/ are not existing words (you will not find them in a dictionary), if you heard someone say:

''I just bought a beautiful new *blick*.''

you might ask: ''What's a 'blick'?'' If you heard someone say:

"I just bought a beautiful new *bkli*."

you would probably reply, "What did you say?"

Your knowledge of English "tells" you that certain strings of phonemes are permissible and others are not. After a consonant like /b/, /g/, /k/, or /p/ another stop consonant is not permitted by the rules of the grammar. If a word begins with an /l/ or an /r/, every speaker "knows" that the next segment must be a vowel. That is why */lbɪk/ does not sound like an English word. It violates the restrictions on the sequencing of phonemes.

Other such constraints exist in English. If the initial sounds of *chill* or *Jill* begin a word, the next sound must be a vowel. /čat/ or /čon/ or /čækari/ are possible words in English, as are /ǰæl/ or /ǰot/ or /ǰalɪk/, but */člit/ and */ǰpurz/ are not. No more than three sequential consonants can occur at the beginning of a word, and these three are restricted to /s/ + /p,t,k/ + /l,r,w,y/. There are even restrictions if this condition is met. For example, /stl/ is not a permitted sequence, so *stlick* is not a possible word in English, but *strick* is.

Other languages have different sequential restrictions. In Polish *zl* is a permissible combination, as in *zloty,* a unit of currency.

Syllable Structure

If we examine these restrictions a little further, we find that they constrain sequences of phonemes not only in words, but also in syllables. That is, only the clusters that can begin a word can begin a syllable in a word. Words like *instruct* /ɪnstrʌkt/ with the medial cluster /nstr/ or *explicit* /ɛksplɪsɪt/ with the medial cluster /kspl/ can be divided into well-formed syllables /ɪn $ strʌkt/ and /ɛk $ splɪsɪt/ (using $ to symbolize a syllable boundary). We as speakers of English know that "constluct" is not a possible word because the second syllable starts with a nonpermissible sequence /stl/. Syllables, then, are important phonological units. (A rule of thumb for determining where syllable boundaries occur in a word is to pronounce the word slowly and see where a "natural" phonetic break occurs. This break will not necessarily coincide with the rules set down by copy editors or dictionaries for using a hyphen to divide a word at the end of a line. For example, *The American College Dictionary* inserts a syllable break between the *t* and *r* in *retrospect* and between the *s* and *t* in *restoration*. Yet, in slow and careful pronunciation most speakers will **syllabify** them as *re $ tro $ spect* and *re $ stor $ a $ tion,* respectively.)

There are also sequential constraints that go across syllable boundaries. One such restriction in English words pertains to medial clusters of syllable-final nasal consonants followed by syllable-initial nonnasal (oral) stops. For the most part, only the labial /m/ occurs before the labials /p/ and /b/, and only the velar /ŋ/ occurs before the velars /k/ and /g/, as in the following examples:[3]

---

[3]There are exceptions to this rule, and we have oversimplified it. In complex words where prefixes like *un-* meaning "not" occur, as in *unbound* or *uncap,* an /n/ is followed by /b/ and /k/ respectively. In Chapter 4, however, we will see that some prefixes ending with nasals obey this constraint.

ample	-mp-	*but no*	*-mt-	*-mk-
amble	-mb-	*but no*	*-md-	*-mg-
antler	-nt-	*but no*	*-np-	*-nk-
handle	-nd-	*but no*	*-nb-	*-ng-
ankle	-ŋk-	*but no*	*-ŋp-	*-ŋt-
angle	-ŋg-	*but no*	*-ŋb-	*-ŋd-

This constraint (which occurs in many languages) states that only homorganic nasal + nonnasal consonant clusters may occur. **Homorganic consonants** are articulated at the same place of articulation—that is, labial, alveolar, palatal, or velar.

All languages have constraints on the permitted sequences of phonemes, though different languages have different constraints. Children learn these rules when they learn the language, just as they learn what the phonemes are and how they are related to phonetic segments. In Asante Twi, a word may end only in a vowel or a nasal consonant. /pik/ is not a possible Twi word, because it breaks the sequential rules of the language; and /ŋŋu/ is not a possible word in English for similar reasons, although it is an actual word in Twi.

Speakers of all languages have the same kinds of knowledge. They know what sounds are part of the language, what the phonemes are, and what phonemic and phonetic sequences may occur. The specific sounds and sound sequences may differ, but the phonological systems include similar kinds of rules.

Natural Classes

The rules in English phonology that determine the conditions under which vowels are nasalized, voiceless stops are aspirated, or which clusters may occur within a word are general rules. They apply to classes of sounds. They also apply to all the words in the vocabulary of the language, and they even apply to nonsense words that are not in the language but could enter the language (like *sint, peeg,* or *sparg,* which would be /sɪnt/, /pig/, and /sparg/ phonemically and [sĩnt], [pʰig], and [sparg] phonetically. Less general rules are also found in all languages, as well as exceptions to these general rules.

Of greater interest is that the more we examine the phonologies of the many thousands of languages of the world, the more we find that phonological rules apply to the same broad general classes of sounds, like the ones we have mentioned—nasals, voiceless stops, alveolars, labials, and so on. This fact is understandable and really not surprising since such rules often have phonetic explanations and these classes of sounds are defined by phonetic features. For this reason such classes are called **natural classes** of speech sounds.

A natural class is one in which the number of features that must be specified to define that class is smaller than the number of features required to distinguish any member of that class.

The class of voiceless stops—/p, t, k/—can be specified by two features:

$$\begin{bmatrix} -\text{continuant} \\ -\text{voiced} \end{bmatrix}.$$ /t/ alone would require four features to distinguish it from all other

consonants: $\begin{bmatrix} -\text{continuant} \\ -\text{voiced} \\ +\text{anterior} \\ +\text{coronal} \end{bmatrix}.$

When we discussed the aspiration of voiceless stops above, we pointed out that all the members of this class became aspirated in the given environments. Therefore aspiration refers to a natural class of sounds, defined by two features. If, instead, only /p/ and /t/ were aspirated, then we would have to refer to the class of

sounds that were $\begin{bmatrix} -\text{continuant} \\ -\text{voiced} \\ +\text{anterior} \end{bmatrix}.$

If only /p/ and /k/ were aspirated and /t/ unaspirated, the number of features that defined these two sounds as distinct from all other phonemes would be even greater. The more features that have to be mentioned, the less general the process. Therefore the class of sounds that includes /p/, /t/, and /k/ is "more natural" than the class of sounds that includes only /p/ and /t/.

If the English vowel nasalization rule applied only before /n/ and not before /m/ or /ŋ/, and this rule were stated using pluses and minuses to define the class before which vowels are nasalized, it would be stated thus:

(3) Nasalize vowels before $\begin{bmatrix} +\text{nasal} \\ +\text{coronal} \\ +\text{anterior} \end{bmatrix}$ segments.

This statement is more complex than the general rule:

(4) Nasalize vowels before [+nasal] segments.

Children should find it easier to learn a rule that applies to a natural class of sounds, because they have to extract fewer features from the speech input than they would if the rule applied to a less natural class. It should also be easier to remember such a rule.

This fact about phonological rules illustrates why individual phonemic segments are better regarded as combinations or complexes of features than as indissoluble whole segments. If such segments were not specified as feature-matrices, the similarities among /p/, /t/, and /k/ or /m/, /n/, and /ŋ/ would not be revealed. It would appear just as easy for a child to learn a rule such as

Nasalize vowels before /p/, /i/, or /z/.

as to learn a rule such as

Nasalize vowels before /m/, /n/, or /ŋ/.

The first rule has no phonetic explanation, whereas the second rule does. It is easier to raise the velum to produce a nasalized vowel in anticipation of a following nasal consonant than to prevent the velum from rising before the consonant closure.

The use of feature notation reveals why certain rules are in some sense "more natural" or "simpler" to learn than others. The phonetic features that were presented in Chapter 2 therefore define the various phonetic and phonological natural classes in the world's languages.

Prosodic Phonology and Suprasegmentals

So far this chapter has been mainly concerned with the **segmental** aspects of phonology. There are, however, other linguistically important phonological features, which have traditionally been called **prosodic** or **suprasegmental** features. We mentioned some of them briefly in Chapter 2. They usually refer to units larger than the segment, such as the syllable, word, or phrase; hence the term *suprasegmental*. More recently features of this kind are called **autosegmental** features and represented by **autosegmental tiers.** They include pitch or tone, melody or intonation, and stress.

Tone

In Chapter 2 we mentioned that speakers of all languages vary the pitch of their voices when they talk, and that the pitch produced depends upon how fast the vocal cords vibrate; the faster they vibrate, the higher the pitch.

The way pitch is used linguistically differs from language to language. In English, it does not much matter whether you say *cat* with a high pitch or a low pitch. It will still mean "cat." However, if you say *ba* with a high pitch in Nupe (a language spoken in Nigeria), it will mean "to be sour," whereas if you say *ba* with a low pitch, it will mean "to count." Languages that use the pitch of individual syllables to contrast meanings are called **tone languages.**

It is probably safe to say that most of the languages in the world are tone languages. There are more than 1000 tone languages in Africa alone; many languages of Asia, such as Chinese, Thai, and Burmese, are tone languages, as are many native American languages.

Thai is a language that has contrasting pitches, or tones. The same string of "segmental" sounds represented by [naa] or [na:] will mean different things when spoken with a low pitch, a mid pitch, a high pitch, a falling pitch from high to low, or a rising pitch from low to high. Thai therefore has five linguistic tones:

naa	[__]	low tone	"a nickname"
naa	[—]	mid tone	"rice paddy"
naa	[⎤]	high tone	"young maternal uncle or aunt"
naa	[⌐¬]	falling tone	"face"
naa	[_⟋]	rising tone	"thick"

These contrastive phonemic tones can be symbolized thus:

low tone = L	mid tone = M	high tone = H
falling tone = HL	rising tone = LH	

and represented on a separate **tier** in the following way:

Phoneme tier:	na:	na:	na:	na:	na:
	|	|	|	/\	/\
Tonal tier:	H	M	L	H L	L H

If phonemes are on one tier and tones on a separate tier, then it is not necessary that there be a one-to-one relationship between each segment and each tone, as the Thai example shows. The word meaning "face" and the word meaning "thick" each have one syllable and two tones.

We can also place diacritics above the vowels to represent the tonal contrasts, as illustrated by the three contrastive tones in Nupe:

bá	[⎤]	"be sour"	bā	[—]	"cut"	bà	[_]	"count"
|			|			|		
H			M			L		

In Twi we see how two tones are used for contrasts in two-syllable words:

dù à	[_]	"tail"	dù á	[_⎤]	"tree"
| |			| |		
L L			L H		

kɔ̀ tɔ́	[_⎤]	"go buy"	kɔ́ tɔ̀	[⌐_]	"crab"
| |			| |		
L H			H L		

In some tone languages the pitch of each tone is "level"; in others, the direction of the pitch (whether it glides from high to low, or from low to high) is important. Tones that "glide" are called **contour tones;** tones that do not are called

level or **register tones.** The contour tones of Thai were easily represented by using the tonal tier, because a falling glide is a high tone followed by a low tone, and a rising tone is a low followed by a high. Some languages have rising-falling [∧] or falling-rising [∨] tones, which would be L H L and H L H, respectively.

In a tone language it is not the absolute pitch of the syllables that is important but the relations among the pitches of different syllables. After all, some individual speakers have high-pitched voices, others low-pitched, and others medium-pitched. In many tone languages we find a falling-off of the pitch, or a "downdrifting."

In the following sentence in Twi, the **relative pitch** rather than the absolute pitch is important:

"Kofi searches for a little food for his friend's child."

```
Kofi   hwehwɛ   aduaŋ   kakra ma  n' adamfo  ba.
| |     |  |  |   |  |    |  |  |  |  | |  |   |
LH      L  H  L   L  H    L  L  L  H L  L     H
```

The actual pitches of these syllables would be rather different from each other, shown as follows (the higher the number, the higher the pitch):

7		fí											
6				hwɛ́	á								
5	Kò							krá					
4			hwè								á		
3						duàŋ	kà						bá
2									mà	ǹ'			
1												dàmfò	

The lowering of the pitch is called **downdrift.** In languages with downdrift— and many tone languages in Africa are downdrift languages—a high tone that occurs after a low tone, or a low tone after a high tone, is lower in pitch than the preceding similarly marked tone. Notice that the first high tone in the sentence is given the pitch value 7. The next high tone (which occurs after an intervening low tone) is 6; that is, it is lower in pitch than the first high tone.

This example shows that in analyzing tones, just as in analyzing segments, all the physical properties need not be considered; only essential features are important in language—in this case, whether the tone is "high" or "low" in relation to the other pitches, but not the specific pitch of that tone.

Intonation

In languages that are not tone languages, such as English, pitch still plays an important role. It is the **pitch contour** of the phrase or sentence that is important. We say

John is going as a statement with a falling pitch, but as a question with the pitch rising at the end.

Languages that use pitch syntactically—for example, to change a sentence from a statement to a question—or in which the changing pitch of a whole sentence is otherwise important to the meaning are called **intonation languages.**

Two sentences in English can be exactly the same phonetically except for the overall **pitch contour** or **intonation** of the utterance. This difference can distinguish between two meanings. Look at sentences a and b:

    a. What did you put in my drink, Jane?
    b. What did you put in my drink, Jane?

In sentence a the questioner is asking what Jane put in the drink. In sentence b the questioner is asking whether someone put Jane into the drink. In sentence a the pitch rises sharply on the word *drink* and then falls off. In sentence b the sharp rise is on *Jane,* and it continues to rise without any decrease.

Sentence c illustrates that a written sentence may be ambiguous (may have two meanings):

    c. Tristram left directions for Isolde to follow.

When spoken the sentence can be disambiguated by changing the intonation. If it means that Tristram wanted Isolde to follow him, it is pronounced with the rise in pitch on the first syllable of *follow,* followed by a fall in pitch, as in d:

    d. Tristram left directions for Isolde to follow.

The sentence can also mean that Tristram left a set of directions he wanted Isolde to use. If this is the intention, the highest pitch comes on the second syllable of directions, as in e:

    e. Tristram left directions for Isolde to follow.

The way we have indicated pitch is of course highly oversimplified. Before the big rise in pitch the voice does not remain on the same monotone low pitch. These pitch diagrams indicate merely when there is a special change in pitch.

Thus pitch plays an important role in both tone languages and intonation languages, but in different ways.

Word Stress

In English and many other languages, one or more of the syllables in each content word (words other than the "little words" like *to, the, a, of,* and so on) are stressed. The stressed syllable is marked by ´ in the following examples:

B.C.   **Johnny Hart**

By permission of Johnny Hart and North America Syndicate, Inc.

pérvert	(noun)	as in	"My neighbor is a pervert."
pervért	(verb)	as in	"Don't pervert the idea."
súbject	(noun)	as in	"Let's change the subject."
subjéct	(verb)	as in	"He'll subject us to criticism."[4]

In some words, more than one vowel is stressed, but if so, one of these stressed vowels receives greater stress than the others. We have indicated the most highly stressed vowel by an acute accent over the vowel (we say this vowel receives the **accent,** or **primary stress,** or **main stress**); the other stressed vowels are indicated by marking a grave accent ` over the vowels (these vowels receive **secondary stress**).

rèsignátion	phònétic	sỳstemátic
fùndaméntal	ìntrodúctory	rèvolútion

Generally, speakers of a language know which syllable receives primary stress or accent, which receives secondary stress, and which are not stressed at all; it is part of their knowledge of the language.

The stress pattern of a word may differ from dialect to dialect. For example, in most varieties of American English the word *láboratòry* has two stressed syllables; in one dialect of British English it receives only one stress (ləbɔ́rətri]. Because the vowel qualities in English are closely related to whether they are stressed or not, the British vowels differ from the American vowels in this word; in fact, in the British version one vowel "drops out" completely because it is not stressed.

Just as stressed syllables in poetry reveal the **metrical structure** of the verse, phonological stress patterns relate to the metrical structure of a language.

We can, then, specify which syllable in the word is stressed by marking the vowel in that syllable (because vowels constitute the syllable peaks) as either [+stress] or [−stress]. We can also designate stress by numbers. The primary stressed or accented vowel can be designated by placing a "1" over the vowel; secondary stress can be designated by a "2"; unstressed vowels are left unmarked.

---

[4]These minimal pairs show that stress is contrastive in English; it distinguishes between nouns and verbs.

```
    2   1          2    1
 resignation    systematic
```

Stress is a property of a syllable rather than a segment, so it is a prosodic or suprasegmental feature. We can also represent the stress pattern of a word by indicating the syllabic units and the degree of stress or lack of stress of that syllable. For example, the stress patterns of the noun-verb pair illustrated above can be specified as follows (with the Greek letter "sigma" representing a syllable):

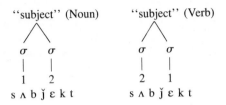

```
"subject" (Noun)      "subject" (Verb)
       /\                    /\
      /  \                  /  \
    σ     σ              σ     σ
    |     |              |     |
    1     2              2     1
  s ʌ b ǰ ɛ k t        s ʌ b ǰ ɛ k t
```

To produce a stressed syllable, we may change the pitch (usually by raising it), make the syllable louder, or make it longer. We often use all three of these phonetic features to stress a syllable.

Sentence and Phrase Stress

© Howie Schneider.

When words are combined into phrases and sentences, one of the syllables receives greater stress than all others. That is, just as there is only one primary stress in a word spoken in isolation (for example, in a list), only one of the vowels in a phrase (or sentence) receives primary stress or accent; all the other stressed vowels are "reduced" to secondary stress. A syllable that receives the main stress when the word is not in a phrase may have only secondary stress in a phrase, as is illustrated by these examples:

$$
\begin{array}{cccc}
1 & 1 & 1 & 2 \\
\end{array}
$$
tight + rope → tightrope   ("a rope for acrobatics")
$$
\begin{array}{cccc}
1 & 1 & 2 & 1 \\
\end{array}
$$
tight + rope → tight rope   ("a rope drawn taut")

$$
\begin{array}{ccc}
1 & 1 & 1\ 2 \\
\end{array}
$$
hot + dog → hotdog   ("frankfurter")
$$
\begin{array}{ccc}
1 & 1 & 2\ 1 \\
\end{array}
$$
hot + dog → hot dog   ("an overheated dog")

$$
\begin{array}{ccc}
1 & 1 & 1\ 2 \\
\end{array}
$$
red + coat → Redcoat   ("a British soldier")
$$
\begin{array}{ccc}
1 & 1 & 2\ 1 \\
\end{array}
$$
red + coat → red coat   ("a coat that is red")

$$
\begin{array}{cccc}
1 & 1 & 1 & 2 \\
\end{array}
$$
white + house → White House   ("the President's house")
$$
\begin{array}{cccc}
1 & 1 & 2 & 1 \\
\end{array}
$$
white + house → white house   ("a house painted white")

In English we place primary stress on an adjective followed by a noun when the two words are combined in a compound noun (usually, but not always, written as one word), but we place the stress on the noun when the words are not joined in this way. The differences between the pairs above are therefore predictable:

Compound Noun	**Adjective 1 Noun**
tightrope	tight rope
Redcoat	red coat
hotdog	hot dog
White House	white house

These minimal pairs show that stress may be predictable if phonological rules include nonphonological information; that is, the phonology is not independent of the rest of the grammar. The stress differences between the noun and verb pairs (*subject* as noun and verb) discussed in the previous section are also predictable from the word category.

In the English sentences we used to illustrate intonation contours, we may also describe the differences by referring to the word on which the main stress is placed, as in the following examples:

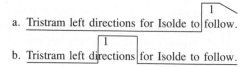

a. Tristram left directions for Isolde to follow.

b. Tristram left directions for Isolde to follow.

In sentence a the primary stress is on the word *follow,* and in b the primary stress is on *directions*.

The Rules of Phonology

No rule is so general which admits not some exception.
Robert Burton, *The Anatomy of Melancholy*

But that to come
Shall all be done by the rule.
Shakespeare, *Antony and Cleopatra*

As discussed above, all who know a language know its basic vocabulary, the phonemic representations of words, their phonetic pronunciations, and what these forms mean. This knowledge is "stored" in mental dictionaries.

If you want to refer to the concept "pot," you say [pʰat] not [tʰat]. You know what sounds represent the meaning you wish to express. You must know that the word meaning "pot" starts with a /p/ rather than a /t/ or a /k/, or you would not be understood. You also know that the initial /p/ is pronounced as a [pʰ], because part of your phonological knowledge is the fact that all syllable-initial voiceless stops before stressed vowels are aspirated. It is not necessary to specify the /p/ as an aspirated [pʰ] in your mental dictionary; there is a general rule that will add this feature. The inclusion of the feature [+aspiration] in the description of the initial segment of this word would be redundant. The fact that the initial voiceless stop is aspirated is not a fact about the word *pot* but about all words that begin with voiceless stops.

The relationship between the phonemic representations that are stored and the phonetic representations that reflect the pronunciation of these words is "rule-governed." These **phonological rules** relate the **minimally specified** phonemic representation to the phonetic representation and are part of a speaker's knowledge of the language. They are part of the mental grammar.

The phonemic representation need only include the nonpredictable distinctive features of the string of phonemes that represent the words. The phonetic representation **derived** by applying these rules includes all the linguistically relevant phonetic aspects of the sounds. It does not include all the physical properties of the sounds of an utterance, because the physical signal may vary in many ways that have little to do with the phonological system. The absolute pitch of the sounds, the rate of speech, or its loudness is not linguistically significant. The phonetic transcription is therefore also an abstraction from the physical signal; it includes the nonvariant phonetic aspects of the utterances, those features that remain relatively the same from speaker to speaker and from one time to another.

The Formalization of Phonological Rules

Form follows function.
Slogan of the Bauhaus school of architecture

Rule 1, the aspiration rule, and Rule 2, the nasalization rule, given above are rules of the grammar of English. They make certain predictions about English pronunciation. We repeat them, with some slight changes, for easy reference.

(1) Nasalize vowels and diphthongs before nasals.
(2) Aspirate voiceless stops before stressed vowels at the beginning of a word or syllable.

Both rules specify the **class of sounds** affected by the rules:

in (1) vowels and diphthongs
in (2) voiceless stops

Both rules state what **phonetic changes** are to occur:

in (1) nasalize (change from [−nasal] to [+nasal])
in (2) aspirate (change from [−aspirated] to [+aspirated])

Both rules specify the **context** or **phonemic environment** of the relevant sounds:

in (1) before nasals
in (2) before stressed vowels at the beginning of a word or syllable

All three kinds of information—segments affected, phonemic environment, phonetic change—must be included in the statement of a phonological rule, or it would not explicitly state the regularities that constitute speakers' phonological knowledge. The rules of grammar written by linguists or posited as being in the grammar should explicitly characterize the actual rules known unconsciously by speakers of the language.

How can we state these rules in the most explicit and simple way? With the development of linguistic theory, **technical notations** began to be used as in other sciences, both to simplify the theoretical statements and to reveal the "laws" of language. Every physicist knows that $E = mc^2$ means "Energy equals mass times the square of the velocity of light."

The phonological rules we have considered so far have been stated in words like the sentence used to "translate" the formula in physics. We have used a few special symbols or "formal devices" or "formal notations" in specifying the + or − values of features and in applying the **cover symbols** like C, V, L, and G to the classes of consonants, vowels, liquids, and glides. The phonetic symbols themselves are technical terms; /e/ represents a "front, mid, tense, unrounded vowel" in the same sense as *"E"* in physics represents "energy" and *"m"* represents "mass." Slashes—/ /—show that the symbols represent phonemes; brackets— [ ]—enclose phonetic segments or phones.

Other such notations can be used to **formalize** phonological rules. These special symbols are part of the theory of phonology. They do more than merely save paper or abbreviate long statements. They provide a way to express the generalizations of the language that may be obscured otherwise.

By using feature notation, rather than phonetic or phonemic cover symbols, "natural" rules are revealed to be simpler than "unnatural rules." We illustrated this idea by reference to a rule that applied to all aspirated stops /p,t,k/ rather than just to /p/ and /t/ and to a rule nasalizing vowels before the natural class of nasals as compared to a rule nasalizing vowels before /p, i, z/. These examples illustrating the explanatory power of the feature notation show that certain kinds of formalization are important in a theory. Perhaps another example will be helpful.

Suppose the phonology of a language included a rule that nasalizes a vowel or glide before, and only before, a /t/. Stating this rule without features, we could say:

(3) Nasalize a vowel or glide before a /t/.

Using the phonemic cover symbol, the rule appears to be simpler than the vowel or glide nasalization rule stated as

(4) Nasalize a vowel or glide before /m/, /n/, or /ŋ/.

because it mentions only /t/, whereas Rule 4 has to include three phonemes. Nevertheless it is a strange and highly unlikely rule, with little phonetic plausibility, and therefore it would undoubtedly be a difficult rule for a child to learn.

The complexity of Rule 3 shows up as soon as it is stated in feature notation:

(5) [−consonantal] becomes [+nasal] before a $\begin{bmatrix} +\text{consonantal} \\ -\text{vocalic} \\ +\text{anterior} \\ +\text{coronal} \\ -\text{voiced} \\ -\text{continuant} \end{bmatrix}$

as opposed to:

(6) [−consonantal] becomes [+nasal] before [+nasal]

We can see at a glance that Rule 5 is more complex (you have to mention more features) than Rule 6, and that the features mentioned have nothing in common. Rule 6 seems like a "natural" rule and Rule 5 does not. This difference is exactly what we want to reveal. Without the use of features the difference between the two rules is hidden. The use of such feature notation to represent phonemes is, then, part of the theory of phonology. The formal notation is not used merely because it is somehow more "elegant" but because it better represents what we know about phonological rules.

We can simplify the rule still further by using other symbols to replace words, just as we use "=" instead of "equals" in mathematical equations and formulas. Instead of writing "becomes," we will use an arrow, →. The segment on the left of the arrow "becomes" or "is" whatever is on the right of the arrow in the specified environment:

(7) [−consonantal] → [+nasal] before a [+nasal]

What occurs on the left of the arrow fulfills the first requirement for a rule: it specifies the class of sounds affected by the rule. What occurs on the right side of the arrow specifies the change that occurs, thus fulfilling the second requirement of a phonological rule.

To fulfill the third requirement of a rule—giving the phonological environment or context where the rule will apply—we can formalize the notions of "environment" or "in the environment" and the notions of "before" and "after," because it is also important to specify whether the vowels to be nasalized occur before or after a nasal. We will see below that in some languages, nasalization occurs after rather than before nasal segments. We will use the following notations:

a slash   /   to mean "in the environment of"
a dash   —   placed before or after the segment(s) that determine the change

Using these notations, we can rewrite Rule 7:

(8) [−consonantal] → [+nasal] /— [+nasal]

This rule reads in words: "A vowel or glide (a segment specified as nonconsonantal) becomes or is (→) nasalized in the environment (/) before (—) a nasal segment."

If the rule were written instead as:

(9) [−consonantal] → [+nasal] / [+nasal] —

it would read: "A vowel or glide becomes nasalized in the environment *after* a nasal." The fact that the dash follows the [+nasal] shows that a vowel that comes after it is changed.

The aspiration rule states that the environment in which a voiceless stop is to become aspirated is at the beginning of a syllable. We can use the symbol $ to represent a syllable **boundary.** The rule also states that aspiration occurs only if the following vowel is **stressed.** The /p/ in *pit* and *repeat* is aspirated, but the /p/ in *in $ spect* or *compass* is not. We can use the feature [±stress] to write the rule as:

(10) $\begin{bmatrix} -\text{continuant} \\ -\text{voiced} \end{bmatrix}$ → [+aspirated] / \$ — $\begin{bmatrix} -\text{consonantal} \\ +\text{stress} \end{bmatrix}$

This version is somewhat oversimplified, because a syllable-initial voiceless stop before a liquid—/l/ or /r/—followed by a stressed vowel is also aspirated. We shall see how to write this fact below.

Because every word-initial segment is also syllable-initial, the rule applies to word-initial voiceless stops. Notice that we do not have to write two rules, one for word-initial voiceless stops and one for syllable-initial voiceless stops before stressed vowels. Where one rule will suffice, to state the process in two rules would obscure the generalization we wish to capture.

In the sections below on the kinds of phonological rules that occur in the world's languages, we will have more to say on formal devices.

Assimilation Rules

The vowel nasalization rule is an **assimilation rule;** it *assimilates* one segment to another by "copying" or "spreading" a feature of a sequential phoneme, making the two phones more similar. Assimilation rules, for the most part, are caused by articulatory or physiological processes. There is a tendency when we speak to increase the ease of articulation. Assimilation rules in languages reflect what phoneticians often call **coarticulation**—the spreading of phonetic features either in anticipation of sounds or the perseveration of articulatory processes. This tendency to "sloppiness" may become regularized as rules of the language.

The following example illustrates how the English vowel nasalization rule applies to the phonemic representation of words and shows the assimilatory nature of the rule; that is, the [−nasal] feature value of the vowel in the phonemic representation changes to a [+nasal] in the phonetic representation:

	"Bob"	**"bomb"**
Phonemic representation	/b a b/	/b a m/
Nasality: phonemic feature value	− − −	− − +
Apply nasal rule (1)	NA*	
Nasality: phonetic feature value	− − −	− + +
Phonetic representation	[b a b]	[b ã m]

*NA = "not applicable."

The nasalization rule applies wherever it is applicable.

There are many other examples of assimilation rules in English and other languages. There is an **optional** ("free variation") rule in English that, particularly in fast speech, devoices the nasals and liquids in words like *snow* /sno/ [sno̥], *slow* /slo/ [slo̥], *smart* /smart/ [sm̥art], *probe* /prob/ [pʰr̥ob], and so on. The feature [−voiced] of the /s/ or /p/ carries over onto the following segment. Because voiceless nasals and liquids do not occur phonemically—do not contrast with voiced sonorants—the vocal cords can "afford" to be "sluggish." The devoicing will not change the meaning of the words; [slat] and [sl̥at] both mean "slot."

Vowels may also become devoiced or voiceless in a voiceless environment. In Japanese, high vowels are devoiced when preceded and followed by voiceless obstruents; in words like *sukiyaki* the /u/ becomes [u̥]. This assimilation rule can be stated as follows:

$$(11) \quad \begin{bmatrix} -\text{consonantal} \\ +\text{syllabic} \end{bmatrix} \rightarrow [-\text{voiced}] \; / \; \begin{bmatrix} -\text{sonorant} \\ -\text{voiced} \end{bmatrix} - \begin{bmatrix} -\text{sonorant} \\ -\text{voiced} \end{bmatrix}$$

This rule states that any Japanese vowel (segment that is nonconsonantal and syllabic) becomes devoiced ([−voiced]) in the environment of, or when it occurs (/) between, voiceless obstruents. Notice that the dash does not occur immediately after the slash or at the end of the rule, but between the segment matrices represented as [−sonorant, −voiced].

This rule includes the three kinds of information required:

a. the class of sounds affected: vowels ($\begin{bmatrix} -\text{consonantal} \\ +\text{syllabic} \end{bmatrix}$)

b. the phonemic environment: between two obstruents

c. the phonetic change: devoicing $\begin{bmatrix} -\text{consonantal} \\ +\text{syllabic} \\ +\text{voiced} \end{bmatrix} \rightarrow \begin{bmatrix} -\text{consonantal} \\ +\text{syllabic} \\ -\text{voiced} \end{bmatrix}$

Rule 11 does not specify the class of segments to the left of the arrow as [+voiced] because phonemically all vowels in Japanese are voiced. It therefore simply has to include the change on the right side of the arrow.

We can illustrate the application of this rule in Japanese as we did the vowel nasalization rule in English:

	"sukiyaki"
Phonemic Representation	/s u k i j a k i/
Voicing: phonemic feature value	− + − + + + − +
Apply Devoicing rule (11)	↓
Voicing: phonetic feature value	− − − + + + − +
Phonetic Representation	[s ṷ k i j a k i]

The English vowel nasalization and devoicing rules and the Japanese devoicing rule change feature specifications. That is, in English the [−nasal] value of phonemic vowels is changed to [+nasal] phonetically when they occur before nasals through a spreading process. Vowels in Japanese are phonemically voiced, and the rule changes vowels that occur in the specified environment into phonetically voiceless segments.

The rules we have discussed are phonetically plausible, as are other assimilation rules, and can be explained by natural phonetic processes. This fact does not mean that all these rules have to occur in all languages. In fact, if they always occurred they would not have to be learned at all; they would apply automatically and universally, and therefore would not have to be included in the grammar of any particular language. They are not, however, universal.

There is a nasal assimilation rule in Akan that nasalizes voiced stops when they follow nasal consonants, as shown in the following example:

/ɔ bá/   [ɔ́bá]   "he comes"   /ɔ ḿ bá/   [ɔ́mmá]   "he doesn't come"
he come   *he not come*

The /b/ of the verb "come" becomes an [m] when it follows the negative /m/.

This assimilation rule also has a phonetic explanation; the velum is lowered to produce the nasal consonant and remains down during the following stop. Although it is a phonetically "natural" assimilation rule, it does not occur in the grammar of English; the word *amber,* for example, shows an [m] followed by a [b]. A child learning Akan must learn this rule, just as a child learning English learns to nasalize all vowels before nasal consonants, a rule that does not occur in the grammar of Akan.

Assimilation rules such as the ones we have discussed in English, Japanese, and Akan often have the function of changing the value of phonemic features. They are feature-changing or feature-spreading rules. Although nasality is nondistinctive for vowels in English, it is a distinctive feature for consonants, and the nasalization rule therefore changes a feature value.

The Akan rule is a feature-changing rule that states that [m] is an allophone of /b/ as well as an allophone of /m/. Thus, there is no one-to-one relationship between phonemes and their allophones. This fact can be illustrated in another way:

Akan Phonemes   /b/   /m/

Akan Phones   [b]   [m]

We will provide more examples of this one-to-many or many-to-one mapping between phonemes and allophones below.

Dissimilation Rules

Given some idea about how speech sounds are produced, assimilation rules seem understandable. It is easier not to require exact timing in the raising or lowering of the velum before or after nasals. It might seem strange, then, to learn that we also find **dissimilation rules** in languages, rules in which a segment becomes *less* similar to another segment rather than more similar.

Such rules do exist. They also have a "natural" explanation, often from the point of view of the **hearer** rather than the speaker. That is, in listening to speech, if sounds are too similar, we may miss the contrast. Many speakers in English "dissimilate" the sequence of two fricatives /fθ/ in the word *diphthong* and pronounce it with a labial stop /p/ instead of the labial fricative /f/. This change may also be due to "ease of articulation" factors. Notice that only one feature value changes [+continuant] to [−continuant]; /f/ and /p/ are both voiceless and labial.

A classic example of such a dissimilation rule, in which the value of a feature of a segment changes to become different from that of a neighboring segment, is provided by Sanskrit, an ancient Indian language in which the Hindu sacred works were written. There is a Sanskrit rule that changes a [+aspirated] segment to [−aspirated] if a [+aspirated] sound occurs earlier in certain words.

Dissimilation rules are quite rare, but they do occur. The African language Kikuyu also has a dissimilation rule, in which a prefix added to a verb begins with a velar fricative if the verb begins with a stop or with a velar stop if the verb begins with a continuant.

Feature Addition Rules

Some phonological rules are neither assimilation nor dissimilation rules. The aspiration rule in English, which aspirates voiceless stops in certain contexts, simply adds a nondistinctive feature. Aspiration is neither present nor absent in any phonemic feature matrices in English. This fact was pointed out above when we discussed why /p/ and /b/ were distinguished by the feature [±voiced] rather than by the feature [±aspirated]. The assimilation rules do not add new features but change phonemic feature values, whereas the aspiration rule adds a new feature not present in phonemic matrices.

/p/ and /b/ (and all such symbols) are simply cover symbols that do not reveal the phonemic distinctions. In the phonemic and phonetic feature matrices, these differences are made explicit, as shown in the following phonemic matrices:

	/p/	/b/	
Consonantal	+	+	
Vocalic	−	−	
Continuant	−	−	
Labial	+	+	
Voiced	−	+	←distinctive difference

The nondistinctive feature "aspiration" is not included in these phonemic representations because aspiration is predictable. The phonemic and phonetic differences between the bilabial stops in *pit, spit,* and *bit* illustrate this reasoning:

	pit	/pɪt/	[pʰɪt]	spit	/spɪt/	[spɪt]	bit	/bɪt/	[bɪt]
Distinctive Features									
Consonantal		+	+		+	+		+	+
Vocalic		−	−		−	−		−	−
Labial		+	+		+	+		+	+
Continuant		−	−		−	−		−	−
Voiced		−	−		−	−		+	+
Apply Rule 10					NA			NA	
Nondistinctive feature									
Aspirated			+						

In the phonemic representations of all three words there is no feature value specified for the nondistinctive feature [±aspirated]. Phonemically, /p/ and /b/ are neither "aspirated" nor "unaspirated." The specification of this feature depends on the context of the /p/—where it occurs in a word. The aspiration rule (10) can apply only to the voiceless stops /p/, /t/, /k/, because the specification of the class of sounds on the left of the arrow is unique to this class, but only when one of these segments occurs in the environment specified after the slash, at the beginning of a syllable (/$—) before a stressed vowel. The rule thus adds the [+aspirated] designation to the voiceless stops in words like *pin, tin, kin, peal, teal, keel, repeal, intend,* and *rekindle* but does nothing to *spin, steal, skin, penumbra, terrific, collect,* and so on, or to any of the voiced stops.

Segment Deletion and Addition Rules

In addition to assimilation (feature-changing) and feature-addition rules, phonological rules can delete or add entire phonemic segments. In French, for example, as demonstrated by Sanford Schane,[5] word-final consonants are deleted when the following word begins with a consonant or a liquid, but are retained when the following word begins with a vowel or a glide:

Before a consonant:	petit tableau	[pəti tablo]	"small picture"
	nos tableaux	[no tablo]	"our pictures"
Before a liquid:	petit livre	[pəti livr]	"small book"
	nos livres	[no livr]	"our books"
Before a vowel:	petit ami	[pətit ami]	"small friend"
	nos amis	[noz ami]	"our friends"
Before a glide:	petit oiseau	[pətit wazo]	"small bird"
	nos oiseaux	[noz wazo]	"our birds"

This general rule in French applies to all word-final consonants. In the chapter on phonetics we distinguished these four classes of sounds by the following features:

	Obstruents	**Liquids**	**Vowels**	**Glides**
Consonantal	+	+	−	−
Syllabic	−	+/−	+	−

Using these classes, and the symbol ø to represent the "null" unit, and # as "word boundary," we can state the French rule simply:

(12) [+consonantal] → ø / — # # [+consonantal]

[5]Sanford Schane. 1968. *French Phonology and Morphology.* M.I.T. Press. Cambridge, Mass.

This rule can be "translated" into words as:

> (12a) A consonantal segment (obstruent or liquid) is deleted or becomes null
> (→ ø) in the environment (/) at the end of a word (— #) which is
> followed by a word beginning with an obstruent or liquid
> (# [+consonantal]).

or simply as "Delete a consonant before a word beginning with a consonant."

In Schane's complete analysis, many words that are pronounced with a final consonant actually have a vowel as their word-final segment in phonemic representation. The vowel prevents the rule of word-final consonant deletion from applying. The vowel itself is deleted by another, later rule. Given this rule in the grammar of French, *petit* would be phonemically /pətit/. It need not be additionally represented as /pəti/, because the rule determines the phonetic shape of the word.

"Deletion rules" also show up as **optional rules** in fast speech or casual speech in English. They result, for example, in the common contractions changing *he is* [hi ɪz] to *he's* [hiz] or *I will* [aj wɪl] to *I'll* [ajl]. In ordinary everyday speech most of us also "delete" the unstressed vowels that are shown in bold type in words like the following:

   mystery   general   memory   funeral   vigorous   Barbara

These words in casual speech sound as if they were written:

   mystry   genral   memry   funral   vigrous   Barbra

Phonological rules therefore can be either optional or obligatory.

Phonological rules may also add whole segments. In Spanish, a rule inserts an [e] at the beginning of a word that otherwise would begin with an [s] followed by another consonant. For example, the word meaning "to transcribe" in Spanish is *transcribir,* and the word meaning "to endorse" is *subscribir.* Both of these words consist of a prefix followed by *scribir,* which means "to write." Without a prefix, however, "to write" is not **scribir* but *escribir;* the segment [e] has been added to the word-initial /skr/ cluster. You will not find a word in Spanish beginning with [sp] or [st] or [sk]; the [e] insertion rule produces the phonetic forms of *escuela* "school," *estampa* "stamp," *España* "Spain," and *espina* "spine," from the phonemic representations that begin with /sk/, /st/, and /sp/.

In English, another optional rule inserts a voiceless stop after a nasal followed by a voiceless consonant. Thus, many speakers pronounce *mince,* which is phonemically /mɪns/, as [mɪnts], identically with *mints* /mɪnt + s/; they pronounce *sense* and *cents* identically as [sɛnts], although the first word phonemically has no /t/. One of the authors of this book regularly receives letters addressed to "Professor Frompkin," a spelling that reflects the writers' pronunciation of her name, which she pronounces [frɔmkɪn] but which others pronounce [frɔmpkɪn]. The voiceless stop that is inserted in these words is always *homorganic*—produced at the same place of articulation—as the nasal. That is, it is the labial [p] after the labial [m], the alveolar [t] after the alveolar [n], or the velar [k] after the velar [ŋ].

Movement (Metathesis) Rules

Phonological rules may also move phonemes from one place in the string to another. Such rules are called **metathesis rules.** They are less common, but they do exist. In some dialects of English, for example, the word *ask* is pronounced [æks], but the word *asking* is pronounced [æskiŋ]. In these dialects a metathesis rule "switches" the /s/ and /k/ in certain contexts. It is interesting that in Old English the verb was *aksian,* with the /k/ preceding the /s/. An historical metathesis rule switched these two consonants, producing *ask* in most dialects of English. Children's speech shows many cases of metathesis (which are later corrected as the child approaches the adult grammar): *aminal* for *animal* and *pusketti* for *spaghetti* are common children's pronunciations.

In Hebrew there is a metathesis rule that reverses a pronoun-final consonant with the first consonant of the following verb if the verb starts with a sibilant. These reversals are in "reflexive" verb forms, as shown in the following examples:

Nonsibilant—Initial Verbs		Sibilant—Initial Verbs	
kabel	"to accept"	*tsadek*	"to justify"
lehit-kabel	"to be accepted"	*lehits-tadek* (not **lehit-tsadek*)	"to apologize"
pater	"to fire"	*šameš*	"to use for"
lehit-pater	"to resign"	*lehiš-tameš* (not **lehit-šameš*)	"to use"
bayeš	"to shame"	*sader*	"to arrange"
lehit-bayeš	"to be ashamed"	*lehis-tader* (not **lehit-sader*)	"to arrange oneself"

We see, then, that phonological rules may produce the following alterations:

1. **Change feature values** (vowel nasalization rule in English).
2. **Add new features** (aspiration in English).
3. **Delete segments** (final consonant deletion in French).
4. **Add segments** (vowel insertion in Spanish).
5. **Reorder segments** (metathesis rule in Hebrew).

These rules, when applied to the phonemic representations of words and phrases, result in phonetic forms that may differ substantially from the phonemic forms. If such differences were unpredictable, we would find it difficult to explain how we can understand what we hear or how we produce utterances that represent the meanings we wish to convey. The more we look at languages, however, the more we see that many aspects of the phonetic forms of utterances which appear at first to be irregular and unpredictable are actually rule-governed. We learn, or construct, these rules when we are learning the language as children. The rules represent "patterns," or general principles.

From One to Many and from Many to One

The discussion on how phonemic representations of utterances are realized phonetically included an example from the African Ghanaian language Akan, to show that the relationship between a phoneme and its allophonic realization may be complex. The same phone may be an allophone of two or more phonemes, as [m] was shown to be an allophone of both /b/ and /m/ in Akan.

We can also illustrate this complex mapping relationship in English. Consider the vowels in the following pairs of words:

	A			**B**	
/i/	compete	[i]	competition	[ə]
/ɪ/	medicinal	[ɪ]	medicine	[ə]
/e/	maintain	[e]	maintenance	[ə]
/ɛ/	telegraph	[ɛ]	telegraphy	[ə]
/æ/	analysis	[æ]	analytic	[ə]
/a/	solid	[a]	solidity	[ə]
/o/	phone	[o]	phonetic	[ə]
/u/	Talmudic	[u]	Talmud	[ə]

In column A all the bold-faced vowels are stressed vowels with a variety of different vowel phones; in column B all the bold-faced unstressed vowels are pronounced [ə]; yet the "reduced" vowels of column B must be derived from different underlying phonemes, because when they are stressed they show up as different vowels in column A. If the vowel of *compete* were not phonemically /i/, there would be no way to account for the particular quality of the stressed vowel. We might say that [ə] is an allophone of all English vowel phonemes. The rule to derive the schwa can be stated simply as:

(13) Change a vowel to a [ə] when it is unstressed.

or as a formal rule:

$$(13\text{a}) \quad \begin{bmatrix} -\text{consonantal} \\ +\text{syllabic} \\ -\text{stress} \end{bmatrix} \rightarrow \begin{bmatrix} -\text{high} \\ -\text{low} \\ +\text{back} \\ -\text{round} \end{bmatrix}$$

Another way of stating this rule, which complies with the three requirements we set above, is as follows:

$$(13\text{b}) \quad \begin{bmatrix} -\text{consonantal} \\ +\text{syllabic} \end{bmatrix} \rightarrow \begin{bmatrix} -\text{high} \\ -\text{low} \\ +\text{back} \\ -\text{round} \end{bmatrix} / \underline{\quad} \begin{bmatrix} -\text{stress} \end{bmatrix}$$

The environment is not before or after a segment, but a feature specification of that segment. That is, any vowel whose matrix includes the feature value [−stress] will undergo this rule.

This rule is oversimplified, because when an unstressed vowel occurs as the final segment of some words it retains its full vowel quality, as shown in words like *confetti, motto,* or *democracy.* In some dialects, all unstressed vowels are reduced.

The rule that "reduces" unstressed vowels to schwas is another example of a rule that changes feature values.

In a phonological description of a language that we do not know, it is not always possible to determine from the phonetic transcription what the phonemic representation is. However, given the phonemic representation and the phonological rules, we can always derive the correct phonetic transcription. Of course, in our internal, mental grammars this derivation is no problem, because the words are listed phonemically and we know the rules of the language.

Another example will illustrate this aspect of phonology. In English, /t/ and /d/ are both phonemes, as is illustrated by the minimal pairs *tie/die* and *bat/bad.* When /t/ or /d/ occurs between a stressed and an unstressed vowel they both become a flap [D]. For many speakers of English, *writer* and *rider* are pronounced identically as [rajDər]; yet these speakers know that *writer* has a phonemic /t/ because of *write* /rajt/, whereas *rider* has a phonemic /d/ because of *ride* /rajd/. The "flap rule" may be stated informally:

> (14) An alveolar stop becomes a voiced flap when preceded by a stressed vowel and followed by an unstressed vowel.

The application of this rule is illustrated as follows:

Phonemic	write	writer	ride	rider
Representation	/rajt/	/rajt + ər/	/rajd/	/rajd + ər/
		↓		↓
Apply Rule 14	NA	D	NA	D
Phonetic				
Representation	[rajt]	[rajDər]	[rajd]	[rajDər]

We are omitting other phonetic details that are also determined by phonological rules, such as the fact that in *ride* the vowel is slightly longer than in *write* because it is followed by a voiced [d], which is a phonetic rule in many languages. We are using the example only to illustrate the fact that two distinct phonemes may be realized phonetically as the same sound.

Such cases show that we cannot arrive at a phonological analysis by simply inspecting the phonetic representation of utterances. If we just looked for minimal pairs as the only evidence for phonology, we would have to conclude that [D] is a phoneme in English because it contrasts phonetically with other phonetic units: *riper* [rajpər], *rhymer* [rãjmər], *riser* [rajzər], and so forth. Grammars are much more complex than this pairing shows. The fact that *write* and *ride* change their phonetic forms when suffixes are added shows that there is an intricate mapping between phonemic representations of words and phonetic pronunciations.

Notice that in the case of the "schwa rule" and the "flap rule" the allophones derived from the different phonemes by rule are different in features from all other phonemes in the language. That is, there is no [D] phoneme, but there is a [D] phone.

The English "flap rule" also illustrates an important phonological process called **neutralization;** the voicing contrast between /t/ and /d/ is *neutralized* in the specified environment. That is, /t/ never contrasts with /d/ in the environment between a stressed and an unstressed vowel.

Similar rules showing there is no one-to-one relation between phonemes and phones are found in other languages. In both Russian and German, when voiced obstruents occur at the end of a word or syllable, they become voiceless. Both voiced and voiceless obstruents do occur in German as phonemes, as is shown by the following minimal pair:

> *Tier*   [ti:r]   "animal"   *dir*   [di:r]   "to you"

At the end of a word, however, only [t] occurs; the words meaning "bundle" *Bund*[6] and "colorful" *bunt* are phonetically identical and pronounced [bŪnt]. Should they, then, be phonemically identical—that is, /bŪnt/?

If *Bund* and *bunt* were represented phonemically as /bŪnt/, identically with the phonetic pronunciation, there would be no way of accounting for the [d] in *Bunde* [bŪndə], which is the plural of *Bund*. If, however, the singular and plural stems are represented phonemically as /bund/ and /bunt/ and there is a rule in the grammar of German that says "Devoice obstruents at the end of a word," the correct phonetic singular and plural forms for both words would result:

	Bund		*bunt*	
	singular	plural	singular	plural
Phonemic *Representation*	/bund/	/bund+ə/	/bunt/	/bunt+ə/
Apply Devoicing Rule	t	NA	NA	NA
Phonetic *Representation*	[bŪnt]	[bŪndə]	[bŪnt]	[bŪntə]

This example shows again that the phonetic realization of two distinct phonemes may be identical in certain environments. As in the English flap rule, the contrast between /t/ and /d/ and all voiceless and voiced obstruents is neutralized in word-final position.

The German devoicing rule, like the vowel reduction rule in English and the

---

[6]In German, nouns are capitalized in written form.

homorganic nasal rule, changes the specifications of features. In German, the phonemic representation of the final stop in *Bund* is /d/, specified as [+voiced]; it is changed by the rule above to [−voiced] to derive the phonetic [t] in word-final position.

This rule in German further illustrates that we cannot decide what the phonemic representation of a word is, given only the phonetic form; [būnt] can be derived from either /bund/ or /bunt/. However, given the phonemic representations and the rules of the language, the phonetic forms are automatically derived.

The Function of Phonological Rules

The function of the phonological rules in a grammar is to provide the phonetic information necessary for the pronunciation of utterances. We may illustrate this point in the following way:

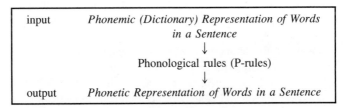

input	*Phonemic (Dictionary) Representation of Words in a Sentence*
	↓
	Phonological rules (P-rules)
	↓
output	*Phonetic Representation of Words in a Sentence*

That is, the input to the P-rules is the phonemic representation; the P-rules apply to or operate on the phonemic strings and produce as output the phonetic representation.

The application of rules in this way is called a **derivation.** We have given a number of examples of derivations, which show how phonemically oral vowels become nasalized, how phonemically unaspirated voiceless stops become aspirated, how contrastive voiced and voiceless alveolar stops in English merge to become flaps, and how German voiced obstruents are devoiced. A derivation is thus an explicit way of showing both the effects of a phonological rule and the function of phonological rules (which we can abbreviate as P-rules) in a grammar.

All the examples of derivations we have so far considered show the application of just one phonological rule. It must be the case, however, that more than one rule may apply to a word. For example, the word *panda* is phonemically /pænda/ but phonetically [pʰǣndə]. Three rules apply to it: the aspiration rule, the vowel nasalization rule, and the schwa rule.

We can derive [pʰǣndə] from /pænda/ as follows:

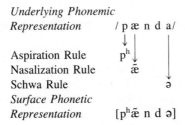

Underlying Phonemic
Representation   / p æ n d a/

Aspiration Rule   pʰ
Nasalization Rule   ǣ
Schwa Rule   ə
Surface Phonetic
Representation   [pʰǣ n d ə]

We are using phonetic symbols instead of matrices in which the feature values are changed. These derivations are equivalent, however, as long as we understand that a phonetic symbol is a *cover term* representing a matrix with all distinctive features marked either + or − (unless, of course, the feature is nondistinctive, such as the nasality value for phonemic vowels in English).

In deriving the pronunciation of the word *panda,* it did not matter which rule was applied first or second or third. The order of rule application does matter in some cases.

In the discussion of the English "flap rule" which specifies that a /t/ or /d/ becomes the voiced [D] between a stressed vowel and an unstressed vowel, we mentioned that there may be a phonetic difference in vowel length between *write* and *ride.* This difference is, of course, due to the rule that lengthens vowels before voiced, but not voiceless, obstruents. It would apply to *ride* /rajd/ to produce [raj:d], but it would not apply to *write* /rajt/, which phonetically is [rajt]. Though *write* and *ride* are pronounced by some speakers with phonetically different lengths of the vowel diphthongs, others pronounce these words with the same vowel length, usually the longer variety. How can this difference be accounted for, when in *writer* and *rider* the phonetic vowels both occur before the voiced flap [D]?

This difference reveals another interesting fact: the application of some rules must be ordered. Speakers who apply the "flap rule" first will have no phonetic contrast; *writer* and *rider* will be identical phonetically—[raj:Dər]. Speakers who apply the vowel lengthening rule before the flap rule will only have a longer vowel in *rider,* as the following derivations show:

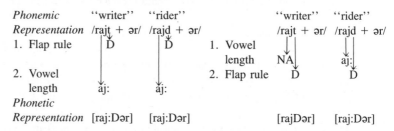

The ordering of the rules, permitted by the theory, is a formal way of showing how a speaker's grammar specifies the pronunciation of words and sentences. We do not necessarily apply rules in sequence when we pronounce these words in speech performance. Just as phonemes are abstractions, explicit rule ordering is also an abstraction. We are not suggesting that we have in our mental grammars +'s and −'s and arrows and slashes. These symbols are abstract devices whose function is to reveal what speakers know about the sound patterns of their language.

Slips of the Tongue: Evidence for Phonological Rules

"Slips of the tongue" or "speech errors" in which we deviate in some way from the intended utterance show phonological rules in action. Some of these tongue slips are called **spoonerisms,** after William Archibald Spooner, a distinguished head of an Oxford College in the early 1900s who is reported to have said to a class of students "You have hissed my mystery lecture" instead of the intended "You have

THE WIZARD OF ID   **By Parker and Hart**

By permission of Johnny Hart and North America Syndicate, Inc.

missed my history lecture," "You have tasted the whole worm" instead of "You have wasted the whole term," and other such errors. We all make speech errors, however, and they tell us interesting things about language and its use. Consider the following speech errors:

Intended Utterance	Actual Utterance
(1) gone to seed	god to seen
[gõn tə sid]	[gɔd tə sĩn]
(2) stick in the mud	smuck in the tid
[stɪk ĩn ðə mʌd]	[smʌk ĩn ðə tʰɪd]
(3) speech production	preach seduction
[spič pʰrədʌkšõn]	[pʰrič sədʌkšõn]

In the first example, the final consonants of the first and third words were reversed. Notice that the reversal of the consonants also changed the nasality of the vowels. The first vowel /a/ was a nasalized [a] in the intended utterance; in the actual utterance the nasalization was "lost," because it no longer occurred before a nasal consonant. The vowel in the third word, which was the nonnasal [i] in the intended utterance, became [i] in the error, because it was followed by /n/. The nasalization rule applied.

In the other two errors, we see the application of the aspiration rule. In the intended *stick,* the /t/ would have been realized as unaspirated because it is not syllable-initial; when it was switched with the /m/ in *mud,* it was pronounced as the aspirated [tʰ], because it occurred initially. The third example also illustrates the application of the aspiration rule in performance.

Rule Simplification

Even if such phonological rules did not show up in slips of the tongue, the generalizations they represent are real ones, as our discussion of these rules has shown. The formalization of the rules and their specified order of application is part of the formal apparatus of the theory of phonology. Their function is to state explicitly the nature of phonological knowledge.

There are other "notational devices" that help to fulfill this function. Consider the two environments in which vowel phonemes are lengthened, becoming [+long] before voiced obstruents, nasals, and nonsyllabic liquids, and at the end of words. We can formalize these two environments in two rules:

$$\text{(15a)} \quad [-\text{consonantal}] \rightarrow [+\bar{\text{l}}\text{ong}] \; / \; \underline{\quad} \begin{bmatrix} +\text{consonantal} \\ -\text{syllabic} \\ +\text{voiced} \end{bmatrix}$$

$$\text{(15b)} \quad [-\text{consonantal}] \rightarrow [+\text{long}] \; / \; \underline{\quad} \; \#$$

Rule 15a. lengthens vowels before voiced obstruents; Rule 15b lengthens them at the end of a word.

By writing two rules, we seem to be missing a generalization; after all, both Rule 15a and Rule 15b apply to vowels and glides, and both add the feature [+long]. To **collapse** or combine two or more rules that have identical parts we can use another device, **braces { }.** Let us collapse Rules 15a and 15b into 15c:

$$\text{(15c)} \quad [-\text{consonantal}] \rightarrow [+\text{long}] \; / \; \underline{\quad} \left\{ \begin{matrix} \begin{bmatrix} +\text{consonantal} \\ -\text{syllabic} \\ +\text{voiced} \end{bmatrix} \\ \# \end{matrix} \right\}$$

The braces signify that the rule applies *either* before voiced consonants *or* before a word boundary. Thus the brace notation permits us to express a rule in a more general fashion.

We will mention only one other "notational device" that helps reveal generalizations in phonology. Consider again Rule 10, the aspiration rule. We have seen that a voiceless stop is aspirated in syllable-initial position when it occurs before a stressed vowel that may or may not be preceded by a liquid. In the formalization of Rule 10, we did not include the optional liquid. Now we can rewrite this rule to account for this fact by using the brace notation. If we use the cover symbols V́ for stressed vowel and L for liquid, the rule can be stated as:

$$\text{(16)} \quad \begin{bmatrix} -\text{continuant} \\ -\text{voiced} \end{bmatrix} \rightarrow [+\text{aspirated}] \; / \; \$ \; \underline{\quad} \left\{ \begin{matrix} \text{V́} \\ \text{LV́} \end{matrix} \right\}$$

This version gives us the result we want; by using the braces we have collapsed two rules, both of which apply to voiceless stops and both of which aspirate them. However, identical parts in the environment of the two rules are still repeated, namely, the stressed vowel. This version seems to miss a generalization we would want to capture. We should have some better notational device that shows that the rule applies before a liquid followed by a stressed vowel or simply before a stressed vowel. To collapse rules like this one, we use parentheses, ( ), around the "optional" segment or segments. The rule really states that a voiceless stop is aspirated before a stressed vowel, which may or may not be preceded by a liquid: the presence of the liquid does not affect the aspiration. Using parentheses, we can state the rule as:

$$(17) \begin{bmatrix} -\text{continuant} \\ -\text{voiced} \end{bmatrix} \rightarrow [+\text{aspirated}] \; / \; \$ \; — \; (\text{L}) \; \acute{\text{V}}$$

The importance of formal devices such as feature notations, arrows, slashes, dashes, braces, and parentheses is that they enable us to express linguistic generalizations. They provide the means to express the function of phonological rules. Because the grammar that linguists write for any particular language aims to express in the most general fashion a speaker's linguistic competence, the notations that permit them to succeed are important to the theory of phonology.

We have not discussed all the formalisms used in phonology to capture linguistic generalizations. Actually, our main purpose here is to help you understand the kinds of phonological processes (rules) found in the languages of the world.

An examination of the phonologies of different languages shows rules that add features, change features, add segments, delete segments, and transpose or switch segments. Evidently human linguistic ability permits us to form such rules. Just as all possible sounds are not found in languages, so all conceivable rules are not. No language has ever been found to include a rule specifying that all the phonemes in a word should be reversed, or that every third phoneme should be deleted, or that an /l/ should be added before a word just in case the word has thirteen phonemes. These rules are logically but not phonologically possible. We see, then, that the forms of grammars and their phonological parts are not as variable as Satie seemed to think. There are universal constraints on the phonological systems that humans can learn.

Summary

Part of knowing a language is knowing the **phonology** or sound system of that language—the inventory of **phones,** the phonetic segments that occur in the language, and the ways in which they pattern. It is this patterning that determines the inventory of **phonemes**—the segments that differentiate words. Phonetic segments are enclosed in square brackets, [ ], and phonemes between slashes, / /.

When phones occur in **complementary distribution,** they are **allophones**—predictable phonetic variants—of phonemes. For example, in English, aspirated voiceless stops such as the initial sounds in the words *pill, till,* and *kill* are in complementary distribution with the unaspirated voiceless stops following the "s" in *spill, still,* and *skill;* the two sets never occur in the same phonological environment. Therefore the aspirated [p^h], [t^h], and [k^h] and the unaspirated [p], [t], and [k] are allophones of the phonemes /p/, /t/, and /k/, respectively. On the other hand, phones that occur in the same environment and that differentiate words, like the [p] and [b] in *pill* and *bill,* represent two distinct phonemes, in this case /p/ and /b/.

Phonological segments—phonemes and phones—are composed of phonetic features or properties, such as the presence or absence of *voicing, nasality, labiality,* and *continuance,* which distinguish one segment from another. When this phonetic difference contrasts words, such as the voicing of /b/ versus the voicelessness of /p/, it is a **distinctive feature.** Therefore, in English, the **binary-valued** feature [±voiced] is a distinctive feature, whereas aspiration is not.

A method that a linguist (or a student of linguistics) can use to discover the phonemes in a language is to look for **minimal pairs,** word pairs that are distinguished by a single phone occurring in the same position. Some pairs, such as *beat* and *meat,* contrast by means of a single distinctive feature, in this case, [±nasal]; /b/ is [−nasal] and /m/ is [+nasal]. Other minimal pairs may show sounds contrasting in more than one feature; for example, in *rip* and *rim,* /p/ is [−voiced, −nasal] and /m/ is [+voiced, +nasal]. The contrast of /b/ and /m/ shows that [±nasal] is a distinctive feature in English.

Phonetic features that are **nondistinctive** in one language may be distinctive in another. Aspiration is distinctive in Thai and nondistinctive in English; both aspirated voiceless stops and unaspirated voiceless stops are phonemes in Thai.

The phonology of a language also includes constraints on the **sequences** of phonemes in the language, as exemplified by the fact that in English two stop consonants may not occur together at the beginning of a word; similarly, the final sound of the word *sing,* the velar nasal, never occurs word initially. These sequential constraints determine what are *possible* but nonoccurring words in a language, and what phonetic strings are ''impossible'' or ''illegal.'' For example, *blick* [blɪk] is not now an English word, but it could become one; whereas *kbli* [kbli] or *ngos* [ŋos] could not.

Words in some languages may also be phonemically distingushed by **prosodic** or **suprasegmental features,** such as **pitch, stress,** and segment **duration or length.** Languages in which the syllables or words are contrasted by pitch are called **tone languages.** Other languages, **intonation languages,** use pitch variations over phrases and sentences to distinguish meaning differences. Thai is a tone language, whereas English is an intonation language.

In English, words and phrases may be differentiated by stress, as in the contrast between the noun *pervert,* in which the first syllable is stressed, and the verb, in which the final syllable is stressed. In the compound noun *hotdog* versus the adjective + noun phrase *hot dog,* the former is stressed on *hot,* the latter on *dog.* Whereas neither **vowel length** nor **consonant length** is phonemic in English, both are contrastive in Japanese, and length is phonemic in many languages.

The relationship between the **phonemic representation** of words and sentences and their **phonetic representation** (the pronunciation) is determined by general **phonological rules.** Phonological rules in a grammar apply to phonemic strings and alter them in various ways to **derive** their phonetic pronunciation:

1. **Assimilation** rules change feature values of segments, thus spreading phonetic properties. The rule that nasalizes vowels in English before nasal consonants is such a rule.
2. **Dissimilation** rules like the Sanskrit aspiration rule change feature values to make two phonemes in a string more dissimilar.

3. **Feature addition** rules add nondistinctive features that are predictable from the context. The rule that aspirates voiceless stops at the beginning of words and syllables in English is such a rule, because aspiration is a nonphonemic, nondistinctive, and predictable *redundant* feature.

4. **Segment addition** rules *insert* segments into the phonemic string. The rule in Spanish that inserts [e] before word-initial /s/ + consonant clusters is an addition or insertion rule.

5. **Segment deletion** rules remove phonemic segments in certain contexts. Contraction rules in English are deletion rules.

6. **Metathesis** rules transpose or move segments in a string. They occur in many languages, such as Hebrew. The rule in certain American English dialects that changes an /sk/ to [ks] in final position is a metathesis rule.

Phonological rules often refer to entire classes of sounds rather than to individual sounds. These **natural classes** are characterized by the phonetic properties or features that pertain to all the members of each class, such as voiceless sounds, voiced sounds, stops, fricatives, consonants, and vowels, or using +'s and −'s, the class specified as [−voiced] or [+consonantal] or [−continuant] or [+nasal].

The phonological rules in a language refer to the distinctive features of phonemes. Such rules show that the phonemic shape of words or phrases is not identical with their phonetic form. The phonemes are not the actual phonetic sounds, but are abstract mental constructs that are realized as sounds by the operation of rules such as those described above. No one teaches us these rules; yet all speakers of a language know the phonology of their language better than any linguist who tries to describe it. The linguist's job is to make explicit what we know unconsciously about the sound pattern of our language.

In the writing of rules, linguists use **formal notations** that reveal linguistic generalizations of phonological processes. Features are used rather than whole segments, and devices such as **braces** and **parentheses** collapse rules that contain similar parts. Such devices are used only if they are able truly to represent what speakers know about the sound patterns of their language.

References

Anderson, Stephen R. 1974. *The Organization of Phonology*. Academic Press. New York.

Anderson, S. R. 1985. *Phonology in the Twentieth Century: Theories of Rules and Theories of Representations*. U. of Chicago Press. Chicago.

Chomsky, N., and M. Halle. 1968. *The Sound Pattern of English*. Harper & Row. New York.

Clements, George N., and Samuel Jay Keyser. 1983. *CV Phonology: A Generative Theory of the Syllable*. M.I.T. Press. Cambridge, Mass.

Dell, François. 1980. *Generative Phonology*. Cambridge University Press. London.

Hyman, Larry M. 1975. *Phonology: Theory and Analysis*. Holt, Rinehart and Winston. New York.

Kenstowicz, Michael, and Charles Kisseberth. 1979. *Generative Phonology: Description and Theory*. Academic Press. New York.

Exercises

Where indicated in the following exercises, you may write your answer in the space provided.

1. Consider the distribution of [r] and [l] in Korean in the following words:

rupi	"ruby"	mul	"water"
kiri	"road"	pal	"big"
saram	"person"	səul	"Seoul"
irɯmi*	"name"	ilkop	"seven"
ratio	"radio"	ipalsa	"barber"

*[ɯ] is a high back unrounded vowel. It does not affect your analysis in this problem.

Are [r] and [l] allophones of one or two phonemes? State your reasons, and give the rule to derive the surface phones if you conclude that they are allophonic.

2. In Southern Kongo, a Bantu language spoken in Angola, the nonpalatal segments [t, s, z] are in complementary distribution with their palatal counterparts [č, š, ž], as shown in the following words:

[tobola]	"to bore a hole"	[čina]	"to cut"
[tanu]	"five"	[čiba]	"banana"
[kesoka]	"to be cut"	[nkoši]	"lion"
[kasu]	"emaciation"	[nselele]	"termite"
[kunezulu]	"heaven"	[ažimola]	"alms"
[nzwetu]	"our"	[lolonži]	"to wash house"
[zevo]	"then"	[zenga]	"to cut"
[žima]	"to stretch"		

a. State the distribution of each pair of segments given below. (Assume that the nonoccurrence of [t] before [e] is an *accidental gap*.)

Example: [t]—[č]: [t] occurs before the back vowels [o, a, u]; [č] occurs before [i].

[s]—[š]
[z]—[ž]

b. Which phones should be used as the basic phoneme for each pair? For instance, should [t] and [č] be derived from /t/ or /č/? State the reasons for your choice.

c. State the *one* phonological rule that will derive all the phonetic segments from the phonemes. Do not state a separate rule for each phoneme, but a general rule for all three phonemes you listed in b.

3. In some dialects of English the following words have different vowels, as is shown by the phonetic transcriptions.

A		B		C	
bite	[bʌjt]	bide	[bajd]	die	[daj]
rice	[rʌjs]	rise	[rajz]	by	[baj]
ripe	[rʌjp]	bribe	[brajb]	sigh	[saj]
wife	[wʌjf]	wives	[wajvz]	rye	[raj]
dike	[dʌjk]	dime	[dajm]	guy	[gaj]
		nine	[najn]		
		rile	[rajl]		
		dire	[dajr]		
		writhe	[rajð]		

a. How may the classes of sounds that end the words in columns A and B be characterized? That is, what feature specifies all the final segments in A and all the final segments in B?

b. How do the words in column C differ from those in columns A and B?

c. Are [ʌj] and [aj] in complementary distribution? Give your reasons.

d. If [ʌj] and [aj] are allophones of one phoneme, should they be derived from /ʌj/ or /aj/? Why?

e. Give the phonetic representations of the following:

life _____ lives _____ lie _____

file _____ bike _____ lice_____

f. State the rule that will relate the phonemic representations to the phonetic representations of the words given above.

4. Pairs like *top* and *chop, dunk* and *junk, so* and *show* reveal that /t/ and /č/, /d/ and /ǰ/, and /s/ and /š/ are distinct phonemes in English. Although it is difficult to find a minimal pair to distinguish /z/ and /ž/, they occur in similar if not identical environments, such as *razor* and *azure*. Consider these same pairs of nonpalatalized and palatalized consonants in the following data. (The palatal forms are optional forms that often occur in casual speech.)

Nonpalatalized		*Palatalized*	
[hɪt mi]	"hit me"	[hɪč ju]	"hit you"
[lid hɪm]	"lead him"	[liǰ ju]	"lead you"
[[pʰæs ʌs]	"pass us"	[pʰæš ju]	"pass you"
[luz ðɛm]	"lose them"	[luž ju]	"lose you"

State the rule that specifies when /t/, /d/, /s/, and /z/ may become palatalized as [č], [ǰ], [š], and [ž]. Use feature notations to reveal generalizations.

5. The following sets of minimal pairs show that English /p/ and /b/ contrast in initial, medial, and final positions.

Initial	*Medial*	*Final*
pit/bit	rapid/rabid	cap/cab

Find similar sets of minimal pairs for each pair of consonants given:

a. /k/–/g/
b. /m/–/n/
c. /l/–/r/
d. /b/–/v/
e. /b/–/m/
f. /p/–/f/
g. /s/–/š/
h. /č/–/ǰ/
i. /s/–/z/

6. Here are some words in Japanese. (The spelling *ch* is [č] and *ts* [ts] is an alveolar affricate.)

tatami	"mat"	tomodachi	"friend"	uchi	"house"
tegami	"letter"	totemo	"very"	otoko	"male"
chichi	"father"	tsukue	"desk"	tetsudau	"help"
shita	"under"	ato	"later"	matsu	"wait"
natsu	"summer"	tsutsumu	"wrap"	chizu	"map"
kata	"person"	tatemono	"building"	te	"hand"

In addition, Japanese words (except for certain loan words) never contain the phonetic sequences *[ti] or *[tu]. Consider *ch* ([č]) and *ts* [ts] to be single phones.

a. Based on these data, are [t], [č], and [ts] in complementary distribution?
b. State the distribution of these phones, first in words, then using features.
c. Give a phonemic analysis of these data insofar as [t], [č], and [ts] are concerned. Identify the phoneme or phonemes, and the allophones.
d. Give the phonemic representation of the following Japanese words.

tatami _____   tomodachi _____   uchi _____

tegami _____   totemo _____   otoko _____

chichi _____   tsukue _____   tetsudau _____

shita _____   ato _____   matsu _____

(Exercise 6 continued on p. 119.)

deguchi	_____	natsu	_____	tsutsumu	_____
chizu	_____	kata	_____	koto	_____
tatemono	_____	te	_____	tsuri	_____

7. Consider the following English verbs. Those in column A have stress on the next-to-last syllable (called the *penultimate*), whereas the verbs in column B have their last syllable stressed.

A	B	C
astonish	collapse	explain
exit	exist	erase
imagine	torment	surprise
cancel	revolt	combine
elicit	adopt	careen
practice	insist	atone
solicit	contort	equate

a. State a rule that predicts where stress occurs in these verbs.
b. In the verbs in column C, stress also occurs on the final syllable. What must you add to the rule to account for this fact? (Hint: For the forms in columns A and B, the final consonants had to be considered; for the forms in column C, consider the vowels.)

8. Below are listed ten "words." Some are English words, some are not words now but could be (they are "possible words"), and others are definitely "foreign" (they violate English sequential constraints.)

Write the English words in regular spelling. Mark the other words "foreign" or "possible." For each word you mark as "foreign," state your reason.

Word	Possible	"Foreign"	Reason
Example:			
[θrot] throat			
[slig]	X		
[lsig]		X	No English word can begin with a liquid followed by an obstruent.
a. [pʰril]			
b. [skrič]			
c. [know]			
d. [may]			

(Exercise 8 continued on p. 120.)

	Word	**Possible**	**"Foreign"**	**Reason**

e. [gnostɪk]

f. [junəkɔrn]

g. [fruit]

h. [blaft]

i. [ŋar]

j. [æpəpʰlɛksi]

9. State the following rules, using the "formal notation" discussed at the end of the chapter.

Example: Aspirate a voiceless stop consonant at the end of a word.

$$\begin{bmatrix} -\text{continuant} \\ -\text{voice} \end{bmatrix} \rightarrow [+\text{aspirated}] \; / - \#$$

a. A vowel is stressed in the environment after a word boundary (at the beginning of a word).
b. A voiced consonant becomes nasal before a nasal.
c. A voiceless segment becomes voiced between two vowels.
d. A voiced consonant becomes voiceless either before a voiceless consonant or at the end of a word.

10. Consider these phonetic forms of Hebrew words:

[v]–[b]		[f]–[p]	
bika	"lamented"	litef	"stroked"
mugbal	"limited"	sefer	"book"
šavar	"broke" (masc.)	sataf	"washed"
šavra	"broke" (fem.)	para	"cow"
ʔikev	"delayed"	mitpaxat	"handkerchief"
bara	"created"	haʔalpim	"the Alps"

Assume that these words and their phonetic sequences are representative of what may occur in Hebrew. In your answers below, consider classes of sounds rather than individual sounds.

a. Are [b] and [v] allophones of one phoneme? (Hint: Are they in complementary distribution?)
b. Does the same rule, or lack of a rule, that describes the distribution of [b] and [v] apply to [p] and [f]? If not, why not?
c. Here is a word with one phone missing. A blank appears in place of the missing sound: hid__ik.

(Exercise 10 continued on p. 121.)

Check the one correct statement.

(1)   [b] but not [v] could occur in the empty slot.   ( )
(2)   [v] but not [b] could occur in the empty slot.   ( )
(3)   Either [b] or [v] could occur in the empty slot.   ( )
(4)   Neither [b] nor [v] could occur in the empty slot.   ( )

d.   Which one of the following statements is correct about the incomplete
     word __ana?

(1)   [f] but not [p] could occur in the empty slot.   ( )
(2)   [p] but not [f] could occur in the empty slot.   ( )
(3)   Either [p] or [f] could fill the blank.   ( )
(4)   Neither [p] nor [f] could fill the blank.   ( )

e.   Now consider the following possible words (in phonetic transcription):

           laval   surva   labal   palar   falu   razif

If these words actually occurred in Hebrew, would they:

(1)   Force you to revise the conclusions about the distribution of labial
      stops and fricatives you reached on the basis of the first group of
      words given above?   ( )
(2)   Support your original conclusions?   ( )
(3)   Neither support nor disprove your original conclusions?   ( )

C H A P T E R

4

Morphology: The Words of Language

A word is dead
When it is said,
Some say.
I say it just
Begins to live
That day.

Emily Dickinson, "A Word"

Every speaker of every language knows thousands, even tens of thousands, of words. Knowing a word means knowing both its sound and its meaning. Someone who does not know English, hearing an utterance like [ð ə kʰ æ t e t ð ə r æ t], would not know where one word begins or ends, or even how many words have been said. A speaker of English, however, has no difficulty in segmenting the sounds into the individual words *the cat ate the rat*. Similarly, someone who does not know the native American language Potawatomi would not know whether [kwapmuknanuk] (which means "They see us.") was one, two, or more words. It is, in fact, only one word.

The sounds (pronunciation) and the meaning of a word are inseparable; they are like two sides of a coin. **Synonyms** like *couch* and *sofa* are two words because their identical meanings are represented by two different phonological forms; **homonyms** like *crab* the crustacean and *crab* meaning "to complain," with identical phonological forms but with different meanings, are also two words. This fact was pointed out by the nineteenth-century Swiss linguist Ferdinand de Saussure, who discussed the *arbitrary* union between the sounds *(form)* and meaning *(concept)* of the **linguistic sign,** or **word.**

We have already seen that speakers of a language know by virtue of their phonological knowledge whether a string of sounds could be a word in their language. If speakers of English do not know the meaning of *plarm*, they would conclude either that it is a word they do not know or that it is not a word in English. They would know, however, that it is a possible English word. If someone told them that a plarm was a particular kind of water rat, *plarm* would become a sound-meaning unit, a linguistic sign, a word. Thus, as illustrated in exercise 8 in Chapter 3, all strings of sounds can be grouped into three sets: (1) existing words *(black)*, (2) possible but nonoccurring words *(blick)*, and (3) impossible "words" *(kbli)*.

Just as a particular string of sounds must be united with a meaning to be a word, so a concept or meaning must be united with specific sounds. Before 1955, the word *googol* [gugəl] did not exist in English. Now, at least among mathematicians and scientists, it is a word. The word was "coined" by the nine-year-old nephew of Dr. Edward Kasner, a mathematician, to mean "the number 1 followed by 100 zeros," a number equal to 10^{100}. The number existed before the word was invented, but no phonological form represented this particular numerical concept. When the concept and sounds were united, a word came into being. In fact, from this word another word, *googolplex,* was formed to mean "1 followed by a googol of zeros."

Dictionaries

B.C.   Johnny Hart

By permission of Johnny Hart and North America Syndicate, Inc.

The words we know form part of our linguistic knowledge; they constitute the dictionary or lexical component of our internalized grammars. Because each word is a sound-meaning unit, each word in our mental dictionaries must be stored with its unique phonological representation, which determines its pronunciation (when the phonological rules are applied), and with its meaning.

Each word must include other information as well. The dictionary representation of a word must include whether it is a noun, a verb, an adjective, an adverb, a preposition, or a conjunction. That is, it must specify to what **grammatical category,** or **syntactic class,** it belongs. A form like *love* must be listed as both a verb and a noun, as shown by the sentences *I love you* and *You are the love of my life.* If such information were not in the mental dictionary, we would not know how to form grammatical sentences, nor be able to distinguish grammatical from ungrammatical sentences. The classes of words—the **syntactic categories** such as nouns, verbs, adjectives, and so on—will be discussed in more detail in Chapter 5. The semantic properties of words, which represent their meanings, will be discussed in Chapter 6.

Dictionaries that we buy in a bookstore contain information also found in our mental dictionaries. The first English dictionary (actually a Latin-English dictionary by Sir Thomas Elyot) was published in 1538, over 400 years ago. One of the best efforts at **lexicography** ("the editing or making of a dictionary"[1]) was the *Dictionary of the English Language* by Dr. Samuel Johnson, published in 1755 in two volumes.

The aim of most early lexicographers was to "prescribe" rather than "describe" the words of a language; to be, as in the stated aim of one Webster's dictionary, the "supreme authority" on the "correct" pronunciation and meaning of a word. It is to Johnson's credit that in his Preface he stated he could not construct the language but only "register the language."

Although probably no speaker of English knows all the 450,000 words listed in *Webster's Third,* all speakers know more about the words in their mental dictionaries than can be found in any published dictionary. Chapter 5 will discuss some of the syntactic information that must be part of a speaker's lexical knowledge but that is not found in even the *Oxford English Dictionary* (often referred to as the OED), called the greatest lexicographic work ever produced.[2]

All dictionaries, from the OED to the more commonly used "collegiate dictionaries," provide the following information about each word: (1) its spelling, (2) the "standard" pronunciation, (3) definitions to represent the word's one or more meanings, and (4) parts of speech, such as noun, verb, or preposition. Other information may be included, such as the **etymology** or history of the word and whether the word is "nonstandard" (such as *ain't*), slang, "vulgar," or "obsolete." Many dictionaries provide quotations from published literature to illustrate the given definitions, as Johnson first did.

It is interesting to think that scholarly lexicographers spend years to write dictionaries that include information that young children store in their mental dictionaries with ease.

Classes of Words

In English, nouns, verbs, adjectives, and adverbs make up the largest part of the vocabulary. They are the **content words** of a language, which are sometimes called the *open class* of lexical items because we can and regularly do add new words to them. *Googol,* for example, was added to the class of nouns. A new verb, *download,* which means "to transfer information from a large computer to a smaller

---

[1] *The Webster's Third New Dictionary of the English Language: Unabridged.*
[2] The twelve volumes of the OED were published in 1933. Many scholars worked without salary from 1888 to 1928 to produce this great piece of scholarship.

computer,'' entered English with the computer revolution. New adverbs like *weatherwise* and *saleswise* have been added in recent years, as well as adjectives like *biodegradable*.

Other syntactic categories include ''grammatical'' or ''function'' words. Conjunctions like *and* and *or*, prepositions like *in* and *of*, and pronouns have been referred to as *''closed'' classes*. It is not easy to think of new conjunctions or prepositions or pronouns that have recently entered the language. There is a small set of personal pronouns such as *I, me, mine, he, she*, and so on. With the growth of the feminist movement some proposals have been made for adding a new neutral singular pronoun, neither masculine nor feminine, which could be used as the general, or **generic,** form. Had such a pronoun existed, it might have prevented the department chairperson in a large university from making the incongruous statement, ''We will hire the best person for the job, regardless of his sex.'' The UCLA psychologist Donald MacKay has suggested that we use ''e'' /i/ for this pronoun, with various alternative forms; others point out that *they* and *their* are already being used as neutral third person singular forms, as in ''Anyone can do it if they try hard enough,'' or ''Everyone can do their best.'' This use of the various forms of *they* is reported to be Standard British English used on the BBC (British Broadcasting System), with *anyone* and *everyone* now considered either singular or plural, similar to such words as *committee* or *government*.

These classes of content and function words appear to have psychological and neurological validity. Some brain-damaged patients have greater difficulty in using or understanding or reading function words than content words. Some interpret a word like *in* to mean *inn* or *which* to mean *witch* when asked to read and use such words in sentences. Other patients do just the opposite. Such effects of brain damage on language will be further discussed in Chapter 11. We mention this fact here merely to show that linguistic analysis of words is validated by research in other areas of science. Notice that the important feature of these two classes is their function rather than their degree of ''openness.'' What is an ''open class'' in one language may be ''closed'' in another. In Akan, for example, there are only a handful of ''adjectives''; most English adjectives are in the verb class in Akan. Instead of saying ''The sun is bright today,'' an Akan speaker will say ''The sun brightens today.''

Word Sets

Most wonderful of all are words, and how they make friends one with another.

O. Henry

Words may be related to each other in a special way. Consider the words below, which are all related in both sound and meaning. They all include the same phonological form with a meaning identical to that of the first word, *phone*.

phone	phonic
phonetic	phoneme
phonetician	phonemic
phonetics	allophone
phonology	telephone
phonologist	telephonic
phonological	euphonious

Phone is a minimal form that cannot be divided into more elemental structures. *ph* does not mean anything, and *pho* [fo] has no relation in meaning to the word *foe*, and *-one* /on/ is not related to the sound unit /on/ meaning "own" or to the word spelled *one* and pronounced /wʌn/; but all the words on the list contain the word *phone* as part of their structure. The phonological rules of English "tell us" that in *phonetic, phonetics, phonology, phonologist, phonemic* the pronunciation is [fən] instead of [fon], but the same element *phone* /fon/ is present, with its identical meaning, "pertaining to sound," in all these words.

Notice further that in the following pairs of words the meanings of all the words in column B consist of the meanings of the words in column A plus the meaning "not":

A	B
desirable	undesirable
likely	unlikely
inspired	uninspired
happy	unhappy
developed	undeveloped
sophisticated	unsophisticated

Webster's *Third New International Dictionary* lists about 2700 adjectives beginning with *un-*, the meaning of which speakers of English would know if they know the word without the *un-*. The "Luann" cartoon reflects the knowledge that speakers have about the meaning of *un-*.

LUANN   **Greg Evans**

© News America Syndicate, 1986, by permission of North America Syndicate, Inc.

If the most elemental units of meaning, the basic linguistic signs, are assumed to be the words of a language, it would be a coincidence that *un-* has the same meaning in all the column B words above, or that *phone* has the same meaning in all the words in the preceding list. Obviously, it is no coincidence. The words *undesirable, unlikely, uninspired, unhappy,* and the others in column B consist of at least two meaningful units: *un + desirable, un + likely,* and so on.

It is also a fact about words that their internal structure is subject to rules. *Uneaten, unadmired,* and *ungrammatical* are words in English, but **eatenun, *admiredun, *grammaticalun* (to mean "not eaten," "not admired," "not grammatical") are not, because we form a negative meaning of a word not by **suffixing** *un* (adding it to the end of the word), but by **prefixing** it (adding it to the beginning).

The study of the internal structure of words and of the rules by which words are formed is called **morphology.** Just as knowledge of a language implies knowledge of the phonology, so it also implies knowledge of the morphology.

Morphemes: The Minimal Units of Meaning

"They gave it me," Humpty Dumpty continued, "for an un-birthday present."
"I beg your pardon?" Alice said with a puzzled air.
"I'm not offended," said Humpty Dumpty.
"I mean, what is an un-birthday present?"
"A present given when it isn't your birthday, of course."

Lewis Carroll, *Through the Looking-Glass*

When Samuel Goldwyn, the pioneer moviemaker, announced: "In two words: im-possible," he was reflecting the common view that words are the basic meaningful elements in a language. We have already seen that this view cannot be right, because some words are formed by combining a number of distinct units of meaning. The traditional term for the most elemental unit of grammatical form is **morpheme.** The word is derived from the Greek word *morphe,* meaning "form." Linguistically speaking, then, Goldwyn should have said: "In two morphemes: im-possible."

A single word may be composed of one or more morphemes:

one morpheme	boy
	desire
two morphemes	boy + ish
	desire + able
three morphemes	boy + ish + ness
	desire + able + ity
four morphemes	gentle + man + li + ness
	un + desire + able + ity
more than four morphemes	un + gentle + man + li + ness
	anti + dis + establish + ment + ari + an + ism[3]

[3] Some speakers would perceive several morphemes in "establish."

A morpheme may be defined as the **minimal linguistic sign,** a grammatical unit that is an arbitrary union of a sound and a meaning and that cannot be further analyzed. As we shall see below, this definition may be too simple, but it will serve our purposes for now. Every word in every language is composed of one or more morphemes.

Bound and Free Morphemes

If we look at the above examples, we can see that some morphemes, like *boy, desire, gentle,* and *man,* can constitute words by themselves. Other morphemes, like *-ish, -able, -ness, -ly, dis-, trans-,* and *un-,* are never words but always parts of words. Thus, *un-* is like *pre- (prefix, predetermine, prejudge, prearrange), dis- (disallow, disobey, disapprove, dislike),* and *bi- (bipolar, bisexual, bivalved);* it occurs only before other morphemes. Such morphemes are called **prefixes.** Other morphemes occur only as **suffixes,** after other morphemes. English examples of such morphemes are *-er (singer, performer, reader, beautifier), -ist (typist, copyist, pianist, novelist, collaborationist, Marxist),* and *-ly (manly, bastardly, sickly, orderly, friendly),* to mention only a few.

These prefix and suffix morphemes have traditionally been called **bound morphemes,** because they cannot occur "unattached," as distinct from **free morphemes** like *man, bastard, sick, prove, allow, judge,* and so on. Of course, in speaking we seldom use even free morphemes alone. We combine all morphemes into larger units—phrases and sentences.

In all languages morphemes are the minimal linguistic signs. In Turkish, if you add *-ak* to a verb, you derive a noun, as in:

dur	"to stop"	dur + ak, "stopping place"
bat	"to sink"	bat + ak, "sinking place" or "marsh/swamp"

In English, in order to express reciprocal action we use the phrase *each other* as in *understand each other, love each other.* In Turkish, one simply adds a morpheme to the verb:

anla	"understand"	anla + s "understand each other"
sev	"love"	sev + is "love each other"

The "reciprocal" suffix in the above examples has the phonological form /s/ after a vowel and /is/ after a consonant.

In Piro, an Arawakan language spoken in Peru, a single morpheme, *kaka,* can be added to a verb to express the meaning "cause to":

cokoruha	"to harpoon"	cokoruha + kaka	"cause to harpoon"
salwa	"to visit"	salwa + kaka	"cause to visit"

In Karok, a native American language spoken in the Pacific Northwest, if you add -*ak* to a noun, it forms a locative adverbial meaning "in, on, or at":

ikrivra:m	"house"	ikrivra:mak	"in a house"
ʔa:s	"water"	ʔa:sak	"in water"

Note that it is accidental that both Turkish and Karok have a suffix -*ak*. Despite the similarity in form, the two meanings are different.

Also in Karok, the suffix -*ara* has the same meaning as our -*y*, that is, "characterized by":

ʔa:x	"blood"	ʔax + ara	"bloody"
apti:k	"branch"	aptikara	"branchy"

The examples illustrate "free" morphemes like *boy* in English: *dur* in Turkish, *salwa* in Piro, and *ʔa:s* in Karok. Suffix morphemes are also illustrated. Some languages also have **infixes,** morphemes that are inserted into a morpheme. Bontoc, a language spoken in the Philippines, is such a language, as is illustrated by the following examples:

Nouns/Adjectives		**Verbs**	
fikas	"strong"	f*um*ikas	"to be strong"
kilad	"red"	k*um*ilad	"to be red"
fusul	"enemy"	f*um*usul	"to be an enemy"

In this language the infix -*um*- is inserted after the first consonant of the noun or adjective. Thus, a speaker of Bontoc who learns that *pusi* means "poor" would understand the meaning of *pumusi* ("to be poor") on hearing the word for the first time. Similarly, a Bontok speaker who knows that *ŋumitad* means "to be dark" would know that the adjective "dark" must be *ŋitad*.

Crans and Huckles

We have already defined a morpheme as the basic element of meaning, as a phonological form that is arbitrarily united with a particular meaning and that cannot be analyzed into simpler elements. This definition has presented problems for linguistic analysis for many years, although it holds for most of the morphemes in a language. Consider words like *cranberry, huckleberry,* and *boysenberry.*[4] The *berry* part is no problem, but *huckle* and *boysen* occur only with *berry,* as did *cran* until the drink *Cranapple* juice came on the market.

To account for bound forms like *huckle-, boysen-,* and *cran-,* we have to redefine the notion "morpheme." Some morphemes are not meaningful in isolation but acquire meaning only in combination with other specific morphemes. Thus the

---

[4]Boysen is the name of the horticulturist who developed the berry. The proper name is therefore a free morpheme, but it occurs in combination with another morpheme only in this word.

morpheme *huckle* when joined with *berry* has the meaning of a special kind of berry, which is small, round, purplish-blue, and so on.

Just as there are some morphemes that occur only in a single word (that is, combined with another morpheme), there are other morphemes that occur in many words, combining with different morphemes, but for which it is difficult to find a constant meaning. How would you define the *-ceive* in *receive, perceive,* and *conceive,* or the *mit* in *remit, permit, commit,* and *submit?* Stems like *-ceive* and *-mit* were productive morphemes in Latin, but their origins have been obscured by time and their borrowings into English.

There are also words that seem to be composed of prefix + stem morpheme in which the stem morphemes, like the *cran* above, never occur alone. Thus we find *inept* but no **ept, inane* but no **ane, incest* but no **cest, inert* but no **ert, disgusted* but no **gusted.*

To complicate things a little further, there are words like *strawberry,* where the *straw* has no relationship to any other kind of *straw, gooseberry,* which is unrelated to *goose,* and *blackberries,* which may be blue or red. Although some of these words have historical origins, there is no present meaningful connection. The OED entry for the word *strawberry* states that "The reason for the name has been variously conjectured. One explanation refers the first element to Straw . . . a particle of straw or chaff, a mote describing the appearance of the achenes scattered over the surface of the strawberry." That may be true of the word's origin, but today, the *straw-* in *strawberry* is not the same morpheme as that found in *strawlike* or *straw-colored.*

A morpheme, like a word, is a linguistic sign—both its phonemic form and its meaning must be constant. The final syllable of the word *gardener* is a morpheme that, although it has the same phonological form as the *-er* in *longer,* is a different morpheme than the comparative *-er* (because it has a different meaning); and the *-er* in the **monomorphemic** (one morpheme) word *brother* or *butter* does not represent a separate morpheme at all.

All morphemes, then, are phonological forms that are bound or free. **Affixes** (prefixes, suffixes, and infixes) are bound morphemes. Nonaffix lexical content morphemes such as *boy* or *cran,* called **root** morphemes, can be bound or free. We can illustrate these facts as follows:

	Free	Bound
Root	*dog, cat, aardvark, corduroy, run, bottle, hot, separate, phone, museum, school* (and thousands more)	*huckle*(berry), (dis)*gruntle,* (un)*couth,* (non)*chalance,* (per)*ceive,* (re)*ceive,* (de)*ceive,* (con)*ceive* (and a few more)
Affix		(friend)*ship,* (lead)*er-ship,* *re*(do), *re*(think), *re*(set), *trans*-(sex)*-ual,* (sad)*ly* (and many others)

Rules of Word Formation

"I never heard of 'Uglification,'" Alice ventured to say. "What is it?"

The Gryphon lifted up both its paws in surprise. "Never heard of uglifying!" it exclaimed. "You know what to beautify is, I suppose?"

"Yes," said Alice doubtfully: "it means—to make—anything—prettier."

"Well, then," the Gryphon went on, "if you don't know what to uglify is, you are a simpleton."

Lewis Carroll, *Alice's Adventures in Wonderland*

When the Mock Turtle listed the different branches of Arithmetic for Alice as "Ambition, Distraction, Uglification, and Derision," Alice was confused. She was not really a simpleton, because *uglification* was not a common word in English until Lewis Carroll invented it. We have already noted that there are gaps in the lexicon, "words" that are not in the dictionary but that can be added. Some of the gaps are due to the fact that a permissible sound sequence has no meaning attached to it (like *blick* or *slarm* or *krobe*). Other gaps are due to the fact that possible combinations of morphemes have not been made (like *ugly + ify* or *linguistic + ism*). The reason morphemes can be combined in this way is that there exist, in every language, rules that relate to the formation of words. Such **morphological rules** determine how morphemes combine to form new words.

The Mock Turtle added *-ify* to the adjective *ugly* and formed a verb. Many verbs in English have been formed in this way: *purify, amplify, simplify, falsify. -ify* conjoined with nouns also forms verbs: *objectify, glorify, personify.* Notice that the Mock Turtle went even further: he added the suffix *-cation* to *uglify* and formed a noun, *uglification,* as in *glorification, simplification, falsification,* and *purification.*

Derivational Morphology

PEANUTS   **Charles Schulz**

Reprinted by permission: © 1974 United Feature Syndicate, Inc.

There are morphemes in English that add new meanings to an existing word. They are sometimes called **derivational morphemes** because when they are conjoined to other morphemes (or words), a new word is derived, or formed. The derived word may even be in a different grammatical class than the underived word. For example, when a verb is conjoined with the suffix *-able,* the result is an adjective, as in *desire + able* or *adore + able*. A few other examples are:

Noun to Adjective	Verb to Noun	Adjective to Adverb	Noun to Verb
boy + ish	acquitt + al	exact + ly	moral + ize
virtu + ous	clear + ance	quiet + ly	vaccin + ate
Elizabeth + an	accus + ation		brand + ish
pictur + esque	confer + ence		
affection + ate	sing + er		
health + ful	conform + ist		
alcohol + ic	predict + ion		
life + like	free + dom		

Other derivational morphemes do not cause a change in grammatical class. Many prefixes fall into this category:

a + moral	mono + theism
auto + biography	re + print
ex + wife	semi + annual
super + human	sub + minimal

There are also suffixes of this type:

vicar + age	Trotsky + ite
long + er	Commun + ist
short + est	music + ian
Americ + an	pun + ster

New words may enter the dictionary in this fashion, created by the application of morphological rules. It is often the case that when such a word as *Commun + ist* enters the language, other possible complex forms will not, such as *Commun + ite* (as in *Trotsky + ite*) or *Commun + ian* (as in *grammar + ian*). There may, however, exist alternative forms: for example, *Marxian* and *Marxist; linguist* and *linguistician; phoneticist* and *phonetician*. Notice, however, that there is no *linguite* or *phoneticite*. The redundancy of such alternative forms, all of which conform to the regular rules of word formation, may explain some of the accidental gaps in the lexicon. It further shows that the actual words in the language constitute only a subset of the possible words.

Some of the morphological rules are **productive:** they can be used freely to form new words from the list of free and bound morphemes. The suffix *-able* is a morpheme that can be freely conjoined with verbs to derive an adjective with the meaning of the verb and the meaning of *-able*, which is something like "able to be," as in *accept + able, blame + able, pass + able, change + able, breathe + able, adapt + able,* and so on. The meaning of *-able* has also been given as "fit for doing" or "fit for being done."

Such a rule might be stated as:

(1) VERB + able = "able to be VERB-ed"
accept + able = "able to be accepted"

The productivity of this rule is illustrated by the fact that we find *-able* in such morphologically complex words as *un + speak + abl(e) + y* and *un + come + at + able.*

We have already noted that there is a morpheme in English meaning "not" that has the form *un-* and that when combined with adjectives like *afraid, fit, free, smooth, American,* and *British* forms the antonyms, or negatives, of these adjectives—for example, *unafraid, unfit, unfree, unsmooth, unAmerican,* and *unBritish.* We can also add the prefix *un-* to derived words that have been formed by morphological rules:

un + believ(e) + able
un + accept + able
un + talk + about + able
un + keep + off + able
un + speak + able

The rule that forms these words may be stated as:

(2) un + ADJECTIVE = "not-ADJECTIVE"

This rule seems to account for all the examples cited; yet we find *happy* and *unhappy, cowardly* and *uncowardly,* but not *sad* and **unsad* or *brave* and **unbrave.*

These starred forms may be merely accidental gaps in the lexicon. If someone referred to a person as being **unsad,* we would know that the person was "not sad," and an **unbrave* person would not be brave. But as the linguist Sandra Thompson[5] points out, it may be the case that the "*un*-Rule" is not as productive for adjectives composed of just one morpheme as for adjectives that are themselves derived from verbs. The rule seems to be freely applicable to an adjectival form derived from a verb, as in *unenlightened, unsimplified, uncharacterized, unauthorized, undistinguished,* and so on.

It is true, however, that we cannot always know the meaning of the words derived from free and derivational morphemes from the morphemes themselves. Thompson has also pointed out that the following *un*-words have unpredictable meanings:

[5] S. A. Thompson. 1975. "On the Issue of Productivity in the Lexikon." *Kritikon Litterarum* 4: 332–349.

unloosen	"loosen, let loose"
unrip	"rip, undo by ripping"
undo	"reverse doing"
untread	"go back through in the same steps"
unearth	"dig up"
unfrock	"deprive (a cleric) of ecclesiastic rank"
unnerve	"fluster"

Therefore, although the words in a language are not the most elemental sound-meaning units, they (plus the morphemes) must be listed in our dictionaries. The morphological rules also are in the grammar, revealing the relation between words and providing the means for forming new words.

Morphological rules may be more or less productive. The rule that adds an -er to verbs in English to produce a noun meaning "one who performs an action (once or habitually)" appears to be a very productive morphological rule; most English verbs accept this suffix: *lover, hunter, predictor* (notice that -or and -er have the same pronunciation), *examiner, exam-taker, analyzer,* and so forth.

Now consider the following

sincerity	from	*sincere*
warmth	from	*warm*
moisten	from	*moist*

The suffix -ity is found in many other words in English, like *chastity, scarcity,* and *curiosity;* and -th occurs in *health, wealth, depth, width,* and *growth.* We find -en in *sadden, ripen, redden, weaken, deepen.* Still, the phrase **The fiercity of the lion* sounds somewhat strange, as does the sentence **I'm going to thinnen the sauce.* Someone may use the word *coolth,* but, as Thompson points out, when such words as *fiercity, thinnen, fullen,* or *coolth* are used, usually it is either an error or an attempt at humor.

It is possible that in such cases a morphological rule that was once productive (as shown by the existence of related pairs like *scarce/scarcity*) is no longer so. Our knowledge of the related pairs, however, may permit us to use these examples in forming new words, by analogy with the existing lexical items.

"Pullet Surprises"

DRABBLE   **Kevin Fagan**

That speakers of a language know the morphemes of that language and the rules for word formation is shown as much by the "errors" made as by the nondeviant forms produced. Morphemes combine to form words. These words form our internal dictionaries. No speaker of a language knows all the words. Given our knowledge of the morphemes of the language and the morphological rules, we can often guess the meaning of a word we do not know. Sometimes we guess wrong.

Amsel Greene collected errors made by her students in vocabulary-building classes and published them in a book called *Pullet Surprises*.[6] The title is taken from a sentence written by one of her high-school students: "In 1957 Eugene O'Neill won a Pullet Surprise." What is most interesting about these errors is how much they reveal about the students' knowledge of English morphology. Consider the creativity of these students in the following examples:

Word	Student's Definition
deciduous	"able to make up one's mind"
longevity	"being very tall"
fortuitous	"well protected"
gubernatorial	"to do with peanuts"
bibliography	"holy geography"
adamant	"pertaining to original sin"
diatribe	"food for the whole clan"
polyglot	"more than one glot"
gullible	"to do with sea birds"
homogeneous	"devoted to home life"

The student who used the word *indefatigable* in the sentence

> *She tried many reducing diets, but remained indefatigable.*

clearly shows morphological knowledge: *in,* meaning "not" as in *ineffective; de* meaning "off" as in *decapitate; fat,* as in "fat"; *able,* as in *able;* and combined meaning, "not able to take the fat off."

Word Coinage

As we have seen, new words may be added to the vocabulary or lexicon of a language by derivational processes. New words may also enter a language in a variety of other ways. Some are created outright to fit some purpose. Madison Avenue has added many new words to English, such as *Kodak, nylon, Orlon,* and *Dacron.* Specific brand names such as *Xerox, Kleenex, Jell-O, Frigidaire, Brillo,*

---

[6]Amsel Greene. 1969. *Pullet Surprises*. Scott, Foresman & Co. Glenview, Ill.

and *Vaseline* are now sometimes used as the general name for different brands of these types of products. Notice that some of these words were created from existing words: *Kleenex* from the word *clean* and *Jell-O* from *gel,* for example.

Compounds

. . . the Houyhnhnms have no Word in their Language to express any thing that is evil, except what they borrow from the Deformities or ill Qualities of the Yahoos. Thus they denote the Folly of a Servant, an Omission of a Child, a Stone that cuts their feet, a Continuance of foul or unseasonable Weather, and the like, by adding to each the Epithet of Yahoo. For instance, Hnhm Yahoo, Whnaholm Yahoo, Ynlhmnawihlma Yahoo, and an ill contrived House, Ynholmhnmrohlnw Yahoo.

Jonathan Swift, *Gulliver's Travels*

PEANUTS   **Charles Schulz**

Reprinted by permission: © 1972 United Feature Syndicate, Inc.

New words may be formed by stringing together other words to create **compound** words. There is almost no limit on the kinds of combinations that occur in English, as the following list of compounds shows:

	-Adjective	**-Noun**	**-Verb**
Adjective-	bittersweet	poorhouse	highborn
Noun-	headstrong	rainbow	spoonfeed
Verb-	carryall	pickpocket	sleepwalk

Frigidaire is a compound formed by combining the adjective *frigid* with the noun *air*.

When the two words are in the same grammatical category, the compound will be in this category: noun + noun—*girlfriend, fighter-bomber, paper clip, elevator-operator, landlord, mailman;* adjective + adjective—*icy-cold, red-hot, wordly-wise.* In many cases, when the two words fall into different categories the class of the second or final word will be the grammatical category of the compound: noun + adjective—*headstrong, watertight, lifelong;* verb + noun—*pickpocket, pinchpenny, daredevil, sawbones.* On the other hand, compounds formed with a preposition are in the category of the nonprepositional part of the compound: *overtake, hanger-on, undertake, sundown, afterbirth, downfall, uplift.*

Though two-word compounds are the most common in English, it would be difficult to state an upper limit: Consider *three-time loser, four-dimensional space-time, sergeant-at-arms, mother-of-pearl, man about town, master of ceremonies,* and *daughter-in-law.*

Spelling does not tell us what sequence of words constitutes a compound; whether a compound is spelled with a space between the two words, with a hyphen, or with no separation at all is idiosyncratic, as shown, for example, in *blackbird, gold-tail,* and *smoke screen.*

Compound Stress Patterns   As was pointed out in Chapter 3, compounds often have different stress patterns from noncompounded word sequences. *Redcoat, greenhouse,* and *lighthouse keeper* have the primary stress on the first part of the compound, whereas *red coat, green house,* and *light housekeeper* do not. There are exceptions to this rule: *Fifth Street* versus *Fifth Avenue, mailman* versus *postman,* among others. Even in complex compounds like *six-cornered hen house annex door* we find the compound stress pattern.

Meaning of Compounds   One of the interesting things about a compound is that you cannot always tell by the words it contains what the compound means. The meaning of a compound is not always the sum of the meanings of its parts; a *blackboard* may be green or white.

B.C.   **Johnny Hart**

By permission of Johnny Hart and North America Syndicate, Inc.

Everyone who wears a red coat is not a *Redcoat,* either. The difference between the sentences *She has a red coat in her closet* and *She has a Redcoat in her closet* could be highly significant under certain circumstances. It is true, as noted above, that the two sentences sound different. In *bedchamber, bedclothes, bedside,* and *bedtime,* though, *bed* is stressed in all of the compounds; yet a *bedchamber* is a room where there is a bed, *bedclothes* are linens and blankets for a bed, *bedside* does not refer to the physical side of a bed but to the place next to it, and *bedtime* is the time one goes to bed.

Other similarly constructed compounds show that underlying the juxtaposition of words, different grammatical relations are expressed. A *boathouse* is a house for boats, but a *cathouse* is not a house for cats. A *jumping bean* is a bean that jumps, a *falling star* is a "star" that falls, and a *magnifying glass* is a glass that magnifies; but a *looking glass* is not a glass that looks, nor is an *eating apple* an apple that eats, and *laughing gas* does not laugh.

In all these examples, the meaning of each compound includes at least to some extent the meanings of the individual parts. However, there are other compounds that do not seem to relate to the meanings of the individual parts at all. A *jack-in-a-box* is a tropical tree, and a *turncoat* is a traitor. A *highbrow* does not necessarily have a high brow, nor does a *bigwig* have a big wig, nor does an *egghead* have an egg-shaped head.

As we pointed out above in the discussion of the prefix *un-,* the meaning of many compounds must be learned as if they were individual simple words. Some of the meanings may be figured out, but not all. If you had never heard the word *hunchback,* it might be possible to infer the meaning; but if you had never heard the word *flatfoot,* it is doubtful you would know it means "detective" or "policeman," even though the origin of the word, once you know the meaning, can be figured out.

Therefore, the words as well as the morphemes must be listed in our dictionaries. The morphological rules also are in the grammar, revealing the relations between words and providing the means for forming new words. Dr. Seuss uses the rules of compounding when he explains that "when tweetle beetles battle with paddles in a puddle, they call it a *tweetle beetle puddle paddle battle.*"[7]

Universality of Compounding   English is not the only language that has rules for conjoining words to form compounds: French *cure-dent,* "toothpick"; German *Panzerkraftwagen,* "armored car"; Russian *cetyrexetaznyi,* "four-storied"; Spanish *tocadiscos,* "record player." In the native American language Papago the word meaning "thing" is *haʔichu,* and it combines with *doakam,* "living creatures," to form the compound *haʔichu doakam,* "animal life."

In Twi, by combining the word meaning "son" or "child," *ɔba,* with the word meaning "chief," *ɔhene,* one derives the compound *ɔheneba,* meaning "prince." By adding the word "house," *ofi,* to *ɔhene,* the word meaning "palace," *ahemfi* is derived. The other changes that occur in the Twi compounds are due to phonological and morphological rules in the language.

---

[7]T. S. Geisel. 1965. *Fox in Sox.* Random House. New York. P. 51.

In Thai the word "cat" is *mɛɛw*, the word for "watch" (in the sense of "to watch over") is *fâw*, and the word for "house" is bâan. The word for "watch cat" (like a watchdog) is the compound *mɛɛwfâwbâan*—literally, "catwatchhouse."

Compounding is therefore a common and frequent process for enlarging the vocabulary of all languages.

Acronyms

Acronyms are words derived from the initials of several words. Such words are pronounced as the spelling indicates: NASA as /næsə/, UNESCO as /junɛsko/, and CARE as /ker/. *Radar*, from "radio detecting and ranging," *laser*, from "light amplification by stimulated emission of radiation," and *scuba*, from "self-contained underwater breathing apparatus," show the creative efforts of word coiners, as does *snafu*, which is rendered in polite circles as "situation normal, all fouled up."

Blends

THE WIZARD OF ID   **Brant Parker and Johnny Hart**

By permission of Johnny Hart and North America Syndicate, Inc.

Blends are compounds that are "less than" compounds. *Smog*, from *smoke* + *fog;* *motel*, from *motor* + *hotel;* and *urinalysis*, from *urine* + *analysis* are examples of blends that have attained full lexical status in English. The word *Cranapple* may be a blend of *cranberry* and *apple*. *Broasted*, from *broiled* + *roasted*, is a blend that has limited acceptance in the language, as does Lewis Carroll's *chortle*, from *chuckle* + *snort*. Carroll is famous for both the coining and the blending of words. In *Through the Looking-Glass* he describes the "meanings" of the made-up words in "Jabberwocky" as follows:

> . . . "Brillig" means four o'clock in the afternoon—the time when you begin broiling things for dinner. . . . "Slithy" means "lithe and slimy." . . . You see it's like a portmanteau—there are two meanings packed up into one word. . . . "Toves" are something like badgers—they're something like lizards—and they're something like corkscrews . . . also they make their nests under sun-dials—also they live on cheese. . . . To "gyre" is to go round and round like a gyroscope. To "gimble" is to make holes like a gimlet. And "the wabe" is the grass-plot

round a sun-dial. . . . It's called "wabe" . . . because it goes a long way before it and a long way behind it. . . . "Mimsy" is "flimsy and miserable" (there's another pormanteau . . . for you).

Carroll's "portmanteaus" are what we have called blends, and such words can become part of the regular lexicon.

Back-Formations

New words may be formed from existing words by "subtracting" an affix thought to be part of the old word; that is, ignorance sometimes can be creative. Thus *peddle* was derived from *peddler* on the mistaken assumption that the *er* was the "agentive" suffix. Such words are called **back-formations.** The verbs *hawk, stoke, swindle,* and *edit* all came into the language as back-formations—of *hawker, stoker, swindler,* and *editor*. *Pea* was derived from a singular word, *pease,* by speakers who thought *pease* /piz/ was a plural. Language purists sometimes rail against back-formations and cite *enthuse* (from *enthusiasm*) and *ept* (from *inept*) as examples of language corruption; but language cannot be corrupt (although the speakers who use it may be), and many words have entered the language this way.

Some word coinage, similar to the kind of wrong morphemic analysis that produces back-formations, is deliberate. The word *bikini* is from the Bikini atoll of the Marshall Islands. Because the first syllable *bi-* in other words, like *bipolar,* means "two," some clever person called a topless bathing suit a *monokini*. Historically, a number of new words have entered the English lexicon in this way. Based on analogy with such pairs as *act/action, exempt/exemption, revise/revision,* new words *resurrect, preempt,* and *televise* were formed from the existing words *resurrection, preemption,* and *television*.

Abbreviations

Abbreviations of longer words or phrases also may become "lexicalized"; *nark* for *narcotics agent, tec* (or *dick*) for *detective; telly,* the British word for *television, prof* for *professor, piano* for *pianoforte,* and *gym* for *gymnasium* are only a few examples of such "short forms" that are now used as whole words. Other examples are *ad, bike, math, gas, phone, bus,* and *van*. This process is sometimes called **clipping.**

Words from Names

The creativity of word coinage (or vocabulary addition) is also revealed by the number of words in the English vocabulary that derive from proper names of individuals or places.

Willard R. Espy[8] has compiled a book of 1500 such words. They include some old favorites:

[8] W. R. Espy. 1978. *O Thou Improper, Thou Uncommon Noun: An Etymology of Words That Once Were Names*. Clarkson N. Potter. New York.

sandwich	Named for the fourth Earl of Sandwich, who put his food between two slices of bread so that he could eat while he gambled.
robot	After the mechanical creatures in the Czech writer Karel Capek's play *R.U.R.*, the initials standing for "Rossum's Universal Robots."
gargantuan	Named for Gargantua, the creature with a huge appetite created by Rabelais.
jumbo	After an elephant brought to the United States by P. T. Barnum. ("Jumbo olives" need not be as big as an elephant, however.)

Espy admits to ignorance of the Susan, an unknown servant, from whom we derived the compound *lazy susan,* or the Betty or Charlotte or Chuck from whom we got *brown betty, charlotte russe,* or *chuck wagon.* He does point out that *denim* was named for the material used for overalls and carpeting, which originally was imported "de Nîmes" ("from Nimes") in France, and *argyle* from the kind of socks worn by the chiefs of Argyll of the Campbell clan in Scotland.

Inflectional Morphology

". . . and even . . . the patriotic archbishop of Canterbury found it advisable—"
"Found what?" said the Duck.
"Found it," the Mouse replied rather crossly; "of course you know what 'it' means."
"I know what 'it' means well enough, when I find a thing," said the Duck; "it's generally a frog or a worm. The question is, what did the archbishop find?"

Lewis Carroll, *Alice's Adventures in Wonderland*

Morphological rules for combining morphemes into words differ from the syntactic rules of a language, which determine how words are combined to form sentences; but there is an interesting relationship between morphology and syntax. In the discussion of derivational morphology, we saw that certain aspects of morphology have syntactic implications—nouns can be derived from verbs, verbs from adjectives, adjectives from nouns, and so on. There are other ways in which morphology is dependent on syntax.

We also saw above that the definition of a morpheme as a minimal unit of meaning was too simple, because some morphemes have constant forms but become meaningful only when combined with other morphemes. For instance, the morpheme *-ceive* or *-mit* cannot be assigned an intrinsic meaning; yet, as speakers of English, we recognize it as a separate grammatical unit.

Sentences are combinations of morphemes. It is not always possible to assign a meaning to some of these morphemes, however. For example, what is the meaning of *it* in the sentence *It's hot in July* or in *The archbishop found it advisable?* What is the meaning of *to* in *He wanted her to go? To* has a grammatical "meaning" as an infinitive marker, and *it* is also a morpheme required by the syntactic, sentence-formation rules of the language.

"My boy, Grand-père is not the one to ask about such things. I have lived eighty-seven peaceful and happy years in Montoire-sur-le-Loir without the past anterior verb form."

Drawing by Opie; © 1973 The New Yorker Magazine, Inc.

Similarly, there are "bound" morphemes that, like *to*, are for the most part purely grammatical markers, representing such concepts as "tense," "number," "gender," "case," and so forth.

Such "bound" grammatical morphemes are called **inflectional morphemes:** they never change the syntactic category of the words or morphemes to which they are attached. They are always attached to complete words. Consider the forms of the verb in the following sentences:

a. I sail the ocean blue.
b. He sail*s* the ocean blue.
c. John sail*ed* the ocean blue.
d. John has sail*ed* the ocean blue.
e. John is sail*ing* the ocean blue.

In sentence b the *s* at the end of the verb is an "agreement" marker; it signifies that the subject of the verb is "third-person," is "singular," and that the verb is in the "present tense." It does not add any "lexical meaning." In sentences c–e the *-ed* and *-ing* endings are morphemes required by the syntactic rules of the language to signal "tense" or "aspect."

English is no longer a highly inflected language, but we do have other inflectional endings. The plurality of a count noun,[9] for example, is usually marked by a

---

[9] Count nouns can be counted: *one boy, two boys,* and so forth. Noncount nouns cannot be counted: **one rice, *two rices,* and so on.

plural suffix attached to the singular noun, as in *boy/boys, cat/cats,* and so on.

An interesting thing about inflectional morphemes in English is that they typically follow derivational morphemes. Thus, to the derivationally complex word *un + like + ly + hood,* we can add a plural ending to form *un + like + ly + hood + s* but not **unlikeslyhood.* However, with "compounds," which will be discussed below, the situation is complicated. For many speakers, the plural of *mother-in-law* is *mothers-in-law,* whereas the possessive form is *mother-in-law's.* With noncompound words, though, the inflectional morphemes do come after the derivational morphemes.

Some grammatical relations can be expressed either inflectionally (morphologically) or syntactically. We can see this option in the following sentences:

The boy's book is blue.	The book of the boy is blue.
He loves books.	He is a lover of books.
The planes that fly are red.	The flying planes are red.
He is hungrier than she.	He is more hungry than she.

Perhaps some of you form the comparative of *beastly* only by adding *-er. Beastlier* is often used interchangeably with *more beastly.* There are speakers who say either. We know the rule that determines when either form of the comparative can be used or when just one can be used, as Lewis Carroll pointed out:

"Curiouser and curiouser!" cried Alice (she was so much surprised, that for the moment she quite forgot how to speak good English).

Some languages are highly inflective. The noun in Finnish, for example, has many different inflectional endings, as shown in the following example (do not be concerned if you do not know what all the specific case endings mean):

mantere	nominative singular (sg.)
mantereen	genitive (possessive) sg.
manteretta	partitive sg.
mantereena	essive sg.
mantereeseen	illative sg.
mantereita	partitive plural (pl.)
mantereisiin	illative pl.
mantereiden	genitive pl.

These forms of the noun meaning "continent" are just some of its inflected forms.[10]

It is interesting to note that what one language signals with inflectional affixes, another does with word order and another with "function words." For example, in English, the sentence *Maxim defends Victor* means something different from *Victor defends Maxim.* The word order is important. In Russian, all the following sentences mean "Maxim defends Victor":

[10]Examples from L. Campbell. 1977. "Generative Phonology vs. Finnish Phonology: Retrospect and Prospect." *Texas Linguistic Forum* 5: 21–58.

Maksim zasčisčajet Viktora.
Maksim Viktora zasčisčajet.
Viktora Maksim zasčisčajet.
Viktora zasčisčajet Maksim.
Zasčisčajet Maksim Viktora.
Zasčisčajet Viktora Maksim.

The inflectional suffix -a added to the name *Viktor* to derive *Viktora* shows that Victor, not Maxim, is defended.

In English, to form the future tense of a verb we must use a function word *will,* as in *John will come Monday.* In French, the verb is inflected for tense. Notice the difference between "John is coming Monday" *Jean **vient** lundi* and "John will come Monday" *Jean **viendra** lundi.*

In discussing derivational and compounding morphology, we noted that knowing the meaning of the distinct morphemes may not always reveal the meaning of the morphologically complex word. This problem is not true of inflectional morphology. If we know the meaning of the word *linguist,* we also know the meaning of the plural form *linguists;* if we know the meaning of the verb *analyze,* we know the meaning of *analyzed* and *analyzes* and *analyzing.* This fact is one difference between derivational and inflectional morphology.

The Pronunciation of Morphemes

In Chapter 3, we presented a number of examples showing that a single morpheme may have different pronunciations (that is, different phonetic forms) in different contexts. Thus *write* is pronounced [rajt] alone but is pronounced [rajDər] or [raj:Dər] when the suffix *-er* is added.

Similarly, different pronunciations of vowels occur in English, depending on whether they are stressed or unstressed. The particular phonetic forms of some morphemes are determined by regular phonological rules that refer only to the phonemic context, as is true of the alternate vowel forms of the following sets:

m[ɛ]ll[ə]dy   h[a]rm[ə]ny   s[ɪ]mph[ə]ny
m[ə]ll[o]dious   h[a]rm[o]nious   s[ɪ]mph[o]nious
m[ə]ll[a]dic   h[a]rm[a]nic   s[ɪ]mph[a]nic

The vowel rules that determine these pronunciations are rather complicated and beyond the scope of this text. The examples are presented simply to show that the morphemes in "melody," "harmony," and "symphony" vary phonetically in these words.

Another example of a morpheme in English with different phonetic forms is the plural morpheme. Consider the following nouns.

A	**B**	**C**	**D**
cab	cap	buss	child
cad	cat	bush	ox
bag	back	buzz	mouse
love	cuff	garage	sheep
lathe	faith	match	criterion
cam		badge	
can			
bang			
call			
bar			
spa			
boy			

All the nouns in column A end in voiced nonsibilant sounds, and to form their plurals you add the voiced [z]. All the words in column B end in voiceless nonsibilant sounds, and you add a voiceless [s]. The words in C end in both voiced and voiceless sibilants, which form their plurals with the insertion of a schwa followed by [z].

Children do not have to learn the plural rule by memorizing the individual sounds that require the [z] or [s] or [əz] plural ending, because these sounds form natural classes, as discussed in Chapter 3. A grammar that included lists of these sounds would not reveal the regularities in the language or what a speaker knows about the regular plural-formation rule.

The regular plural rule does not work for a word like *child*, which in the plural is *children*, or for *ox*, which becomes *oxen*, or for *sheep*, which is unchanged phonologically in the plural. *Child, ox,* and *sheep* are exceptions to the regular rule. We learn these exceptional plurals when learning the language.

If the grammar represented each unexceptional or regular word in both its singular and plural forms—for example, *cat* /kæt/, *cats* /kæts/; *cap* /kæp/, *caps* /kæps/; and so on—it would imply that the plurals of *cat* and *cap* were as irregular as the plurals of *child* and *ox*. Of course, they are not. If a new toy appeared on the market called a *glick* /glɪk/, a young child who wanted two of them would ask for two *glicks* /glɪks/ and not two *glicken*, even if the child had never heard the word *glicks*. The child knows the regular rule to form plurals. An experiment conducted by the linguist Jean Berko Gleason showed that very young children can apply this rule to words they never have heard previously. This fact is further discussed in Chapter 10. A grammar that describes such knowledge (the internalized mental grammar) must then include the general rule.

This rule, which determines the phonetic representation or pronunciation of the plural morpheme, is somewhat different from some of the other phonological rules we have discussed. The "aspiration rule" in English applies to a word whenever the phonological description is met; it is not the case, for example, that a /t/ is aspirated only if it is part of a particular morpheme. The "flap rule," which changes the phonetic forms of the morphemes *write* and *ride* when a suffix is added, is also completely automatic, depending solely on the phonological environment. The plural rule, however, applies only to the inflectional plural morpheme. To see that it is not "purely" phonological in nature, consider the following words:

race	[res]	ray	[re]	ray + pl.	[rez]	*[res]
sauce	[sɔs]	saw	[sɔ]	saw + pl.	[sɔz]	*[sɔs]
rice	[rajs]	rye	[raj]	rye + pl.	[rajz]	*[rajs]

The examples show that the [z] in the plural is not determined by the phonological context, because in an identical context an [s] occurs.

Morphophonemics

FRANK AND ERNEST   **Bob Thaves**

The rule that determines the phonetic form of the plural morpheme has traditionally been called a **morphophonemic rule,** because its application is determined by both the morphology and the phonology. When a morpheme has alternate phonetic forms, these forms are called **allomorphs** by some linguists. [z], [s], and [əz] would be allomorphs of the regular plural morpheme, and determined by rule.

To show how such a rule may be applied, assume that the regular, productive, plural morpheme has the phonological form /z/, with the meaning "plural." The regular "plural rule" can be stated in a simple way:

(3a) Insert an [ə] before the plural ending when a regular noun ends in a sibilant—/s/, /z/, /š/, /ž/, /č/, or /ǰ/.

(3b) Change the voiced /z/ to voiceless [s] when it is preceded by a voiceless sound.

If neither 3a nor 3b applies, then /z/ will be realized as [z]; no segments will be added and no features will be changed.

The plural-formation rule will derive the phonetic forms of plurals for all regular nouns (remember, this plural is /z/):

	bus + pl.	*butt* + pl.	*bug* + pl.
Phonemic *Representation*	/bʌs + z/	/bʌt + z/	/bʌg + z/
	↓		
apply rule 3a	ə	NA*	NA
apply rule 3b	NA	s	NA
Phonetic *Representation*	[bʌsəz]	[bʌts]	[bʌgz]

*NA means "not applicable."

As we have formulated these rules, 3a must be applied before 3b. If we applied the two parts of the rule in reverse order, we would derive incorrect phonetic forms:

Phonemic Representation	/bʌs + z/
	↓
apply rule 3b	s
apply rule 3a	ə
Phonetic Representation	*[bʌsəs]

The plural-formation rule illustrates once again that phonological rules can insert entire segments into the phonemic string: an [ə] is added by the first rule. It also illustrates the importance of *ordered rules* in phonology.

An examination of the rule for the formation of the past tense of verbs in English shows some interesting parallels with the plural formation of nouns.

A	B	C	D
grab	reap	state	is
hug	peak	raid	run
seethe	unearth		sing
love	huff		have
buzz	kiss		go
rouge	wish		hit
judge	pitch		
fan			
ram			
long			
kill			
care			
tie			
bow			
hoe			

The productive regular past tense morpheme in English is /d/, *phonemically,* but [d] (column A), [t] (column B), or [ə] (column C) *phonetically,* again depending on the final phoneme of the verb to which it is attached.

The past-tense rule in English, like the plural-formation rule, must include morphological information. Notice that after a vowel or diphthong the form of the past tense is always [d], even though no phonological rule would be violated if a [t] were added, as shown by the words *tight, bout, rote.* When the word is a verb, and when the final alveolar represents the past tense morpheme, however, it must be a voiced [d] and not a voiceless [t].

There is a plausible explanation for why a [ə] is inserted in the past tense of regular verbs ending with alveolar stops (and in nouns ending with sibilants). Because in English we do not contrast long and short consonants, it is difficult for English speakers to perceive a difference in consonantal length. If we added a [z] to *squeeze* we would get [skwizz], which would be hard for English speakers to distinguish from [skwiz]; similarly, if we added [d] to *load,* it would be [lodd] phonetically in the past and [lod] in the present, which would also be difficult to perceive.

Exceptions and Suppletions

PEANUTS   **Charles Schulz**

© 1960 United Feature Syndicate, Inc.

Just as there are no regular rules to determine the plural forms of exceptional nouns like *child/children, man/men, sheep/sheep, criterion/criteria,* so also there are no regular rules to specify the past tense of the verbs in column D.

When, as children, we are acquiring (or constructing) the grammar, we have to learn specifically that the plural of *man* is *men* and that the past of *go* is *went.* For this reason we often hear children say *mans* and *goed;* they first learn the regular rules, and until they learn the exceptions to these rules, they apply them generally to all the nouns and verbs. These children's errors, in fact, support our position that the regular rules exist.

The irregular forms, then, must be listed separately in our mental dictionaries, as **suppletive forms.** When a new word enters the language it is the regular inflectional rules that apply. The plural of *Bic* is *Bics,* not **Bicken.*

The past tense of the verb *hit,* as in the sentence *Yesterday John hit the roof,* and the plural of the noun *sheep,* as in *The sheep are in the meadow,* show that some morphemes seem to have no phonological shape at all. We know that *hit* in the above sentence is *hit + past* because of the time adverb *yesterday,* and we know that *sheep* is the phonetic form of *sheep* + *plural* because of the plural verb form *are*. Thousands of years ago the Hindu grammarians suggested that some morphemes have a **zero-form;** that is, they have no phonological representation. In our view, however, because we would like to hold to the definition of a morpheme as a constant sound-meaning form, we will suggest that the morpheme *hit* is marked as both present and past in the dictionary, and the morpheme *sheep* is marked as both singular and plural.

More Sequential Constraints

Some of the sequential constraints on phonemes that were discussed in Chapter 3 may show up as phonological and morphophonemic rules. The English homorganic nasal constraint applies between some morphemes as well as within a morpheme. The negative prefix *in-*, which, like *un-*, means "not," has three allomorphs:

[ĭn] before vowels:	inexcusable, inattentive, inorganic
and alveolars:	intolerable, indefinable, insurmountable
[ĭm] before labials:	impossible, imbalance
[ĭŋ] before velars:	incomplete, inglorious

The pronunciation of this morpheme is often revealed by the spelling as *im-* when it is prefixed to morphemes beginning with /p/ or /b/. Because we have no letter "ŋ" in our alphabet (although it exists in alphabets used in other languages), the velar [ŋ] is written as *n* in words like *incomplete.* You may not realize that you pronounce the *n* in *inconceivable, inglorious, incongruous,* and other such words as [ŋ] because your homorganic nasal rule is as unconscious as other rules in your grammar. It is the job of linguists and phoneticians to bring such rules to consciousness or to reveal them as part of the grammar. If you say these words in normal tempo without pausing after the *in-*, you should feel the back of your tongue rise to touch the velum.

In Akan the negative morpheme also has three nasal allomorphs: [m] before /p/, [n] before /t/, and [ŋ] before /k/, as is shown in the following cases:

mɪ pɛ	"I like"		mɪ mpɛ	"I don't like"
mɪ tɪ	"I speak"		mɪ ntɪ	"I don't speak"
mɪ kɔ	"I go"		mɪ ŋkɔ	"I don't go"

We see, then, that one morpheme may have different phonetic forms or allomorphs. We have also seen that more than one morpheme may occur in the language with the same meaning but different forms—like *in-, un-,* and *not* (all meaning "not"). It is not possible to predict which of these forms will occur, so they are separate synonymous morphemes. It is only when the phonetic form is predictable by general rule that we find different phonetic forms of a single morpheme.

The plural and past-tense formation rules both change feature values of segments (for example, the voiced /z/ and /d/ to voiceless [s] and [t] after voiceless sounds) and also insert a [ə] in given environments. The nasal homorganic rule is also a feature-changing rule. Because the allomorph [īn] occurs before vowels, where there is no consonant following by which we can determine the place of articulation features, the phonemic representation of this morpheme is /ɪn/ and the rule will assimilate the /n/ to a following consonant by changing feature values of the /n/.

In some cases different phonetic forms of the same morpheme may be derived by segment-deletion rules, as in the following examples:

	A		**B**
sign	[saj̃n]	signature	[sɪgnəčər]
design	[dəzaj̃n]	designation	[dɛzɪgnešən]
paradigm	[pʰærədaj̃m]	paradigmatic	[pʰærədɪgmæDək]

In none of the words in column A is there a phonetic [g], but in each corresponding word in column B a [g] occurs. Our knowledge of English phonology accounts for these phonetic differences. The "[g]–no [g]" alternation is regular, and we apply it to words that we never have heard before. Suppose someone says:

"He was a salignant [səlɪgnənt] man."

Even if you do not know what the word means, you might ask (perhaps to hide your ignorance):

"Why, did he salign [səlajn] somebody?"

It is highly doubtful that a speaker of English would pronounce the verb form with the -ant dropped as [səlɪgn], because the phonological rules of English would "delete" the /g/ when it occurred in this context. This rule might be stated as:

(4) Delete a /g/ when it occurs before a final nasal consonant.[11]

Given this rule, the phonemic representation of the stems in *sign/signature, design/designation, resign/resignation, repugn/repugnant, phlegm/phlegmatic, paradigm/paradigmatic,* and *diaphragm/diaphragmatic* will include a phonemic /g/ that will be deleted by the regular rule if a suffix is not added. By stating the class of sounds that follow the /g/ (nasal consonants) rather than any specific nasal consonant, the rule deletes the /g/ before both /m/ and /n/.

The phonological rules that delete whole segments, add segments and features, and change features also account for the various phonetic forms of some morphemes. This point can be further illustrated by the following words:

[11] The /g/ may be deleted under other circumstances as well, as indicated by its absence in *signing* and *signer.*

A			B		
bomb	/bamb/	[bãm]	bombardier	/bambədir/	[bãmbədir]
iamb	/ajæmb/	[ajæ̃m]	iambic	/ajæmbɪk/	[ajæ̃mbək]
crumb	/krʌmb/	[kʰʌ̃m]	crumble	/krʌmbl/	[kʰrʌ̃mbəl]

A speaker of English knows when to pronounce a final /b/ and when not to. The relationship between the pronunciation of the A words and their B counterparts is regular and can be accounted for by the following rule:

(5) Delete a word-final /b/ when it occurs after an /m/.

Notice that the underlying phonemic representation of the A and B stems is the same.

Phonemic Representation	/bamb/	/bamb + adir/	/bʌlb/
apply /b/ deletion rule (5)	ø	NA	NA
unstressed vowel rule	NA	ə	NA
nasalization rule	ã	ã	NA
Phonetic Representation	[bãm]	[bãmbədir]	[bʌlb]

The rules that delete the segments discussed above are general phonological rules, but their application to phonemic representations results in deriving different phonetic forms of the same morpheme. We also find different morphemes with the same phonological form but different meanings. This concept follows from defining the morpheme as a sound-meaning unit. As discussed above, the morpheme *-er* means "one who does" in words like *singer, painter, lover, worker*, but the same sounds represent the "comparative" morpheme, meaning "more," in *nicer, prettier, taller*. In *butcher*, the sounds represented by the spelling *-er* do not represent any morpheme, since a butcher is not one who *butches. (In an earlier form of English the word *butcher* was *bucker*, "one who dresses bucks." The *-er* in this word was then a separate morpheme.) Similarly, in *water* the *-er* is not a distinct morpheme ending; *butcher* and *water* are single morphemes, or **monomorphemic words.**

We can summarize what we have been discussing regarding the morpheme as a sound-meaning unit:

1. A morpheme may be represented by a single sound, such as the "without" morpheme *a-* in *amoral* or *asexual*.
2. A morpheme may be represented by a syllable, such as *child* and *-ish* in *child + ish*.
3. A morpheme may be represented by more than one syllable: by two syllables, as in *aardvark, lady, water*; or by three syllables, as in *Hackensack* or *crocodile*; or by four or more syllables, as in *salamander*.

4. Two different morphemes may have the same phonological representation: *-er* as in *singer* and *-er* as in *skinnier.*

5. A morpheme may have alternate phonetic forms: the regular plural /z/, which is either [z], [s], or [əz]; *sign* in *sign* [sãyn] and *signature* [sɪgn].

6. For most words, the different pronunciations can be predicted from the regular phonological rules of the language. The deletion of the final /b/ after /m/ applies automatically, without reference to any particular morphemes.

7. In some cases the rules that predict the various phonetic forms of morphemes must refer to particular morphemes. Thus the homorganic nasal rule applies to /ɪn-/ as in *incomplete* and *impossible* but not to /ʌn-/ as in *unclean, unglamorous,* and *unbecoming.*

The grammar of the language that is internalized by the language learner includes the morphemes and the derived words of the language. The morphological rules of the grammar permit you to use and understand the morphemes and words in forming and understanding sentences and new words.

Summary

Knowing a language means knowing the words of that language. When you know a word you know both its **form** (sound) and its **meaning;** these are inseparable parts of the *linguistic sign.* Each word is stored in our mental dictionaries with its phonological representation, its meaning (semantic properties), and its syntactic class or category.

Words are not the most elemental sound-meaning units; some words are structurally complex. The most elemental grammatical units in a language are *morphemes.* Thus, *moralizers* is an English word composed of four morphemes: *moral + ize + er + s.*

The study of word formation and the internal structure of words is called **morphology.** Part of linguistic competence is knowledge of the morphemes, the words, their pronunciation, their meanings, and how they are combined. Morphemes combine according to the morphological rules of the language.

Some morphemes are **bound;** they must be joined to other morphemes as parts of words and never are words by themselves. Other morphemes are **free;** they need not be attached to other morphemes. *Free, king, serf,* and *bore* are free morphemes; *-dom,* as in *freedom, kingdom, serfdom,* and *boredom,* is a bound morpheme. **Affixes,** that is **prefixes, suffixes,** and **infixes,** are bound morphemes.

Some morphemes, like *huckle* in *huckleberry* and *-ceive* in *perceive* or *receive,* have constant phonological form but meanings determined only by the words in which they occur. They are therefore also bound morphemes; they are similar, however, to **lexical content** or **root morphemes,** which constitute the major word classes—nouns, verbs, adjectives, adverbs.

Morphemes may also be classified as derivational or inflectional. **Deriva-

tional morphological rules are lexical rules of word formation. **Inflectional morphemes** are determined by the rules of syntax. They are added to complete words, simple **monomorphemic** words or complex **polymorphemic** words with more than one morpheme. Derivational morphemes can change the syntactic category of the word with which they combine; adding *ish* to the noun *boy* derives an adjective, for example. Inflectional morphemes never change the syntactic category of the word.

Some grammatical morphemes or "function words" constitute a "closed class" of morphemes. Like inflectional morphemes, they are inserted according to the syntactic structure. The past tense morpheme represented by /d/ is added as a suffix to a verb, but the future tense morpheme *will* is inserted in a sentence according to specific rules.

Grammars also include other ways of increasing the vocabulary. Words can be coined outright so that former nonsense words or possible but nonoccurring words become words. Morphological **compounding** rules combine two or more morphemes or words to form complex compounds like *lamb chop, deep-sea diver,* and *ne'er-do-well.* Frequently the meaning of compounds cannot be predicted from the meanings of their individual morphemes. **Acronyms** are words derived from the initials of several words, like AWOL /ewɔl/, which came into the language as the initials for "away without leave." **Blends** are similar to compounds but usually combine shortened forms of two or more morphemes or words. *Carpeteria* is a store selling carpets, and the name derives from *carpet* plus the end of *cafeteria.* **Backformations, abbreviations,** and words formed from proper nouns also add to our given stock of words.

A morpheme may have different phonetic representations, which are determined by the **morphophonemic** and phonological rules of the language. Thus the regular plural morpheme is phonetically [z], [s], or [əz], depending on the final phoneme of the noun to which it is attached. In some cases the alternate forms are not predictable by regular or general rules; such forms are called **suppletive forms.** Examples are *man/men, datum/data,* and *go/went, bring/brought.* These forms constitute a small set of the lexical items in a language; most of the morphemes are subject to regular rules.

Although the particular morphemes and the particular morphological rules are language-dependent, the same general processes occur in all languages.

References

Aronoff, Mark. 1976. "Word Formation in Generative Grammar." *Linguistic Inquiry.* Monograph 1. M.I.T. Press. Cambridge, Mass.

Marchand, Hans. 1969. *The Categories and Types of Present-Day English Word-Formations.* 2d ed. C. H. Beck'sche Verlagsbuchhandlung. Munich.

Matthews, P. H. 1976. *Morphology: An Introduction to the Theory of Word Structure.* Cambridge University Press. Cambridge, England.

Exercises

1. Divide these words by placing a + between their separate morphemes. (Some of the words may be *monomorphemic* and therefore indivisible.)

   Example: replaces   re + place + s

   a. retroactive   _____

   b. befriended   _____

   c. televise   _____

   d. margin   _____

   e. endearment   _____

   f. psychology   _____

   g. unpalatable   _____

   h. holiday   _____

   i. grandmother   _____

   j. morphemic   _____

   k. cursive   _____

   l. Massachusetts   _____

2. Below are some data from Samoan:

manao	"he wishes"	mananao	"they wish"
matua	"he is old"	matutua	"they are old"
malosi	"he is strong"	malolosi	"they are strong"
punou	"he bends"	punonou	"they bend"
atamaki	"he is wise"	atamamaki	"they are wise"
savali	"he travels"	pepese	"they sing"
laga	"he weaves"		

   a. What is the Samoan for:

   (1) they weave _____

   (2) they travel _____

(3) he sings _____

b. Formulate a general statement (a morphological rule) that states how to form the plural verb form from the singular verb form.

3. Consider the following data from Ewe, a West African language. (Ewe is a tone language, but the tones are unmarked in these examples, since tone is not relevant to the problem.)

Ewe	English
uwa ye xa amu	"The chief looked at a child."
uwa ye xa ufi	"The chief looked at a tree."
uwa xa ina ye	"A chief looked at the picture."
amu xa ina	"A child looked at a picture."
amu ye vo ele ye	"The child wanted the chair."
amu xa ele ye	"A child looked at the chair."
ika vo ina ye	"A woman wanted the picture."

a. The morpheme meaning "the" is _____.

b. The morpheme meaning "a" is: (Circle the correct answer)
   (1) xa   (2) amu   (3) ye   (4) none of these

c. List all the other morphemes occurring in the Ewe sentences above. (Give the Ewe morpheme and the English "gloss.")

_____   _____

_____   _____

_____   _____

_____   _____

_____   _____

_____   _____

    d. How would you say in Ewe "The woman looked at the tree"?

_____

    e. If *oge de abo* means "A man drank wine," what would the Ewe sentence meaning "A man wanted the wine" be?

_____

4. In the African language Maninka, the suffix *-li* has more than one pronunciation (like the *-ed* past tense ending on English verbs, as in *reaped* [t], *robbed* [d], and *raided* [əd]). This suffix is similar to the derivational suffix *-ing*, which when added to the verb *cook* makes it a noun as in "Her cooking was great," or the suffix *-ion*, which also derives a verb from a noun as in *create + ion*, permitting "the creation of the word."

Consider these data from Maninka:

bugo	"hit"	bugoli	"hitting"
dila	"repair"	dilali	"repairing"
don	"come in"	donni	"coming in"
dumu	"eat"	dumuni	"eating"
gwen	"chase"	gwenni	"chasing"

    a. What are the two forms of the morpheme meaning "the _____ing"?

       (1) _____ (2) _____

    b. Can you predict which phonetic form will occur? If so, state the rule.
    c. What are the "-ing" forms for the following verbs?

       da   "lie down" _____   famu   "understand" _____

       men "hear"   _____   sunogo "sleep"   _____

5. List five suffix morphemes. Give their meaning, the types of stems they may be suffixed to, and two examples of each.

    Example: -er meaning: "doer of"; makes an agentive noun
             stem type: added to verbs
             examples: *rider*   "one who rides"
                      teacher "one who teaches"

    a. _____ meaning:
                  stem type:
                  examples:

b. _____ meaning:
                         stem type:
                         examples:

c. _____ meaning:
                         stem type:
                         examples:

d. _____ meaning:
                         stem type:
                         examples:

e. _____ meaning:
                         stem type:
                         examples:

6. List five morpheme prefixes. Give their meaning, the types of stems they may be prefixed to, and two examples of each.

a.

b.

c.

d.

e.

7. Here are some Japanese verb forms that you may consider to be phonetic transcriptions. They represent two different styles (informal and formal) of present tense verbs.

	Informal	**Formal**	**Basic Verb Stem**
"call"	yobu	yobimasu	_____
"write"	kaku	kakimasu	_____
"eat"	taberu	tabemasu	_____
"see"	miru	mimasu	_____
"lend"	kasu	kashimasu	_____
"wait"	matsu	machimasu	_____
"leave"	deru	demasu	_____

"go out"	dekakeru	dekakemasu	_____
"read"	yomu	yomimasu	_____
"die"	shinu	shinimasu	_____
"close"	shimeru	shimemasu	_____
"wear"	kiru	kimasu	_____

   a. List the underlying or basic verb stems for each of these Japanese verbs.
   b. State the rule for deriving the present-tense informal verb forms from the underlying verb stems.
   c. State the rule for deriving the present-tense formal verb forms from the underlying verb stems.
   d. State a rule that will derive the formal forms from the informal forms.

8. Below are some sentences in Swahili:

mtoto	amefika	"The child has arrived."
mtoto	anafika	"The child is arriving."
mtoto	atafika	"The child will arrive."
watoto	wamefika	"The children have arrived."
watoto	wanafika	"The children are arriving."
watoto	watafika	"The children will arrive."
mtu	amelala	"The man has slept."
mtu	analala	"The man is sleeping."
mtu	atalala	"The man will sleep."
watu	wamelala	"The men have slept."
watu	wanalala	"The men are sleeping."
watu	watalala	"The men will sleep."
kisu	kimeanguka	"The knife has fallen."
kisu	kinaanguka	"The knife is falling."
kisu	kitaanguka	"The knife will fall."
visu	vimeanguka	"The knives have fallen."
visu	vinaanguka	"The knives are falling."
visu	vitaanguka	"The knives will fall."
kikapu	kimeanguka	"The basket has fallen."
kikapu	kinaanguka	"The basket is falling."
kikapu	kitaanguka	"The basket will fall."
vikapu	vimeanguka	"The baskets have fallen."
vikapu	vinaanguka	"The baskets are falling."
vikapu	vitaanguka	"The baskets will fall."

One of the characteristic features of Swahili (and Bantu languages in general) is the existence of noun classes. There are specific singular and plural prefixes that occur with the nouns in each class. These prefixes are also used for purposes of agreement between the subject-noun and the verb. In the sentences given, two of these classes are included (there are many more in the language).

a. Identify all the morphemes you can detect, and give their meanings. Example: -toto "child"

        m- noun prefix attached to singular nouns of Class I

        a- prefix attached to verbs when the subject is a singular noun of Class I

Be sure to look for the other noun and verb markers, including tense markers.

b. How is the "verb" constructed? That is, what kinds of morphemes are strung together and in what order?

c. How would you say in Swahili:

  (1) The child is falling.   _____

  (2) The baskets have arrived. _____

  (3) The man will fall.   _____

9. Consider the following phonetic data from the Bantu language Luganda. (The data have been somewhat altered to make the problem easier.) In each line, the same root or stem morpheme occurs in both columns A and B, but it has one prefix in column A, meaning "a" or "an," and another prefix in column B, meaning "little."

A		**B**	
[ēnato]	"a canoe"	[akaato]	"little canoe"
[ēnapo]	"a house"	[akaapo]	"little house"
[ēnobi]	"an animal"	[akaoobi]	"little animal"
[ēmpipi]	"a kidney"	[akapipi]	"little kidney"
[ēŋkoosa]	"a feather"	[akakoosa]	"little feather"
[ēmmããmmo]	"a peg"	[akabããmmo]	"little peg"
[ēŋŋõõmme]	"a horn"	[akagõõmme]	"little horn"
[ēnnīmiro]	"a garden"	[akadīmiro]	"little garden"
[ēnugēni]	"a stranger"	[akatabi]	"little branch"

In answering the following questions, base your answers on only these forms. Assume that all the words in the language follow the regularities shown here. You may need to use scratch paper to work out your analysis before writing your answers in the space provided. (Hint: The phonemic representation of the morpheme meaning "little" is /aka/.)

a. Are nasal vowels in Luganda phonemic? _____

Are they predictable? _____

b. Is the phonemic representation of the morpheme meaning "garden" /dimiro/?

c. What is the phonemic representation of the morpheme meaning

"canoe"? _____

d. Are [p] and [b] allophones of one phoneme?

e. If /am/ represents a bound prefix morpheme in Luganda, can you conclude that [amdano] is a possible phonetic form for a word in this language starting with this prefix?

f. Is there a phonological homorganic nasal rule in Luganda?

g. If the phonetic representation of the word meaning "little boy" is [akapoobe], give the phonemic and phonetic representations for "a boy."

Phonemic _____ Phonetic _____

h. Which of the following forms is the *phonemic* representation for the prefix meaning "a" or "an"?
(1) /en/   (2) /ẽn/   (3) /ẽm/   (4) /em/   (5) /eŋ/

i. What is the *phonetic* representation of the word meaning "a branch"?

_____

j. What is the *phonemic* representation of the word meaning "little stranger"? _____

k. State in general terms any phonological rules revealed by the Luganda data.

10. Below are listed some words followed by incorrect definitions. (All these errors are taken from Amsel Greene's *Pullet Surprises*.)

Word	Student Definition
stalemate	"husband or wife no longer interested"
effusive	"able to be merged"

tenet	"a group of ten singers"
dermatology	"a study of derms"
ingenious	"not very smart"
finesse	"a female fish"

For each of these incorrect definitions, give some possible reasons why the students made the guesses they did. Where you can exemplify by reference to other words or morphemes, giving their meanings, do so.

Syntax:
The Sentence
Patterns of
Language

Grammatical or Ungrammatical?

> ... The fundamental aim in the linguistic analysis of a language L
> is to separate the grammatical sequences which are sentences of L
> from the ungrammatical sequences which are not sentences of L
> and to study the structure of the grammatical sequences.
>
> Noam Chomsky, *Syntactic Structures*

In the previous chapters we have discussed how the grammar of a language represents the speaker's linguistic knowledge of *phonetics, phonology,* and *morphology.*
Knowing a language also means being able to put words together to form phrases
and sentences that express our thoughts. The part of the grammar that concerns the
structure of phrases and sentences is called **syntax.**

Part of the meaning of a sentence is found in the words of which it is composed, but sentence meaning is more than the sum of the meanings of words. The
sentence

> The children sang songs for the teacher.

does not have the same meaning as

> The teacher sang songs for the children.

and the string of words

> songs sang for the the children teacher

has no linguistic meaning, even though it is made up of meaningful units. A sentence is a string of words or morphemes, but every such string is not a sentence. Rules of grammar determine how morphemes and words can combine to express a specific meaning.

When you know a language, then, you know which combinations or strings of morphemes are permitted by the syntactic rules and which are not. Those strings that conform to the syntactic rules are called the **sentences** or **grammatical sentences** of the language, and strings of morphemes that do not are called **ungrammatical.**

What Grammaticality Is Based On

You do not have to study linguistics or the grammar of English to know that

> The boy kissed the girl.

is a "good" sentence, but that something is wrong or funny with

> *Girl the boy the kissed.

In Chapter 1 you were asked to distinguish between grammatical and ungrammatical strings of words by marking the ungrammatical strings with an asterisk. Here is a similar list. According to *your* knowledge or intuitions about English, which of the following would you "star"?

(1) (a) The boy found the ball.
    (b) The boy found.
    (c) The boy found in the house.
    (d) The boy found the ball in the house.
    (e) The boy put the ball.
    (f) Zachary looked up the number.
    (g) Zachary looked the number up.
    (h) Jill walked up the hill.
    (i) Jill walked the hill up.
    (j) Disa slept the baby.
    (k) Disa slept.
    (l) Emily drinks water every day.
    (m) Emily drinks a soda every day.
    (n) Emily drinks a water every day.
    (o) Robert is fond of his children.
    (p) Robert is amazed that his children dislike TV.
    (q) Robert is fond that his children dislike TV.
    (r) Robert is amazed of his children.

We predict that speakers of English would "star" sentences **b, c, e, i, j, n, q,** and **r** as ungrammatical. If we are right, it shows that grammaticality judgments are not idiosyncratic or capricious, but are rule-governed.

The syntactic rules that account for our intuitions about these strings are more than just rules of word order. The rules additionally specify, for example, that *found* must be immediately followed by some expression similar to *the ball,* but not by *in the house,* as illustrated in strings a–d. The rules also allow *up* to occur either just after the verb *looked* (f) or at the end of the sentence (g), but it may only occur after the verb in h, as the strangeness of i attests. *Slept* works the opposite of *found;* it may occur without anything following it (j and k). For English speakers the word *soda* can be preceded by the word *a,* but *water* sounds funny in the same circumstances, as evinced by l–n. The last four examples indicate that a phrase beginning with *of* may follow *fond* but not *amazed,* whereas a phrase beginning with *that* plus a complete sentence may follow *amazed* but not *fond.*

Sentences are not simply random strings of words and morphemes, but conform to specific patterns determined by the syntactic rules of the language. This statement is true of all human languages. The fact that all speakers can distinguish grammatical from ungrammatical combinations of words in their own language, and often know how to repair ungrammatical ones to make them grammatical, demonstrates their knowledge of the rules of syntax.

What Grammaticality Is Not Based On

Grammaticality is *not* based on what is taught in school but on the rules acquired or constructed unconsciously as children. Much grammatical knowledge is "in place" before we learn to read.

The ability to make grammaticality judgments does not depend on having heard the sentence before. You may never have heard or read the sentence

Enormous crickets in pink socks danced at the prom.

but your syntactic knowledge will tell you that it is grammatical.

Grammaticality judgments do not depend on whether the sentence is meaningful or not, as shown by the following sentences:

Colorless green ideas sleep furiously.
A verb crumpled the milk.

Although these sentences do not make much sense, they are syntactically well formed. They sound "funny," but they differ in their "funniness" from the following strings:

*Furiously sleep ideas green colorless.
*Milk the crumpled verb a.

Grammatical sentences may be uninterpretable if they include nonsense strings, that is, words with no agreed-on meaning, as shown by the first two lines of "Jabberwocky" by Lewis Carroll:

> 'Twas brillig, and the slithy toves
> Did gyre and gimble in the wabe;

Such nonsense poetry is amusing because the sentences "obey" syntactic rules and sound like good English. Ungrammatical strings of nonsense words are not entertaining:

> *Toves slithy the and brillig 'twas
> wabe the in gimble and gyre did . . .

Grammaticality does not depend on the truth of sentences either—if it did, lying would be impossible—nor on whether real objects are being discussed, nor on whether something is possible or not. Untrue sentences can be grammatical, sentences discussing unicorns can be grammatical, and sentences referring to pregnant fathers can be grammatical.

Unconscious knowledge of the syntactic rules of grammars permits speakers to make grammaticality judgments.

What Else Do You Know About Syntax?

TUMBLEWEEDS   **Tom K. Ryan**

© 1978 United Feature Syndicate, Inc., by permission of North America Syndicate, Inc.

Syntactic knowledge goes beyond being able to decide which strings are grammatical and which are not. It accounts for the double meaning, or *ambiguity,* of expressions like the one illustrated in the cartoon above. The humor of the cartoon depends on the ambiguity of the phrase *synthetic buffalo hides,* which can mean buffalo hides that are synthetic, or hides of synthetic buffalo. The ambiguity results because syntactic rules allow the following *two* structures:

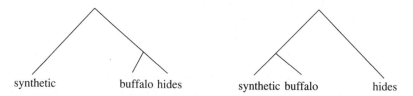

synthetic   buffalo hides   synthetic buffalo   hides

It is therefore due to the syntactic structure that the expression has two meanings, rather than to any ambiguous words. The same is true of the following sentences.

> It's a miracle that the old magician was able to work.
> Visiting professors can be interesting.
> He decided on the train.

Syntactic knowledge also plays a role in determining when two nonidentical sentences have the same meaning and when they do not. For example, the following sentences mean approximately the same thing, although they differ in syntactic structure:

> Pleasing Disa is fun for Vicki.
> It is fun for Vicki to please Disa.

Knowledge of English syntactic rules also enables us to determine how different parts of a sentence are related. In the sentences

> The student solved the problem.
> The problem was solved by the student.

the student is the grammatical or structural subject only of the first sentence, but it is logically the subject of both sentences (the notions of logical subject and object will be discussed in a later section). Syntactic rules specify such grammatical and logical relations, which, together with semantic rules, reveal the meaning associations in sentences.

Finally, syntactic rules permit speakers to produce and understand an unlimited number of sentences never produced or heard before—the creative aspect of language mentioned in Chapter 1.

Thus syntactic rules in a grammar must at least account for:

1. the grammaticality of sentences
2. the ordering of words and morphemes
3. structural ambiguity
4. the fact that sentences with different structures can have the same meaning
5. the grammatical and logical relations within a sentence

6. speakers' creative ability to produce and understand any of an infinite set of possible sentences

A major goal of linguistics is to show clearly and explicitly how syntactic rules account for this knowledge. A theory of grammar must provide a complete characterization of what speakers implicitly know about their language. This chapter will discuss some of this knowledge and the rules that account for it. A full description of syntax goes beyond the scope of this book; however, the works by Chomsky, Sells, and Van Riemsdijk and Williams cited in the References section at the end of this chapter are excellent sources for further reading.

Sentence Structure

THE FAR SIDE   **Gary Larson**

Beginning duck

© 1986 Universal Press Syndicate. Reprinted with permission. All rights reserved.

Syntactic rules determine the correct order of words in a sentence. In English we know that an article like *the* or *an* precedes a noun like *animal,* but sentences are more than words placed one after another like beads on a string. As *synthetic buffalo hides* showed, the words of a sentence can be divided into two or more groups, and within each group the words can be divided into subgroups, and so on, until only single words remain. For example, the sentence

The child found the puppy.

is composed of two main groups, or **constituents:**

the child   found the puppy

corresponding to the ''subject'' and ''predicate'' of the sentence. These groups can be further subdivided until the original sentence is represented in the following branching diagram:

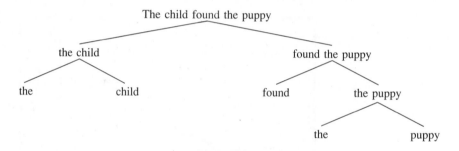

Such a diagram is called a **constituent structure tree.** The ''tree'' is upside down with the ''root'' at the top and the ''leaves'' at the bottom. At each point where the tree ''branches,'' there is a group of words that form a part or **structural constituent** of the sentence. At the bottom of the tree are the individual words or morphemes. In addition to revealing linear order, a constituent structure tree has **hierarchical structure.** This expression means that the groups and subgroups of words composing the structural constituents are shown by the level on which they appear in the tree.

The diagram shows that the phrase *found the puppy* is naturally divided into the two parts *found* and *the puppy*. A different division, say *found the* and *puppy,* makes ''unnatural'' groups that are not constituents. Notice that an answer to the question, ''What did you find?'' might be ''the puppy,'' but no question about what happened could be answered by saying ''found the.'' This test shows that *the puppy* is a *structural constituent*, whereas *found the* is not.

The expression *synthetic buffalo hides* has two possible constituent structure tree representations (see the diagram at the top of page 169). Each tree represents one of the possible meanings. Thus constituent structure can explicitly explain why the phrase is ambiguous.

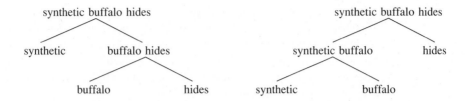

All sentences in all languages can be represented by constituent structure trees, and all languages have syntactic rules that determine the linear order of words and their hierarchical structure, that is, how the words are grouped into structural constituents.

The constituent structure of sentences also reveals which constituents can be substituted for other constituents without affecting the grammaticality of the sentence (although the meaning may change). For example, the constituents *the child* and *the puppy* can be substituted for each other in the diagram on page 168 to produce:

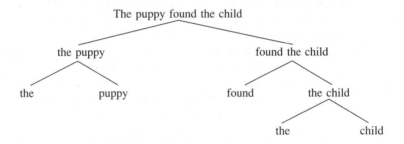

Constituents that can be substituted for one another without loss of grammaticality belong to the same **syntactic category.** *The child* and *the puppy* belong to the syntactic category **Noun Phrase (NP).** Noun Phrases may be easily identified because they can function as "subject" or "object" in a sentence, and only Noun Phrases may do so. Noun Phrases generally contain a Noun or Pronoun. Part of syntactic knowledge is knowing the syntactic categories of your language. You know what a Noun Phrase is even if you have never heard the term before.

You can identify which of the following expressions are Noun Phrases by inserting them into the spaces in "Who found _____?" and "_____ was lost." The ones that "feel right" will be the Noun Phrases:

(2) (a) a bird
    (b) the red banjo
    (c) have a nice day
    (d) with a balloon
    (e) the woman who was laughing
    (f) it
    (g) John
    (h) run

We predict you were able to identify a, b, e, f, and g as Noun Phrases.

There are other syntactic categories. The constituent *found the puppy* is a **Verb Phrase (VP).** Verb Phrases always contain a Verb, which may be followed by other constituents, such as a Noun Phrase. A syntactic category may contain other syntactic categories. You can determine which of the following are Verb Phrases by trying to substitute each one into "The child _____."

(3) (a) saw a duck
    (b) a bird
    (c) slept
    (d) smart
    (e) is smart
    (f) found the cake
    (g) found the cake in the cupboard

The Verb Phrases are a, c, e, f, and g.

Other syntactic categories we will encounter in this section are **Sentence (S), Article (Art), Noun (N),** and **Verb (V).** Some of these syntactic categories should be familiar; they have traditionally been called "parts of speech." All languages have such syntactic categories; in fact, categories such as Noun, Verb, and Noun Phrase are universally found in the grammars of all human languages. Speakers know the syntactic categories of their language, even if they do not know the technical terms.

We can now explicitly represent the constituent structure of *The child found the puppy* by indicating the syntactic category of each constituent:

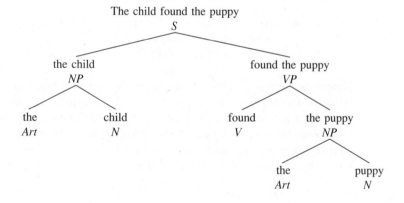

Three aspects of the syntactic knowledge of sentence structure are revealed in this constituent structure tree:

(4) (a) the linear order of the words
    (b) the grouping of the words into structural constituents
    (c) the syntactic category of each structural constituent

Every sentence of English, and of every other human language, can be represented by a constituent structure tree that explicitly reveals these three kinds of information.

The above diagram is correct, but it is redundant, and it can be drawn more simply:

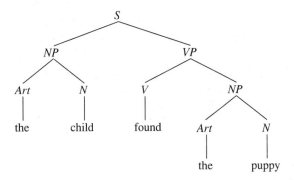

No information is lost by this "streamlining." If you trace each word up the tree, you will see that *puppy* is a Noun, *the puppy* is a Noun Phrase, *found the puppy* is a Verb Phrase, *the child found the puppy* is a sentence, that *child* is also a Noun and *the child,* like *the puppy,* is also a Noun Phrase, and so on.

The tree diagram also shows that the sentence *The child found the puppy* consists of two structural constituents: a Noun Phrase *the child* and a Verb Phrase *found the puppy.* The Verb Phrase *found the puppy* consists of two structural constituents: the Verb *found* and the Noun Phrase *the puppy,* and so on. The article *the* and the Noun *puppy* are constituents contained in a larger constituent Noun Phrase *the puppy,* but individually neither is a Noun Phrase.

A constituent includes *all* the smaller constituents beneath it in the tree. Each branching point in the tree is called a **node,** and sometimes the syntactic category associated with the node is called its **label.**

Another example is given below:

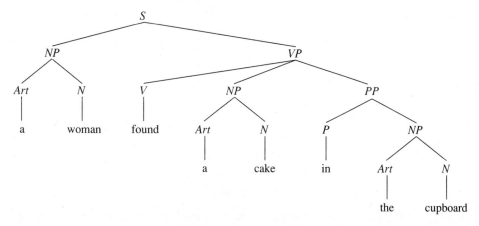

This tree shows that a Verb Phrase may also consist of a Verb followed by a Noun Phrase followed by a **Prepositional Phrase (PP).** Additionally, a Prepositional Phrase is a **Preposition (P)** followed by a Noun Phrase. This tree illustrates that a Noun Phrase may occur in three different structural positions: below the S node, below the VP node, and below the PP node.

Just as constituent structure reveals ambiguities such as *synthetic buffalo hides,* it explains other cases of ambiguity. This function is further evidence that constituent structure trees represent linguistic knowledge, as shown by the following examples:

> The old men and women left.
> The boy saw the man with the telescope.

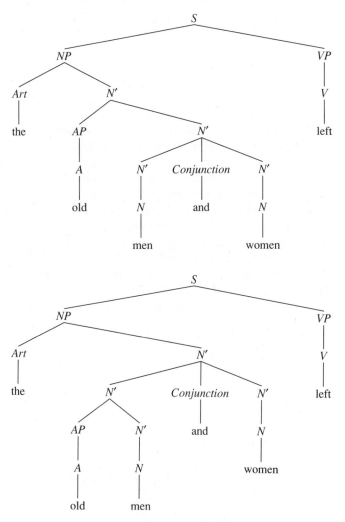

The first sentence can mean either that the old men and the old women left, or that the old men and all of the women, young and old, left, as shown by the constituent structure trees on page 172.[1]

In interpreting the second sentence, it is not clear whether the boy saw a man who had a telescope, or whether the boy used the telescope to see the man. Structurally the two versions can be distinguished by the following constituent structure trees:

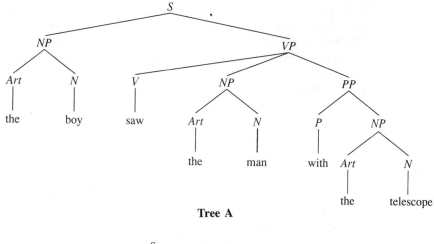

Tree A

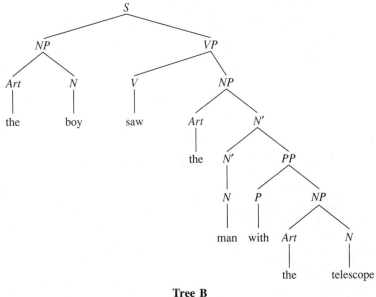

Tree B

In Tree B the PP *with the telescope* is under the same N′ node as *man*, both preceded by the Article *the*, showing that it is the man with the telescope whom the boy saw.

---

[1]The category N′ will be explained in a later section.

Phrase Structure Rules

Everyone who is master of the language he speaks . . . may form new . . . Phrases, provided they coincide with the genius of the language.
Michaelis, *Dissertation* (1769)

If we looked at many more constituent structure trees of English sentences, we would begin to see certain patterns emerging. In ordinary sentences, the S is always subdivided into NP VP. NPs always contain Nouns, VPs always contain Verbs, PPs consist in a Preposition followed by a Noun Phrase.

Of all *possible* tree structures, few represent actual sentence structure, just as of all possible word combinations, few turn out to be actual sentences. For example,

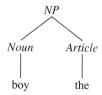

is a possible but nonoccurring tree structure in English.

This grammatical knowledge is represented through **Phrase Structure Rules,** which state explicitly *all* and *only* the possible combinations of constituents of the language.

For example, in English a Noun Phrase (NP) can be an Article (Art) followed by a Noun (N). Thus a "piece" of a tree, called a *subtree,* may look like this:

The Phrase Structure Rule that states this generalization is:

(5) NP → Art N

This rule conveys two facts:

(a) A Noun Phrase *may be* an Article followed by a Noun.
(b) An Article followed by a Noun *is always* a Noun Phrase.

The left side of the arrow is the constituent whose components are defined on the right side. The right side of the arrow also shows the linear order of these components. Phrase Structure Rules reveal speakers' knowledge of the linear order of words, the grouping of words into constituents, and the syntactic categories of each constituent.[2]

The constituent structure trees of the previous section show that the following Phase Structure Rules are part of the grammar of English.

(6a) VP → V NP
(6b) VP → V NP PP

Rule 6a states that a Verb Phrase may be a Verb followed by a Noun Phrase. Rule 6b states that a Verb Phrase may also be a Verb followed by a Noun Phrase followed by a Prepositional Phrase. These rules are *general* statements, which do not refer to any specific Verb Phrase, Verb, Noun Phrase, or Prepositional Phrase.

Rules 6a and 6b can be summed up in one statement: A Verb Phrase may be a Verb followed by a Noun Phrase, which may be followed by a Prepositional Phrase. The Prepositional Phrase may or may not be there. By putting parentheses around optional elements, we can abbreviate rules 6a and 6b with the single rule 7. (This formal way of stating *optional* elements was also discussed in Chapter 3.)

(7) VP → V NP (PP)

In fact the NP is also optional, as shown in the following trees:

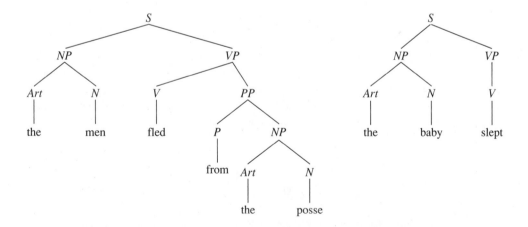

In the first case we have a Verb Phrase consisting of a Verb plus a Prepositional Phrase, corresponding to the rule VP → V PP. In the second case, the Verb Phrase

[2]There is general agreement concerning these facts about language, which may be expressed differently in different theories.

consists of a Verb alone, corresponding to the rule VP → V. All the facts about the Verb Phrase we have seen so far are revealed in the single rule:

(8) VP → V (NP) (PP)

This rule states that a Verb Phrase may consist of a Verb followed optionally by a Noun Phrase and/or a Prepositional Phrase.

Other rules of English that are evident are:

(9) S → NP VP
(10) PP → P NP

Growing Trees

I think that I shall never see
A poem lovely as a tree

Joyce Kilmer, "Trees"

Constituent Structure Trees may not be lovely to look at, but if a poem is written in grammatical English, its sentences can be represented as trees. Rules 5, 8, 9, and 10, repeated here, tell us in part what Constituent Structure Trees are valid for English.

S → NP VP
NP → Art N
VP → V (NP) (PP)
PP → P NP

S is designated as the "root" of the tree or the node from which all trees must begin. The rules specify or **generate** trees in the following way.

Starting with the root S, the branches from S are the constituents specified by the category labels on the right side of any S rule, in that order.

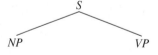

Applying the rules for NP and VP in the same way, new branches are added.

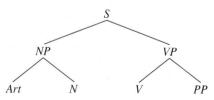

In the case of the VP rule, which abbreviates four rules, any of the four versions can be used, as shown in another possible expansion.

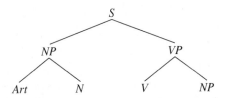

Rules apply until no category on the bottom of the tree appears on the left side of any rule. The terminal categories that never appear on the left side are **lexical categories**—the Articles, Nouns, Verbs, and Prepositions.

Because many words belong to the same lexical categories, a single tree structure represents many sentences, such as:

(11) The boy kissed the girl.
A child found a puppy.
An artist painted the mural.

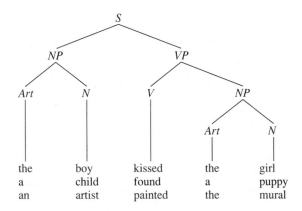

There are infinitely many trees in any language, but only a handful of Phrase Structure Rules. The rules are a formal way of specifying the trees allowed by the grammar of the language.

Trees That Won't Grow

Who climbs the grammar-tree distinctly knows
Where noun and verb and participle grows.
John Dryden, "Juvenal's Satire," vi

The Phrase Structure Rules of a language tell us not only what structures are found in the language, but which ones are not found. The rules provide an *explicit* account of linguistic knowledge. Assuming the rule

$$S \rightarrow NP\ VP$$

is the only "S-rule" in the grammar of English, the following fragments are not sentences for the reasons given:

*The man	(lacks a VP)
*Saw a buffalo	(lacks an NP)
*Saw a buffalo the man	(NP and VP in wrong order)

Similarly, *boy the* cannot be an NP, because no NP rule of English syntax specifies that an article can follow a noun.

Other languages have different Phrase Structure Rules. In Swedish, for example, the article may follow the Noun in some NPs, for example, in *mannen* "the man" (*mann* "man" + *en* "the"). Other languages have "Post-positions" instead of *Pre*positions in which the "Preposition" comes after the Noun Phrase instead of preceding it. For example, *Tokyo kara* means "from Tokyo" in Japanese. These differences are reflected in the Phrase Structure Rules of the grammars of these languages.

In German, the Verb may be the last constituent in the Verb Phrase, following any NPs or PPs that may occur. This particular characteristic of German inspired Mark Twain to write:

> Whenever the literary German dives into a sentence, that is the last you are going to see of him till he emerges on the other side of the Atlantic with his Verb in his mouth.[3]

Despite these differences in detail, all grammars of all languages have the *type* of rule we are calling Phrase Structure Rules that determine the constituent structure of sentences of the language and its syntactic categories.

More Phrase Structure Rules

Normal human minds are such that . . . without the help of anybody, they will produce 1000 (sentences) they never heard spoke of . . . inventing and saying such things as they never heard from their masters, nor any mouth.
Huarte De San Juan, c. 1530–1592

There are many sentences of English whose structure we have not yet accounted for:

(12) (a) The man with the hat smiled.
     (b) A very large black dog looked out the window.
     (c) The nurse thought that the patient died.

[3]Mark Twain, *A Connecticut Yankee in King Arthur's Court.*

In 12a the Noun Phrase is more than just an article followed by a noun. The Noun is modified by the Prepositional Phrase *with the hat*. In 12b the Noun *dog* is modified by adjectives, although no Phrase Structure Rule mentions adjectives. Finally, in 12c the Verb *thought* is followed by a complete sentence, *the patient died,* although our rules, as they stand, do not generate this sentence.

To account for these sentences we will use the category N̄, called **N-Bar,** which is also symbolized as **N'.** This category can be thought of as a Noun Phrase without any articles or other premodifiers (such as *every* or *some*). A constituent structure representation of 12a using this new category would be:

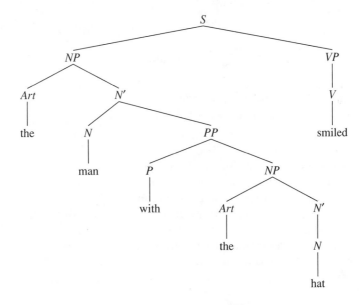

This analysis suggests that we modify our NP rule 5 to read:

(5') NP → Art N'

We must also describe in a Phrase Structure Rule what N' is. In part it must be a Noun alone, to account for simple NPs that contain an Article plus a Noun; it must also be a Noun followed by an optional Prepositional Phrase, giving us the new rule:

(13) N' → N (PP)

To account for the presence of adjectives, as in 12b, we must introduce the category of **Adjective (Adj)** and ''degree'' words **(Deg)** such as *very, quite,* and *mostly.* The ''higher'' category **Adjective Phrase (AP)** is also needed. A tree diagram of 12b would be:

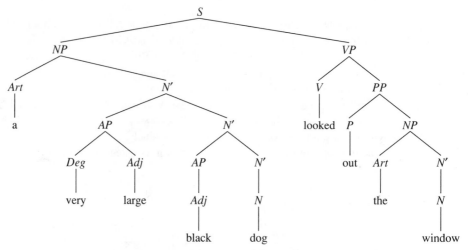

This tree indicates the need for two additional rules:

(14) N′ → AP N′
(15) AP → (Deg) Adj

Rule 14 is different in one respect from the other rules we have discussed: the category on the left side of the arrow is repeated on the right side. This rule is a **recursive** rule, and repeated applications of it allow indefinitely many adjectives to precede a noun, a fact about English we discussed in Chapter 1. We will study more about recursive rules in a later section.

In 12c the Verb Phrase contains a Verb followed by the word *that* followed by a complete sentence. *That* belongs to a very small class of words representing the category **Complementizer (Comp).** Whenever an S node is "embedded"—that is, when it is *not* the topmost S node—it is preceded by a Comp. The category

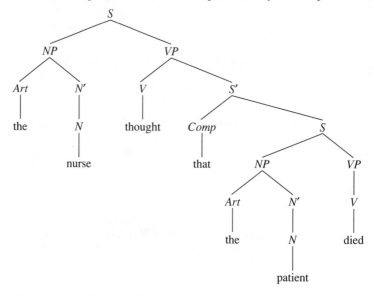

Comp + S is called **S' (S-Bar).** It is shown in the constituent structure tree on the bottom of page 180.

The addition of just two rules allows us to account for this new type of constituent structure.

(16) VP → V S'
(17) S' → Comp S

We now summarize all the Phrase Structure Rules for the grammar of English presented so far:

(18) S → NP VP

S' → Comp S

NP → Art N'

N' → AP N'
N' → N (PP)   or equivalently[4] N' → $\left\{ \begin{array}{l} \text{AP N'} \\ \text{N (PP)} \end{array} \right\}$

VP → V (NP) (PP)
VP → V S'   or VP → V $\left\{ \begin{array}{l} \text{(NP) (PP)} \\ \text{S'} \end{array} \right\}$

AP → (Deg) A

PP → P NP

With these nine rules (actually 14 conflated individual rules) we can characterize infinitely many sentences of English, with a large variety of constituent structures. Phrase Structure Rules with recursive properties explain how language is "creative," and how speakers with "finite" minds have the ability to produce and understand an infinite set of sentences. The rules presented here are only a fraction of the rules needed for a complete description of the language.

Many generalizations about English are contained in these rules. For example, Noun Phrases always contain a Noun, Adjective Phrases an Adjective, Prepositional Phrases a Preposition, and Verb Phrases a Verb. Put more briefly, X-phrases always contain an X, where X stands for Noun, Adjective, Preposition, or Verb.

Such generalizations have led some linguists to formulate Phrase Structure Rules using Xs to capture general properties. This approach is called "X-bar" theory.

NPs and APs seem to share several structural properties. Both may begin with "specifier" words: Articles like *a* and *the* in the case of NPs; degree words like *rather* and *very* in the case of APs. Both may end in a Prepositional Phrase or Sentence:

her happiness *about the prize* (NP + PP)
rather miserable *over the burglary* (AP + PP)
a belief that *the patient recovered* (NP + S)
very proud that *the child succeeded* (AP + S)

---

[4]The use of curly braces means either the top or bottom line within the braces may be chosen to be the right side of the arrow, as in phonological rules.

By letting the more abstract symbol X″ (X double bar) stand for either NP or AP, X′ stand for N′ or A′, and X stand for N or A, we can write a general rule that covers both Noun Phrases and Adjective Phrases:[5]

$$X'' \rightarrow \text{Specifier } X'$$
$$X' \rightarrow X \text{ (Complement)}$$

where *Specifier* is Art for NPs and Deg for APs. *Complement* is either PP or S′. This rule "schema" stands for the six rules:

$$NP \rightarrow \text{Art } N'$$
$$AP \rightarrow \text{Deg } A'$$
$$N' \rightarrow N \text{ (PP)}$$
$$N' \rightarrow N \text{ (S')}$$
$$A' \rightarrow A \text{ (PP)}$$
$$A' \rightarrow A \text{ (S')}$$

The reason to conflate these six rules is that by so doing we reveal a generality about all grammars—a linguistic universal. Our goal is to reflect such knowledge of universals explicitly in the grammars that we write and in a theory of grammar.

The Lexicon

We next went to the School of Languages, where three Professors sat in Consultation upon improving that of their own Country.

The first Project was to shorten Discourse by cutting Polysyllables into one, and leaving out Verbs and Participles; because in Reality all things imaginable are but Nouns.

The other was a Scheme for entirely abolishing all Words whatsoever; and this was urged as a great Advantage in Point of Health as well as Brevity. For it is plain, that every Word we speak is in some degree a Diminution of our Lungs by Corrosion. . . .

Jonathan Swift, *Gulliver's Travels*

The learned professors of languages in Laputa proposed a scheme for abolishing all words, thinking it would be more convenient if "Men [were] to carry about them, such Things as were necessary to express the particular Business they are to discourse on." We doubt that this scheme could ever come to fruition, even in Laputa, not only because it would be difficult to carry around an unobservable *atom* or an abstract *loyalty*, but because our thoughts are expressed by sentences that have structure and cannot be represented by things pulled from a sack.

---

[5]Verb Phrases pattern similarly insofar as Complement goes:

He sent *for his three fiddlers.* (PP)
He believes that *the patient recovered.* (S)

Speakers of any language know thousands of words. They know how to pronounce them in all contexts, they know their meaning (see Chapter 6), and they know how to combine them in Phrases or Sentences, which means that they know their *syntactic category* (or *word class,* or "part of speech"). All of this knowledge is contained in a component of the grammar called **the Lexicon.**

The Lexicon contains all the words and morphemes in our vocabulary and can be thought of as our "mental dictionary." Together with the Phrase Structure Rules, the Lexicon provides the information needed for complete, well-formed constituent structure trees. The Phrase Structure Rules account for the entire tree except for the words at the bottom. The words in the tree belong to the same syntactic categories as the label of the nodes immediately above them. Through *lexical insertion,* words of the specified category are chosen from the Lexicon and put into the tree. Only words that are specified as verbs in the Lexicon are inserted under a node labeled *verb,* and so on. Words such as *fish,* which belong to two or more categories, have separate entries in the Lexicon.

Subcategorization

The Lexicon contains more syntactic information than simply the syntactic category of each word. If it did not, speakers of English would be unable to make the following grammatical distinctions:

> *John found.
> *John found in the house.
> John found the ball.

In the Lexicon, the Verb *find,* in addition to being specified as a verb, is specified as being a **transitive** verb. A transitive verb must be followed by a Noun Phrase, its "direct object." This additional specification is called **subcategorization.**

Most words in the Lexicon are subcategorized for certain contexts. Subcategorization accounts for the ungrammaticality of:

> (19a) *John put the meat.
> (19b) *The teachers identified that the students were late.
> (19c) *Suzanne slept the baby.

The Verb *put* in 19a is subcategorized to occur with *both* a Noun Phrase and a Prepositional Phrase, as in *John put the meat **in the refrigerator**.* 19b is ungrammatical because *identify* is not subcategorized for an embedded sentence, but only for a Noun Phrase: *They identified **the students**. Sleep* is subcategorized as an **intransitive verb,** so it cannot take an object, which is why 19c is ungrammatical.

Other categories besides the Verb are subcategorized. For example, within the AP, the Adjective *fond* is subcategorized for a PP, but not for an S (20ab), whereas *hopeful* is subcategorized for an S, but not a PP (20cd):

(20) (a) Robert is fond of his children.
     (b) *Robert is fond that his children love animals.
     (c) *Robert is hopeful of his children.
     (d) Robert is hopeful that his children will write.

Nouns are also subcategorized, so within the NP, a Noun such as *belief* may be followed by a PP or an S:

    their belief in a supreme being
    their belief that a supreme being exists

Knowledge about subcategorization is accounted for in the Lexicon as follows:

A Fragment of the Lexicon	Comment
put, V, ___ NP PP	*put* is a Verb and must be followed by both an NP and a PP within the Verb Phrase
identify, V, ___ NP	*identify* is a Verb and must be followed by an NP within the Verb Phrase
sleep, V, ___	*sleep* is a Verb and must not be followed by any category within the Verb Phrase
fond, Adj, ___ PP	*fond* is an Adjective and must be followed by a PP within the Adjective Phrase
hopeful, Adj, ___ S	*hopeful* is an Adjective and must be followed by an S within the Adjective Phrase
belief, N, ___ PP, ___ S	*belief* is a Noun and may be followed by either a PP or an S within the Noun Phrase

Subcategorization takes place between the **head** of a phrase—the Noun in a Noun Phrase, the Adjective in an Adjective Phrase, and so on—and the other categories that may occur in the phrase. In general, if X'' is a phrase, X is its head and is subcategorized as to what its complement may be. This generalization supports the ''X-bar'' theory discussed above, which makes the important claim that all phrasal categories share certain basic properties.

More Co-occurrence Restrictions

Subcategorization is a special kind of **co-occurrence restriction** that is syntactically based. There are other co-occurrence restrictions that are somewhat different from the ones we have been discussing. Consider

    *The ball found the boy.
    *The rock cried.
    *Lunch ate John.

According to one theory of grammar, these sentences are semantically deviant. The semantic rules of the language, many of which will be discussed in the next chapter, will indicate the anomaly of such sentences. These **selectional restrictions** state, for example, that the Verb *cry* must co-occur with an "animate" subject.

Even though such sentences are **semantically anomalous,** they are syntactically well-formed and can be represented by constituent structure trees similar to the ones that underlie the normal sentences:

> The boy found the house.
> The child cried.
> John ate lunch.

Some of the poetry of E. E. Cummings and others illustrates that sentences in a language may be syntactically well-formed but semantically deviant. The Noun Phrase *the six subjunctive crumbs* from one of Cummings' poems can be diagramed thus:

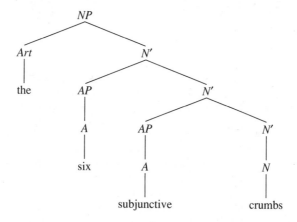

In this way we might diagram the more meaningful NP *the six subjunctive sentences;* but since *subjunctive* normally refers to a grammatical concept, and *crumbs* never does (unless we speak metaphorically of "sentence crumbs"), the result is semantic deviance, or oddness, or anomaly.

Nonsense poetry such as Carroll's "Jabberwocky" also shows that phrases and sentences can be syntactically well-formed, yet semantically uninterpretable, because the words belong to no lexicon and have no "agreed-on" meaning, even though they "look like" words—that is, they are *possible* words. A final example is the poem "Uffia," by Harriet R. White:

> When sporgles spanned the floreate mead
> And cogwogs gleet upon the lea,
> Uffia gopped to meet her love
> Who smeeged upon the equat sea.

The Infinitude of Language

So, naturalists observe, a flea
Hath smaller fleas that on him prey;
And these have smaller fleas still to bite 'em,
And so proceed ad infinitum.

Jonathan Swift, "On Poetry. A Rhapsody"

PEANUTS   **Charles Schulz**

© 1986 United Feature Syndicate, Inc.

There is no longest sentence in any language, because speakers can lengthen any sentence by various means, such as adding an adjective. Even children know how to produce and understand very long sentences, and know how to make them even longer, as illustrated by the children's rhyme about the house that Jack built.

> This is the farmer sowing the corn,
> that kept the cock that crowed in the morn,
> that waked the priest all shaven and shorn,
> that married the man all tattered and torn,
> that kissed the maiden all forlorn,
> that milked the cow with the crumpled horn,
> that tossed the dog,
> that worried the cat,
> that killed the rat,
> that ate the malt,
> that lay in the house that Jack built.

This rhyme begins with the line *This is the house that Jack built,* continues by lengthening it to *This is the malt that lay in the house that Jack built,* and so on.

You can add any of the following phrases to the beginning of the rhyme and still have a grammatical, even longer, sentence:

> I think that . . .
> What is the name of the unicorn that noticed that . . .
> Ask someone if . . .
> Do you know whether . . .

What is it about sentence structure and syntactic rules that allows a speaker to make any sentence longer? Suppose we start with the sentence *The happy child laughed,* which has the following constituent structure:

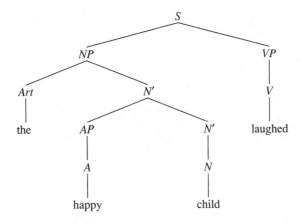

To form this sentence the rule

N′ → AP N′

was applied once. To form *The tall, happy child laughed,* the rule is applied twice, giving this constituent structure:

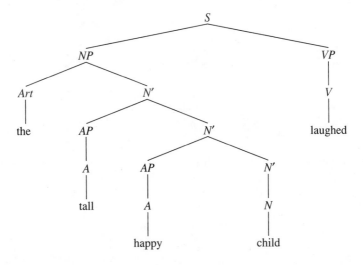

Because it is a *recursive* rule—the category on the left of the arrow is repeated on the right—it can be applied repeatedly to its own "output," and it is this property that captures the ability to add "one more adjective."

A somewhat more complicated example is suggested in the "B.C." cartoon.

B.C.   **Johnny Hart**

By permission of Johnny Hart and North America Syndicate, Inc.

The sentence in the final box consists of five sentences combined together as shown:[6]

> *You mean   you didn't know   (that) I knew   she didn't know   you knew that?*

To see what the constituent structure of the "B.C." cartoon sentence must look like, let us first examine a similar but simpler case. Consider *You mean that you knew that I knew:*[7]

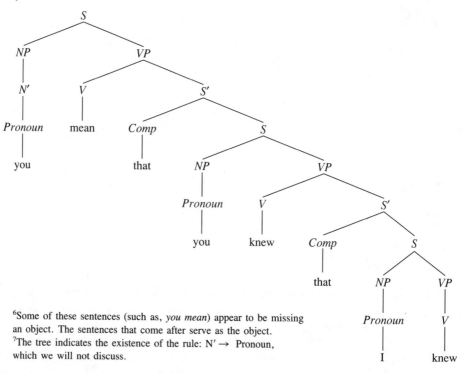

[6]Some of these sentences (such as, *you mean*) appear to be missing an object. The sentences that come after serve as the object.
[7]The tree indicates the existence of the rule: N′ → Pronoun, which we will not discuss.

In this tree the final sentence *I knew* is in the higher sentence *you knew* . . . , which itself is in the highest sentence *You mean*. . . . The lower sentences are **embedded** in the higher ones.

Three rules allow the S node to repeat indefinitely:

$$S \rightarrow NP\ VP$$
$$VP \rightarrow V\ S'$$
$$S' \rightarrow Comp\ S$$

In this set of rules the S node occurs on the left side of the arrow in one rule, and through the VP and the S', eventually appears on the right side of another rule. Such a *set* of rules is *recursive* and allows the same syntactic category to appear repeatedly in a constituent structure tree. In the above tree the set of rules has been applied twice, resulting in two occurrences of an embedded S. Recursive rules represent our linguistic ability to construct and understand longer and longer complex sentences that comply with the rules of grammar.

Recursion is common in all languages. It allows speakers to "recycle" syntactic constituents within the same sentence. With a small number of rules and syntactic categories, an infinite set of sentences can be generated.

Recursive rules give a speaker access to infinitely many sentences, but no speaker utters infinitely many, or hears infinitely many, in a lifetime; nor is any sentence of infinite length, although there is no upper limit on sentence length. Nevertheless the ability to produce longer and longer sentences allows them to be more and more varied, hence as descriptive and creative as the speaker wishes.

The Function of Constituents

Conjunction junction, what's your function?
Song on the children's TV program *The Electric Company*

Knowledge of a language permits us to distinguish between the *structural* and *logical* functional relations of constituents, also called the **grammatical relations.** This distinction is illustrated in:

(21) (a) The dog bit the man.
    (b) The man was bitten by the dog.
    (c) John loved Mary.
    (d) It was Mary John loved.

In both 21a and 21b the **logical subject**—the doer of the action—is the dog. Only in 21a is *the dog* the **structural subject** (the first NP under the S node). Similarly the **logical object** in both sentences is *the man,* but only in 21a is *the man* the **structural object** or direct object (the first NP under the VP node). In 21b *the man* is the *logical object,* but the *structural subject.*

In both 21c and 21d *John* is the logical subject and *Mary* is the logical object, but in 21d the **focus** is different. By changing the sentence around so that *Mary* comes first, our attention is focused on who it was that John loved. This version can also be used for contrastive purposes, as in

It was Mary John loved, not Susan.

Contrast or emphasis can also be reflected phonologically by stressing the word without a change in word order:

John loved MARY, not Susan.

Many sentences include a **topic** (what is being talked about) and a **comment** (what is being said about the topic). The topic often corresponds to the *structural* subject of a sentence. In 21a the topic is *the dog* and the comment is *bit the man,* whereas in 21b the topic is *the man* and the comment is *was bitten by the dog.* Thus two sentences may have the same logical relationships, but differ in topic and comment.

The topic of a sentence is also called the **old information,** because it represents something already under discussion. The comment, on the other hand, is **new information,** because it represents information added to the discourse. In many languages there is a tendency to state old information at the beginning of the sentence, followed by the new information; in English the structural subject occurs first in the sentence.

Some languages have grammatical morphemes or particles that explicitly mark the topic of the sentence. In Japanese this particle is *wa,* and nouns followed by *wa* in Japanese generally occur at the beginning of the sentence.

In English the structural subject and the topic are often the same, but it is possible for them to be different. In such sentences, the topic is stated first, followed by a complete sentence containing its own subject:

As for pets, sheepdogs are the best.

In the above sentence, the topic is ''pets'' and the subject is ''sheepdogs.'' Sentences like this one are not ''basic'' sentences of English, and are infrequent in formal, written English. In languages such as Mandarin Chinese, however, which have been described as ''topic prominent,''[8] such sentential forms are considered basic, as the following sentence illustrates.

Nèike shù yèzi   dà
that   tree leaves big
''As for that tree, the leaves are big.''

Knowledge of language includes knowing the grammatical relations of a sen-

---

[8]For more information, see S. A. Thompson and C. N. Li, 1975. ''Subject and Topic: A New Typology of Language.'' In *Subject and Topic.* C. N. Li, ed. Academic Press. New York.

tence, knowing ways of contrasting and focusing different parts of a sentence, and knowing the topic and comment of a sentence.

Types of Languages

All the Oriental nations jam tongue and words together in the throat, like the Hebrews and Syrians. All the Mediterranean peoples push their enunciation forward to the palate, like the Greeks and the Asians. All the Occidentals break their words on the teeth, like the Italians and Spaniards. . . .

Isadore of Seville, 7th century c.e.

There are many ways to classify languages. One way, to be discussed in Chapter 8, is according to the language "family." This method would be like classifying people according to whether they were Smiths, Johnsons, Fromkins, or Rodmans. Another way of classifying languages is by certain linguistic traits, regardless of family. With people, this method would be like classifying them according to height and weight, or hair and eye color.

Every language has sentences that include a Subject (S),[9] an Object (O), and a Verb (V), although some sentences do not have all three elements. Languages have been classified according to the "basic" or **unmarked** order in which these constituents occur in the language.

There are six possible orders—SOV (Subject, Object, Verb), SVO, VSO, VOS, OVS, OSV—permitting six possible language types. Here are examples of some of the languages in these classes:[10]

> SVO: English, French, Swahili, Hausa, Thai
> VSO: Tagalog, Irish, (Classical) Arabic, (Biblical) Hebrew
> SOV: Turkish, Japanese, Persian, Georgian, Eskimo
> OVS: Apalai (Brazil), Barasano (Colombia), Panare (Venezuela)
> OSV: Apurina and Xavante (Brazil)
> VOS: Cakchiquel (Guatemala), Coeur d'Alene (Idaho), Huave (Oaxaca, Mexico)

The most frequent word orders in languages are SVO, VSO, and SOV. The "basic" sentences in such languages may be illustrated as follows:

> SVO English: The cat ate the rat.
> VSO Tagalog: Sumagot siya sa propesor
>   answered he   the professor
>   "He answered the professor."
> SOV Turkish: Romalɨlar barbarlarɨ yendiler
>   Romans   barbarians defeated
>   "The Romans defeated the Barbarians."

[9]In this section *only,* S will abbreviate Subject rather than Sentence.
[10]The examples of VOS, OVS, and OSV languages are from G. K. Pullum, 1981. "Languages with Object Before Subject: A Comment and a Catalogue." *Linguistics* 19: 147–155.

The order of other sentence constituents in a language is most frequently correlated with the language type. If a language is of a type in which the Verb precedes the Object—a "VO" language, which includes SVO, VSO, or VOS—then the Auxiliary Verb tends to precede the Verb, Adverbs tend to follow the Verb, and Prepositions tend to precede the Noun, among other such ordering relationships. English exhibits all these tendencies.

In "OV" languages, most of which are SOV, the opposite tendency occurs: Auxiliary Verbs tend to follow the Verb, Adverbs tend to precede the Verb, and there are "Postpositions," which are "Prepositions" that follow the noun. Japanese, an SOV language, has Postpositions, as we saw above. Also, in Japanese, the Auxiliary Verb follows the Verb, as illustrated by the following sentence:

> Akiko   wa   sakana   o   tabete   iru
> Akiko   *topic*   fish   *object* eating   is
>   *marker*   *marker*
> "Akiko is eating fish."

It must be emphasized that the correlations between language type and the word order of various constituents in sentences are "tendencies," not inviolable rules, and different languages follow them to a greater or lesser degree.

The knowledge that speakers of the various languages have about word order is revealed in the particular Phrase Structure Rules of the language. In English, an SVO language, the V precedes its NP Object: VP → V NP. In Turkish or Japanese, SOV languages, the NP Object precedes the Verb in the corresponding Phrase Structure Rule of that language. Similarly, the rule PP → P NP occurs in SVO languages, whereas the rule PP → NP P is the correlate occurring in SOV languages.

Just because a language is, say, an SVO language does not mean that SVO is the only possible word order. We find sentences such as *Mary, I believe* (OSV) in English, but, as discussed in the previous section, they are not basic sentences, and they have the purpose of contrasting or putting into focus some part of the sentence.

When we look at the languages of the world and attempt to classify them, we find both diversity—the differing orders of Subject, Object, and Verb—and fundamental commonalities: all languages have Verbs; all languages have NPs that may function as Subjects and Objects; and all languages have rules that "linearize" these constituents into some basic order. No language randomly orders its constituents.

Transformational Rules

Method consists entirely in properly ordering and arranging the things to which we should pay attention.

Descartes, *Oeuvres, Vol. X*

THE WIZARD OF ID   **Brant Parker and Johnny Hart**

By permission of Johnny Hart and North America Syndicate, Inc.

The Phrase Structure Rules and the Lexicon characterize an infinite set of sentences of varying constituent structure. Nevertheless there still remain many types of common English sentences that they do not account for.

We have not considered sentences with "verbs" such as *is* in *The boy is sleeping* or *will* in *The boy will sleep.* This class of **Auxiliary Verbs** or **Auxiliary (Aux)** includes *to be* as well as *will, can, would, could,* and several others. They occur in such structures as this one:

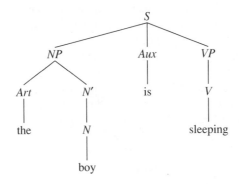

Another rule for expanding the S node accounts for such structures:

S → NP Aux VP

but this rule will not account for the following sentences:

Is the boy sleeping?
Can the boy sleep?
Will the boy sleep?

The Auxiliary Verb is the first word in these sentences, rather than in its "normal" position. One analysis accounts for these sentences by another Phrase Structure Rule, say S → Aux NP VP, or something similar.

Another analysis proposes that the interrogative (question) sentences are formed by the **movement** of the Auxiliary Verb to the front of the sentence. This operation is applied to an already formed constituent structure tree, to give another constituent structure tree that differs from the first in that some element has been relocated. Such operations are called **Transformations** or **Transformational Rules.**

A sentence like *The boy is sleeping* is the direct result of applying the Phrase Structure Rules; but a sentence like *Is the boy sleeping?* is the result of a two-step process. First the Phrase Structure Rules apply to give the "normal" word order: *The boy is sleeping*. Then the movement transformation applies, giving *Is the boy sleeping?*

Consider another interrogative sentence: *What will the boy find?* We observed earlier that *find* is a transitive verb, which must therefore be followed by an NP; yet here is a grammatical sentence in which it is not followed by an NP. It seems that we need a different subcategorization rule for *find* in sentences beginning with *what*. That is, *find* cannot be followed by an NP in questions beginning with *what*, whereas in other sentences the NP must be present. (Notice the ungrammaticality of *What will the boy find the ball?* and *Will the boy find?*)

The knowledge speakers have about words that is captured by subcategorization rules does not change from sentence type to sentence type, any more than the meaning of a word changes depending on whether it occurs in a statement or a question. We require an analysis in which *find* has one subcategorization rule that covers all types of sentences.

Just as we use Phrase Structure Rules to generate *The boy is sleeping* and a Movement Transformation to prepose the Auxiliary for *Is the boy sleeping?*, we will use Phrase Structure Rules to generate *The boy will find what?*,[11] and further apply the Movement Transformation to the "Wh-word" to give *What will the boy find?*[12]

By proposing that *The boy will find what?* and *What will the boy find?* come from applying the same Phrase Structure Rules, we establish the general fact that *find* is transitive (*what* is the NP logical object) and requires one subcategorization rule. The Transformation is responsible for changing the position of *what* in the second sentence.

This analysis also explains speakers' knowledge that *what* in *What will the boy find?* is the logical object of *find*. Logical subject and logical object are determined by the Phrase Structure Rules and are not affected by the Transformational Rules.

Such an analysis will, with appropriate modification, account for speakers' ability to form other kinds of questions, such as:

> Which book will the boy read?
> Who is sleeping?
> In what park have you seen the man with the telescope?
> The girl wondered what the boy had found.[13]

---

[11]Although unusual in written form, this string is a grammatical sentence when spoken as an "echo" question or as an expression of surprise. When spoken, *what* has rising intonation ending with high pitch.
[12]The movement transformation is also applied to the Auxiliary Verb in the derivation of this sentence: notice the position of *will* in the sentence. "Wh-words" are *what, who, which, where*, and so on.
[13]This sentence is a so-called indirect question. Notice the position of *what*.

A Movement Rule

The Tranformational Rules that move the Auxiliary Verb and the Wh-word are specific examples of a general transformation rule ''move any constituent,'' or **Move α (Move Alpha).** For example, this rule may move constituents to the right, called **postposing,** or to the left, called **preposing.**

As a postposing rule, the Move α Transformation accounts for the following pair of synonymous sentences:

> The people elected the man who spent the most money senator.
> The people elected senator the man who spent the most money.

Here, the NP *the man who spent the most money* is postposed around the word *senator,* to the end of the sentence.

As a preposing rule, Move α preposes the adjective *small* in accounting for:

> Though the girl was small, she could lift my sheepdog.
> Small though the girl was, she could lift my sheepdog.

Transformations that *delete* rather than *move* elements in constituent structure trees have also been proposed. In the ''B.C.'' cartoon from the ''Infinitude'' section above, only one embedded S is preceded by the complementizer *that*:[14]

> You mean   you didn't know   that I knew   she didn't know   you knew that.

All the embedded Sentences come from the Phrase Structure Rules VP $\rightarrow$ V S' and S' $\rightarrow$ Comp S, so after the Phrase Structure Rules have applied, every embedded sentence is preceded by a complementizer:

> You mean *that* you didn't know *that* I knew *that* she didn't know *that* you knew that.

Under certain circumstances, however, the Comp node may be deleted by a ''Comp Deletion'' Transformation. The transformation applied three times in this case.

Structure Dependence and Conditions

Just as Phrase Structure Rules generate *classes* of constituent structure trees, Transformations also apply to *classes* of trees. Any structure with an Aux or a Wh-word may have that word moved to the front of the sentence by Move α. Similarly, any structure with a Comp node is subject to the Comp Deletion Transformation. Transformations are **structure-dependent;** they do not apply because of particular words or meanings, but because of particular structures that contain specific syntactic categories.

Because transformations are *structure-dependent,* they may apply to *any* con-

---

[14]The final *that* is not a complementizer, but a ''demonstrative pronoun.''

stituent structure tree of the "appropriate" structure. Consider Move α as applied to Wh-words. It applies to any tree with a Wh-word. Thus Move α applies to

> The boy believes who to be arriving tonight?
> The members think that the president is doing what?

to produce

> Who does the boy believe to be arriving tonight?
> What do the members think that the president is doing?

In some cases "correctly" applying Move α gives ungrammatical results. Consider these two sentences, which the Phrase Structure Rules could generate:

> The president will deny the rumor that the Pentagon did what?
> Emily is visiting the lady who owns which house?

Move α is applicable, and if it applies we get the following:

> *What will the president deny the rumor that the Pentagon did?
> *Which house is Emily visiting the lady who owns?

As one linguist once put it, "Word hash!" But Move α applied legally, so something is wrong.

The problem is solved by general or universal conditions on Move α that prevent it from applying in certain cases. One such condition, the "Subjacency Condition," would prevent Move α from deriving the ungrammatical examples given above. In general, this condition states that there are restrictions on what can be moved where.

Other conditions on transformations have been proposed, such as **recoverability.** That means that enough information must be left in the tree after the transformation has applied to indicate what was deleted or moved. This condition constrains the power of transformations and explains why transformations do not change logical relations.

If this topic seems incredibly complex to you, it is! Language *is* incredibly complex, and in an introductory text we are unable to present the details and specific arguments in support of many of these concepts. (Works cited in the References section are a source of further information.) Despite the syntactic complexities of English or any language, children learn them at a very early age.

The model of grammar we have presented contains a relatively small number of Phrase Structure Rules, a large Lexicon with detailed information representing what speakers know about their vocabulary, and a few very general Transformational Rules constrained by conditions that reflect language universals. Evidence for all of these components of grammar is found in all languages of the world. This fact points up the *empirical* nature of linguistic studies. All the rules and types of rules we are discussing result from a careful investigation of linguistic phenomena in a large number of languages.

Summary

Speakers of a language recognize the grammatical sentences of their language and know how the words and morphemes in a grammatical sentence must be arranged. All speakers are capable of producing and understanding an unlimited number of new sentences never before spoken or heard. They also recognize ambiguities, know when different sentences are paraphrases, and correctly perceive the grammatical relations in a sentence. All this knowledge, and much more, is accounted for in the grammar by the **rules of syntax.**

Sentences have structure that can be represented by **constituent structure trees** whose nodes are labeled with **syntactic category** names. Such a representation reveals three kinds of structural information about sentences:

1.   Linear order of words
2.   Grouping of words into structural constituents
3.   The syntactic category of each structural constituent

Linguists often describe sentences in terms of constituent structure trees.

The **Lexicon** represents the knowledge speakers have about the vocabulary of their language, including the meaning, syntactic category, and phonology of each word and morpheme. Additionally, the Lexicon contains **subcategorization** restrictions, such as the fact that a **transitive** Verb must be followed by a Noun Phrase, but an **intransitive** Verb must not.

A grammar is a formally stated, explicit characterization of linguistic knowledge. **Phrase Structure Rules** characterize the basic or underlying constituent structure trees of the language, including such facts as that a Noun Phrase may be an Article followed by a Noun, but never a Noun followed by an Article (in English). The **X-bar** convention, in which Phrase Structure Rules are expressed using X'', X', and X, reveals general facts about syntactic categories, such as that Noun Phrases always contain Nouns, Adjective Phrases always contain Adjectives, and so on.

Phrase Structure Rules may be **recursive.** A recursive rule or set of rules repeats on the right side of the arrow a category that appears on the left side. Recursive rules allow the same syntactic category to appear repeatedly in a constituent structure tree, which reflects speakers' ability to produce sentences without length limitations.

The grammar includes the **function** of constituents in phrases and sentences. **Grammatical relations** are one such function, indicating the **logical subject, structural subject, logical object,** and **structural object** of phrases and sentences. For example, in an **active** sentence such as *John kissed Mary, John* functions as both the logical subject and the structural subject, whereas *Mary* functions as the logical and structural object of *kissed.* In the **passive** *Mary was kissed by John, John* is still the logical subject, and *Mary* is still the logical object of *kiss,* but *Mary* has replaced *John* as the structural subject. Other functions discussed in the text are **focus, topic/comment,** and **old versus new information.**

Not all linguistic knowledge is revealed by the Phrase Structure Rules and the Lexicon. In related pairs of sentences, such as a statement and its corresponding yes-no question, an operation that moves the **Auxiliary Verb** to the front of the sentence appears to be needed. Such an operation is called a **Transformational Rule.** Transformations operate on fully specified constituent structure trees to give new trees. Transformations are **structure-dependent:** they apply to trees with appropriate structures, and they are not dependent on the occurrence of particular words or meanings.

Move α is a general transformation that reorders nodes in trees. There may be other types of Transformational Rules, such as **deletion** transformations. Because transformations are so general, they can ''overapply'' to produce ungrammatical results. There are **conditions on transformations** that limit the applicability of transformations to those cases where grammatical results are obtained.

The syntax of human language is sufficiently complex to require Phrase Structure Rules, a Lexicon, Transformational Rules, and conditions on transformations to account for speakers' knowledge.

References

Akmajian, A., R. A. Demers, and R. M. Harnish. 1979. *Linguistics: An Introduction to Language and Communication*. 2d ed. M.I.T. Press. Cambridge, Mass.

Chomsky, Noam. 1957. *Syntactic Structures*. Mouton. The Hague.

Chomsky, Noam. 1965. *Aspects of the Theory of Syntax*. M.I.T. Press. Cambridge, Mass.

Chomsky, Noam. 1972. *Language and Mind*. Rev. ed. Harcourt Brace Jovanovich. New York.

Chomsky, Noam. 1982. *Some Concepts and Consequences of the Theory of Government and Binding*. M.I.T. Press. Cambridge, Mass.

Gazdar, Gerald, E. Klein, G. Pullum, and I. Sag. 1985. *Generalized Phrase Structure Grammar*. Harvard University Press. Cambridge, Mass.

Newmeyer, Frederick J. 1981. *Linguistic Theory in America: The First Quarter Century of Transformational-Generative Grammar*. Academic Press. New York.

Sells, Peter. 1985. *Lectures on Contemporary Syntactic Theories: An Introduction to Government-Binding Theory, Generalized Phrase Structure Grammar, and Lexical-Functional Grammar*. Center for the Study of Language and Information. Ventura Hall. Stanford University. Stanford, Calif. 94305.

Stockwell, R. P. 1977. *Foundations of Syntactic Theory*. Prentice-Hall. Englewood Cliffs, N.J.

Stockwell, R. P., M. Bean, and D. Elliot. 1977. *Workbook for Foundations of Syntactic Theory*. Prentice-Hall. Englewood Cliffs, N.J.

Van Riemsdijk, Henk, and E. Williams. 1986. *Introduction to the Theory of Grammar*. M.I.T. Press. Cambridge, Mass.

Exercises

1. Besides distinguishing grammatical from ungrammatical strings, the rules of syntax account for other kinds of linguistic knowledge, such as

   a. when a sentence is structurally ambiguous.
   b. when two sentences of different structure mean the same thing.
   c. what the grammatical relations are in sentences.

   In each case a–c, draw on your own linguistic knowledge of English to provide an example different than the ones in the chapter, and explain why your example illustrates the point. If you know a language other than English, provide examples in that language, if possible.

   a. Structural ambiguity:
   b. Paraphrases:
   c. Grammatical relations:

2. Consider the following sentences:

   a. I hate war.
   b. You know that I hate war.
   c. He knows that you know that I hate war.

      A. Write another sentence that includes sentence *c*.
      B. What does this set of sentences reveal about the nature of language?
      C. How is this characteristic of human language related to the difference between linguistic competence and performance? (Hint: Review these concepts in Chapter 1.)

3. Paraphrase each of the following sentences in two different ways to show that you understand the ambiguity involved:

   > Example: Smoking grass can be nauseating.
   > i. Putting grass in a pipe and smoking it can make you sick.
   > ii. Fumes from smoldering grass can make you sick.

   a. Dick finally decided on the boat.

      i.
      ii.

   b. The professor's appointment was shocking.

      i.
      ii.

   c. Old men and women are hard to live with.

      i.
      ii.

   d.   That sheepdog is too hairy to eat.

     i.

     ii.

   e.   Could this be the invisible man's hair tonic?
     i.
     ii.

   f.   The governor is a dirty street fighter.

     i.

     ii.

   g.   I cannot recommend him too highly.

     i.

     ii.

   h.   Terry loves his wife and so do I.

     i.

     ii.

   i.   They said she would go yesterday.

     i.

     ii.

   j.   How much do you want to cut the grass? (Hint: Look at the following cartoon.)

HI & LOIS

Reprinted with special permission of King Features Syndicate, Inc.

     i.

     ii.

4.   Consider the trees underlying the ambiguous sentence

    The boy saw the man with the telescope.

given at the end of the section on Sentence Structure (p. 173). Paraphrase each meaning and indicate which tree goes with which meaning.

Paraphrase of meaning of Tree A:

Paraphrase of meaning of Tree B:

5. In spaces a–n write out the fourteen phrase structure rules that the following seven rules abbreviate. (They make up the rules in 18 on p. 181.)

(i) $S \rightarrow NP\ VP$

(ii) $S' \rightarrow Comp\ S$

(iii) $NP \rightarrow Art\ N'$

(iv) $N' \rightarrow \left\{ \begin{array}{l} AP\ N' \\ N\ (PP) \end{array} \right\}$

(v) $VP \rightarrow V \left\{ \begin{array}{l} (NP)\ (PP) \\ \quad S' \end{array} \right\}$

(vi) $AP \rightarrow (Deg)\ A$

(vii) $PP \rightarrow P\ NP$

a.   b.

c.   d.

e.   f.

g.   h.

i.   j.

k.   l.

m.   n.

6. In all languages, sentences can occur within sentences. For example, in exercise 2, sentence *b* contains sentence *a*, and sentence *c* contains sentence *b*. Put another way, sentence *a* is *embedded* in sentence *b*, and sentence *b* is embedded in sentence *c*. Sometimes embedded sentences appear slightly changed from their "normal" form, but you should be able to recognize and underline the embedded sentences in the sentences below. Underline in the non-English sentences, when given, not in the translations. (The first one is done as an example):

a. Yesterday I noticed <u>my accountant repairing the toilet and my plumber computing my taxes</u>.

b. Becky said that Jake would play the piano.

c. I deplore the fact that bats have wings.

d. That Guinevere loves Lorian is known to all my friends.

e. Who promised the teacher that Maxine wouldn't be absent?

f. It's ridiculous that he washes his own Rolls-Royce.

g. The woman asked for the waiter to bring a glass of ice water.

h. The person who answers this question will win $100.

    i.   The idea of Romeo marrying a 13-year-old is upsetting.

    j.   I gave my hat to the nurse who helped me cut my hair.

    k.   For your children to spend all your royalty payments on recreational drugs is a shame.

    l.   Give this fork to the person I'm getting the pie for.

    m.   khǎw chŷa   wǎa   khruu maa. (Thai)

        He   believe *complementizer* teacher come

        He believes the teacher is coming.

    n.   Je me demande quand il partira. (French)

        I me ask   when he will leave

        I wonder when he'll leave.

    o.   Jan zei dat Piet dit boek niet heeft gelezen. (Dutch)

        Jan said that Piet this book not has   read

        Jan said that Piet has not read this book.

7. Following the patterns of the various tree examples in the text, expecially in the two sections on phrase structure rules, draw constituent structure trees for the following sentences:

    a.   The puppy found the child.
    b.   A frightened passenger landed the crippled airplane.
    c.   The house on the hill collapsed in the wind.
    d.   The ice melted.
    e.   The hot sun melted the ice.
    f.   A quaint old ivy-covered house appeared.
    g.   The old tree swayed in the wind.
    h.   The children put the toy in the box.
    i.   The reporter realized that the senator lied.

8. Use rule 18 on page 181 to create five constituent structure trees of sentences of 6, 7, 8, 9, and 10 words long not given in the chapter. Use your own "mental lexicon" to fill in the bottom of the tree.

9. We stated that the rules of syntax specify all and only the grammatical sentences of the language. Why is it important to say "only"? What would be wrong with a grammar that specified as grammatical sentences all of the truly grammatical ones plus a few that were not grammatical?

10. Here is a set of made-up Phrase Structure Rules. The "initial" symbol is still

S, and the "terminal symbols" (the ones that do not appear to the left of an arrow) are actual words:

    (i) S → A B C
    (ii) A → *the*
    (iii) B → *children*
    (iv) C → *ran*
    (v) C → C *and* D
    (vi) D → *ran and* D
    (vii) D → *ran*

  a. Give three constituent structure trees that these rules characterize.
  b. How many constituent structure trees could these rules characterize? (Hint: Look for recursive rules.)

11. Because languages have recursive properties, there is no limit to the potential length of sentences, and the set of sentences of any language is infinite. Give two examples (different from the ones in the text) of:

  a. Adjective recursion
  b. Noun recursion
  c. Noun Phrase recursion
  d. Verb Phrase recursion
  e. Sentence recursion

In one example the relevant category should appear twice in the constituent structure, and in the other example at least three times. Diagram one of the constituent structure trees in each case, being careful to illustrate the recursion.

12. State at least three differences between English and the following languages, using just the sentence(s) given. Ignore lexical differences—that is, the different vocabulary. Then give the language *type:* SVO, SOV, and so on. Here is an example:

    Thai: dèg   khon   níi   kamlang   kin
            boy *classifier* this *progressive* eat
            "This boy is eating."

            măa   tua   nán   kin   khâaw
            dog *classifier* that eat rice
            "That dog ate rice."

Three differences are: (1) Thai has "classifiers." They have no English equivalent. (2) The demonstratives "this" and "that" follow the noun in Thai, but precede the noun in English. (3) The "progressive" is expressed by a separate word in Thai. The verb does not change form. In English, the progressive is indicated by the presence of the verb *to be* and the adding of *-ing* to the verb. Thai is an SVO language.

a. French:

    cet   homme   intelligent   arrivera
    this   man   intelligent   will arrive
    "This intelligent man will arrive."

    ces   hommes   intelligents   arriveront
    these men   intelligent   will arrive
    "These intelligent men will arrive."

b. Japanese:

    watashi ga   sakana o   tabete   iru
    I   *subject* fish   *object*   eat (*ing*) am
          marker   *marker*
    "I am eating fish." ·

c. Swahili:

    mtoto   alivunja kikombe
    m-   toto   a-   li-   vunja ki-   kombe
    class   child   he   *past* break *class*   cup
    marker   *marker*
    "The child broke the cup."

    watoto   wanavunja   vikombe
    wa-   toto   wa- na-   vunja vi-   kombe
    class   child they *present* break *class*   cup
    marker   *marker*
    "The children break the cups."

d. Korean:

    kɨ   sonyɔn-nɨn   wɨyu-lɨl   masi-ass-ta
    kɨ   sonyɔn- nɨn   wɨyu- lɨl   masi- ass- ta
    the boy   *subject* milk *object* drink *past* *assertion*
             marker   *marker*
    "The boy drank milk."

    kɨ-nɨn muɔs-lɨl mɔk-ass-nya
    kɨ   nɨn   muɔs- lɨl   mɔk- ass- nya
    he   *subject* what *object* eat   *past* *question*
         marker   *marker*
    "What did he eat?"

e. Tagalog:

    nakita ni   Pedro   -ng   puno   na   ang
    saw   *article* Pedro *complementizer* full   already *topic*
                                                      marker

    "Pedro saw the bus was already full."

Semantics:
The Meanings
of Language

Language without meaning is meaningless.
Roman Jakobson

B.C.   **Johnny Hart**

By permission of Johnny Hart and North America Syndicate, Inc.

For thousands of years philosophers have been pondering the meaning of "meaning"; yet speakers of a language can understand what is said to them and can produce strings of words that convey meaning.

Learning a language includes learning the "agreed-upon" meanings of certain strings of sounds and learning how to combine these meaningful units into larger units that also convey meaning. We are not free to change the meanings of these words at will, for if we did we would be unable to communicate with anyone.

Humpty Dumpty, however, was unwilling to accept this fact when he said:

205

"There's glory for you!"

"I don't know what you mean by 'glory,'" Alice said.

Humpty Dumpty smiled contemptuously. "Of course you don't—till I tell you. I meant 'there's a nice knock-down argument for you!'"

"But 'glory' doesn't mean 'a nice knock-down argument,'" Alice objected.

"When *I* use a word," Humpty Dumpty said, in rather a scornful tone, "it means just what I choose it to mean—neither more nor less."

"The question is," said Alice, "whether you *can* make words mean so many different things."

Alice is quite right. You cannot make words mean what they do not mean. Of course, if you wish to redefine the meaning of each word as you use it, you are free to do so, but you would be making an artificial, clumsy use of language, and most people would not wait around long to talk to you. A new word may be created, but it enters the language with its sound–meaning relationship already determined.

Fortunately there are few Humpty Dumptys; all the speakers of a language share the basic vocabulary—the sounds and meanings of words. All speakers know how to combine words to produce phrase and sentence meaning. The study of the linguistic meaning of words, phrases, and sentences is called **semantics.**

Word Meanings

"My name is Alice . . ."

"It's a stupid name enough!" Humpty Dumpty interrupted impatiently. "What does it mean?"

"Must a name mean something?" Alice asked doubtfully.

"Of course it must," Humpty Dumpty said with a short laugh. "My name means the shape I am—and a good handsome shape it is, too. With a name like yours, you might be any shape, almost."

Lewis Carroll, *Through the Looking-Glass*

Not only do we know what the morphemes of our language are, we also know what they *mean*. Dictionaries are filled with words and their meanings. So is the head of every human being who speaks a language. You are a walking dictionary. You know the meaning of thousands of words. Your knowledge of their meanings permits you to use them appropriately in sentences and to understand them when heard, even though you probably seldom stop and ask yourself: "What does *boy* mean?" or "What does *walk* mean?" The meaning of words is part of linguistic knowledge and is therefore a part of the grammar. Your mental storehouse of information about words and morphemes is what we have been calling **the Lexicon.**

Semantic Properties

Words and morphemes have meanings. We shall talk about the meaning of words, even though words may be composed of several morphemes.

B.C.

Johnny Hart

By permission of Johnny Hart and North America Syndicate, Inc.

Suppose someone said:

> The assassin was stopped before he got to Mr. Thwacklehurst.

If the word *assassin* is in your mental dictionary, you know that it was some *person* who was prevented from *murdering* some *important person* named Thwacklehurst. Your knowledge of the meaning of *assassin* tells you that it was not an animal that tried to kill the man and that Thwacklehurst was not likely to be a little old man who owned a tobacco shop. In other words, your knowledge of the meaning of *assassin* includes knowing that the individual to whom that word refers is *human,* is a *murderer,* and is a killer of *important people.* These pieces of information, then, are some of the **semantic properties** of the word upon which speakers of the language agree. The meaning of all nouns, verbs, adjectives, and adverbs—the "content words"—and even some of the "function words" such as *with* or *over* can at least partially be specified by such properties.

The same semantic property may be part of the meaning of many different words. "Female" is a semantic property that helps to define

tigress	hen	actress	maiden
doe	mare	debutante	widow
ewe	vixen	girl	woman

The words in the last two columns are also distinguished by the semantic property "human," which is also found in

doctor	dean	professor	bachelor	parent	baby	child

The last two of these words are also specified as "young." That is, part of the meaning of the words *baby* and *child* is that they are "human" and "young." (We will continue to indicate words by using *italics* and semantic "properties" by using double quotation marks.)

The meanings of words have other properties. The word *father* has the properties "male" and "adult," as does *uncle* and *bachelor;* but *father* also has the property "parent," which distinguishes it from the other two words.

Mare, in addition to "female" and "animal," must also denote a property of "horseness." Words have general semantic properties such as "human" or "parent," as well as more specific properties that give the word its particular meaning.

The same semantic property may occur in words of different categories. "Female" is part of the meaning of the noun *mother,* of the verb *breast-feed,* and of the adjective *pregnant.* "Cause" is a verbal property of *darken, kill, uglify,* and so on.

darken	cause to become dark
kill	cause to die
uglify	cause to become ugly

Other semantic properties that help account for the meaning of verbs are shown in the following table:

Semantic Property	**Verbs Having It**
motion	bring, fall, plod, walk, run . . .
contact	hit, kiss, touch . . .
creation	build, imagine, make . . .
sense	see, hear, feel . . .

For the most part no two words have exactly the same meaning (but see the discussion of synonyms below). Additional semantic properties make for finer and finer distinctions in meaning. *Plod* is distinguished from *walk* by the property "slow," and *stalk* from *plod* by a property such as "purposeful."

The humor of the cartoon at the head of this section is that the verb "roll over" has a specific semantic property, something like "activity about the longest axis." The snake's attempt to roll about its shortest axis indicates trouble with semantic *properties.*

Semantic Features   Words may be in intersecting semantic classes. For example *woman* is in the class with the property "female"; *child* is in the class "young," and *girl* is in the intersecting class with the two properties "female" and "young."

Additionally, there are semantic relations between words, and certain semantic categories may imply others. For example, the property "human" implies "animate."

Such relationships can be expressed by **semantic features,** similar to phonetic features. In this case the lexical entries for words such as *father, girl,* and *mare* would have the following (incomplete) appearance:

woman	*father*	*girl*	*mare*	*stalk*
+female	+male	+female	+female	+motion
+human	+human	+human	−human	+slow
−young	+parent	+young	−young	+purposeful
. . .	. . .	. . .	+horseness	. . .
			. . .	

Intersecting classes share the same features, such as the class of human females, which are marked "plus" for the features *human* and *female*.

Additional facts, such as that "human" implies "animate," could be stated using **redundancy rules** on these features, for example:

$$[+\text{human}] \rightarrow [+\text{animate}]$$

This rule means that if *any* word contains the feature [+human], it "automatically" contains the feature [+animate]. Therefore the feature [+animate] need not be specifically mentioned in the lexical entry for *father* (or *girl, professor, child*); it can be inferred from the feature [+human] by the redundancy rule.

Some semantic redundancy rules reveal "negative" properties. For example, if something is "human" it is not "abstract"; an activity that is "slow" is not "fast." Thus we could state:

$$[+\text{human}] \rightarrow [-\text{abstract}]$$
$$[+\text{slow}] \rightarrow [-\text{fast}]$$

Meaning Postulates   We have a great deal of linguistic knowledge about words, their properties, and the relationships among them. Consider the following information about words that speakers of English share:

> If something is *metal,* it is a concrete object.
> If something *swims,* it is in a liquid.
> If something is *open,* it is not closed.

These statements are true due to the meaning of the italicized words. This lexical knowledge can be revealed through **meaning postulates,** which are formal rules, similar to semantic redundancy rules. For example,

$$(x) \text{ metal} \rightarrow (x) \text{ concrete}$$

is a meaning postulate that states that if anything is metal, it must be a concrete object. (Thus **metal idea* is semantically odd unless it is a metaphor, because *idea* is [−concrete].) Similarly,

$$(x) \text{ open} \rightarrow not (x) \text{ closed}$$

means open things are not closed.

Meaning postulates reveal even more complex knowledge. If you *own* something, then that something *belongs to you,* and vice versa. This connection follows from the meanings of the words, and it is expressed by the following meaning postulate, which goes in *both* directions (notice the two-headed arrow):

$$(x) \text{ owns } (y) \leftrightarrow (y) \text{ belongs to } (x)$$

Meaning postulates and redundancy rules are a part of the *lexicon.* These "formal" devices reveal knowledge about the meanings of words that all speakers have.

Evidence for the existence of semantic properties is found in the speech errors, or "slips of the tongue," that we all produce. In Chapter 3 on phonology some errors were cited that reveal the internalized phonological system of the language. Other errors, which result in the substitution of a word for an intended word, reveal semantic classes. Consider the following word-substitution errors that some speakers have actually produced:

Intended Utterance	Actual Utterance (Error)
bridge of the nose	bridge of the neck
when my gums bled	when my tongues bled
he came too late	he came too early
Mary was young	Mary was early
the lady with the dachshund	the lady with the Volkswagen
that's a horse of another color	that's a horse of another race
he has to pay her alimony	he has to pay her rent

These errors and thousands we and others have collected, reveal that the incorrectly substituted words are not random substitutions but share some semantic property with the intended words. *Nose* and *neck, gums* and *tongues* are all "body parts" or "parts of the head." *Young, early,* and *late* are related to "time." *Dachshund* and *Volkswagen* are both "German" and "small." The semantic relationships between *color* and *race* and even between *alimony* and *rent* are rather obvious.

The semantic properties that describe the linguistic meaning of a word should not be confused with other properties, such as physical properties. Scientists know that water is composed of hydrogen and oxygen. We know that water is an essential ingredient of lemonade or a bath. We need not know any of these things, though, to know what the word *water* means, and to be able to use and understand this word in a sentence.

Linguistic knowledge includes knowing the meaning of words and morphemes. Meaning is specified in part by a set of semantic properties, some of which may be specific to the word, together with redundancy rules and meaning postulates that reveal more general relationships. This system enables speakers to use and understand words and to combine them to produce meaningful utterances.

Ambiguity

"Mine is a long and sad tale!" said the Mouse, turning to Alice and sighing.

"It is a long tail, certainly," said Alice, looking with wonder at the Mouse's tail, "but why do you call it sad?"

Lewis Carroll, *Alice's Adventures in Wonderland*

We said above that knowing a word means knowing its sounds and meaning. Both are necessary, for the same sounds can sometimes mean different things. **Homo-**

nyms or **homophones** are different words that are pronounced the same. They may have the same or different spelling. *To, too,* and *two* are homophones because they are all pronounced /tu/; *will* as in *last will and testament, Will* the man's name, and *will* to denote future tense mean different things but are spelled and pronounced identically.

THE BORN LOSER   **Art Sansom**

© 1983 Newspaper Enterprise Association, Inc.

Homonyms may create ambiguity. A word or a sentence is **ambiguous** if it can be understood or interpreted in more than one way. The sentence

> She cannot bear children.

may be understood to mean "She is unable to give birth to children" or "She cannot tolerate children." The ambiguity is due to the two words *bear* with two different meanings. Sometimes additional context can help to disambiguate the sentence:

> She cannot bear children if they are noisy.
> She cannot bear children because she is sterile.

Both words *bear* as used in the above sentences are verbs. There is another homonym *bear,* the animal, which is a noun with different semantic properties. The adjective *bare,* despite its different spelling, is homophonous with the above words and also has a different meaning. *Bare* as a verb is yet another homonym.

Homonyms are good candidates for humor as well as for confusion.

> "How is bread made?"
> "I know *that*!" Alice cried eagerly.
> "You take some flour—"
> "Where do you pick the flower?" the White Queen asked. "In a garden, or in the hedges?"
> "Well, it isn't *picked* at all," Alice explained; "it's *ground*—"
> "How many acres of ground?" said the White Queen.

The humor of this passage is based on two sets of homonyms: *flower* and *flour* and the two meanings of *ground.* Alice means *ground* as the past tense of *grind,* whereas the White Queen is interpreting *ground* to mean "earth."

Thus, sentences may be ambiguous because they contain one or more ambiguous words. This condition is **lexical ambiguity.** Some other examples of such lexically ambiguous sentences are:

(1) (a) The Rabbi married my sister.
    (b) Do you smoke after sex?
    (c) It takes two mice to screw in a light bulb.

Item c is also an example of **structural ambiguity,** which was examined in Chapter 5 on syntax, in which the two or more meanings are not the result of lexical ambiguity but the result of two or more *structures* underlying the same string of words. The word *screw* has two meanings, and the sentences have two structures:

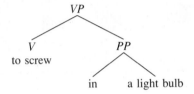

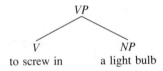

Such examples of homonyms and ambiguous sentences show that there is no one-to-one relation between sounds and meanings, and that we cannot always determine the precise meaning from the sound alone. They are further evidence that the sound–meaning relationship in language is arbitrary, and that we must learn how to relate sounds and meanings when learning the language.

Paraphrases

Does he wear a turban, a fez or a hat?
Does he sleep on a mattress, a bed or a mat, or a Cot,
The Akond of Swat?
Can he write a letter concisely clear,
Without a speck or a smudge or smear or Blot,
The Akond of Swat?

Edward Lear, "The Akond of Swat"

There are not only words that sound the same but have different meanings; there are also words that sound different but have the same or nearly the same meaning. Such words are called **synonyms.** There are dictionaries of synonyms that contain many hundreds of entries, such as:

apathetic/phlegmatic/passive/sluggish/indifferent
pedigree/ancestry/genealogy/descent/lineage

It has been said that there are no perfect synonyms—that is, no two words ever have *exactly* the same meaning. Still, the following pairs of sentences have very similar meanings.

I'll be happy to come./I'll be glad to come.
He's sitting on the sofa./He's sitting on the couch.

Some individuals may always use *sofa* instead of *couch,* but if they know the two words they will understand both sentences and interpret them to mean the same thing. The degree of semantic similarity between words depends to a great extent on the number of semantic properties they share. *Sofa* and *couch* refer to the same type of object and share most, if not all, of their semantic properties.

There are words that have many semantic properties in common but that are not synonyms or near synonyms. *Man* and *boy* both refer to male humans; the meaning of *boy* includes the additional semantic property of "youth," whereby it differs from the meaning of *man.* Thus the semantic system of English permits you to say *A sofa is a couch* or *A couch is a sofa* but not *A man is a boy* or *A boy is a man,* except when you wish to describe "boylike" qualities of the man or "man-like" qualities of the boy.

Often a word with several meanings, called a **polysemous** word, will share one of its meanings with another word. Thus *mature* and *ripe* are synonymous when applied to fruit, but only *mature* can apply to animals. *Deep* and *profound* are another such pair. Both apply to thought, but only *deep* applies to water. Sometimes words that are ordinarily opposites can mean the same thing in certain contexts; thus a *good* scare is the same as a *bad* scare. Similarly, a word with a positive meaning in one form, such as the adjective *perfect,* when used adverbially, undergoes a "weakening" effect, so that a "perfectly good bicycle" is neither perfect nor always good. "Perfectly good" means something more like "adequate."

When synonyms occur in otherwise identical sentences, the sentences will be paraphrases. Sentences are **paraphrases** if they have the same meaning (except possibly for minor differences in emphasis). Thus the use of synonyms may create **lexical paraphrase,** just as the use of homonyms may create lexical ambiguity.

Sentences may also be paraphrases because of *structural differences* that are not essential to their meanings. Some examples were cited in the previous chapter. We noted that a pair of sentences may be paraphrases in terms of the *logical relations,* but differ in the matter of *focus* or in terms of the *topic/comment* structure. Thus many active/passive pairs of sentences such as *John kissed Mary* and *Mary was kissed by John* differ in meaning only in that John is the topic of the first, whereas Mary is the topic of the second. The two sentences may still be considered to be paraphrases.

Other instances of paraphrases will be described later on in this chapter.

Antonyms

As a rule, man is a fool;
When it's hot, he wants it cool;
When it's cool, he wants it hot;
Always wanting what is not.

Anonymous

The meaning of a word may be partially defined by saying what it is *not*. *Male* means *not female*. *Dead* means *not alive*. Words that are opposite in meaning are often called **antonyms.** Ironically, the basic property of two words that are antonyms is that they share all but one semantic property. *Beautiful* and *tall* are not antonyms; *beautiful* and *ugly*, or *tall* and *short*, are. The property they do not share is present in one and absent in the other. Thus, in order to be opposites, two words must be semantically similar or in the same semantic category, such as "gender" or "height."

There are several kinds of antonymy. There are **complementary pairs:**

alive/dead   present/absent   awake/asleep

They are complementary in that *not alive = dead* and *not dead = alive,* and so on.

There are **gradable** pairs of antonyms:

big/small   hot/cold   fast/slow   happy/sad

With gradable pairs the negative of one word is not synonymous with the other. For example, someone who is *not happy* is not necessarily *sad.* It is also true of gradable antonyms that more of one is less of another. More bigness is less smallness; wider is less narrow, and taller is less short. Another characteristic of many pairs of gradable antonyms is that one is **marked** and the other **unmarked.** The unmarked member is the one used in questions of degree. We ask, "How *high* is it?" (not "How *low* is it?") or "How *tall* is she?" We answer "One thousand feet high" or "Five feet tall" but never "Five feet short," except humorously. *High* and *tall* are the unmarked members of *high/low* and *tall/short.* Notice that the meaning of these adjectives and other similar ones is relative. The words themselves provide no information about absolute size. Because of our knowledge of the language, and of things in the world, this relativity normally causes no confusion. Thus we know that "a small elephant" is much bigger than "a big mouse."

Another kind of "opposite" involves pairs like

give/receive, buy/sell, teacher/pupil

They are called **relational opposites,** and they display symmetry in their meaning. If X *gives* Y to Z, then Z *receives* Y from X. If X is Y's *teacher,* then Y is X's *pupil*. Pairs of words ending in *-er* and *-ee* are usually relational opposites. If Mary is Bill's employ*er*, then Bill is Mary's employ*ee*.

These relationships may be expressed formally through *meaning postulates:*

> *(x)* gives *(y,z)* ↔ *(z)* receives *(y,x)*
> *(x)* teacher *(y)* ↔ *(y)* pupil *(x)*

Comparative forms of gradable pairs of adjectives often form relational pairs. Thus, if Sally is *taller* than Alfred, then Alfred is *shorter* than Sally. If a Cadillac is *more expensive* than a Ford, then a Ford is *cheaper* than a Cadillac.

If meanings of words were indissoluble wholes, there would be no way to make the interpretations that we do. We know that *big* and *red* are not opposites because they have too few semantic properties in common. They are both adjectives, but *big* is in the semantic class involving size, whereas *red* is a color. On the other hand, *buy/sell* are relational opposites because both contain the semantic property "transfer of property," and they differ only in one property, "direction of transfer."

Redundancy rules on semantic features can reveal our knowledge about antonyms. Consider:

> [+married] → [−single]   [+single] → [−married]

These rules show that any word that bears the semantic property "married," such as *wife,* is understood to lack the semantic property "single"; and conversely, any word that bears the semantic property "single," such as *bachelor,* will not have the property "married."

BROOM HILDA   **Russell Myers**

Reprinted by permission: Tribune Media Services.

In English there are a number of ways to form antonyms. You can add the prefix *un:*

> likely/unlikely   able/unable   fortunate/unfortunate

or you can add *non:*

> entity/nonentity   conformist/nonconformist

or you can add *in:*

> tolerant/intolerant   discreet/indiscreet   decent/indecent

Because we know the semantic properties of words, we know when two words are antonyms, synonyms, or homonyms, or are unrelated in meaning.

Names

Her name was McGill and she called herself Lil
But everyone knew her as Nancy.

John Lennon and Paul McCartney, "Rocky Raccoon"[1]

TUMBLEWEEDS   **T.K. Ryan**

"What's in a name?" is a question that has occupied philosophers of language for centuries. Plato was concerned with whether names were "natural," though the question did not bother Adam when he named the animals; Humpty Dumpty thought his name meant his shape, and in part it does.

Usually when we think of names we think of names of people or places,

[1]© 1969 by Northern Songs Ltd. All rights for the U.S.A., Mexico, and the Philippines controlled by Maclen Music, Inc., c/o ATV Music Corp. Used by permission; all rights reserved.

which are **proper names.** We do not think of *Canis familiaris* as being named "dog." Still, the old view persists that all words name some object, though that object may be abstract. This view presents difficulties. We are unable to identify the objects named by *sincerity* or *forgetfulness,* not to mention *into, brave,* and *think.*

Proper names can refer to objects. The objects may be extant, such as those designated by

> Disa Karin Viktoria Lubker
> Lake Michigan
> The Empire State Building

or extinct, such as

> Socrates
> Troy

or even fictional

> Sherlock Holmes
> Dr. John H. Watson
> Oz

Proper names are **definite,** which means they refer to a unique object insofar as the speaker and listener are concerned. If I say

> Mary Smith is coming to dinner.

my spouse understands Mary Smith to refer to our friend Mary Smith, and not to one of the dozens of Mary Smiths in the phone book.

Because they are inherently definite, proper names are not in general preceded by *the:*

> *the John Smith
> *the California

There are some exceptions, such as the names of rivers, ships, and erected structures:

> the Mississippi
> the *Queen Mary*
> the Empire State Building
> the Eiffel Tower
> the Golden Gate Bridge

and there are special cases such as *the John Smiths* to refer to the family of John Smith. Also, for the sake of clarity or literary effect, it is possible to precede a proper name by an article if the resulting noun phrase is followed by a modifying expression such as a prepositional phrase or a sentence:

> The Paris of the 1920s . . .
> The New York that everyone knows and loves . . .

Proper names cannot usually be pluralized, though they can be plural, like *the Great Lakes* or *the Pleiades*. There are exceptions, such as *the John Smiths* mentioned above, or expressions like *the Linguistics Department has three Bobs,* meaning three people named Bob, but they are special locutions used in particular circumstances. Because proper names generally refer to unique objects, it is not surprising that they occur mainly in the singular.

For the same reason, proper names cannot in general be preceded by adjectives. Many adjectives have the semantic effect of narrowing down the field of reference, so that the noun phrase *a red house* is a more specific description than simply *a house;* but what proper names refer to is already completely narrowed down, so modification by adjectives seems peculiar. Again, as in all these cases, extenuating circumstances give rise to exceptions. Language is nothing if not flexible, and we find expressions such as *young John* used to discriminate between two people named John. We also find adjectives applied to emphasize some quality of the object referred to, such as *the wicked Borgias* or *the brilliant Professor Einstein*.

Names may be coined or drawn from the stock of names that the language provides; but once a proper name is coined, it cannot be pluralized or preceded by *the* or any adjective (except for cases like those cited above), and it will be used to refer uniquely, for these rules are among the many rules already in the grammar, and speakers know they apply to all proper names, even new ones.

Phrase and Sentence Meaning

"Then you should say what you mean," the March Hare went on.

"I do," Alice hastily replied, "at least—I mean what I say—that's the same thing, you know."

"Not the same thing a bit!" said the Hatter. "You might just as well say that 'I see what I eat' is the same thing as 'I eat what I see'!"

"You might just as well say," added the March Hare, "that 'I like what I get' is the same thing as 'I get what I like'!"

"You might just as well say," added the Dormouse . . . "that 'I breathe when I sleep' is the same thing as 'I sleep when I breathe'!"

"It is the same thing with you," said the Hatter.

Lewis Carroll, *Alice's Adventures in Wonderland*

Words and morphemes are the smallest meaningful units in language. For the most part, however, we communicate in phrases and sentences, which also have meaning. The meaning of a phrase or sentence depends on both the meaning of its words and how these words are structurally combined. (Idioms are exceptional and will be discussed later.) Some of the semantic knowledge we have about words can be applied to sentences. Words are synonyms; sentences are paraphrases. Words may be homonyms; sentences may be ambiguous. Words have opposites; sentences can be negated. Words are used for naming purposes; sentences can be used that way too. Both words and sentences can be used to refer to, or point out, objects; and both may have some further meaning beyond this referring capability, as we shall see in the following section.

Sense and Reference

You mentioned your name as if I should recognize it, but beyond the obvious facts that you are a bachelor, a solicitor, a Freemason, and an asthmatic, I know nothing whatever about you.

Sir Arthur Conan Doyle, "The Norwood Builder," *The Memoirs of Sherlock Holmes*

Take care of the sense, and the sounds will take care of themselves.

Lewis Carroll, *Alice's Adventures in Wonderland*

We hinted earlier that the name *Humpty Dumpty* not only referred to a fictional object, but had some further meaning, something like "a good round shape." Do proper names have a meaning over and above referring to objects? Certainly, the name *Sue* has the semantic property "female," as evinced by the humor in "A Boy Named Sue," a song sung by Johnny Cash. *The Pacific Ocean* has the semantic properties of *ocean*, and even such names as *Fido* and *Bossie* are associated with dogs and cows, respectively.

Words other than proper names both have a meaning and can be used to refer to objects, and so can larger units such as phrases and sentences. The German philosopher Gottlob Frege proposed that the meaning of an expression be called **sense** *(Sinn)*, and if the expression refers to something, it has **reference** (Bedeutung).

Noun Phrases normally have sense and can be used to refer. Thus the noun phrase

The man who is my father

refers to a certain individual and has a certain sense or meaning that is different from that of

The man who married my mother

although both expressions may have the same referent.

Phrases may, however, have sense but no reference. If not, we would be unable to understand sentences like these:

The present king of France is bald.
By the year 3000, our descendants will have left Earth.

Speakers of English can understand these sentences, even though France now has no king, and our descendants of a millennium from now do not exist.

Combining Words into Sentences

. . . I placed all my words with their interpretations in alphabetical order. And thus in a few days, by the help of a very faithful memory, I got some insight into their language.

Jonathan Swift, *Gulliver's Travels*

Although it is widely believed that learning a language is merely learning the words of that language and what they mean—a myth apparently accepted by Gulliver— there is more to it than that, as you know if you have ever tried to learn a foreign language. We comprehend sentences because we know the meaning of individual words, *and we know rules for combining their meanings.*

We know the meanings of *red* and *balloon*. The semantic rule to interpret the combination *red balloon* adds the property "redness" to the properties of *balloon*. The phrase *the red balloon,* because of the presence of the definite article *the,* means "a particular instance of redness and balloonness." A semantic rule for the interpretation of *the* accounts for this fact.

The phrase *large balloon* would be interpreted by a different semantic rule, because part of the meaning of *large* is that it is a relative concept. *Large balloon* means "large *for a balloon.*" What is large for a balloon may be small for a house and gargantuan for a cockroach; yet we correctly comprehend the meanings of *large balloon, large house,* and *large cockroach.*

There are many more rules involved in the semantics of noun phrases. Because noun phrases may contain prepositional phrases, semantic rules are needed for such expressions as *The house with the white picket fence*. We have seen how the rules account for *the house,* and *the white picket fence.* The semantic rule for prepositions indicates that two objects stand in a relationship determined by the meaning of the particular preposition. For *with,* that relationship is "accompanies" or "is part of." A preposition like *on* means a certain spatial relationship, and so on for other prepositions.

The syntactic structure of a phrase is important to its meaning. *The dog on the bed* has a different meaning than *the bed on the dog; red brick* is different than *brick red.*

Meanings build on meanings. Thus the meaning of *on* combines the meanings of the noun phrases on either side of it. In turn, the noun phrases may be the combinations of meanings of articles, adjectives, nouns, prepositional phrases, and even sentences.

Thematic Relations

B.C. **Johnny Hart**

By permission of Johnny Hart and North America Syndicate, Inc.

In the chapter on syntax, we observed that verbs are subcategorized for zero, one, or two "objects," and that these objects have a "logical relation" to the verb. *Sleep* was an example of a zero-object or intransitive verb; *find* was subcategorized for one object, and *put* for two.

A verb is related in various ways to the constituents in a sentence. The relations depend on the meaning of the particular verb. For example the NP *the boy* in *the boy found a red brick* is called the **agent** or "doer" of the action of finding. The NP *a red brick* is the **theme** (sometimes called **patient**) or "recipient" of the action. (The boldfaced words are technical terms of semantic theory.) Part of the meaning of *find* is that its subject is an agent and its logical object is a theme. That fact is reflected in the entry for *find* in the lexicon.

The noun phrases that follow the verb *put* have the relation of theme and **location.** In the verb phrase *put the red brick on the wall, the red brick* is the theme and *on the wall* is the location. The entire verb phrase is interpreted to mean that the theme of *put* changes its position to the location. The location, itself a prepositional phrase, will have its own meaning, which is combined with the meaning of *put* and the meaning of *the red brick. Put*'s subject is also an agent, so that in *The boy put the red brick on the wall,* "the boy" performs the action. Semantic rules do all this work, revealing speaker knowledge about the meaning of such sentences.

The semantic relationships that we have called *theme, agent,* and *location* are among the **thematic relations** or **θ-roles** of the verb. Other thematic relations are **goal,** where the action is directed, **source,** where the action originated, and **instrument,** an object used to accomplish the action. Consider the following example:

The boy carried the red brick from the wall to the wagon.

The boy is the agent; *the red brick* is the theme; *the wall* is the source; *the wagon* is the goal. In

The boy broke a window with the red brick.

The boy is again the agent, *a window* is the theme, and *the red brick* is the instrument. These examples show that the same noun phrase *(the red brick)* can function in a different thematic role depending on the sentence.

The lexical entries for *find* and *put* would now look something like this:

find, V, ___ NP, (Agent, Theme)
put, V, ___ NP PP, (Agent, Theme, Location)

The thematic relations are contained in parentheses. The first one states that the logical subject is an agent. The remaining thematic relations belong to the constituents for which the verb is subcategorized. The logical object of both *find* and *put* will be a theme. The Prepositional Phrase for which *put* subcategorizes will be a location.

Our knowledge of verbs includes their syntactic category, how they are subcategorized, and the thematic relations that their NP subject and object(s) have, and this knowledge is explicitly represented in the lexicon.

Thematic relations are the same in sentences that are paraphrases. In both these sentences

The dog bit the man.
The man was bitten by the dog.

the dog is the agent and *the man* is the theme.

Thematic relations may remain the same in sentences that are *not* paraphrases, as in the following instances:

The boy opened the door with the key.
The key opened the door.
The door opened.

In all three of these sentences, *the door* is the theme, the thing that gets opened. In the first two sentences, *the key,* despite its different structural role, retains the thematic role of instrument.

In many languages thematic roles are reflected in the **case** assumed by the noun. The *case* or *grammatical case* of a noun is the particular morphological shape that it takes. English nouns do not have extensive case, but the possessive form of a noun, as in *the boy's red brick,* is called the genitive or possessive case.

In other languages such as Finnish, the noun assumes a morphological shape according to its thematic role in the sentence. For example, in Finnish *koulu-* is the root meaning ''school,'' and *-sta* is a case ending that means ''directional source.'' Thus *koulusta* means ''from the school.'' Similarly, *kouluun (koulu + un)* means ''to the school.''

Some of the information carried by grammatical case in languages like Finnish is borne by prepositions in English. Thus *from* and *to* often indicate the thematic relations of Source and Goal. Instrument is marked by *with*, Location by prepositions such as *on* and *in*, and Agent by *by* in passive sentences. The role of Theme is generally unaccompanied by a preposition, as is Agent when it is the structural subject of the sentence. What we are calling thematic relations or roles in this section has sometimes been studied as *case theory*.

Irrespective of how we label the semantic relations that exist between verbs and noun phrases, they are a part of every speaker's linguistic competence and account for much of the meaning of language.

The "Truth" of Sentences

. . . Having Occasion to talk of Lying and false Representation, it was with much Difficulty that he comprehended what I meant. . . . For he argued thus: That the Use of Speech was to make us understand one another and to receive Information of Facts; now if any one said the Thing which was not, these Ends were defeated; because I cannot properly be said to understand him. . . . And these were all the Notions he had concerning that Faculty of Lying, so perfectly well understood, and so universally practiced among human Creatures.

Jonathan Swift, *Gulliver's Travels*

Some philosophers and linguists would say that the meaning of a sentence is the set of conditions that determine the truth of the sentence. *The boy found a red brick* is true just in case *someone aptly described as "the boy" had a "finding relationship" with something aptly described as "a red brick."* The meaning of the sentence would be this italicized set of conditions, or something similar to it.

Part of the meaning of a sentence is certainly knowledge of its "truth conditions." Those truth conditions would contain much of the information about meaning discussed in the previous section. In the world as we know it, the sentence

The Declaration of Independence was signed in 1776.

is true, and the sentence

The Declaration of Independence was signed in 1976.

is false. We know the meaning of both sentences equally well, and knowing their meaning means knowing their truth conditions. We compare their truth conditions with "the real world" or historical fact, and can thus say which one is true and which one false.

You can, however, understand well-formed sentences of your language without knowing their truth value. Knowing the truth conditions is not the same as knowing the actual facts. Rather, the truth conditions, the meaning, permit you to examine the world and learn the actual facts. If you did not know the linguistic meaning—if the sentence were in an unknown language—you could never determine its truth, even if you had memorized an encyclopedia. You may not know the truth of

> The Mecklenburg Charter was signed in 1770.

but if you know its meaning you know *in principle* how to discover its truth, even if you do not have the means to actually do so. For example, consider the sentence

> The moon is made of green cheese.

We knew before space travel that going to the moon would test the truth of the sentence.

Now consider this sentence:

> Rufus believes that the Declaration of Independence was signed in 1976.

This sentence is true if some individual named Rufus does indeed believe the statement, and it is false if he does not. Those are its truth conditions.

It does not matter that a subpart of the sentence is false. An entire sentence may be true even if one or more of its parts are false, and vice versa. Truth is determined by the semantic rules, which permit you to combine the subparts of a sentence and still know under what conditions the sentence is true or false.

Knowing a language includes knowing the semantic rules for combining meanings and the conditions under which sentences are true or false.

Discourse Meaning

Though this be madness, yet there is method in't.
William Shakespeare, *Hamlet*

Linguistic knowledge accounts for speakers' ability to combine phonemes into morphemes, morphemes into words, and words into sentences. Knowing a language also permits combining sentences together to express complex thoughts and ideas. This linguistic ability makes language an excellent medium for communication. These larger linguistic units are called **discourse.**

The study of discourse, or **discourse analysis,** involves many aspects of *linguistic performance* and of "sociolinguistics" (taken up in the next chapter), as well as linguistic competence. Discourse analysis involves questions of style, appropriateness, cohesiveness, rhetorical force, topic/subtopic structure, differences between written and spoken discourse, and so on.

Maxims of Conversation

With a little hoard of maxims preaching down a daughter's heart.
Tennyson, "Locksley Hall"

Speakers recognize when a series of sentences "hangs together" or when it is "disjointed." The discourse below, which gave rise to Polonius' remark quoted at the head of this section, does not seem quite right—it is not **coherent.**

POLONIUS: What do you read, my lord?
HAMLET: Words, words, words.
POLONIUS: What is the matter, my lord?
HAMLET: Between who?
POLONIUS: I mean, the matter that you read, my lord.
HAMLET: Slanders, sir: for the satirical rogue says here that old men have grey beards, that their faces are wrinkled, their eyes purging thick amber and plum-tree gum, and that they have a plentiful lack of wit, together with most weak hams: all which, sir, though I most powerfully and potently believe, yet I hold it not honesty to have it thus set down; for yourself, sir, should grow old as I am, if like a crab you could go backward.[2]

Hamlet, who is feigning insanity, refuses to answer Polonius' questions "in good faith." He has violated certain conversational conventions or **maxims of conversation.**[3] One such maxim, the **cooperative principle,** states that a speaker's contribution to the discourse should be as informative as is required—neither more nor less. Hamlet has violated this maxim in both ways. In answering "Words, words, words" to the question of what is being read, he is providing too little information. His final remark goes to the other extreme in providing more information than required.

He also violates the **maxim of relevance,** when he "misinterprets" the question about the reading matter as a matter between two individuals.

The "run on" nature of Hamlet's final remark is another source of incoherence. This effect is increased in the final sentence by the somewhat bizarre choice of phrasing to compare growing younger with walking backward.

Conversational conventions such as the requirement to "be relevant" allow the various sentence meanings to be sensibly connected into discourse meaning, much as rules of sentence grammar allow word meanings to be sensibly (and grammatically) connected into sentence meaning.

Most of the rules of grammar we have studied are for phrases and sentences. Such rules interact heavily with nonlinguistic knowledge in discourse.

The Articles *the* and *a*

There are discourse rules that apply regularly, such as those that determine the occurrence of the articles *the* and *a*. The article *the* is used to indicate that the referent of a noun phrase is agreed upon by speaker and listener. If someone says

I saw the boy.

---

[2]*Hamlet*, Act II, Scene ii.
[3]These maxims were first discussed by H. Paul Grice in the William James Lectures, delivered at Harvard University in 1967.

it is assumed that a certain boy is being discussed. No such assumption accompanies

> I saw a boy.

which is more of a description of what was seen than a reference to a particular individual.

Often a discourse will begin with the use of indefinite articles, and once everyone agrees on the referents, definite articles start to appear. A short example illustrates this transition:

> I saw *a* boy and *a* girl holding hands and kissing.
> Oh, it sounds lovely.
> Yes, *the* boy was quite tall and handsome, and he seemed to like *the* girl a lot.

This example also illustrates that the use of pronouns is often discourse-dependent. The use of *he* to refer to the boy in the final clause is necessary to avoid the stilted-sounding:

> Yes, the boy was quite tall and handsome, and *the boy* seemed to like the girl a lot.

There are rules of discourse, which may be considered performance rules, that determine when a pronoun can be used in the place of a more complete expression.

Anaphora

When two expressions refer to the same thing, they are said to be **coreferential.** Discourses are filled with pronouns that are coreferential with other expressions, their **antecedents.** Rules of discourse determine when a pronoun can or should be used instead of a longer expression. The process of replacing a longer expression by a pronoun or another kind of "pro-form" is called **anaphora.** Here are three examples of the use of anaphoric expressions, or pro-forms:

> I love Disa and Jack loves *Disa* too.
> I love Disa and Jack loves *her* too.   (Pronoun)
>
> Emily hugged Cassidy and Zachary hugged Cassidy too.
> Emily hugged Cassidy and Zachary *did* too.   (Pro–verb phrase)
>
> I am sick and *my being sick* makes me sad.
> I am sick, *which* makes me sad.   ("Pro-sentence")

Performance discourse conventions permit us to "violate" in regular ways many of the rules of grammar. For example, the rules of syntax would not generate as a well-formed sentence *My uncle has, too,* but in the following discourse it is perfectly acceptable:

> First speaker: My aunt has been dieting strenuously.
> Second speaker: My uncle has, too.

The second speaker is understood to mean "My uncle has been dieting strenuously." The missing part of the verb phrase is understood from previous discourse.

Entire sentences may be "filled in" this way:

> First speaker: My aunt has been dieting strenuously, and she has lost a good deal of weight.
> Second speaker: My mother has, too.

The second speaker is understood to have meant "My mother has been dieting strenuously, and she has lost a good deal of weight."[4] Rules of discourse not only provide the missing parts of the verb phrase, but provide the entire second sentence meaning.

Much discourse is "telegraphic" in nature. Verb phrases are not specifically mentioned, entire clauses are left out, pronouns abound, "you know" is everywhere. People still understand people, and part of the reason is that rules of grammar and rules of discourse combine with contextual knowledge to fill in missing gaps and make the discourse cohere.

Pragmatics

We have referred to the "context" of a sentence or discourse, and the importance of context in interpreting language. The general study of how context influences the way sentences convey information is called **pragmatics.**

Pragmatics is as complex a subject as syntax or semantics. The term *pragmatics* comes from the field of **semiotics,** or the study of signs. Linguistic signs are one kind of sign, which we have examined in this book. Within semiotics, *syntax* means "the way signs are arranged," *semantics* means "what signs mean or signify," and *pragmatics* means "the relationship between signs and their users."

Pragmatics has to do with people's use of language in contexts, so it is a part of what we have been calling *linguistic performance*.

Speech Acts

Reprinted by permission: © 1961 United Feature Syndicate, Inc.

---

[4]Some speakers would say the reply is ambiguous: it may or may not mean that the mother lost weight. The point is, it *can* be interpreted with the "missing" sentence in place.

You can do things with speech. You can make promises, lay bets, issue warnings, christen boats, place names in nomination, offer congratulations, or swear testimony. By saying *I warn you that there is a sheepdog in the closet,* you not only say something, you *warn* someone. Verbs like *bet, promise, warn,* and so on are **performative verbs.** Using them in a sentence does something extra over and above the statement.

There are hundreds of performative verbs in every language. The following sentences illustrate their usage:

(2) I *bet* you five dollars the Yankees win.
I *challenge* you to a match.
I *dare* you to step over this line.
I *fine* you $100 for possession of oregano.
I *move* that we adjourn.
I *nominate* Batman for mayor of Gotham City.
I *promise* to improve.
I *resign!*

In all these sentences the speaker is the subject (that is, they are in ''first person'') who by uttering the sentence is accomplishing some additional action, such as daring, nominating, or resigning. Also, all these sentences are affirmative, declarative, and in the present tense. They are typical **performative sentences.**

An informal test to see whether a sentence contains a performative verb is to begin it with the words *I hereby.* . . . Only performance sentences sound right when begun this way. Compare *I hereby apologize to you* with the somewhat strange *I hereby know you.* The first is generally taken as an act of apologizing. In all the examples in (2), insertion of *hereby* would be acceptable. As the cartoon at the beginning of this section shows, Snoopy is aware that using *hereby* will ensure that his statement is taken as an act of despising.

Actually, every utterance is some kind of speech act. Even when there is no explicit performative verb, as in *It is raining,* we recognize an implicit performance of *stating.* On the other hand, *Is it raining?* is a performance of *questioning,* just as *Leave!* is a performance of *ordering.* In all these instances we could use, if we chose, an actual performative verb: *I **state** that it is raining; I **ask** if it is raining; I **order** you to leave.*

The study of how we do things with sentences is the study of **speech acts.** In studying speech acts, we are acutely aware of the importance of the *context of the utterance.* In some circumstances *There is a sheepdog in the closet* is a warning, but the same sentence may be a promise or even a mere statement of fact, depending on circumstances. We call this purpose—a warning, a promise, a threat, or whatever—the **illocutionary force** of a speech act.

Speech act theory aims to tell us when we appear to ask questions but are really giving orders, or when we say one thing with special (sarcastic) intonation and mean the opposite. Thus, at a dinner table, the question *Can you pass the salt?* means the order *Pass the salt!* It is not a request for information, and *yes* is an inappropriate response.

Because the illocutionary force of a speech act depends on the context of the utterance, speech act theory is a part of pragmatics.

Presuppositions

Speakers often make implicit assumptions about the real world, and the sense of an utterance may depend on those assumptions, which some linguists term **presuppositions.**[5] Consider the following sentences:

(3) (a) Have you stopped hugging your sheepdog?
    (b) Who bought the badminton set?
    (c) John doesn't write poems in the bathroom.
    (d) The present King of France is bald.
    (e) Would you like another beer?

In sentence 3a the speaker has *presupposed* that the listener has at some past time hugged his sheepdog. In 3b there is the presupposition that someone has already bought a badminton set, and in 3c it is assumed that John writes poetry.

We have already run across the somewhat odd 3d, which we decided we could understand even though France does not currently have a king. The use of the definite article *the* usually presupposes an existing referent. When presuppositions are inconsistent with the actual state of the world, the utterance is felt to be strange, unless a fictional setting is agreed upon by the conversants, as in a play, for example.

Sentence 3e presupposes or implies that you have already had at least one beer. Part of the meaning of the word *another* includes this presupposition. The Hatter in *Alice's Adventures in Wonderland* would not agree with us.

> "Take some more tea," the March Hare said to Alice, very earnestly.
>
> "I've had nothing yet," Alice replied in an offended tone, "so I can't take more."
>
> "You mean you can't take *less*," said the Hatter: "It's very easy to take *more* than nothing."

The humor in this passage comes from the fact that knowing English includes knowing the meaning of the word *more*, which in this usage presupposes some earlier amount.

These phenomena may also be described as **implication** or **entailment.** Part of the meaning of *more* implies or entails that there has already been something. The definite article *the*, in these terms, entails or implies the existence of the referent within the current context.

Presuppositions can be used to communicate information indirectly. If someone says *My brother is rich*, we assume that person has a brother, even though that fact is not explicitly stated. Much of the information that is exchanged in a conver-

---

[5]Other linguists call the same phenomenon **implication.** *Presupposition* is used here because it seems to be more widely accepted.

sation or discourse is of this kind. Often, after a conversation has ended, we will realize that some fact was imparted to us that was not specifically mentioned. That fact is often a presupposition.

The use of language in a courtroom is restricted so that presuppositions cannot influence the court or jury. The famous type of question *Have you stopped beating your wife?* is disallowed in court, because accepting the validity of the question means accepting its presuppositions; the question imparts ''information'' in a way that is difficult to cross-examine and even difficult to detect. Presuppositions are so much a part of natural discourse that they become second nature and we do not think of them, any more than we are directly aware of the many other rules and maxims that govern discourse.

Deixis

DENNIS THE MENACE   **Hank Ketcham**

''Dennis the Menace''® used by permission of Hank Ketcham and © by North America Syndicate.

In all languages there are many words and expressions whose references rely entirely on the circumstances of the utterance and can only be understood in light of these circumstances. This aspect of pragmatics is called **deixis.** Pronouns are often deictic.

> I   my   mine   you   your   yours

These pronouns require identification of speaker and listener for interpretation. Proper names as well as expressions such as

> this person
> that man
> these women
> those men

are deictic, for they require pragmatic information in order for the listener to make a "referential connection" and understand what is meant. The above examples illustrate **person deixis.** They also show that the use of **demonstrative articles** like *this* and *that* is deictic.

There is also **time deixis** and **place deixis.** The following examples are all deictic expressions of time:

now	then	tomorrow
this time	that time	seven days ago
two weeks from now	last week	next April

In order to understand what specific times such expressions refer to, we need to know when the utterance was said. Clearly, *next week* has a different reference when uttered today than a month from today. If you found an advertising leaflet on the street that said "BIG SALE NEXT WEEK" with no date given, you would not know whether the sale had already taken place.

Expressions of place deixis require contextual information about the place of the utterance, as shown by the following examples:

here	there	this place
that place	this ranch	those towers over there
this city	these parks	yonder mountains

The "Dennis the Menace" cartoon at the beginning of this section indicates what can happen if the deictic conventions are not observed.

Directional terms such as

before/behind left/right front/back

are deictic insofar as you need to know which way the speaker is facing. In Japanese the verb *kuru* "come" can only be used for motion toward the place of utterance. A Japanese speaker cannot call up a friend and ask

May I *kuru* to your house?

as you might, in English, ask "May I come to your house?"
The correct verb is *iku,* "go," which indicates motion away from the place of utterance. These verbs thus have a deictic aspect to their meaning.

Deixis abounds in language use and marks one of the boundaries of semantics and pragmatics. The pronoun *I* certainly has a meaning independent of context—its semantic meaning, which is "the speaker"; but context is necessary to know who the speaker is, hence what "I" refers to.

When Rules Are Broken

For all a rhetorician's rules
Teach nothing but to name his tools.
Samuel Butler, *Hudibras*

The rules of language are not laws of nature. Only by a "miracle" can the laws of nature be broken, but the rules of language are broken every day by everybody. This lawlessness is not human perversity, but rather another way in which language is put to use.

There are three kinds of rule violation that we will discuss: **anomaly,** a violation of semantic rules to create "nonsense"; **metaphor,** or nonliteral meaning; and **idioms,** in which the meaning of an expression may be unrelated to the meaning of its parts.

Anomaly: No Sense and Nonsense

Don't tell me of a man's being able to talk sense; everyone can talk sense. Can he talk nonsense?
William Pitt

If in a conversation someone said to you

My brother is an only child.

you might think that he was making a joke or that he did not know the meaning of the words he was using. You would know that the sentence was strange, or **anomalous;** yet it is certainly an English sentence. It conforms to all the grammatical rules of the language. It is strange because it represents a contradiction; the meaning of *brother* includes the fact that the individual referred to is a male human who has at least one sibling.

The sentence

That bachelor is pregnant.

is anomalous for similar reasons; the word *bachelor* contains the semantic property "male," whereas the word "pregnant" has the semantic property "female." Through a semantic redundancy rule *pregnant* will also be marked [−male]. The anomaly arises from trying to equate something that is [+male] with something that is [−male].

The semantic properties of words determine what other words they can be combined with. One sentence that is used by linguists to illustrate this fact is

Colorless green ideas sleep furiously.[6]

The sentence seems to obey all the syntactic rules of English. The subject is *colorless green ideas* and the predicate is *sleep furiously*. It has the same syntactic structure as the sentence

Dark green leaves rustle furiously.

but there is obviously something wrong *semantically* with the sentence. The meaning of *colorless* includes the semantic property "without color," but it is combined with the adjective *green,* which has the property "green in color." How can something be both "without color" and "green in color" simultaneously? Other such semantic violations also occur in the sentence.

There are other sentences that sound like English sentences but make no sense at all because they include words that have no meaning; they are **uninterpretable.** One can only interpret them if one dreams up some meaning for each "no-sense" word. Lewis Carroll's "Jabberwocky" is probably the most famous poem in which most of the content words have no meaning—they do not exist in the lexicon of the grammar. Still, all the sentences "sound" as if they should be or could be English sentences:

'Twas brillig, and the slithy toves
   Did gyre and gimble in the wabe;
All mimsy were the borogoves,
   And the mome raths outgrabe.
   . . .

He took his vorpal sword in hand:
   Long time the manxome foe he sought—
So rested he by the Tumtum tree,
   And stood awhile in thought.

Without knowing what *vorpal* means, you nevertheless know that

He took his vorpal sword in hand.

means the same thing as

He took his sword, which was vorpal, in hand.
It was in his hand that he took his vorpal sword.

Knowing the language, and assuming that *vorpal* means the same thing in the three sentences (because the same sounds are used), you can decide that the "truth value" of the three sentences is identical. In other words, you are able to decide that two things mean the same thing even though you do not know what either one

---

[6]Noam Chomsky. 1957. *Syntactic Structures.* Mouton. The Hague.

means. You decide by assuming that the semantic properties of *vorpal* are the same whenever it is used.

We now see why Alice commented, when she had read "Jabberwocky":

"It seems very pretty, but it's *rather* hard to understand!" (You see she didn't like to confess, even to herself, that she couldn't make it out at all.) "Somehow it seems to fill my head with ideas—only I don't exactly know what they are! However, *somebody* killed *something:* that's clear, at any rate—"

The semantic properties of words show up in other ways in sentence construction. For example, if the meaning of a word includes the semantic property "human" in English, we can replace it by one sort of pronoun but not another. This semantic feature determines that we call a boy *he* and a table *it,* and not vice versa.

According to Mark Twain, Eve had such knowledge in her grammar, for she writes in her diary:

If this reptile is a man, it ain't an *it,* is it? That wouldn't be grammatical, would it? I think it would be *he.* In that case one would parse it thus: nominative *he;* dative, *him;* possessive, *his'n.*

The linguist Samuel Levin has shown that in poetry semantic violations may form strange but interesting aesthetic images. He cites Dylan Thomas's phrase *a grief ago* as an example. *Ago* is ordinarily used with words specified by some temporal semantic feature:

a week ago		*a table ago
an hour ago	but not	*a dream ago
a month ago		*a mother ago
a century ago		

When Thomas used the word *grief* with *ago* he was adding a durational feature to *grief* for poetic effect.

In the poetry of E. E. Cummings there are phrases like

the six subjunctive crumbs twitch
a man . . . wearing a round jeer for a hat
children building this rainman out of snow.

Though all of these phrases violate some semantic rules, we can understand them; it is the breaking of the rules that creates the imagery desired. The ability to understand these phrases and at the same time recognize their anomalous or deviant nature shows knowledge of the semantic system and semantic properties of the language.

Metaphor

Our doubts are traitors.

Shakespeare

Walls have ears.

Cervantes

The night has a thousand eyes
and the day but one.

Frances William Bourdillon

Sometimes the breaking of semantic rules can be used to convey a particular idea. *Walls have ears* is certainly anomalous, but it can be interpreted as meaning "you can be overheard even when you think nobody is listening." In some sense the sentence is ambiguous, but the literal meaning is so unlikely that listeners stretch their imagination for another interpretation. That "stretching" is based on semantic properties that are inferred or that provide some kind of resemblance. Such non-literal interpretations of sentences are called **metaphor.**

The literal meaning of a sentence such as

My new car is a lemon.

is anomalous. You could, if driven to the wall (another metaphor), provide some literal interpretation that is plausible if given sufficient context. For example, the *new car* may be a miniature toy carved out of a piece of citrus fruit. The more common meaning, however, would be metaphorical and interpreted as referring to a newly purchased automobile that breaks down and requires constant repairs. The imagination stretching in this case may relate to the semantic property "tastes sour" that *lemon* possesses.

Metaphors are not necessarily anomalous when taken literally. The literal meaning of the sentence

Dr. Jekyll is a butcher.

is that a physician named Jekyll also works as a retailer of meats or a slaughterer of animals used for food. The metaphorical meaning is that the doctor named Jekyll is harmful, possibly murderous, and apt to operate unnecessarily.

Similarly, the sentence

John is a snake in the grass.

can be interpreted literally to refer to a pet snake on the lawn named John. Meta-phorically the sentence has nothing to do with a scaly, limbless reptile.

To interpret metaphors we need to understand both the literal meaning and facts about the world. To understand the metaphor

Time is money.

it is necessary to know that in our society we are often paid according to the number of hours or days worked. To recognize that the sentence

Jack is a pussycat.

has a different meaning than

Jack is a tiger.

requires knowledge that the metaphorical meaning of each sentence does *not* depend on the semantic property "feline." Rather, other semantic properties of these two words are referred to.

Metaphorical use of language is language creativity at its highest. Nevertheless, the basis of metaphorical use is the ordinary linguistic knowledge about words, their semantic properties, and their combining powers that all speakers possess.

Idioms

PEANUTS   **Charles M. Schulz**

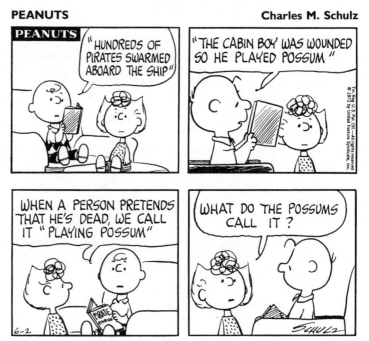

© 1972 United Feature Syndicate, Inc.

Knowing a language includes knowing the morphemes, simple words, compound words, and their meanings. In addition it means knowing fixed phrases, consisting of more than one word, with meanings that cannot be inferred from the meanings of the individual words. The usual semantic rules for combining meanings do not apply. Such expressions are called **idioms.** All languages contain many idiomatic phrases, as in these English examples:

sell down the river
haul over the coals
eat my hat
let their hair down
put his foot in his mouth
throw her weight around
snap out of it
cut it out
hit it off
get it off
bite your tongue
give a piece of your mind

Idioms are similar in structure to ordinary phrases except that they tend to be frozen in form and do not readily enter into other combinations or allow the word order to change. Thus,

(4) She put her foot in her mouth.

has the same structure as

(5) She put her bracelet in her drawer.

but whereas

The drawer in which she put her bracelet was hers.
Her bracelet was put in her drawer.

are sentences related to sentence 5,

The mouth in which she put her foot was hers.
Her foot was put in her mouth.

do not have the idiomatic sense of sentence 4.

On the other hand, the words of some idioms can be moved without affecting the idiomatic sense:

The FBI kept tabs on radicals.
Tabs were kept on radicals by the FBI.
Radicals were kept tabs on by the FBI.

Idioms can break the rules on combining semantic properties. The object of *eat* must usually be something with the semantic property "edible," but in

he ate his hat
eat your heart out

this restriction is violated.

Idioms, grammatically as well as semantically, have special characteristics. They must be entered into the lexicon or mental dictionary as single "items," with their meaning specified, and speakers must learn the special restrictions on their use in sentences.

Many idioms may have originated as metaphorical expressions that "took hold" in the language and became frozen in their form and meaning.

Summary

Knowing a language is knowing how to produce and understand sentences with particular meanings. The study of linguistic meaning, called **semantics,** is concerned with the meaning of words, morphemes, phrases, and sentences.

The meanings of morphemes and words are defined in part by their **semantic properties** or **features.** Relationships between semantic properties, such as that "human" implies "animate," can be expressed through **redundancy rules.** Other relationships between words, such as that "open" implies "not closed," are expressed in **meaning postulates.**

When two words have the same sounds but different meanings, they are **homonyms** or **homophones** (for example, *bear* and *bare*). The use of homophones in a sentence may lead to **ambiguity,** which occurs when a single utterance has more than one meaning. Ambiguity may also occur because of the structure of the sentence. *Flying planes can be dangerous* is both structurally and lexically ambiguous. *Planes* can refer to special woodworking tools or airplanes. If the *airplane* meaning is intended, the sentence can be interpreted to mean "To fly planes can be dangerous" or "Planes that are flying can be dangerous." These two meanings result from the sentence structure.

Sentences with the same meaning are **paraphrases.** Sentences may be paraphrases of one another because they contain **synonyms** (different words that mean the same thing, such as *couch* and *sofa*) or because they differ structurally in ways that do not affect meaning *(They gave the boy help/They gave help to the boy).*

A word that has several meanings is **polysemous.** For example, the word *good* means "well-behaved" in *good child* and "sound" in *good investment.*

Two words that are "opposite" in meaning are **antonyms.** Antonyms have the same semantic properties except for the one that accounts for their oppositeness. There are antonymous pairs that are **complementary** *(alive/dead),* **gradable** *(hot/cold),* and **relational opposites** *(buy/sell, employer/employee).*

Proper names are special morphemes used to designate particular objects uniquely; that is, they are **definite.** Proper names cannot ordinarily be preceded by an article or an adjective, or be pluralized.

Words, phrases, and sentences have **sense** and can be used to **refer.** Frege showed that meaning is more than reference alone. Some meaningful expressions (for example, *the present King of France*) have sense but no reference.

Languages have rules for combining the meanings of words. For example, a *red balloon* is a balloon with the additional property of redness. Sentence meaning is determined in part by the **thematic relations** of the noun phrases to the verb. These semantic relationships indicate who, to whom, toward what, from which, with what, and so on to make up sentence meaning.

The meaning of a sentence determines under what conditions the sentence is true or false. You can understand a sentence without knowing its "truth value," but you cannot determine the truth value without knowing the meaning.

Discourse consists of several sentences. Discourse analysis involves questions of style, appropriateness, cohesiveness, rhetorical force, topic/subtopic structure, differences between written and spoken discourse, and so on. Well-structured discourse follows certain rules and **maxims,** such as "be relevant," that make the discourse **coherent.** There are also grammatical rules that affect discourse, such as those which determine when to use the definite article *the,* when to use pronouns, and when to draw "missing information" from previous parts of the discourse.

The general study of how context affects linguistic interpretation is **pragmatics.** Pragmatics includes **speech acts, presuppositions,** and **deixis.** Speech act theory is the study of what an utterance does beyond just saying something. The effect of what is done is called the **illocutionary force** of the utterance. For example, use of a **performative verb** like *bequeathe* may be an act of bequeathing, which may even have legal status.

Presuppositions are implicit assumptions that accompany certain utterances. *Have you stopped beating your wife?* carries with it the presupposition that at one time you beat your wife.

Deictic terms such as *you, there, now* require knowledge of the circumstances (the person, place, or time) of the utterance to be interpreted referentially.

Pragmatics itself is part of the linguistic theory of performance.

Sentences are **anomalous** when they deviate from certain semantic rules. *The six subjunctive crumbs twitched* and *The stone ran* are anomalous. Other sentences are **uninterpretable** because they contain "words" without meaning, such as *An orkish sluck blecked nokishly.*

Many sentences have both a literal and nonliteral or **metaphorical** interpretation. *He's out in left field* may be a literal description of a baseball player or a metaphorical description of someone mentally deranged.

Idioms are phrases whose meaning is *not* the combination of the meanings of the individual words (for example, *put her foot in her mouth*). Idioms often violate co-occurrence restrictions of semantic properties.

Everything you know about linguistic meaning is included in the semantic system of your grammar, including how to interpret sentences within context.

References

Austin, J. L. 1962. *How to Do Things with Words*. Harvard University Press. Cambridge, Mass.

Brown, G., and G. Yule, 1983. *Discourse Analysis*. Cambridge University Press. Cambridge, England.

Davidson, D., and G. Harman, eds. 1972. *Semantics of Natural Languages*. Reidel. Dordrecht, The Netherlands.

Dillon, G. L. 1977. *Introduction to Contemporary Linguistic Semantics*. Prentice-Hall. Englewood Cliffs, N.J.

Hurford, J. R., and B. Heasley. 1983. *Semantics: A Coursebook*. Cambridge University Press. Cambridge, England.

Katz, J. 1972. *Semantic Theory*. Harper & Row. New York.

Levinson, S. C. 1983. *Pragmatics*. Cambridge University Press. Cambridge, England.

Lyons, J. 1977. *Semantics*. Cambridge University Press. Cambridge, England.

Searle, John R. 1969. *Speech Acts: An Essay in the Philosophy of Language*. Cambridge University Press. Cambridge, England.

Exercises

1. For each group of words given below, state what semantic property or properties are shared by the (a) words and the (b) words, and what semantic property or properties distinguish between the classes of (a) words and (b) words.

> Example: a. widow, mother, sister, aunt, seamstress
> b. widower, father, brother, uncle, tailor
> The (a) and (b) words are "human."
> The (a) words are "female" and the (b) words are "male."

A. a. bachelor, man, son, paperboy, pope, chief
    b. bull, rooster, drake, ram

The (a) and (b) words are _____.

The (a) words are _____.

The (b) words are _____.

B. a. table, stone, pencil, cup, house, ship, car
    b. milk, alcohol, rice, soup, mud

The (a) and (b) words are _____.

The (a) words are _____.

The (b) words are _____.

C. a. book, temple, mountain, road, tractor
    b. idea, love, charity, sincerity, bravery, fear

The (a) and (b) words are _____.

The (a) words are _____.

The (b) words are _____.

D. a. pine, elm, ash, weeping willow, sycamore
    b. rose, dandelion, aster, tulip, daisy

The (a) and (b) words are _____.

The (a) words are _____.

The (b) words are _____.

E. a. book, letter, encyclopedia, novel, notebook, dictionary
   b. typewriter, pencil, ballpoint, crayon, quill, charcoal, chalk

The (a) and (b) words are _____.

The (a) words are _____.

The (b) words are _____.

F. a. walk, run, skip, jump, hop, swim
   b. fly, skate, ski, ride, cycle, canoe, hang-glide

The (a) and (b) words are _____.

The (a) words are _____.

The (b) words are _____.

G. a. ask, tell, say, talk, converse
   b. shout, whisper, mutter, drawl, holler

The (a) and (b) words are _____.

The (a) words are _____.

The (b) words are _____.

H. a. alive, asleep, dead, married, pregnant
   b. tall, smart, interesting, bad, tired

The (a) and (b) words are _____.

The (a) words are _____.

The (b) words are _____.

I. a. alleged, counterfeit, false, putative, accused
   b. red, large, cheerful, pretty, stupid
      (*Hint:* Is an alleged murderer always a murderer?)

The (a) and (b) words are _____.

The (a) words are _____.

The (b) words are _____.

2. Knowing the meaning of words like *swim* or *fly* includes knowledge such as "swimming takes place in a liquid medium," or "flying occurs through the air." Such facts are expressed in the lexicon by *meaning postulates*, with the formal appearance:

> *(x)* swims → *(x)* in liquid
> "If something swims, it must be in liquid."

For each of the verbs in the table below identify one meaning postulate. (The first one is done as an example):

Verb	Meaning Postulate
walk	*(x)* walks → *(x)* uses legs
run	_____
skip	_____
jump	_____
hop	_____
swim	_____
fly	_____
skate	_____
ski	_____
cycle	_____

3. Explain the semantic ambiguity of the following sentences by providing two sentences that paraphrase the two meanings. Example: *She can't bear children* can mean either *She can't give birth to children* or *She can't tolerate children.*

a. He waited by the bank.

Meaning one: _____

Meaning two: _____

b. Is he really that kind?

Meaning one: _____

Meaning two: _____

c. The proprietor of the fish store was the sole owner.

Meaning one: _____

Meaning two: _____

d. The long drill was boring.

Meaning one: _____

Meaning two: _____

e. When he got the clear title to the land, it was a good deed.

Meaning one: _____

Meaning two: _____

f. It takes a good ruler to make a straight line.

Meaning one: _____

Meaning two: _____

g. He saw that gasoline can explode.

Meaning one: _____

Meaning two: _____

4. The following sentences are ambiguous when written. After figuring out the ambiguity, circle the letter of the ones that can be disambiguated in speech by special intonation or pauses.

a. The lamb is too hot to eat.
b. Old men and women will be served first.
c. Kissing girls is what Stephen likes best.
d. They are moving sidewalks.
e. Becky left directions for Jack to follow.
f. John loves Richard more than Martha.

5. There are several kinds of antonymy. By writing a *c*, *g*, or *r* in column *C*, indicate whether the pairs in columns *A* and *B* are complementary, gradable, or relational opposites:

A	*B*	*C*
good	bad	
expensive	cheap	
parent	offspring	
beautiful	ugly	
false	true	
lessor	lessee	
pass	fail	
hot	cold	
legal	illegal	
larger	smaller	
poor	rich	
fast	slow	
asleep	awake	
husband	wife	
rude	polite	

6. The following sentences consist of a verb, its noun phrase subject, and various objects. Identify the thematic relation of each noun phrase by writing the letter *a*, *t*, *l*, *i*, *s*, or *g* above the noun, standing for *agent, theme, location, instrument, source,* or *goal*.

>   *a*   *t*   *s*
> Example: *The boy took the books from the cupboard with a*
>
>   *i*
> *handcart.*

a. Mary found a ball in the house.

b. The children ran from the playground to the wading pool.

c. One of the men unlocked all the doors with a paper clip.

   d. John melted the ice with a blowtorch.

   e. The sun melted the ice.

   f. The ice melted.

   g. Broken ice still melts in the sun.

   h. The farmer's daughter loaded hay onto the truck.

   i. The farmer's daughter loaded the hay with a pitchfork.

   j. The hay was loaded onto the truck by the farmer.

7. It is often the case that the subject of the sentence has the thematic role of agent, as can be seen in the previous exercise. With verbs like *receive*, however, the subject is not the agent. Think of five other verbs in which the subject is clearly not the agent. Can you identify the actual thematic role of the subject in your examples? For instance, we would surmise that the subject of *receive* has the thematic role of goal.

   i. _____ ii. _____ iii. _____

   iv. _____ v. _____

8. Some linguists and philosophers distinguish between two kinds of truthful statements: one follows from the definition or meaning of a word; the other simply happens to be true in the world as we know it. Thus, *kings are monarchs* is true because the word *king* has the semantic property "monarch" as part of its meaning; but *kings are rich* is circumstantially true. We can imagine a poor king, but a king who is not a monarch is not truly a king. Sentences like *kings are monarchs* are said to be **analytic,** true by virtue of meaning alone. Write *A* by any of the following sentences that are analytic, and *T* by the ones that are circumstantially true.

   a. Queens are monarchs.   _____

   b. Queens are female.   _____

   c. Queens are mothers.   _____

   d. Dogs are four-legged.   _____

   e. Dogs are animals.   _____

   f. Cats are felines.   _____

g. Cats are stupid.   _____

h. George Washington is George Washington.   _____

i. George Washington was the first president.   _____

j. Uncles are male.   _____

9. The opposite of *analytic* (see previous exercise) is **contradictory.** A sentence that is false due to the meaning of its words alone is contradictory. *Kings are female* is an example. Write a *C* by the contradictory sentences and an *F* by the sentences that are false due to circumstance.

a. My aunt is a man.   _____

b. Witches are wicked.   _____

c. My brother is an only child.   _____

d. The evening star isn't the morning star.   _____

e. The evening star isn't the evening star.   _____

f. Babies are adults.   _____

g. Babies can lift one ton.   _____

h. Puppies are human.   _____

i. My bachelor friends are all married.   _____

j. My bachelor friends are all lonely.   _____

10. In sports and games many expressions are "performative." By shouting *you're out*, the first-base umpire performs an act. Likewise for *checkmate* in chess. Think up a half-dozen or so similar examples and explicate their use.

11. A criterion of a "performance sentence" is whether you can begin it with *I hereby*. Notice that if you say sentence *a* aloud it sounds like a genuine apology, but to say sentence *b* aloud sounds funny because you cannot perform an act of knowing:

a. I hereby apologize to you.
b. I hereby know you.

Test whether the following sentences are performance sentences by inserting *hereby* and seeing whether they sound "right." Circle the letter of any that are performance sentences.

   c. I testify that she met the agent.
   d. I know that she met the agent.
   e. I suppose the Yankees will win.
   f. He bet her $2500 that Reagan would win.
   g. I dismiss the class.
   h. I teach the class.
   i. We promise to leave early.
   j. I owe the I.R.S. $1,000,000.
   k. I bequeath $1,000,000 to the I.R.S.
   l. I swore I didn't do it.
   m. I swear I didn't do it.

12.   The following sentences make certain presuppositions. What are they? (The first one has been done for you.)

   a. The police ordered the minors to stop drinking.
      Presupposition: The minors were drinking.

   b. Please take me out to the ball game again.

      Presupposition: _____

   c. Valerie regretted not receiving a new T-bird for Labor Day.

      Presupposition: _____

   d. That her pet turtle ran away made Emily very sad.

      Presupposition: _____

   e. The administration forgot that the professors support the students. (Compare *The administration believes that the professors support the students,* in which there is no such presupposition.)

      Presupposition: _____

   f. It is strange that the United States invaded Cambodia in 1970.

      Presupposition: _____

   g. Isn't it strange that the United States invaded Cambodia in 1970?

      Presupposition: _____

   h. Disa wants more popcorn.

Presupposition: _____

i. Why don't pigs have wings?

Presupposition: _____

j. Who discovered America in 1492?

Presupposition: _____

13. Circle the letter of any of the following sentences that contain deictic expressions. (*Hint:* Which ones require you to know the circumstances—participants, time, place, and so on—of the utterance in order to be understood?)

a. I saw you standing there.
b. Dogs are animals.
c. Yesterday all my troubles seemed so far away.
d. Abraham Lincoln was the sixteenth president of the United States.
e. He was born in a log cabin.
f. It was then that she pulled him toward her.
g. Both authors of this book were born in May.
h. The Declaration of Independence was signed in 1776.
i. Germany invaded Poland on September 1, 1939.
j. Once you're inside, the treasure will be found on your right.

14. Although language could not function properly if those who conversed failed to agree on the meanings of the words used, there are many situations where one person does not know all the words used in a sentence. Identify some of these situations, and in each case tell what the person might do to increase understanding. (For example, in a conversation with a linguist, a reference is made to your "organs of articulation," but you are not sure what *articulation* means.)

15. We passed lightly over the distinction between homophony (different words with the same pronunciation) and polysemy (one word with more than one meaning). In practice, it is not always easy to make this distinction. For instance, are the two meanings of *fathom,* as illustrated in the cartoon on page 250, an example of homophony or polysemy?

Dictionary writers must make thousands of decisions of this kind. In a dictionary, homophonous words have separate entries, whereas the various meanings of a polysemous word occur within the same entry.[7] Using any up-to-date dictionary, look up ten sets of homophones (some homophones have four or five entries; for example, *peak*). Then look up ten polysemous

---

[7]Often, word etymologies are used as the basis for decision. If two different meanings of a form come from historically different sources, the forms are considered to be homophones and receive separate entries.

THE WIZARD OF ID   **Parker and Hart**

By permission of Johnny Hart and North America Syndicate, Inc.

words with five or more given meanings (for example, *gauge*). List both sets with their meanings.

16.   The following sentences may be either lexically or structurally ambiguous, or both. Provide paraphrases showing you comprehend all the meanings.

> Example: I saw him walking by the bank.
> Meaning one: I saw him and he was walking by the river bank.
> Meaning two: I saw him and he was walking by the financial institution.
> Meaning three: I was walking by the river bank when I saw him.
> Meaning four: I was walking by the financial institution when I saw him.

a.   We laughed at the colorful ball.
b.   He was knocked over by the punch.
c.   The police were urged to stop drinking by the fifth.
d.   I said I would file it on Thursday.
e.   I cannot recommend visiting professors too highly.

Social Aspects of Language

Speech is civilization itself. The word, even the most contradictious word, preserves contact—it is silence which isolates.

Thomas Mann, *The Magic Mountain*

Children raised in isolation do not use language; it is used by human beings in a social context, communicating their needs, ideas, and emotions to one another. . . .

William Labov, *Sociolinguistic Patterns*

Language in Society

Language is a city to the building of which every human being brought a stone.

Ralph Waldo Emerson, *Letters and Social Aims*

Dialect words—those terrible marks of the beast to the truly genteel.

Thomas Hardy, *The Mayor of Casterbridge*

Dialects

All speakers of English can talk to each other and pretty much understand each other; yet no two speak exactly alike. Some differences are due to age, sex, state of health, size, personality, emotional state, and personal idiosyncrasies. That each person speaks somewhat differently from all others is shown by our ability to recognize acquaintances by hearing them talk. The unique characteristics of the language of an individual speaker are referred to as the speaker's **idiolect.** English may then be said to consist of 400,000,000 idiolects, or the number equal to the number of speakers of English.

Beyond these individual differences, the language of a group of people may show regular variations from that used by other groups of speakers of that language. When the English of speakers in different geographical regions and from different social groups shows *systematic* differences, the groups are said to speak different **dialects** of the same language. The dialects of a single language may thus be defined as **mutually intelligible** forms of a language that differ in **systematic** ways from each other.

It is not always easy to decide whether the systematic differences between two speech communities reflect two dialects or two different languages. A rule-of-thumb definition can be used: ''When dialects become mutually unintelligible—when the speakers of one dialect group can no longer understand the speakers of

253

another dialect group—these 'dialects' become different languages.'' However, to define ''mutually intelligible'' is itself a difficult task. Danes speaking Danish and Norwegians speaking Norwegian and Swedes speaking Swedish can converse with each other; yet Danish and Norwegian and Swedish are considered separate languages because they are spoken in separate countries and because there are regular differences in their grammars. Similarly, Hindi and Urdu are mutually intelligible ''languages'' spoken in Pakistan and India, although the differences between them are not much greater than between the English spoken in America and Australia. On the other hand, the various languages spoken in China, such as Mandarin and Cantonese, although mutually unintelligible, have been referred to as dialects of Chinese because they are spoken within a single country and have a common writing system.

Because neither mutual intelligibility nor the existence of political boundaries is decisive, it is not surprising that a clear-cut distinction between language and dialects has evaded linguistic scholars. We shall, however, use the rule-of-thumb definition and refer to dialects of one language as mutually intelligible versions of the same basic grammar, with systematic differences between them.

Regional Dialects

Phonetics . . . the science of speech. That's my profession. . . . (I) can spot an Irishman or a Yorkshireman by his brogue. I can place any man within six miles. I can place him within two miles in London. Sometimes within two streets.

George Bernard Shaw, *Pygmalion*

Dialectal diversity develops when people are separated from each other geographically and socially. The changes that occur in the language spoken in one area or group do not necessarily spread to another. Within a single group of speakers who are in regular contact with one another, the changes are spread among the group and ''relearned'' by their children. When some communication barrier separates groups of speakers—be it a physical barrier such as an ocean or a mountain range, or social barriers of a political, racial, class, or religious kind—linguistic changes are not easily spread and dialectal differences are reinforced.

Dialect differences tend to increase proportionately to the degree of **communicative isolation** between the groups. Communicative isolation refers to a situation such as existed between America, Australia, and England in the eighteenth century. There was some contact through commerce and emigration, but an Australian was less likely to talk to an Englishman than to another Australian. Today the isolation is less pronounced because of the mass media and travel by jet, but even within one country, regionalisms persist. In fact, there is no evidence to show that any **dialect leveling** occurs due to the mass media, and recent studies even suggest that dialect variation is increasing, particularly in urban areas.

Changes in the grammar do not take place all at once within the speech community. They take place gradually, often originating in one region and slowly spreading to others, and often taking place throughout the lives of several generations of speakers.

A change that occurs in one region and fails to spread to other regions of the language community gives rise to dialect differences. When enough such differences give the language spoken in a particular region (for example, the city of Boston or the southern area of the United States) its own "flavor," that version of the language is referred to as a regional dialect.

Accents

Regional phonological or phonetic distinctions are often referred to as different **accents.** A person is said to have a Boston accent, a Southern accent, a Brooklyn accent, a Midwestern drawl, and so on. Thus, *accent* refers to the characteristics of speech that convey information about the speaker's dialect, which may reveal in what country or what part of the country the speaker grew up or to which sociolinguistic group the speaker belongs. People in the United States often refer to someone as having a British accent or an Australian accent; in Britain they refer to an American accent.

The term *accent* is also used to refer to the speech of someone who speaks a language nonnatively; for example, a French person speaking English is described as having a French accent. In this sense, accent refers to phonological differences or "interference" from a different language spoken elsewhere. Unlike the regional dialectal accents, such "foreign" accents do not reflect differences in the language of the community where the language was acquired.

Dialects of American English

The educated Southerner has no use for an r except at the beginning of a word.
Mark Twain, Life on the Mississippi

Regional dialects tell us a great deal about how languages change, which will be discussed at greater length in the next chapter. The origins of many regional dialects of American English can be traced to the people who first settled North America in the seventeenth and eighteenth centuries. The early settlers came from different parts of England, speaking different dialects. Therefore regional dialect differences existed in the first colonies.

By the time of the American Revolution, there were three major dialect areas in the British colonies: the Northern dialect spoken in New England and around the Hudson River; the Midland dialect spoken in Pennsylvania; and the Southern dialect. These dialects differed from each other, and from the English spoken in England, in systematic ways. Some of the changes that occurred in British English spread to the colonies; others did not.

How regional dialects developed may be illustrated by changes in the pronunciation of words with an *r*. The British in southern England were already dropping their *r*'s before consonants and at the end of words as early as the eighteenth century. Words such as *farm, farther,* and *father* were pronounced as [fa:m], [fa:ðə], and [fa:ðə], respectively. By the end of the eighteenth century, this practice was a general rule among the early settlers in New England and the southern Atlantic seaboard. Close commercial ties were maintained between the New England colonies and London, and Southerners sent their children to England to be educated, which reinforced the ''*r*-dropping'' rule. The ''*r*-less'' dialect still spoken today in Boston, New York, and Savannah maintained this characteristic. Later settlers, however, came from northern England, where the *r* had been retained; as the frontier moved westward so did the *r*.

Pioneers from all three dialect areas spread westward. The intermingling of their dialects ''leveled'' or ''submerged'' many of their dialectal differences, which is why the English used in large sections of the Midwest and the West is similar.

In addition to the English settlers, other waves of immigration brought speakers of other dialects and other languages to different regions. Each group left its imprint on the language of the communities in which they settled—the Germans who in the last half of the eighteenth century settled the southeastern section of Pennsylvania, the Welsh west of Philadelphia, the Germans and Scotch-Irish in the

Midlands area. Later groups of immigrants in the nineteenth and twentieth centuries from Europe and from Asia also enriched the regional dialects in the communities where they settled.

Phonological Differences

I have noticed in traveling about the country a good many differences in the pronunciation of common words. . . . Now what I want to know is whether there is any right or wrong about this matter. . . . If one way is right, why don't we all pronounce that way and compel the other fellow to do the same? If there isn't any right or wrong, why do some persons make so much fuss about it?

Letter quoted in "The Standard American," in J. V. Williamson and V. M. Burke, eds., *A Various Language*

A comparison between the "*r*-less" dialect and other dialects illustrates phonological differences between dialects. There are many such differences in the United States, which created difficulties for the authors of this book in writing Chapter 2, where they had to illustrate the different sounds of English by reference to words in which the sounds occur. Some students pronounce *caught* as /kɔt/ with the vowel /ɔ/ and *cot* as /kat/ with /a/, whereas other students will pronounce them identically. Some readers pronounce *Mary, marry,* and *merry* identically; others pronounce all three words differently as /meri/, /mæri/, and /mɛri/; and still others pronounce two of them the same. In the southern area of the country, *creek* is pronounced with a tense /i/ as /krik/, and in the north Midlands, it is pronounced with a lax /ɪ/ as /krɪk/. Many speakers of American English pronounce *pin* and *pen* identically, whereas others pronounce the first as /pɪn/ and the second as /pɛn/. If variety is indeed the spice of life, then American English dialects add zest to our existence.

Lexical Differences

Regional dialects may differ in the words people use for the same object, as well as in phonology. Hans Kurath,[1] an eminent dialectologist, in his paper "What Do You Call It?" asked:

> Do you call it a *pail* or a *bucket?* Do you draw water from a *faucet* or from a *spigot?* Do you pull down the *blinds,* the *shades,* or the *curtains* when it gets dark? Do you *wheel* the baby, or do you *ride* it or *roll* it? In a *baby carriage,* a *buggy,* a *coach,* or a *cab?*

People take a *lift* to the *first floor* (our *second floor*) in England, but an *elevator* in the United States; they get five gallons of *petrol* (not *gas*) in London; in Britain a *public school* is "private" (you have to pay), and if a student showed up there wearing *pants* ("underpants") instead of *trousers* ("pants"), he would be sent

---

[1]Hans Kurath. 1971. "What Do You Call It?" In Juanita V. Williamson and Virginia M. Burke, eds., *A Various Language: Perspective on American Dialects.* Holt, Rinehart and Winston. New York.

home to get dressed. If you ask for a *tonic* in Boston you will get a drink called *soda* or *soda-pop* in Los Angeles; and a *freeway* in Los Angeles is a *thruway* in New York, a *parkway* in New Jersey, a *motorway* in England, and an *expressway* or *turnpike* in other dialect areas.

Dialect Atlases

Kurath produced **dialect maps** and **dialect atlases** of a region (an example of which may be seen on page 259), on which dialect differences are geographically plotted. For instance, black dots may mark every village whose speakers retain the voiceless /ʍ/ pronunciation of *wheelbarrow,* and white dots where voiced /w/ is pronounced. The black dots often fall together, as do the white dots. These concentrations define **dialect areas.** A line drawn on the map separating the areas is called an **isogloss.** When you "cross" an isogloss, you are passing from one dialect area to another. Sometimes several isoglosses will coincide, often at a political boundary or at a natural boundary such as a river or mountain range. Linguists call these groupings a **bundle of isoglosses.** Such a bundle will define a particular regional dialect.

The first volume of a long-awaited *Dictionary of Regional English* by Frederick G. Cassidy was published in 1985. This work represents years of research and scholarship by Cassidy and other American dialectologists and promises to be a major resource for those interested in American English dialectal differences.

Syntactic Differences

Systematic syntactic differences also distinguish dialects. In most American dialects sentences may be conjoined as follows:

John will eat and Mary will eat → John and Mary will eat.

In the Ozark dialect the following conjunction is also possible:

John will eat and Mary will eat → John will eat and Mary.

Speakers of some American dialects say *Have them come early!* where others would say *Have them to come early!* Some American speakers use *gotten* in a sentence such as *He should have gotten to school on time;* in British English, only the form *got* occurs. In a number of American English dialects the pronoun *I* occurs when *me* would be used in other dialects. This difference is a syntactically conditioned morphological difference.

Dialect 1	**Dialect 2**
between you and I	between you and me
Won't he let you and I swim?	Won't he let you and me swim?

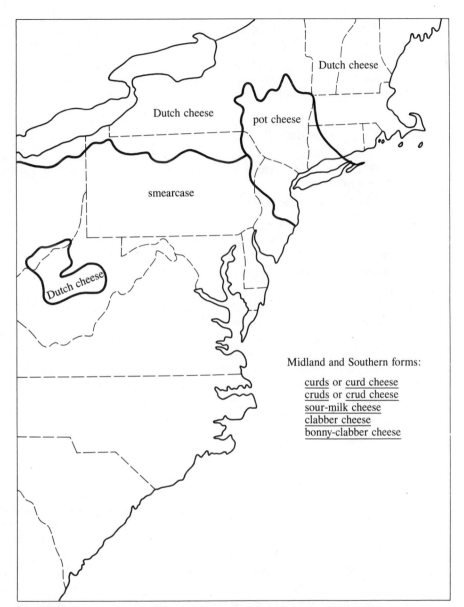

FIGURE 7–1 A dialect map from Hans Kurath's *A Word Geography of the Eastern United States,* showing the isoglosses separating the use of different words referring to the same cheese.

In British English the pronoun *it* in the sentence *I could have done it* can be deleted to form *I could have done,* which is not permitted in the American English grammar.

With all such differences we are still able to understand speakers of another dialect. Even though regional dialects differ as to pronunciation, vocabulary, and syntactic rules, they are minor differences when compared with the totality of the grammar. The largest part of the vocabulary, the sound–meaning relations of words and the syntactic rules, are shared, which is why dialects of one language are mutually intelligible.

The "Standard"

We don't talk fancy grammar and eat anchovy toast. But to live under the kitchen doesn't say we aren't educated.

Mary Norton, *The Borrowers*

Standard English is the customary use of a community when it is recognized and accepted as the customary use of the community. Beyond this is the larger field of good English, any English that justifies itself by accomplishing its end, by hitting the mark.

George Philip Krapp, *Modern English: Its Growth and Present Use*

Even though every language is a composite of dialects, many people talk and think about a language as if it were a ''well-defined'' fixed system with various dialects diverging from this norm. Such was the view of Mario Pei,[2] the author of a number of books on language that were quite popular at one time. He accused the editors of Webster's *Third New International Dictionary,* published in 1961, of confusing ''to the point of obliteration the older distinction between standard, substandard, colloquial, vulgar, and slang,'' attributing to them the view that ''Good and bad, right and wrong, correct and incorrect no longer exist'' (p. 82).

Language Purists

A woman who utters such depressing and disgusting sounds has no right to be anywhere—no right to live. Remember that you are a human being with a soul and the divine gift of articulate speech: that your native language is the language of Shakespeare and Milton and The Bible; and don't sit there crooning like a bilious pigeon.

George Bernard Shaw, *Pygmalion*

Prescriptive grammarians, or language ''purists,'' usually consider the dialect used by political leaders and the upper socioeconomic classes, the dialect used for literature or printed documents, the dialect taught in the schools, as the correct form of the language.

Otto Jesperson, the great Danish linguist, ridiculed the view that a particular dialect is better than any other when he wrote: ''We set up as the best language that

[2]M. Pei. 1964. ''A Loss for Words.'' *Saturday Review.* Nov. 14: 82–84.

which is bound in the best writers, and count as the best writers those that best write the language. We are therefore no further advanced than before."[3]

The dominant or prestige dialect is often called the standard dialect. **Standard American English** (SAE) is a dialect of English that many Americans *almost* speak; divergences from this "norm" are labeled "Philadelphia dialect," "Chicago dialect," "Black English," and so on.

SAE is an idealization. Nobody speaks this dialect; and if somebody did, we would not know it, because SAE is not defined precisely. Several years ago there was an entire conference devoted to one subject: a precise definition of SAE. This meeting did not succeed in satisfying everyone as to what SAE should be. It used to be the case that the language used by national newsbroadcasters represented SAE, but today many of these people speak a regional dialect, or themselves "violate" the English preferred by the purists.

Deviations from this "standard" that no one can define, let alone use, are seen by many as reflecting a "language crisis." Edwin Newman, in his best seller *Strictly Speaking,* asks "Will Americans be the death of English?" and answers "My mature, considered opinion is that it will." All this fuss is reminiscent of Mark Twain's cable to the Associated Press, after reading his obituary: "The reports of my death are greatly exaggerated."

The idea that language change equals corruption goes back at least as far as the Greek grammarians at Alexandria, of around 100–200 B.C.E. They were concerned that the Greek spoken in their time was different from the Greek of Homer, and they believed that the earlier forms were purer. They also tried to "correct" the imperfections but failed as miserably as do any modern counterparts. Similarly, the Moslem Arabic grammarians working at Basra in the eighth and ninth centuries C.E. attempted to purify Arabic to restore it to the perfection of Arabic in the Koran.

For many years after the American Revolution, British writers and journalists railed against American English. Thomas Jefferson was an early target in a commentary on his *Notes on the State of Virginia,* which appeared in the *London Review:*

> For shame, Mr. Jefferson! Why, after trampling upon the honour of our country, and representing it as little better than a land of barbarism—why, we say, perpetually trample also upon the very grammar of our language. . . . Freely, good sir, we will forgive all your attacks, impotent as they are illiberal, upon our *national character;* but for the future spare—O spare, we beseech you, our mother-tongue!

The fears of the British journalists in 1787 proved unfounded, and so will the fears of Edwin Newman. One dialect is neither better nor worse than another, nor purer nor more corrupt; it is simply different.

Those who wish to stem change in language or dialect differentiation are not confined to speakers of English. In France, a notion of the "standard" as the only correct form of the language is promulgated by an official academy of "scholars"

---

[3]O. Jesperson. 1925 (reprinted 1964). *Mankind, Nation, and Individual.* Indiana University Press. Bloomington, Indiana.

who determine what usages constitute the "official French language." A number of years ago, this Academy enacted a law forbidding the use of "Franglais" words in advertising (words of English origin like *le parking, le weekend,* and *le hotdog*), but the French continue to use them. Many of the hundreds of local village dialects (called **patois** [patwa] by the Academy) are actually separate languages, derived from Latin as are French, Spanish, and Italian.

In the past (and to some extent in the present) a Frenchman or Frenchwoman from the provinces who wished to succeed in French society nearly always had to learn Parisian French and be bidialectal. In recent years in France the regional "nationalist" movements made a major demand for the right to use their own languages in their schools and for official business. In the section of France known as l'Occitanie, the popular singers sing in the regional language, Languedoc, both as a protest against the official "standard language" policy and as part of the cultural revival movement. Here is the final chorus of a popular song sung in Languedoc (shown below with its French and English translations):

Languedoc	French	English
Mas perqué, perqué	Mais pourquoi, pourquoi	But why, why
M'an pas dit à l'escóla	Ne m'a-t-on pas dit à l'école	Did they not speak to me at school
La lega de mon pais?	La langue de mon pays?	The language of my country?

In the province of Brittany in France there has also been a strong movement for the use of Breton in the schools, as opposed to the "standard" French. Breton is not even in the same language family as French, which is a Romance language; Breton is a Celtic language in the same family as Irish, Gaelic, and Welsh. (We will discuss such family groupings in Chapter 8.) It is not, however, the structure of the language or the genetic family grouping that has led to the Breton movement. It is rather the pride of a people who speak a language or a dialect not considered as good as the "standard," and their efforts to change this political view of language use.

These efforts have proved successful. In 1982, the newly elected French government decreed that the languages and cultures of Brittany (Breton), the southern Languedoc region, and other areas would be promoted through schooling, exhibitions, and festivals. No longer would school children who spoke Breton be punished by having to wear a wooden shoe tied around their necks, as had been the custom.

There is no reference to a national language in the Constitution of the United States. John Adams proposed that a national academy be established, similar to the French Academy, to standardize American English, but this view was roundly rejected as not in keeping with the goals of "liberty and justice for all."

There is an Academy of the Hebrew Language in Israel, which was established to accomplish a task never before done in the history of humanity—to revive an ancient written language to serve the daily colloquial needs of a modern people.

Twenty-three lexicologists work with the Bible and the Talmud in order to add new words to the language. Although there is some attempt to keep the language "pure," the Academy has given way to popular pressure. Thus, a bank check is called a *check* /ček/ in the singular and pluralized by adding the Hebrew suffix to form *check-im,* although the Hebrew word *hamcha* was proposed. Similarly, *lipstick* has triumphed over *faton* and *pajama* over *chalifatsheina.*

No academy and no guardians of language purity can stem language change, nor should anyone attempt to do so, because such change does not mean corruption. The fact that for the great majority of American English speakers, *criteria* and *data* are now mass nouns like *information* is no cause for concern. Information can include one fact or many facts, but we would still say "The information is." For some speakers it is equally correct to say "The criteria is" or "The criteria are." Those who say "The data are" would or could say "The datum (singular) is."

A difficulty faced by those who wish to dictate the correct forms of words and syntax is that it is not always clear which forms are correct. An article in the April 17, 1977, issue of the *Los Angeles Times,* discussing a letter from a farmer to a zoo, reveals this confusion:

> "Would you send me a couple of mongooses to kill off the snakes on my farm?"
>
> That didn't sound right and he began again: "Would you send me a couple of mongeeses?"
>
> That didn't sound right, either, and, on the third try, this plain man of the land found the answer to a dilemma that has been vexing linguists for centuries:
>
> "Would you send me a mongoose to kill off the snakes on my farm? And, while you're at it, you might as well send me another one."

A standard dialect (or prestige dialect) may have social functions—to bind people together or to provide a common written form for multidialectal speakers. It is, however, neither more expressive, more logical, more complex, nor more regular than any other dialect. Any judgments, therefore, as to the superiority or inferiority of a particular dialect are social judgments, not linguistic or scientific ones.

Black English

LUTHER   **Brumsic Brandon, Jr.**

© 1982, Los Angeles Times Syndicate. Reprinted with permission of the artist.

Whereas the majority of United States dialects are, to a great extent, free from stigma, especially the many regional dialects, one dialect of North American English has been a victim of prejudicial ignorance. This dialect (actually a group of closely related dialects) is spoken by a large section of non-middle-class blacks; it is usually referred to as Black English (BE) or Negro English or Nonstandard Negro English. The distinguishing features of this English dialect persist for social, educational, and economic reasons. The historical discrimination against black Americans[4] has created ghetto living and segregated schools. Where social isolation exists, dialect differences are intensified. In addition, particularly in recent years, many blacks no longer consider their dialect to be inferior, and it has become a means of positive black identification.

Since the onset of the civil-rights movement in the 1960s, Black English has been the focus of national attention. There are critics who attempt to equate the use of Black English with inferior "genetic" intelligence and "cultural deprivation," justifying these incorrect notions by stating that BE is a "deficient, illogical, and incomplete" language. Such epithets cannot be applied to any language, and they are as unscientific in reference to BE as to Russian, Chinese, or Standard American English. The cultural-deprivation myth is as false as the idea that some dialects or languages are inferior. A person may be "deprived" of one cultural background but rich in another.

Some people, white and black, think they can identify someone's race by hearing an unseen person talk, believing that different races inherently speak differently. This assumption is equally false; a black child raised in an upper-class British household will speak RP English.[5] A white child raised in an environment where Black English is spoken will speak Black English. Children construct grammars based on the language they hear.

There are, however, systematic differences between BE and SAE, just as there are systematic differences between Australian and American English.

Phonology of Black English

Deletion of r and l   As stated above, a number of dialects of both British and American English include the phonological rule that can be stated as "Delete /r/ except before a vowel." Black English has the same rule. Pairs of words like *guard* and *god, nor* and *gnaw, sore* and *saw, poor* and *pa, fort* and *fought,* and *court* and *caught* are pronounced identically in BE because of the presence of this phonological rule in the grammar.

Other words that do not rhyme in SAE do rhyme in BE: *yeah* and *fair, idea* and *fear*. In BE (and other Southern dialects) the "*r*-deletion" rule has been extended in some cases, so that *r* is also deleted between vowels. *Carol* is pronounced identically with *Cal,* and *Paris* with *pass.*

---

[4]As used here, "American" refers to the United States.
[5]Received Pronunciation (commonly called RP) has traditionally been considered the most prestigious British pronunciation because it is the dialect "received" ("proper") at the royal court.

For some speakers of BE an "*l*-deletion" rule also occurs, creating homo-phones like *toll* and *toe*, *all* and *awe*, *help* and *hep* [hɛp].

Consonant Cluster Simplification

A regular phonological rule in BE and not in SAE simplifies consonant clusters at the end of words when one of the two conso-nants is an alveolar (/t/, /d/, /s/, /z/). The application of this rule may delete the past-tense morpheme, so *past* and *passed (pass + ed)* are both pronounced like *pass* /pæs/. When speakers of this dialect say *I pass the test yesterday*, they are not showing an ignorance of past and present, but are pronouncing the past tense ac-cording to the rule present in their grammar, similar to *I hit the ball yesterday*.

Because of this deletion rule, *meant* and *mend* are both pronounced the same as *men*. When the rule is combined with the "*l*-deletion" rule, *told*, *toll*, and *toe* have identical pronunciations:

	told	**toll**	**toe**
Phonemic Representation	/told/	/tol/	/to/
Consonant cluster deletion rule	ø	NA	NA
l-deletion rule	ø	ø	NA
Phonetic Representation	[to]	[to]	[to]

The merging of the past and present tense forms in words such as *pass* [pʰæs] and *passed* [pʰæs] is clearly due to a phonological deletion rule rather than a syntac-tic merging of tenses. The deletion rule is optional; it does not always apply, and studies have shown that it is more likely to apply when the final [t] or [d] does not represent the past tense morpheme, as in nouns like *past* [pʰæs] or *paste* [pʰes], as opposed to verbs like *passed* [pʰæast] or *chased* [čʰest]. Such a distinction has also been found with final [s] or [z], which will be retained more often by speakers of BE in words like *seats* [sit + s], where the [s] represents "plural," than in words like *Keats* [kʰit].

There are other systematic differences between the phonology of BE and SAE. BE shares with many regional dialects the lack of any distinction between /ɪ/ and /ɛ/ before nasal consonants, producing identical pronunciations of *pin* and *pen*, *bin* and *Ben*, *tin* and *ten*, and so on. The vowel used in these words is roughly between the [ɪ] of *pit* and the [ɛ] of *pet*.

In BE the phonemic distinction between /aj/ and /aw/ has been lost, both having become /a/. Thus *why* and *wow* are pronounced [wa]. Another change has reduced the /ɔy/ (particularly before /l/) to the simple vowel [ɔ] without the glide, so that *boil* and *boy* are pronounced [bɔ]. One other regular feature is the change of a final /θ/ to /f/ so that *Ruth* is pronounced [ruf] and *death* [dɛf]. It is interesting that this [θ]–[f] correspondence also is true of some dialects of British English, where, in fact, /θ/ is not even a phoneme in the language. *Think* is regularly [fiŋk] in Cockney English.

All these differences are systematic, rule-governed, and similar to sound changes that have taken place in languages all over the world, including Standard English.

Syntactic Differences Between BE and SAE

Syntactic differences, as noted above, also exist between dialects. Linguists such as William Labov have investigated the syntactic structures of Black English. It is the syntactic differences that have often been used to illustrate the "illogic" of BE; yet it is just such differences that point up the fact that BE is as syntactically complex and as "logical" as SAE.

Following the lead of early "prescriptive" grammarians, some "scholars" and teachers conclude that it is illogical to say *he don't know nothing* because two negatives make a positive. Because such negative constructions occur in BE, it has been concluded by some "educators" that speakers of BE are deficient because they use language "illogically." Consider the following sentences:

	SAE	**BE**
Affirmative:	He knows something.	He know something.
Negative:	He doesn't know anything.	He don't know nothing.
	He knows nothing.	He know nothing.
Affirmative:	He likes somebody.	He like somebody.
Negative:	He doesn't like anybody.	He don't like nobody.
	He likes nobody.	He like nobody.
Affirmative:	He has got some.	He got some.
Negative:	He hasn't got any.	He ain't got none.
	He's got none.	He got none.

In Black English, when the verb is negated, the indefinite pronouns *something, somebody,* and *some* become the negative indefinites *nothing, nobody,* and *none.* The rule is simple and elegant and of a type quite common in the world's languages. This same rule existed in earlier periods for all dialects of English. In Standard English, if the verb is negated the indefinites become *anything, anybody,* and *any.* If in the negative sentences in SAE the forms *nothing, nobody,* and *none* are used, then the verb is not negated. The speakers of both SAE and BE know how to negate sentences. The rules are essentially the same, but differ in detail. Both dialects are strictly rule-governed, as is every syntactic process of every dialect in every language in the world.

As the examples above show, Black English also regularizes the present-tense verb forms. In SAE the third-person singular verb forms are inflected by adding to the verb the particular phonetic form that is the same as the plural ending (for example, [z] as in *loves* or *knows,* [s] as in *kicks,* or [əz] as in *kisses*). The absence of this ending in Black English may be the result of the application of phonological rules such as those discussed above.

It has also been said that BE is "illogical" because a form of the verb *to be* is deleted in sentences such as *He nice*. Consider the following sentences from SAE and BE:

SAE	BE
He is nice/He's nice.	He nice.
They are mine/They're mine.	They mine.
I am going to do it/I'm gonna do it.	I gonna do it.

Wherever the standard can use a contraction *(he + is → he's)*, Black English can delete the form of *be*. The following sentences, however, will show that where a contraction cannot be used in SAE, the *be* cannot be deleted in BE:[6]

SAE	BE
*He is as nice as he says he's.	*He as nice as he say he.
*How beautiful you're.	*How beautiful you.
*Here I'm.	*Here I.

These examples further illustrate that syntactic rules may operate slightly differently from one dialect to another, and that the surface forms of the sentences are derived by rule. Many languages have similar deletion rules.

In Black English, however, an uninflected form of *be* is required if the speaker is referring to **habitual** action. In SAE the sentence *John is happy* can be interpreted to mean John is happy at the moment and may be constantly happy. To make the distinction clear in SAE, we would have to say *John is always happy*. In BE, this distinction is made syntactically, as follows:

John be happy.	"John is always happy."
John happy.	"John is happy now."
He be late.	"He is habitually late."
He late.	"He is late this time."
Do you be tired?	"Are you generally tired?"
You tired?	"Are you tired now?"

This syntactic distinction between habitual aspect and nonhabitual occurs in languages other than BE, but not in SAE.

Another regular rule in BE deletes the possessive morpheme -'*s* whenever possession is redundantly specified by word order:

[6]Sentences taken from W. Labov. 1969. "The Logic of Nonstandard English." Georgetown University, 20th Annual Round Table, No. 22.

SAE	BE
That is John's house.	That John house.
That is your house.	That you house.
That house is John's.	That house John's.
	(but not: *That house John.)
That house is yours.	That house yours.
	(but not: *That house your.)

There are many more differences between the grammars of BE and SAE than those we have discussed; but the ones we have listed are enough to show the regularity of BE and to dispel the notion that there is anything "illogical" or "primitive" about this dialect.

The study of Black English is important for nonlinguists such as teachers, as well as for linguists. There would be less of a communication breakdown between teachers and their students who speak Black English if this dialect were not considered to be an inferior version of the standard. Children who read *your brother* as *you bruvver* are using their own pronunciation rules. They would be more likely to respond positively to the statement "In the dialect we are using, the 'th' sound is not pronounced [v], as it is in yours" than they would be to a teacher who expressed an attitude of contempt toward their grammar.

Another important reason for studying these dialects is that such study shows the extent to which dialects differ and leads to a better knowledge of human language. Furthermore, the history of any dialect reveals important information about language change in general, as will be discussed in the next chapter.

History of Black English

It is simple to date the beginning of Black English—the first blacks arrived in Virginia in 1619. There are, however, different theories as to the factors that led to the systematic differences between Black English and other American English dialects.

One view suggests that Black English originated when the Negro slaves learned English from their white masters as a second language. (The difficulties of second-language learning are discussed in Chapter 10.) Although the basic grammar was learned, many surface differences persisted, which were reflected in the grammars constructed by the children of the slaves, who heard English primarily from their parents. Had the children been exposed to the English spoken by the whites, their grammars would have been more similar if not identical to the general Southern dialect. The dialect differences persisted and grew because blacks in America were isolated by social and racial barriers. The proponents of this theory point to the fact that the grammars of Black English and Standard American English are basically identical except for a few syntactic and phonological rules, which produce surface differences.

Another view is that many of the unique features of Black English are traceable to influences of the African languages spoken by the slaves. During the seventeenth and eighteenth centuries, Africans who spoke different languages were purposefully grouped together to discourage communication and to prevent slave revolts. In order to communicate, the slaves were forced to use the one common language all had access to, namely, English. They invented a simplified form—called a pidgin (to be discussed below)—which incorporated many features from West African languages. According to this view, the differences between BE and other dialects are due more to basic syntactic differences than to surface distinctions.

It is apparent that Black English is closer to the Southern dialect of English than to other dialects. The theory that suggests that the Negro slaves learned the English of white Southerners as a second language explains these similarities. They might also be explained by the fact that for many decades a large number of Southern white children were raised by black women and played with black children. It is not unlikely that many of the distinguishing features of Southern dialects were acquired from Black English in this way. A publication of the American Dialect Society in 1908–1909 makes this point clearly:

> For my part, after a somewhat careful study of east Alabama dialect, I am convinced that the speech of the white people, the dialect I have spoken all my life and the one I tried to record here, is more largely colored by the language of the negroes [sic] than by any other single influence.[7]

The two-way interchange still goes on. Standard American English is constantly enriched by words, phrases, and usage originating in Black English; and Black English, whatever its origins, is influenced by the changes that go on in the many other dialects of English.

Hispanic English

A major group of American English dialects is spoken by native Spanish speakers or their descendants. The dialects spoken by Puerto Rican and Cuban immigrants or their children are somewhat different from each other and also from those spoken by Mexican Americans in the Southwest and California, called Chicano English (ChE), although they share many features.

These dialects are spoken mainly by bilingual speakers, and the Spanish influence is reinforced by border contact between the United States and Mexico and the social cohesion of a large segment of this population. Like BE, ChE is not simply an incorrect version of SAE; it differs systematically.

In addition to using ChE, many bilingual Hispanics switch from English to Spanish and vice versa, sometimes within a single sentence, a process called **code-switching.**

ChE is, like other dialects, the result of many factors, a major one being the

---

[7]L. W. Payne. 1909. "A Word-List from East Alabama," *Dialect Notes* 3:279–328, 343–391.

influence of Spanish. Phonological differences between ChE and SAE reveal this influence. Chapters 2 and 3 discussed the fact that English has eleven stressed vowel phonemes (not counting the three diphthongs): /i, ɪ, e, ɛ, æ, u, ʊ, o, ɔ, a, ʌ/. Spanish, however, has only five: /i, e, u, o, a/. Chicano speakers substitute the Spanish vowel system for the English, producing a number of homophones that have distinct pronunciations in SAE. Thus *ship* and *sheep* are both pronounced like *sheep* /šip/, *rid* is pronounced like *read* /rid/, and so on.

Here are other systematic differences:[8]

1. Alternation of *ch* /č/ and *sh* /š/; *show* is pronounced as if spelled with a *ch* /čo/ and *check* as if spelled with an *sh* /šɛk/.
2. Devoicing of some consonants, such as /z/ in *easy* /ɪsɪ/ and *guys* /gajs/.
3. /t/ for /θ/ and /d/ for /ð/ word initially, as in /tiŋ/ for *thing* and /de/ for *they*.
4. Word-final consonant cluster simplification. *War* and *ward* are both pronounced /war/; *star* and *start* are /star/. This process may also delete past tense suffixes (*poked* becomes /pok/) and third person singular agreement (*He loves her* becomes *he love her*), by a process similar to that in BE.

Prosodic aspects of speech in ChE, that is, the suprasegmentals such as stress and intonation, also differ from SAE. Stress, for example, may occur on a different syllable in ChE than in SAE.

The Spanish sequential constraint, which does not permit a word to begin with an /s/ cluster, is sometimes carried over to ChE. Thus, *scare* may be pronounced *escare* /ɛsker/.

There are also regular syntactic differences between ChE and SAE. In Spanish, a negative sentence includes a negative morpheme before the verb even if another negative appears; thus, in ChE, "double negatives" occur:

SAE	ChE
I don't have any money.	I don have no money.
I don't want anything.	I no want nothin.

Another regular difference between ChE and SAE is in the use of the comparative *more* to mean *more often,* as in the following:

SAE	ChE
I use English more often.	More I use English.
They use Spanish more often.	They use more Spanish.

Lexical differences also occur, such as the use of *borrow* in ChE for *lend* in SAE *(Borrow me a pencil.)* as well as many other substitutions.

Many Chicano speakers (and speakers of Black English) are bidialectal; they

[8]Joyce Penfield and Jacob L. Ornstein-Galicia. 1985. *Chicano English: An Ethnic Contact Dialect.* John Benjamin. Philadelphia.

can use either ChE (or BE) or SAE, depending on the social situation. The use of these dialects thus is clearly not evidence of language deviance but of language expertise.

Lingua Francas

Language is a steed that carries one into a far country.
Arab proverb

Many areas of the world are populated by people speaking divergent languages. In such areas, where groups desire social or commercial communication, one language is often used by common agreement. Such a language is called a **lingua franca.**

In medieval times, a trade language came into use in the Mediterranean ports. It consisted of Italian mixed with French, Spanish, Greek, and Arabic, and it was called Lingua Franca, "Frankish language." The term *lingua franca* was generalized to other languages similarly used. Thus, any language can be a lingua franca.

English has been called "the lingua franca of the whole world," French, at one time, was "the lingua franca of diplomacy," and Latin and Greek were the lingua francas of Christianity in the West and East, respectively, for a millennium. Among Jews, Yiddish has long served as a lingua franca.

More frequently, lingua francas serve as "trade languages." East Africa is populated by hundreds of tribes, each speaking its own language, but most Africans of this area learn at least some Swahili as a second language, and this lingua franca is used and understood in nearly every marketplace. A similar situation exists in West Africa, where Hausa is the lingua franca.

Hindi and Urdu are the lingua francas of India and Pakistan, respectively. The linguistic situation of this area of the world is so complex that there are often regional lingua francas—usually the popular dialects near commercial centers. The same situation existed in Imperial China.

In modern China, the Chinese language as a whole is often referred to as *Zhongwen,* which technically refers to the written language, whereas *Zhongguo hua* refers to the spoken language. Ninety-four percent of the people living in the People's Republic of China are said to speak Han languages, which can be divided into eight major dialects (or language groups) that for the most part are mutually unintelligible. Within each group there are hundreds of dialects. In addition to these Han languages, there are more than fifty "national minority" languages, including the five principal ones: Mongolian, Uighur, Tibetan, Zhuang, and Korean. The situation is clearly complex, and for this reason an extensive language reform policy was inaugurated to spread a standard language, called *Putonghua,* which embodies the pronunciation of the Beijing (Peking) dialect, the grammar of Northern Chinese dialects, and the vocabulary of modern colloquial Chinese. The native languages and dialects are not considered inferior; rather, the approach is to spread the "common speech'' (the literal meaning of Putonghua) so that all may communicate with each other in this lingua franca.

Certain lingua francas arise naturally; others are developed by government policy and intervention. In many places of the world, however, people still cannot speak with neighbors only a few miles away.

Pidgins and Creoles

Padi dɛm; kɔntri; una ɔl we de na Rom.
Mɛk una ɔl kak una yes. A Kam bɛr siza,
a nɔ kam prez am.

William Shakespeare, *Julius Caesar* III: ii, translated to Krio by Thomas Decker

Pidgins

A lingua franca is typically a language with a broad base of native speakers, likely to be used and learned by persons whose native language is in the same language family. Often in history, however, missionaries and traders from one part of the world have visited and attempted to communicate with peoples residing in another area. In such cases the contact is too specialized and the cultures too widely separated for the usual kind of lingua franca to arise. Instead, the two (or possibly more) groups use their native languages as a basis for a rudimentary language of few lexical items and ''straightforward'' grammatical rules. Such a ''marginal language'' is called a **pidgin.**

There are a number of such languages in the world, including about sixty varieties of English-based pidgins. One such pigdin, called **Tok Pisin,** originally was called Melanesian Pidgin English. It is widely used in Papua, New Guinea. Like most pidgins, many of its lexical items and much of its structure are based on only one language of the two or more contact languages, in this case English. Tok Pisin has about 1500 lexical items, of which about 80 percent are derived from English.

Although pidgins are in some sense rudimentary, they are not devoid of grammar. The phonological system is rule-governed, as in any human language. The inventory of phonemes is generally small, and each phoneme may have many allophonic pronunciations. In Tok Pisin, for example, [č], [š], and [s] are all possible pronunciations of the phoneme /s/; [masin], [mašin], and [mačin] all mean ''machine.''

Tok Pisin has its own writing system, its own literature, and its own newspapers and radio programs, and it has even been used to address a United Nations meeting.

With their small vocabularies, however, pidgins are not good at expressing fine distinctions of meaning. Many lexical items bear a heavy semantic burden, with context being relied upon to remove ambiguity. Much circumlocution and metaphorical extension is necessary. All of these factors combine to give pidgins a unique flavor. What could be a friendlier definition of "friend" than the Australian aborigine's *him brother belong me,* or more poetic than this description of the sun: *lamp belong Jesus?* A policeman is *gubmint catchum-fella,* whiskers are *grass belong face,* and when a man is thirsty *him belly allatime burn.*

Pidgin has come to have negative connotations, perhaps because the best-known pidgins are all associated with European colonial empires. The *Encyclopaedia Britannica* once described Pidgin English as "an unruly bastard jargon, filled with nursery imbecilities, vulgarisms and corruptions." It no longer uses such a definition. In recent times there is greater recognition of the fact that pidgins reflect human creative linguistic ability, as is beautifully revealed by the Chinese servant asking whether his master's prize sow had given birth to a litter: *Him cow pig have kittens?*

Some people would like to eradicate pidgins. A pidgin spoken on New Zealand by the Maoris was replaced, through massive education, by Standard English, and the use of Chinese Pidgin English was forbidden by the government of China. It, too, has died out. Pidgins have been unjustly maligned; they may serve a useful function.[9] For example, a New Guinean can learn Tok Pisin well enough in six months to begin many kinds of semiprofessional training. To learn English for the same purpose might require ten times as long. In an area with well over 500 mutually unintelligible languages, Tok Pisin plays a vital role in unifying similar cultures.

During the seventeenth, eighteenth, and nineteenth centuries many pidgins sprang up along the coasts of China, Africa, and the New World to accommodate the Europeans. Chinook Jargon is a pidginized native American language used by various tribes of the Pacific Northwest to carry on trade. The original Lingua Franca was an Italian-based pidgin used in Mediterranean ports; and Malay, the language of Indonesia and Malaysia, has been highly influenced by a Dutch-based pidgin. Some linguists have even suggested that Proto-Germanic was originally a pidgin, arguing that ordinary linguistic change cannot account for certain striking differences between the Germanic tongues and other Indo-European languages. They theorized that in the first millennium B.C.E., the primitive Germanic tribes that resided along the Baltic Sea traded with the more sophisticated, seagoing cultures. The two people communicated by means of a pidgin, which either significantly affected Proto-Germanic or actually became Proto-Germanic. If this theory is true, English, German, Dutch, and Yiddish had their beginnings as a pidgin.

Case, tense, mood, and voice are generally absent from pidgins. We cannot, however, speak an English pidgin by merely using English without inflecting verbs or declining pronouns. Pidgins are not "baby talk" or Hollywood's version of native Americans talking English. *Me Tarzan, you Jane* may be understood, but it is not pidgin as it is used in West Africa.

Pidgins are simple, but they are rule-governed. In Tok Pisin, verbs that take a

---

[9]Robert A. Hall. 1955. *Hands Off Pidgin English.* Pacific Publications. New South Wales.

direct object must have the suffix *-m*, even if the direct object is absent in surface structure; here are examples of this "rule" of the language:

Tok Pisin:	Mi driman long kilim wanpela snek.
English:	I dreamed that I killed a snake.
Tok Pisin:	Bandarap em i kukim.
English:	Bandarap cooked (it).

Other rules determine word order, which, as in English, is usually quite strict in pidgins because of the lack of case endings on nouns.

The set of pronouns is often simpler in pidgins. In Cameroonian Pidgin (CP), which is also an English-based pidgin, for example, the pronoun system does not show gender or all the case differences that exist in standard English (SE).[10]

CP			**SE**		
a	mi	ma	I	me	my
yu	yu	yu	you	you	your
i	i/am	i	he	him	his
i	i/am	i	she	her	her
wi	wi	wi	we	us	our
wuna	wuna	wuna	you	you	your
dɛm	dɛm/am	dɛm	they	them	their

Pidgins also may have fewer prepositions than the languages on which they are based. In CP, for example, *fɔ* means "to," "at," "in," "for," and "from," as shown in the following examples:

Gif di buk fɔ mi.	"Give the book to me."
I dei fɔ fam.	"She is at the farm."
Dɛm dei fɔ chɔs.	"They are in the church."
Du dis wan fɔ mi, a bɛg.	"Do this for me, please."
Di mɔni dei fɔ tebul.	"The money is on the table."
You fit muf tɛn frangk fɔ ma kwa.	"You can take ten francs from my bag."

Characteristics of pidgins differ in detail from one pidgin to another, and often vary depending on the native language of the pidgin speaker. Thus the verb generally comes at the end of a sentence for a Japanese pidgin speaker (as in "The poor people all potato eat") whereas a Filipino speaker of pidgin puts it before the subject ("Work hard these people").

---

[10]The data from CP are from Loreto Todd. 1984. *Modern Englishes: Pidgins & Creoles*. Basil Blackwell's. Oxford, England.

Creoles

One distinguishing characteristic of pidgin languages is that no one learns them as native speakers. When a pidgin comes to be adopted by a community as its native tongue, and children learn it as a first language, that language is called a creole; the pidgin has become creolized. Creoles become fully developed languages, having more lexical items and a broader array of grammatical distinctions than pidgins. In time, they become languages as complete in every way as other languages.

Creoles often arose on slave plantations in certain areas where Africans of many different tribes could communicate only through the plantation pidgin. Haitian Creole, based on French, developed in this way, as did the "English" spoken in parts of Jamaica. Gullah is an English-based creole spoken by the descendants of African slaves on the islands off the coast of Georgia and South Carolina. Louisiana Creole, related to Haitian Creole, is spoken by large numbers of blacks and whites in Louisiana. Krio, the language spoken by as many as 200,000 Sierra Leoneans, developed, at least in part, from an English-based pidgin.

The study of pidgins and creoles has contributed a great deal to our understanding of the nature of human language and the genetically determined constraints on grammars, as is pointed out by Bickerton:

> Because the grammatical structures of creole languages are more similar to one another than they are to the structures of any other language, it is reasonable to suppose most if not all creoles were invented by the children of pidgin-speaking immigrants. Moreover, since creoles must have been invented in isolation, it is likely that some general ability, common to all people, is responsible for the linguistic similarities.[11]

Styles, Slang, and Jargon

Slang is language which takes off its coat, spits on its hands—and goes to work.
Carl Sandburg

Styles

Most speakers of a language know many "dialects." They use one "dialect" when out with friends, another when on a job interview or presenting a report in class, and another when talking to their parents. These "situation dialects" are called **styles.**

Nearly everybody has at least an informal and a formal style. In an informal style the rules of contraction are used more often, the syntactic rules of negation and agreement may be altered, and many words are used that do not occur in the formal style. Many speakers have the ability to use a number of different styles, ranging

---

[11]Derek Bickerton. 1983. "Creole Languages." *Scientific American* 249: 116–122.

between the two extremes of formal and informal. Speakers of minority dialects sometimes display virtuosic ability to slide back and forth along a continuum of styles that range from the informal patterns learned in a ghetto to "formal standard." When Labov was studying Black English used by Harlem youths, he encountered difficulties because the youths (subconsciously) adopted a different style in the presence of white strangers. It took time and effort to gain their confidence to the point where they would "forget" that their conversations were being recorded and so use their less formal style.

Many cultures have rules of social behavior that strictly govern style. In some Indo-European languages there is the distinction between "you (familiar)" and "you (polite)." German *du* and French *tu* are to be used only with "intimates"; *Sie* and *vous* are more formal and used with nonintimates. French even has a verb *tutoyer,* which means "to use the *tu* form," and German uses the verb *duzen* to express the informal or less honorific style of speaking.

Other languages have a much more elaborate code of style usage. Speakers of Thai use *kin* "eat" to their intimates, informally; but *thaan* "eat" is used informally with strangers, *rabprathaan* "eat" on formal occasions or when conversing with dignitaries or esteemed persons (such as parents), and *chan* "eat" when referring to Buddhist monks. Japanese and Javanese are also languages with elaborate styles that must be adhered to in certain social situations.

Slang

> Police are notorious for creating new words by shortening existing ones, such as *perp* for *perpetrator, ped* for *pedestrian* and *wit* for *witness.* More baffling to court reporters is the gang member who . . . might testify that he was in his *hoopty* around *dimday* when some *mud duck* with a *tray-eight* tried to *take him out of the box.* Translation: The man was in his car about dusk when a woman armed with a .38 caliber gun tried to kill him.
>
> Los Angeles *Times,* August 11, 1986.

One mark of an informal style is the frequent occurrence of **slang.** Almost everyone uses slang on some occasions, but it is not easy to define the word. Slang has been defined as "one of those things that everybody can recognize and nobody can define."[12] The use of slang, or colloquial language, introduces many new words into the language by recombining old words into new meanings. *Spaced out, right on, hangup,* and *rip-off* have all gained a degree of acceptance. Slang may also introduce an entirely new word, such as *barf, flub,* and *pooped.* Finally, slang often consists of ascribing totally new meanings to old words. *Grass* and *pot* widened their meaning to "marijuana"; *pig* and *fuzz* are derogatory terms for "policeman"; *rap, cool, dig, stoned, bread,* and *split* have all extended their semantic domain.

The words we have cited sound "slangy" because they have not gained total acceptability. Words such as *dwindle, freshman, glib,* and *mob* are former slang

---

[12]Paul Roberts. 1958. *Understanding English.* Harper & Row. New York. P. 342.

words that in time overcame their "unsavory" origin. It is not always easy to know where to draw the line between "slang" words and "regular" words. This confusion seems always to have been around. In 1890, John S. Farmer, coeditor with W. E. Henley of *Slang and Its Analogues,* remarked: "The borderland between slang and the 'Queen's English' is an ill-defined territory, the limits of which have never been clearly mapped out."

One generation's slang is another generation's standard vocabulary. *Fan* (as in "Dodger fan") was once a slang term, short for *fanatic. Phone,* too, was once a slangy, clipped version of *telephone,* as *TV* was of *television.* In Shakespeare's time, *fretful* and *dwindle* were slang, and more recently *blimp* and *hot dog* were both "hard-core" slang.

The use of slang varies from region to region, so slang in New York and slang in Los Angeles differ. The word *slang* itself is slang in British English for "scold."

Slang words and phrases are often "invented" in keeping with new ideas and customs. They may represent "in" attitudes better than the more conservative items of the vocabulary. Their importance is shown by the fact that it was thought necessary to give the returning Vietnam prisoners of war a glossary of eighty-six new slang words and phrases, from *acid* to *zonked.* The words on this list—prepared by the Air Force—had come into use during only five years. Furthermore, by the time this book is published, many of these terms may have passed out of the language, and many new ones will have been added.

A number of slang words have entered English from the "underworld," such as *crack* for a special form of cocaine, *payola, C-note, G-man, to hang paper* ("to write 'bum' checks"), *sawbuck,* and so forth.

The now ordinary French word meaning "head," *tête,* which was once a slang word derived from the Latin *testa,* which meant "earthen pot." Some slang words seem to hang on and on in the language, though, never changing their status from slang to "respectable." Shakespeare used the expression *beat it* to mean "scram" (or more politely, "leave!"), and *beat it* would be considered by most English speakers still to be a slang expression. Similarly, the use of the word *pig* for "policeman" goes back at least as far as 1785, when a writer of the time called a Bow Street police officer a "China Street pig."

Jargon and Argot

It is common knowledge that students have a language that is quite peculiar to them and that is not understood very well outside student society . . . But if the code of behaviour somewhere is particularly lively, then the language of the students is all the richer for it—and vice versa.

Friedrich Ch. Laukhard, 1792

Practically every conceivable science, profession, trade, and occupation has its own set of words, some of which are considered to be "slang" and others "technical," depending on the status of the people using these "in" words. Such words are sometimes called **jargon** or **argot.** Linguistic jargon, some of which is used in this book, consists of terms such as *phoneme, morpheme, case, lexicon, phrase structure rule,* and so on.

The existence of argots or jargons is illustrated by the story of a seaman witness being cross-examined at a trial, who was asked if he knew the plaintiff. Indicating that he did not know what *plaintiff* meant brought a chide from the attorney: ''You mean you came into this court as a witness and don't know what 'plaintiff' means?'' Later the sailor was asked where he was standing when the boat lurched. ''Abaft the binnacle,'' was the reply, and to the attorney's questioning stare he responded: ''You mean you came into this court and don't know where abaft the binnacle is?''

Because the jargon terms used by different professional groups are so extensive (and so obscure in meaning), court reporters in the Los Angeles Criminal Courts Building have a library that includes books on medical terms, guns, trade names, and computer jargon, as well as street slang.

The computer age not only ushered in a technological revolution; it also introduced a huge jargon of ''computerese'' used by computer ''hackers,'' including the words *modem* (a blend of *modulator* and *demodulator*), *bit* (a contraction of *binary digit*), *byte* (a collection of some number of bits), *floppy* (a noun or adjective referring to a flexible *disk*), *ROM* (an acronym for *Read Only Memory*), *RAM* (an acronym for *Random Access Memory),* and *morf* (an abbreviation for the question *Male or female?*).

Many jargon terms pass into the standard language. Jargon, like slang, spreads from a narrow group until it is used and understood by a large segment of the population.

Taboo or Not Taboo?

Sex is a four-letter word.
Bumper-sticker slogan

A recent item in a newspaper included the following paragraph (the names have been deleted to protect the guilty):

> ''This is not a Sunday school, but it is a school of law,'' the judge said in warning the defendants he would not tolerate the ''use of expletives during jury selection.'' ''I'm not going to have my fellow citizens and prospective jurors subjected to filthy language,'' the judge added.

How can language be filthy? In fact, how can it be clean? The filth or beauty of language must be in the ear of the listener, or in the collective ear of society.

There cannot be anything about a particular string of sounds that makes it intrinsically clean or dirty, ugly or beautiful. If you say that you pricked your finger when sewing, no one would raise an eyebrow; but if you refer to your professor as a prick, the judge quoted above would undoubtedly censure this "dirty" word.

Certain words in all societies are considered **taboo**—they are not to be used, or at least, not in "polite company." The word *taboo* was borrowed from Tongan, a Polynesian language, in which it refers to acts that are forbidden or to be avoided. When an act is taboo, reference to this act may also become taboo. That is, first you are forbidden to do something; then you are forbidden to talk about it.

What acts or words are forbidden reflect the particular customs and views of the society. Some words may be used in certain circumstances and not in others; for example, among the Zuni Indians, it is improper to use the work *takka,* meaning "frogs," during a religious ceremony; a complex compound word must be used instead, which literally translated would be "several-are-sitting-in-a-shallow-basin-where-they-are-in-liquid."[13]

In certain societies, words that have religious connotations are considered profane if used outside of formal or religious ceremonies. Christians are forbidden to "take the Lord's name in vain," and this prohibition has been extended to the use of curses, which are believed to have magical powers. Thus *hell* and *damn* are changed to *heck* and *darn,* perhaps with the belief or hope that this change will fool the "powers that be." In England the word *bloody* is a taboo word, perhaps because it originally referred to the blood of Christ. The Oxford English Dictionary states that *bloody* has been in general colloquial use from the Restoration and is "now constantly in the mouths of the lowest classes, but by respectable people considered 'a horrid word' on a par with obscene or profane language, and usually printed in the newspapers 'b_____y.'" It further states that the origin of the term is not quite certain. This uncertainty itself gives us a clue about "dirty" words: people who use them often do not know why they are taboo, only that they are, and to some extent, this is why they remain in the language, to give vent to strong emotion.

Words relating to sex, sex organs, and natural bodily functions make up a large part of the set of taboo words of many cultures. Some languages have no native words to mean "sexual intercourse" but do borrow such words from neighboring people. Other languages have many words for this common and universal act, most of which are considered taboo.

Two or more words or expressions can have the same linguistic meaning, with one acceptable and the others the cause of embarrassment or horror. In English, words borrowed from Latin sound "scientific" and therefore appear to be technical and "clean," whereas native Anglo-Saxon counterparts are taboo. This fact reflects the opinion that the vocabulary used by the upper classes was superior to that used by the lower classes, a distinction going back at least to the Norman conquest in 1066, when, as Farb puts it, "a duchess perspired and expectorated and menstruated—while a kitchen maid sweated and spat and bled."

There is no linguistic reason why the word *vagina* is "clean" whereas *cunt* is "dirty"; or why *prick* or *cock* is taboo, but *penis* is acknowledged as referring to part of the male anatomy; or why everyone *defecates,* but only vulgar people *shit.* Many people even avoid words like *breast, intercourse,* and *testicles* as much as

[13]Peter Farb. 1975. *Word Play.* Bantam Books. New York. P. 85.

words like *tits, fuck,* and *balls.* There is no linguistic basis for such views, but pointing this fact out does not imply advocating the use or nonuse of any such words.

Euphemisms

Banish the use of the four letter words
   Whose meaning is never obscure.
The Anglos, the Saxons, those bawdy old birds
   Were vulgar, obscene, and impure.
But cherish the use of the weaseling phrase
   That never quite says what it means;
You'd better be known for your hypocrite ways
   Than vulgar, impure, and obscene.

Ogden Nash, "Ode to the Four Letter Words"

The existence of taboo words or taboo ideas stimulates the creation of **euphemisms.** A euphemism is a word or phrase that replaces a taboo word or serves to avoid frightening or unpleasant subjects. In many societies, because death is feared, there are a number of euphemisms related to this subject. People are less apt to *die* and more apt to *pass on* or *pass away.* Those who take care of your *loved ones* who have passed away are more likely to be *funeral directors* than *morticians* or *undertakers.*

Ogden Nash's poem, quoted above, exhorts against such euphemisms, as another verse demonstrates:

When in calling, plain speaking is out;
When the ladies (God bless 'em) are milling about,
You may wet, make water, or empty the glass;
You can powder your nose, or the "johnny" will pass.
It's a drain for the lily, or man about dog
When everyone's drunk, it's condensing the fog;
But sure as the devil, that word with a hiss,
It's only in Shakespeare that characters ___.

There are scholars who are as bemused as Ogden Nash with the attitudes revealed by the use of euphemisms in society. A journal, *Maledicta,* subtitled "The International Journal of Verbal Aggression" and edited by Reinhold Aman, "specializes in uncensored glossaries and studies of all offensive and negatively valued words and expressions, in all languages and from all cultures, past and present." A review of this journal by Bill Katz in the *Library Journal* (November 1977) points out, "The history of the dirty word or phrase is the focus of this substantial . . . journal [whose articles] are written in a scholarly yet entertaining fashion by professors . . . as well as by a few outsiders."

A scholarly study of Australian English euphemisms shows the considerable creativity involved:[14]

urinate:	drain the dragon
	syphon the python
	water the horse
	squeeze the lemon
	drain the spuds
	wring the rattlesnake
	shake hands with wife's best friend
	point Percy at the porcelain
	train Terence on the terracotta
have intercourse:	shag
	root
	crack a fat
	dip the wick
	play hospital
	hide the ferret
	play cars and garages
	hide the egg roll (sausage, salami)
	boil bangers
	slip a length
	go off like a beltfed motor
	go like a rat up a rhododendron
	go like a rat up a drain pipe
	have gin on the rocks
	have a northwest cocktail

These euphemisms, as well as the difference between the accepted Latinate "genteel" terms and the "dirty" Anglo-Saxon terms, show that a word or phrase not only has a linguistic **denotative meaning** but also has a **connotative meaning,** reflecting attitudes, emotions, value judgments, and so on. In learning a language, children learn which words are "taboo," and these taboo words differ from one child to another, depending on the value system accepted in the family or group in which the child grows up.

Racial and National Epithets

The use of epithets for people of different religions, nationalities, or color tell us something about the users of these words. The word *boy* is not a taboo word when used generally, but when a 20-year-old white man calls a 40-year-old black man "boy," the word takes on an additional meaning; it reflects the racist attitude of the speaker. So also words like *kike, wop, nigger,* and so forth express racist and chauvinist views of society. If racial and national and religious bigotry and oppres-

[14]Jay Powell. 1972. Paper delivered at the Western Conference of Linguistics, University of Oregon.

sion did not exist, then in time these words would either die out or lose their racist connotations.

Language and Sexism

doctor, n. . . . a man of great learning.
The American College Dictionary, 1947

A businessman is aggressive; a businesswoman is pushy. A businessman is good on details; she's picky. . . . He follows through; she doesn't know when to quit. He stands firm; she's hard. . . . His judgments are her prejudices. He is a man of the world; she's been around. He isn't afraid to say what is on his mind; she's mouthy. He exercises authority diligently; she's power mad. He's closemouthed; she's secretive. He climbed the ladder of success; she slept her way to the top.
From "How to Tell a Businessman from a Businesswoman," Graduate School of Management, UCLA, The Balloon XXII, (6).

The discussion of obscenities, blasphemies, taboo words, and euphemisms showed that words of a language cannot be intrinsically good or bad but may reflect individual or societal values. In addition, one speaker may use a word with positive connotations while another may select a different word with negative connotations to refer to the same person. For example, the same individual may be referred to as a *terrorist* by one group and as a *freedom fighter* by another. A woman may be called a *castrating female* (or *ballsy women's libber*) or may be referred to as a *courageous feminist advocate*. The words we use to refer to certain individuals or groups reflect our individual nonlinguistic attitudes and may also reflect the culture and views of society.

Language reflects sexism in society. Language itself is not sexist, just as it is not obscene; but it can connote sexist attitudes as well as attitudes about social taboos or racism.

Dictionaries often give clues to social attitudes. In the 1969 edition of the *American Heritage Dictionary*, examples used to illustrate the meaning of words include "manly courage" and "masculine charm." Women do not fare as well, as exemplified by "womanish tears" and "feminine wiles." In Webster's *New World Dictionary of the American Language, honorarium* is defined as "a payment to a professional man for services on which no fee is set or legally obtainable."

Sections in history textbooks still in use are headed "pioneers and their wives"; children read that "courageous pioneers crossed the country in covered wagons with their wives, children, and cattle." Presumably women are not considered to be as courageous as their husbands.

The U.S. American Men of Science did not change its name to include *and Women* until 1921. The editors were much in advance of Columbia University. Until 1972, the women's faculty toilet doors were labeled "Women," whereas the men's doors were labeled "Officers of Instruction."

Language also reflects sexism in society by the way we interpret neutral (non-gender-specific) terms. Most people, hearing *My cousin is a professor* (or *a doctor,* or *the Chancellor of the University,* or *a steel worker*), assume the cousin is a man. This assumption has nothing to do with the English language but a great deal to do with the fact that, historically, women have not been prominent in these positions. Similarly, if you heard someone say *My cousin is a nurse* (or *elementary school teacher,* or *clerk-typist,* or *houseworker*), you would probably conclude that the speaker's cousin is a woman. It is less evident why the sentence *My neighbor is a blond* is understood as referring to a woman; perhaps the physical characteristics of women in our society assume greater importance than those of men because women are constantly exploited as sex objects.

Studies analyzing the language used by men in reference to women, which often has derogatory or sexual connotations, indicate that such terms go far back into history, and sometimes enter the language with no pejorative implications but gradually gain them. Thus, from Old English *huswif* "housewife," the word *hussy* was derived. In their original employment, "a laundress made beds, a needlewoman came to sew, a spinster tended the spinning wheel, and a nurse cared for the sick. But all apparently acquired secondary duties in some households, because all became euphemisms for a mistress or a prostitute at some time during their existence."[15]

Words for women—all with abusive or sexual overtones—abound: *dish, tomato, piece, piece of ass, chick, piece of tail, bunny, pussy, pussycat, bitch, doll, slut, cow,* to name just a few. Far fewer such pejorative terms exist for men.

Marked and Unmarked Forms

PEANUTS   **Charles Schulz**

Reprinted by permission: © 1977 United Feature Syndicate, Inc.

[15]Muriel R. Schulz. 1975. "The Semantic Derogation of Woman." In B. Thorne and N. Henley, eds., *Language and Sex.* Newbury House Publishers. Rowley, Mass. PP. 66–67.

One striking fact about the asymmetry between male and female terms in many languages is that when there are male/female pairs, the male form for the most part is **unmarked** and the female term is created by adding a bound morpheme or by compounding. We have many such examples in English:

Male	Female
prince	princess
author	authoress
count	countess
actor	actress
host	hostess
poet	poetess
heir	heiress
hero	heroine
Paul	Pauline

Given these asymmetries, **folk etymologies** (nonscientific speculations about the origin of words) arise that misinterpret a number of nonsexist words. For example, *female* is not the feminine form of *male,* but came into English from the Latin word *femina,* with the same morpheme *fe* that occurs in the Latin *fecundus* meaning "fertile" (originally derived from an Indo-European word meaning "to give suck to"). It entered English through the Old French word *femme* and its diminutive form *femelle* "little woman."

Other male/female gender pairs have interesting meaning differences. Although a *governor* governs a state, a *governess* takes care of children; a *mistress,* in its most widely used meaning, is not a female master, nor is a *majorette* a woman major. We talk of "unwed mothers" but not "unwed fathers," of "career women" but not "career men," because there has been historically no stigma for a bachelor to father a child, and men are supposed to have careers. It is only recently that the term *househusband* has come into being, again reflecting changes in social customs.

Possibly as a protest against the reference to new and important ideas as being *seminal* (from *semen*), Clare Booth Luce updated Ibsen's drama *A Doll's House* by having Nora tell her husband that she is pregnant "in the way only men are supposed to get pregnant." When he asks "Men pregnant?" she replies, "With ideas. Pregnancies there (she taps her head) are masculine. And a very superior form of labor. Pregnancies here (she taps her stomach) are feminine—a very inferior form of labor."

Neutral nongender words become compounded when the basic form becomes associated with either sex. Thus, people talk of a *male nurse* because it is expected that a nurse will be a female, and for parallel reasons we have the compounds *lady doctor, career woman,* and *woman athlete.*

The unmarked male nouns also serve as the general terms, as do the male pronouns. The *brotherhood of man* includes women, but *sisterhood* does not include men.

When Thomas Jefferson wrote in the Declaration of Independence that "all *men* are created equal" and "governments are instituted among *men* deriving their just powers from the consent of the governed," he was not using *men* as a general term to include women. His use of the word *men* was precise at the time that women could not vote. In the sixteenth and seventeenth centuries, masculine pronouns were not used as the **generic** terms; the various forms of *he* were used when referring to males, and of *she* when referring to females. By the eighteenth century, scholars (males, to be sure) created the rule designating the male pronouns as the general term, but it was not until the nineteenth century that the rule was applied widely.

Changes in English are taking place that reflect the feminist movement and the growing awareness on the part of both men and women that language may reflect attitudes of society and reinforce stereotypes and bias. More and more the word *people* is replacing *mankind, personnel* is used instead of *manpower, nurturing* instead of *mothering,* and *to operate* instead of *to man. Chair* or *moderator* is used instead of *chairman* (particularly by those who do not like the "clumsiness" of *chairperson*), and terms like *postal worker, fire fighter,* and *public safety officer* are replacing *mailman, fireman,* and *policeman.*

More Asymmetries

Other linguistic asymmetries exist, such as the fact that most women continue to adopt their husbands' names in marriage. This name change can be traced back to early (and to a great extent, current) legal practices. Thus we often refer to a woman as Mrs. Jack Fromkin, but seldom refer to a man as Mr. Vicki Fromkin, except in an insulting sense. We talk of Professor and Mrs. John Smith but seldom, if ever, of Mr. and Dr. Mary Jones. At a UCLA alumni association dinner, place cards designated where "Dr. Fromkin" and "Mrs. Fromkin" were to sit, although both individuals have doctoral degrees.

It is insulting to a woman to be called a *spinster* or an *old maid,* but it is not insulting to a man to be called a *bachelor*. There is nothing inherently pejorative about the word *spinster*. The connotations reflect the different views society has about an unmarried woman as opposed to an unmarried man. It is not the language that is sexist; it is society.

Female Language

An increasing number of researchers have been investigating language and sex and language and sexism. One area of research concerns the differences between male and female speech styles. In Japanese, male and female speech comprise two distinct dialects of the language. So different are these two styles that "seeing eye" guide dogs in Japan are trained in English, because the sex of the owner is not known in advance and it is easier and more socially acceptable for a blind person to use English than the "wrong" sex's language style.

DENNIS THE MENACE

"WHEN A LADY NEVER MARRIES, SHE'S AN *OLD MAID*." "THEN WHEN A MAN NEVER MARRIES, IS HE AN OLD BUTLER?"

DENNIS THE MENACE® used by permission of Hank Ketcham and © by North America Syndicate.

In the Muskogean language, Koasati, spoken in Louisiana, words that end in an /s/ when spoken by men, end in /l/ or /n/ when used by women; for example, the word meaning "lift it" is *lakawhol* for women and *lakawhos* for men. Early explorers reported that the men and women of the Carib Indians used different dialects. In Chiquita, a Bolivian language, the grammar of male language includes a noun class gender distinction, with names for males and supernatural beings morphologically marked in one way, and nouns referring to females marked in another.

There is nothing inherently wrong in the development of different styles, which may include intonation, phonology, syntax, and lexicon. It is wrong, however, to continue stereotypes regarding female speech, which are more myths than truth. For example, a common stereotype is that women talk a lot; yet controlled studies show just the opposite is true when men and women are together.

One characteristic of female speech is the higher pitch used by women, due, to a great extent, to the shorter vocal tracts of women. However, a study conducted by Caroline Henton showed that the difference in the pitch between male and female British voices was greater, on the average, than could be accounted for by physiology alone, suggesting that some social factor must be involved during the acquisition period, or perhaps during puberty when male voices "change."

This chapter has stressed the fact that language is neither good nor evil, but its use may be. A person who views women or blacks or Hispanics as inferior will consider their special speech characteristics inferior. Furthermore, when society itself institutionalizes such attitudes, the language reflects this bias. When everyone in society is truly created equal and treated as such, there will be little concern for the asymmetries that exist in language.

Artificial Languages

La inteligenta persono lernas la interlingvon Esperanton rapide kaj facile. (Esperanto for: "The intelligent person learns the international language Esperanto rapidly and easily.")

Since the scattering at Babel, many people have hoped for a return to the blissful state when everyone spoke a universal language. Lingua francas are a step in that direction, but none has gone far enough. Since the seventeenth century, scholars have been inventing artificial languages with the hope that they would achieve universal acceptance and that universal language would bring universal peace. With stubborn regularity the world has rejected every attempt. Perhaps the world has seen too many civil wars to accept this idea.

The obituary column of artificial languages indicates the constant attempts and regular failures: Bopal, Kosmos, Novial, Parla, Spokil, Universala, and Volapuk are but a few of the deceased hundreds. Most artificial languages never get beyond their inventors, because they are abstruse and difficult and uninteresting to learn.

One artificial language has enjoyed some success. **Esperanto** was invented by the Polish scholar Zamenhof, who wrote under the pseudonym of Dr. Esperanto ("one who hopes"). He gave his "language" the advantages of extreme grammatical regularity, ease of pronunciation, and a vocabulary based mainly on European languages. Esperanto is spoken by several million speakers throughout the world, including some who learned it as one of their native languages. There is a literature written in it, a number of institutions teach it, and it is officially recognized by some international organizations.

Esperantists claim that their language can be learned easily by any intelligent person; but despite the claims of its proponents, it is not maximally simple. There is an obligatory accusative case (*Ni lernas Esparanton* "We're learning Esperanto"), and adjectives and nouns must agree in number (*inteligenta persono* "intelligent person," but *inteligentaj personoj* "intelligent persons"). Speakers of Chinese or

Malaysian (and even English) find these rules different from those of their own grammars. Esperanto is regular insofar as all nouns end in *-o*, with plural *-oj*; all adjectives end in *-a*, with plural *-aj*; the present tense of all verbs ends in *-as*, the future in *-os*, and the past in *-is*; and the definite article is always *la*. However, to speakers of Thai, a language that does not have a definite article at all, Esperanto is far from "simple," and speakers of the many languages that indicate tenses without verb endings (as English indicates the future tense with *shall* or *will*) may find that aspect of Esperanto difficult to learn.

A modification of Esperanto, called **Ido** ("offspring" in Esperanto), has further simplified the language by eliminating the accusative case and abolishing adjective and noun agreement, but the basic problem remains. Esperanto is essentially a Romance-based pidgin with Greek and Germanic influence, albeit a highly developed one with an immense vocabulary. It therefore remains "foreign" to most people; speakers of Russian, Hungarian, Hausa, or Hindi would find Esperanto as unfamiliar as French or Spanish.

The problems besetting the world community are basically nonlinguistic, despite the linguistic problems that do exist. Language problems may intensify social and economic problems, but they do not generally cause wars, unemployment, poverty, pollution, and disease.

Summary

Every person has an individual way of speaking, called an **idiolect.** The language used by a group of speakers may also show systematic differences called **dialects.** The dialects of a language are the mutually intelligible forms of that language that differ in systematic ways from each other. Dialects develop and are reinforced because languages change, and the changes that occur in one group or area may differ from those that occur in another. **Regional dialects** and **social dialects** develop for this reason. Some of the differences in the regional dialects of the United States may be traced to the different dialects spoken by the colonial settlers from England; those from southern England, who arrived first, spoke one dialect, and those from the north spoke another. In addition, the colonists who maintained close contact with England reflected the changes occurring in British English, while earlier forms were preserved among colonists who spread westward and broke contact with England and the Atlantic coast. The study of regional dialects has produced **dialect atlases** with **dialect maps** showing the areas where specific dialectal characteristics occur in the speech of the region. Each area is delineated by a boundary line called an **isogloss.**

Dialect differences include phonological or pronunciation differences (often called **accents**), vocabulary distinctions, and syntactic rule differences. The differences between dialects are not as great as the similarities, permitting speakers of different dialects to communicate with each other.

In many countries, one dialect or dialect group is viewed as the **standard,** such as **Standard American English** (SAE). Although this particular dialect is not linguistically superior, it may be considered by some to be the only "correct" form of the language. Such a view has led to the idea that some nonstandard dialects are "deficient," as is erroneously suggested regarding **Black English.** A study of Black English shows it to be as logical, complete, rule-governed, and expressive as any other dialect. So are the dialects spoken by Hispanic–Americans, whose native language (or that of their parents) is Spanish. One such dialect, **Chicano English** (ChE), shows interesting systematic phonological and syntactic differences from SAE, stemming from the influence of Spanish.

In areas where many languages are spoken, one language may become a **lingua franca** to ease communication among the people. In other cases, where traders or missionaries or travelers need to communicate with people who speak a language unknown to them, a **pidgin** may develop, based on one language that is simplified lexically, phonologically, and syntactically. When a pidgin is widely used and is learned by children as their first language, it is **creolized.** The grammars of creole languages are similar to those of other languages, and languages of creole origin now exist in many parts of the world.

Besides regional and social dialects, speakers may use different **styles** of their dialect depending on the particular context. **Slang** is not often used in formal situations or writing, but is widely used in speech; **argot** and **jargon** refer to the unique vocabulary used by a professional or trade group and not shared "outside."

In all societies certain acts or behaviors are frowned on, forbidden, or considered taboo. The words or expressions referring to these taboo acts are then also avoided or considered "dirty." Language itself cannot be obscene or clean; the rejection of specific words or linguistic expressions only reflects the culture of a given society. At times slang words may be taboo, whereas scientific or standard terms with the same meaning are acceptable in "polite society." Taboo words and acts give rise to **euphemisms,** which are words or phrases that replace the expressions to be avoided. Thus, *powder room* is a euphemism for *toilet,* which itself started as a euphemism for *lavatory,* which is now more acceptable than its replacement.

Just as some words reflect society's views of sex, natural bodily functions, or religion, so also some words reflect racist, chauvinist, and sexist attitudes in society. The language itself is not racist or sexist, but its use reflects these views. Such terms, however, may perpetuate and reinforce biased views, and be demeaning and insulting to those addressed. Popular movements and changes in the institutions of society may then be reflected in changes in the language.

The communication barriers that exist because of the thousands of languages used in the world have led to the invention of artificial languages, which, the inventors hope, could be used universally. All such attempts have failed. Most such languages, including the most widely known, Esperanto, are not "universal" in any sense; they are pidgins based on a small number of languages from one language family and may still be difficult to learn.

References

Baugh, John. 1983. *Black Street Speech*. University of Texas. Austin.

Burling, Robbins. 1970. *Man's Many Voices*. Holt, Rinehart and Winston. New York.

Cassidy, Frederick G. 1985. *Dictionary of American Regional English*. The Belknap Press of Harvard University Press. Cambridge, Mass.

Dillard, J. L. 1972. *Black English: Its History and Usage in the United States*. Random House. New York.

Ferguson, Charles, and Shirley Brice Health, eds. 1981. *Language in the USA*. Cambridge University Press. Cambridge, England.

Folb, E. 1980. *Runnin' Down Some Lines: The Language and Culture of Black Teenagers*. Harvard University Press. Cambridge, Mass.

Frank, Francine, and Frank Ashen. 1983. *Language and the Sexes*. State University of New York Press. Albany, New York.

Labov, W. 1969. "The Logic of Nonstandard English." Georgetown University 20th Annual Round Table. Monograph Series on Languages and Linguistics, No. 22.

Penfield, Joyce, and Jacob L. Ornstein-Galicia. 1985. *Chicano English: An Ethnic Contact Dialect*. John Benjamin. Amsterdam/Philadelphia.

Reed, Carroll E. 1977. *Dialects of American English*. Rev. ed. University of Massachusetts Press. Amherst, Mass.

Todd, Loreto. 1984. *Modern Englishes: Pidgins & Creoles*. Basil Blackwell. Oxford, England.

Williamson, Juanita V., and Virginia M. Burke. 1971. *A Various Language: Perspectives on American Dialects*. Holt, Rinehart and Winston. New York.

Exercises

1. Each pair of words is pronounced as shown phonetically in at least one American English dialect. Write in phonetic transcription your pronunciation of each word that you pronounce differently.

a.	"horse"	[hɔrs]	_____	"hoarse"	[hors]	_____
b.	"morning"	[mɔrnĩŋ]	_____	"mourning"	[mornĩŋ]	_____
c.	"for"	[fɔr]	_____	"four"	[for]	_____
d.	"ice"	[ʌjs]	_____	"eyes"	[ajz]	_____
e.	"knife"	[nʌjf]	_____	"knives"	[najvz]	_____
f.	"mute"	[mjut]	_____	"nude"	[njud]	_____
g.	"din"	[dĩn]	_____	"den"	[dẽn]	_____
h.	"hog"	[hɔg]	_____	"hot"	[hat]	_____
i.	"marry"	[mæri]	_____	"Mary"	[meri]	_____
j.	"merry"	[mɛri]	_____	"marry"	[mæri]	_____
k.	"rot"	[rat]	_____	"wrought"	[rɔt]	_____
l.	"lease"	[lis]	_____	"grease" (v.)	[griz]	_____
m.	"what"	[ʌat]	_____	"watt"	[wat]	_____
n.	"ant"	[æ̃nt]	_____	"aunt"	[ãnt]	_____
o.	"creek"	[kʰrɪk]	_____	"creak"	[kʰrik]	_____

2. Below is a passage from *The Gospel According to St. Mark* in Cameroon English Pidgin. See how much you are able to understand before consulting the English translation given below. State some of the similarities and differences between CEP and SAE.

1. Di fos tok fo di gud nuus fo Jesus Christ God yi Pikin.
2. I bi sem as i di tok fo di buk fo Isaiah, God yi nchinda (Prophet), "Lukam, mi a di sen man nchinda fo bifo yoa fes weh yi go fix yoa rud fan."

3. Di vos fo som man di krai fo bush: "Fix di ples weh Papa God di go, mek yi rud tret."

Translation:
1. The beginning of the gospel of Jesus Christ, the Son of God;
2. As it is written in the book of Isaiah the prophet, Behold, I send my messenger before thy face, which shall prepare thy way before thee.
3. The voice of one crying in the wilderness, Prepare ye the way of the Lord, make his paths straight.

3. In the period from 1890 to 1904, the book *Slang and Its Analogues* by J. S. Farmer and W. E. Henley was published in seven volumes. The following entries are included in this dictionary. For each item: (1) state whether the word or phrase still exists; (2) if not, state what the modern slang term would be; (3) if the word remains but its meaning has changed, provide the modern meaning.

all out: completely, as in "All out the best." (The expression goes back to as early as 1300.)

to have apartments to let: be an idiot; one who is empty-headed.

been there: in "Oh, yes, I've been there." Applied to a man who is shrewd and who has had many experiences.

belly-button: the navel.

berkeleys: a woman's breasts.

bitch: most offensive appellation that can be given to a woman, even more provoking than that of *whore*.

once in a blue moon: extremely seldom.

boss: master; one who directs.

bread: employment (1785—"out of bread" = "out of work.")

claim: to steal.

cut dirt: to escape.

dog cheap: of little worth. (Used in 1616 by Dekker: "Three things there are Dog-cheap, learning, poorman's sweat, and oathes.")

funeral: as in "It's not my funeral." "It's no business of mine."

to get over: to seduce, to fascinate.

groovy: settled in habit; limited in mind.

grub: food.

head: toilet (nautical use only).

hook: to marry.

hump: to spoil.

hush money: money paid for silence; blackmail.

itch: to be sexually excited.

jam: a sweetheart or a mistress.

leg bags: stockings.

to lie low: to keep quiet; to bide one's time.

to lift a leg on: to have sexual intercourse.

looby: a fool.

malady of France: syphilis (used by Shakespeare in 1599).

nix: nothing.

noddle: the head.

old: money. (1900—''Perhaps it's somebody you owe a bit of the old to, Jack.'')

to pill: talk platitudes.

pipe layer: a political intriguer; a schemer.

poky: cramped, stuffy, stupid.

pot: a quart; a large sum; a prize; a urinal; to excel.

puny: a freshman.

puss-gentleman: an effeminate.

4. Suppose someone asked you to help compile items for a new dictionary of slang. List ten ''slang'' words that you know, and provide a short definition for each.

1)

2)

3)

4)

5)

6)

7)

8)

9)

10)

5. Below are given some words used in British English for which different words are usually used in American English. See if you can match the British and American equivalents.

	British		American		British		American
a.	clothes peg	A.	candy	k.	biscuits	K.	baby buggy
b.	braces	B.	truck	l.	queue	L.	elevator
c.	lift	C.	line	m.	torch	M.	can
d.	pram	D.	main street	n.	underground	N.	cop
e.	waistcoat	E.	crackers	o.	high street	O.	wake up
f.	shop assistant	F.	suspenders	p.	crisps	P.	trunk
g.	sweets	G.	wrench	q.	lorry	Q.	vest
h.	boot (of car)	H.	flashlight	r.	holiday	R.	subway
i.	bobby	I.	potato chips	s.	tin	S.	clothes pin
j.	spanner	J.	vacation	t.	knock up	T.	clerk

6. This chapter has discussed various types of dialects that represent mutually intelligible systematic variations of a single language. In addition to such dialects, which arise historically, "secret" languages are invented that "distort" the language, often to prevent understanding by those who have not learned the language "game."

Pig Latin is a common language game of English; but even Pig Latin has dialects, forms of the "language game" with different rules.

A. Consider the following data from three dialects of Pig Latin, each with its own rule applied to words beginning with vowels:

	Dialect 1	*Dialect 2*	*Dialect 3*
"eat"	[itme]	[ithe]	[ite]
"arc"	[arkme]	[arkhe]	[arke]

(1) State the rule that accounts for the Pig Latin forms in each dialect.

Dialect 1:

Dialect 2:

Dialect 3:

(2) How would you say *honest, admire,* and *illegal* in each dialect? Give the phonetic transcription of the Pig Latin forms.

honest   1. _____   2. _____   3. _____

admire   1. _____   2. _____   3. _____

illegal   1. _____   2. _____   3. _____

B. In one dialect of Pig Latin, the word "strike" is pronounced [ajkstre], and in another dialect it is pronounced [trajkse]. In the first dialect "slot" is pronounced [atsle] and in the second dialect, it is pronounced [latse].

(1) State the rules for each of these dialects that account for these different Pig Latin forms of the same words.

Dialect 1:

Dialect 2:

(2) Give the phonetic transcriptions for the following words in both dialects.

1	2

spot

crisis

scratch

7. Thousands of language games such as Pig Latin exist in the world's languages. In some, a suffix is added to each word; in others a syllable is inserted after each vowel; there are rhyming games and games in which phonemes are reversed. There is a game used by the Walbiri, natives of central Australia, in which the meanings of words are distorted rather than the phonological forms. In this language, all nouns, verbs, pronouns, and adjectives are replaced by their semantic opposites. Thus, the sentence *Those men are small* means *This woman is big*. These language games provide evidence for the phonemes, words, morphemes, semantic features, and so on that are posited by linguists for descriptive grammars.

Below are some sentences representing different English language games. Write each sentence in its undistorted form; state the language-game "rule."

a.   /aj-o tʊk-o maj-o dɔg-o awt-o sajd-o/

b.   /hirli ɪzli əli mɔrli kamliplɪliketliədli gemli/

c.   Mary-shmary can-shman talk-shmalk in-shmin rhyme-shmyme.

d.   Betpetterper latepate thanpan nevpeverper.

e.   thop-e fop-oot bop-all stop-a dop-i op-um blop-ew dop-own /ðapə fapʊt bapɔl stape dapi apəm blapu dapawn/

f.   /kʌbən jʌbu spʌbik ðʌbəs kʌbajnd ʌbəv ʌbənglʌbɪš/ (This sentence is in "Ubby Dubby" from a children's television program popular in the 1970s.)

8. Compile a list of argot (or jargon) terms from some profession or trade (for example, lawyer, musician, doctor, longshoreman, and so forth). Give a definition for each term in "nonjargon" terms.

9. "Translate" the first paragraph of any well-known document or speech—such as the Declaration of Independence, the Gettysburg Address, or the Preamble to the Constitution—into informal, colloquial language.

C H A P T E R 8

Language Change: The Syllables of Time

The language of this country being always upon the flux, the Struldbruggs of one age do not understand those of another, neither are they able after two hundred years to hold any conversation (farther than by a few general words) with their neighbors the mortals, and thus they lie under the disadvantage of living like foreigners in their own country.

Jonathan Swift, *Gulliver's Travels*

All living languages change with time. It is fortunate that they do so rather slowly compared to the human life span. It would be inconvenient to have to relearn our native language every twenty years. In the field of astronomy we find a similar situation. Because of the movement of individual stars, the stellar configurations we call constellations are continuously changing their shape. Fifty thousand years from now we would find it difficult to recognize Orion or the Big Dipper; but from year to year the changes are not noticeable. Linguistic change is also slow, in human—if not astronomical—terms. If we were to turn on a radio and miraculously receive a broadcast in our "native language" from the year 3000, we would probably think we had tuned in some foreign language station; yet from year to year we hardly notice any change in our language.

Many of the changes are revealed when languages have written records. We know a great deal of the history of English because it has been written for about 1000 years. Old English, spoken in England around the end of the first millennium, is scarcely recognizable as English. (Of course, our linguistic ancestors did not call their language Old English!) A speaker of Modern English would find the language unintelligible. There are college courses in which Old English is studied as a foreign language,

The following excerpt from *Caedmon's Hymn*, composed in the seventh century C.E., shows why Old English is studied as a "foreign" language:

Nū sculon herigean heofonrīces Weard,
Now we must praise heaven-kingdom's Guardian,

Meotodes meahte ond his mōdgeþanc,
The Creator's might and his mind-plans,

weorc Wuldorfæder, swā hē wundra gehwæs,
the work of the glory-father, when he of wonders of every one,

ēce Drihten, ōr onstealde.
eternal lord the beginning established.

A line from *Beowulf* further illustrates why Old English must be translated for us to enjoy (the letter þ, called "thorn," is pronounced like the *th* in *think*):

Wolde guman findan þone þe him on sweofote sare geteode
He wanted to find the man who harmed him while he slept

Approximately 500 years after *Beowulf,* Chaucer wrote *The Canterbury Tales* in what is now called Middle English, spoken from around 1100 to 1500. It is more easily understood by present-day readers, as seen by looking at the opening of the *Tales*.

Whan that Aprille with his shoures soote
The droghte of March hath perced to the roote . . .

When April with its sweet showers
The drought of March has pierced to the root . . .

Two hundred years after Chaucer, in a language that can be considered an earlier form of Modern English, Shakespeare's Hamlet says:

A man may fish with the worm that hath eat of a king, and eat of the fish that hath fed of that worm.

Shakespeare wrote in the sixteenth century. A passage from *Everyman,* written about 1485, illustrates why it is claimed that Modern English was already spoken by 1500:

The Summoning of Everyman called it is,
That of our lives and ending shows
How transitory we be all day.
The matter is wonder precious,
But the intent of it is more gracious
And sweet to bear away.

The division of English into Old English (449–1100 C.E.), Middle English (1100–1500), and Modern English (1500–present) is somewhat arbitrary, being marked by the dates of events in English history, such as the Norman invasion of 1066, that profoundly influenced the English language. Thus the history of English and the changes that occurred in the language reflect, to some extent, nonlinguistic history.

Changes in a language are actually changes in the grammars of the speakers of the language. An examination of the changes that have occurred in English during the past 1500 years shows that the sound system and morphological system have changed, the syntactic rules have changed, and the semantic system has changed. Thus all parts of the grammar may change. Although most of our examples are from English, the histories of other languages show similar changes.

The Regularity of Sound Change

That's not a regular rule: you invented it just now.
Lewis Carroll, *Alice's Adventures in Wonderland*

The southern United States represents a major dialect area of American English. For example, words pronounced with the diphthong /aj/ in nonsouthern English will usually be pronounced with the monophthong /a/ in the South. Thus, you may be greeted by /ha/ instead of /haj/ ''hi'' in Atlanta, where many residents will also order apple or pecan /pa/ ''pie.'' This /aj/ – /a/ correspondence between these two dialects is an example of a **regular sound correspondence;** when /aj/ occurs in a word in nonsouthern dialects, /a/ occurs in the southern dialect.

The different pronunciations of *I*, *pie*, and so on did not always exist in English. This chapter will discuss how such dialect differences arose and why the sound differences are usually regular and not confined to just a few words.

In Chaucer's time, over 600 years ago, the small rodent we call a mouse [maws] was called a *mūs* [mu:s], and this mūs may have lived in someone's *hūs* [hu:s], which is the way *house* [haws] was pronounced at that time. In general, where we now pronounce [aw], speakers of Chaucer's time pronounced [u:]. This is a regular correspondence like the one between [aj] and [a:]. Thus *out* [awt] was pronounced *ūt* [u:t], *south* [sawθ] was pronounced [su:θ], and so on. Many such regular correspondences can be found, relating older and newer forms of English. All languages exhibit similar correspondences in their history.

Regular sound correspondences are also found among different languages as well as among dialects of one language. If you have studied a Romance language such as French or Spanish, you may have noticed that where an English word begins with *f*, the corresponding word in a Romance language often has a *p*. Thus *father* is French *père*, Spanish *padre*; and English *fish* is French *poisson*, Spanish *pescado*. This *f–p* correspondence is another example of a regular sound correspondence.[1]

The native American languages Cree and Ojibwa show a *t–n* correspondence: Cree *atim*, Ojibwa *anim,* ''dog''; Cree *nitim*, Ojibwa *ninim,* ''my sister-in-law.''

Languages change in time, and the regular sound correspondences we observe

---

[1]The individual histories of English and the Romance languages have somewhat obscured the regularity of this correspondence, but even so it is striking.

between older and modern forms of a language, or between two dialects or two related languages, are due to changes in the languages' phonological system that affect certain sounds, or classes of sounds, rather than individual words. Centuries ago, as illustrated above, English underwent a sound shift in which [u:] became [aw]. We observe regularity precisely because *sounds* change, not words.

The process of sound shift can also account for dialect differences. At an earlier stage of American English a sound change of [aj] to [a:] took place among certain speakers in the southern region of the country. The change did not spread, perhaps because these speakers were somewhat isolated, or perhaps because the pronunciation of [a:] for [aj] became a "regionalism" that others did not imitate. Whatever the case, many dialect differences in pronunciation result from a sound shift whose spread is limited.

Regional dialect differences in pronunciation arise from the natural linguistic phenomenon of sound change. Many of the world's modern languages were at first regional dialects that became widely spoken and survived as separate languages. The Romance languages were once dialects of Latin spoken in the Roman Empire. As discussed in Chapter 7, there is nothing "degenerate" or "illiterate" about regional pronunciations. They are simply a result of natural sound change that failed to spread.

English and German are languages said to be **genetically related** because they developed from the same "parent" language. All genetically related languages were dialects of the same language at an earlier stage. Regular sound correspondences between languages indicate this fact. Consider the diagram in Figure 8–1 on page 300.

Suppose the phonemic inventory of Language L included the sound A, and the speakers of this language split into two groups with little contact between them. Perhaps half of them migrated to the other side of a mountain or ocean. One group underwent a sound shift A→B: words in L which were pronounced with an A now were pronounced with a B (for example, pronouncing /aw/ in the place of /u:/). The other group underwent a different sound shift of A→C. When the sound shifts are complete, there are two languages (or different dialects) L1 and L2, which exhibit the sound correspondence B↔C. The B↔C correspondence shows that the two languages descended from a common source, the parent language L. (Chance alone cannot explain a regular sound correspondence.)

If records of L were available, it would be possible to observe a regular sound correspondence between L and L1, namely A↔B, and between L and L2, namely A↔C. Such observations would confirm the relatedness of L1 and L2.

Similar circumstances resulted in the *f–p* correspondence between English and the Romance languages. Speakers of Indo-European, the language from which both English and French descended, once divided into smaller groups. One of those groups underwent a sound change of *p→f*. Their descendants eventually spoke "Germanic" languages (for example, English and German). Other Indo-Europeans, whose descendants spoke Romance languages, did not experience the change. This ancient sound change resulted in the *f–p* sound correspondence.

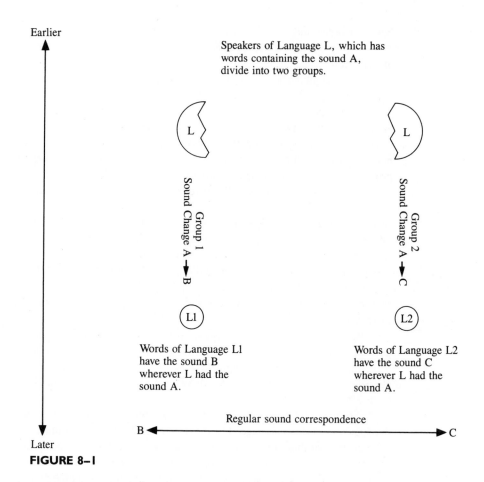

Earlier

Speakers of Language L, which has words containing the sound A, divide into two groups.

L

L

Group 1
Sound Change A → B

Group 2
Sound Change A → C

L1

L2

Words of Language L1 have the sound B wherever L had the sound A.

Words of Language L2 have the sound C wherever L had the sound A.

Regular sound correspondence

B ◄──────────────────────────────► C

Later

FIGURE 8–1

Phonological Change

Etymologists . . . for whom vowels did not matter and who cared not a jot for consonants.
Voltaire

Regular sound correspondences illustrate changes in the phonological system. In earlier chapters we discussed speakers' knowledge of their phonological system including knowledge of the phonemes and phonological rules of the language. Any of these aspects of the phonology is subject to change.

Speakers of most Modern English dialects know that /x/, the velar fricative, is not part of their phonemic inventory. In the history of English this sound was lost. *Night* was once pronounced [nɪxt], *drought* was pronounced [druxt], and *saw* was pronounced [saux]. This phonological change—the loss of /x/—took place between the times of Chaucer and Shakespeare. All words once pronounced with a /x/ no longer include this sound. In some cases it disappeared, as in *night* and *light*. In other cases the /x/ became a /k/, as in *elk* (Old English *eolh* [ɛɔlx]). In yet other cases it became a vowel, as in *hollow* (Old English *holh* [hɔlx]) or *sorrow* (Old English *sorh* [sɔrx]). There are dialects of Modern English such as Scottish that have retained the /x/ sound in some words, such as *loch* [lɔx] meaning ''lake.''

These examples show that the **inventory** of sounds can change by the loss of phonemes. The inventory can also change by the *addition* of new phonemes. Old English did not have the phoneme /ž/ of *leisure* [ližər] or *confusion* [kə̃nfjužə̃n]. Through a process of ''palatalization,'' certain occurrences of /z/ were pronounced as [ž]. Eventually the [ž] sound became a phoneme in its own right, reinforced by the fact that it is a common phoneme in French, which exerted a major influence on English after the Norman Conquest.

A phonetically predictable allophone may become a distinctive phoneme. In Old English the phoneme /f/ was pronounced as [f] in initial and final word position, but as [v] between two vowels. Just as [p] and [pʰ] are allophones of the same /p/ phoneme in modern English, [f] and [v] were variants of the phoneme [f] in Old English. Both [f] and geminate /f:/ occurred between vowels; for example, /ofer/ ''over'' was pronounced [ɔvɛr] and /of:a/ (a person's name) was pronounced [ɔf:a]. (Geminate /f:/ was not voiced between vowels.) When the geminate [f:] was simplified to [f], a contrast between [f] and [v] was created. In addition, other [f]/[v] contrasts arose, and [v] became a separate phoneme /v/.

This example shows that phonemes may be lost (/x/), or added (/ž/), or result from a change in the status of allophones (the allophones of /f/—[f] and [v]— becoming separate phonemes /f/ and /v/).

Such changes occur in the history of all languages. Neither /č/ nor /š/ were phonemes of Latin, but /č/ is a phoneme of modern Italian and /š/ a phoneme of modern French, both of which evolved from Latin. In an older stage of Russian the phoneme /æ/ occurred, but in modern Russian, [æ] is merely an allophone of /a/. Thus a phoneme was lost due to a change in the allophones.

Phonological Rules

An interaction of phonological rules may result in the addition or loss of phonemes, and in changes in the lexicon. For example, the nouns *house* and *bath* were once differentiated from the verbs *house* and *bathe* by the fact that the verbs ended with a short vowel sound (still reflected in the spelling). Furthermore, a rule in English (alluded to above in relation to [f] and [v]) said: ''When a voiceless consonant phoneme occurs between two vowels, voice that consonant.'' Thus the /s/, which was followed by a vowel in the verb *house*, was pronounced [z], and the /θ/ in the verb *bathe* was pronounced [ð] for the same reason.

Later a rule was added to the grammar of English deleting unstressed short vowels at the end of words. The final vowel was thus deleted from the verbs *house* and *bathe,* which resulted in the present pronunciation with final voiced consonants. The addition of this rule also resulted in the new phonemes /z/ and /ð/. Prior to this change, they were simply the allophones of the phonemes /s/ and /θ/ between vowels.

Eventually, both the unstressed vowel deletion rule and the intervocalic-voicing rule were lost from the grammar of English. Thus the set of phonological rules can change both by addition and loss of rules.

Five hundred years ago, Fante, a language of Ghana, did not have the sounds [ts] or [dz] ([ts] is a *single* sound, a voiceless alveolar affricate; [dz] is a voiced alveolar affricate). The *addition* of a phonological rule to the language "created" these sounds; this rule said "pronounce a /d/ as [dz] and a /t/ as [ts] when these phonemes occur before /i/." The addition of this rule to the grammar of Fante did not create new phonemes; [dz] and [ts] are predictable phonetic realizations of the underlying phonemes /d/ and /t/. That is, they are allophones of /d/ and /t/. The grammar, however, was changed in that a new rule was added.

The addition of phonological rules can result in dialect differences. In Chapter 7 we discussed the addition of an "*r*-dropping" rule in English that did not spread throughout the language (/r/ is not pronounced unless followed by a vowel). Today, we see the effect of that rule in the "*r*-less" pronunciation of British English and of American English dialects spoken in the Boston area and the southern United States.

From the standpoint of the language as a whole, phonological changes occur gradually over the course of many generations of speakers, although a given speaker's grammar may or may not reflect the change. The changes are not "planned" any more than we are presently planning what changes will take place in English by the year 2300. Speakers are aware of the changes only through dialect differences.

The Great Vowel Shift

A major change in the history of English that resulted in new phonemic representations of words and morphemes took place approximately between 1400 and 1600. It is known as the **Great Vowel Shift.** The seven long, or tense, vowels of Middle English underwent the following change:

Shift			Example			
Middle English		Modern English	Middle English		Modern English	
[i:]	→	[aj]	[mi:s]	→	[majs]	*mice*
[u:]	→	[aw]	[mu:s]	→	[maws]	*mouse*
[e:]	→	[i:]	[ge:s]	→	[gi:s]	*geese*
[o:]	→	[u:]	[go:s]	→	[gu:s]	*goose*
[ɛ:]	→	[e:]	[brɛ:ken]	→	[bre:k]	*break*
[ɔ:]	→	[o:]	[brɔ:ken]	→	[bro:k]	*broke*
[a:]	→	[e:]	[na:mə]	→	[ne:m]	*name*

By diagraming the Great Vowel Shift on a vowel chart (Figure 8–2), we can see that the highest vowels [i:] and [u:] "fell off" to become the diphthongs [aj] and [aw], while the long vowels underwent an increase in tongue height, as if to fill in the space left when the highest vowels became diphthongs. In addition, [a] was "fronted."

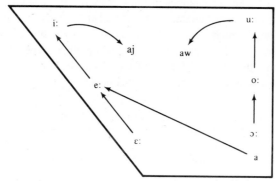

FIGURE 8–2 The Great Vowel Shift.

These changes are among the most dramatic examples of regular sound shift. The phonemic representation of many thousands of words changed. Today, some reflection of this vowel shift is seen in the alternating forms of morphemes in English: *please, pleasant; serene, serenity; sane, sanity; crime, criminal; sign, signal;* and so on. In each pair of words, the first had a long vowel in Middle English and is therefore pronounced differently today.

The Great Vowel Shift is a primary source of many of the spelling "inconsistencies" of English, because our spelling system still reflects the way words were spelled before the Great Vowel Shift took place.

Morphological Change

*Of all the words of witch's doom
There's none so bad as which and whom.
The man who kills both which and whom
Will be enshrined in our Who's Whom.*

Fletcher Knebel

Like phonological rules, rules of morphology may be lost, added, or changed. We can observe some of these changes by comparing older and newer forms of the language, or by looking at different dialects.

The suffix *-ize*, which changes nouns and adjectives into verbs meaning "to make _____," as in *finalize* "to make final," is changing to become "productive" in American English. Speakers are attaching this suffix to more and more words that previously did not take it. Words like *privatize* "to make private" and *rigidize* "to make rigid" are achieving the status of *optimize, stabilize,* and *vitalize.* This change in the morphology of American English is reflected in additions to the lexicon. The change seems to be upsetting the neoprescriptivists. In his book *A Civil Tongue*[2] Edwin Newman devotes an entire chapter, entitled "Ize Front," to lamenting this change in the use of *-ize.*

Extensive changes in rules of morphology have occurred in the history of the Indo-European languages. In Classical Latin there was a complex system of *case endings,* which were added to the noun stem according to its function in the sentence. Latin had seven cases. Below are the different forms (the *declension*) for the noun *lupus* "wolf" for six of the cases (the "locative" case is not shown because its use was restricted to place names):

Case	Noun Stem		Case Ending		
nominative	lup	+	us	lupus	The *wolf* runs.
genitive	lup	+	i	lupi	A sheep in *wolf's* clothing.
dative	lup	+	ō	lupō	Give food *to the wolf.*
accusative	lup	+	um	lupum	I love *the wolf.*
ablative	lup	+	ō	lupō	Run *from a wolf.*
vocative	lup	+	e	lupe	*Wolf,* come here!

In *Alice's Adventures in Wonderland,* Lewis Carroll has Alice give us a brief lesson in grammatical case. Alice has become very small and is swimming around in a pool of her own tears with a mouse whom she wishes to befriend:

> "Would it be of any use, now," thought Alice, "to speak to this mouse? Everything is so out-of-the-way down here, that I should think very likely it can talk: at any rate, there's no harm in trying." So she began: "O Mouse, do you know the way out of this pool? I am very tired of swimming about here, O Mouse!" (Alice thought this must be the right way of speaking to a mouse: she had never done such a thing before, but she remembered having seen in her brother's Latin Grammar, "A mouse—of a mouse—to a mouse—a mouse—O mouse!")

Alice gives an English "translation" of the nominative, genitive, dative, accusative, and vocative cases (she omits the ablative and locative).

Such an extensive case system (of which we have seen only part) was present in Latin, Ancient Greek, and Sanskrit. It was also present in Indo-European, the ancestor of all these languages. Modern languages such as Lithuanian and Russian retain much of the Indo-European case system, but these languages are in the minor-

---

[2]E. Newman. 1976. *A Civil Tongue.* Bobbs-Merrill. New York.

ity. In most modern Indo-European languages, changes have all but obliterated the case system. English still retains the genitive case, calling it possessive (as in *a sheep in wolf's clothing*). Pronouns retain a few more traces: for example, *he/she* corresponds to the nominative, *him/her* to the accusative and dative, and *his/hers* to the genitive case.

English has replaced its depleted case system with an equally expressive system of prepositions and with stricter constraints on word order (a "trade-off" between morphological and syntactic rules). For example, in Latin *lupus donum viro dat*, literally "the wolf a gift to the man gives," is only one of many possible word orders. In English this same meaning is normally conveyed in two ways: *The wolf gives a gift to the man*, in which the preposition *to* "marks" the dative case; or *The wolf gives the man a gift*, in which the word order determines the case structure, hence the meaning.

Old English also had a rich case-ending system, as illustrated by the following noun forms:

Case	OE Singular		OE Plural	
nominative	stān	"stone"	stānas	"stones"
genitive	stānes	"stone's"	stāna	"stones'"
dative	stāne	"stone"	stānum	"stones"
accusative	stān	"stone"	stānas	"stones"

and pronoun forms:

Case	OE Singular		OE Dual		OE Plural	
nominative	ic	"I"	wit	"we two"	wē	"we"
genitive	min	"my-mine"	uncer	"our two"	ūre	"our-ours"
dative	mē	"me"	unc	"us two"	ūs	"us"
accusative	mec	"me"	uncit	"us two"	ūsic	"us"

In these examples, *stān* represents the principal "strong" masculine noun declension. There were "weak" declensions also. The plural of this strong declension in the nominative and accusative cases became generalized to all the English regular nouns in the following way.

In becoming Middle English, Old English underwent a change that lengthened the "stem" vowel and reduced the "suffix" vowel of certain word classes. Thus Old English *stānas*, /stɔnas/, "stones" became Middle English /stɔ:nəs/. Another phonological rule change, mentioned earlier, resulted in the dropping out of certain short unstressed vowels, and this rule, together with the Great Vowel Shift, applied to the Middle English /stɔ:nəs/ to give Modern English /stonz/ (with vowel length not indicated because it is not distinctive in Modern English). This change,

OE /stɔnas/ → ME /stɔ:nəs/ → Mod. Eng. /stonz/

is representative of thousands of similar changes. When the ''weak'' syllables representing case endings in the forms of the singular, genitive plural, and dative plural were similarly dropped, only two distinct forms of the noun were left: *stone* and *stones*. English thus lost much of its case system; this morphological change resulted from changes that took place in the phonological rules of English.

Syntactic Change

The loss of case endings in English occurred together with changes in the rules of syntax, which constrained word order more than it had been. In Old English, word order was freer because the case endings alone disclosed the thematic or meaning relations in a sentence. Thus, the following sentences were all grammatical in Old English, and all meant ''The man slew the king'':

> Se man sloh þone kyning.
> þone kyning sloh se man.
> Se man þone kyning sloh.
> þone kyning se man sloh.
> Sloh se man þone kyning.
> Sloh þone kyning se man.

(*Se* was a definite article used only with the subject noun, and þone was the definite article used only with the object noun.)

In Modern English only the first of the literal translations below means what the original meant, and four of the six are ungrammatical sentences:

> The man slew the king.
> The king slew the man.
> *The man the king slew.
> *The king the man slew.
> *Slew the man the king.
> *Slew the king the man.

The syntactic rules of Modern English permit less variation in word order. Additionally, Modern English, as discussed in Chapter 5, is an SVO (Subject-Verb-Object) language. Old English was more of an SOV language;[3] thus the phrase-structure rules that determine the word order of the basic sentences of the language changed in the history of English.

The syntactic rules relating to the English negative construction also underwent a number of changes from Old English to the present. In Modern English, negation is expressed by adding *not* or *do not*. We may also express negation by adding words like *never* or *no*:

---

[3]Old English had both SVO and SOV characteristics. Despite the freer word order, SVO and SOV were still the preferred word order of the basic sentences of the language.

I am going → I am not going
I went → I did not go
I go to school → I never go to school
I want food → I don't want any food; I want no food

In Old English the main negation element was *ne*. It usually occurred before the *auxiliary verb* or the verb, as illustrated by these examples from Old English manuscripts:[4]

þæt he *na*   siþþan geboren *ne* wurde
that he never after   born   not would-be
that he should never be born after that

ac hie *ne* dorston þær on cuman
but they not dared   there on come
but they dared not land there

In the first example the word order is different from that of Modern English, and there are two negatives: *na* (a contraction of *ne* + *a*; "not" + "ever" = "never") and *ne*. As shown, a "double negative" was grammatical in Old English, although double negatives are ungrammatical in Modern Standard American English.

In addition to the contraction of *ne* + *a* → *na*, other negative contractions occurred in Old English: *ne* could be attached to *habb-* "have," *wes-* "be," *wit-* "know," and *will-* "will" to form *nabb-*, *nes-*, *nyt-*, and *nyll-*, respectively.

Modern English has "contraction" rules that change *do* + *not* into *don't*, *will* + *not* into *won't*, and so on. In these contractions the phonetic form of the negation element always comes at the *end* of the word, because Modern English word order puts the *not* after the auxiliary. In Modern English, *not* must precede the main verb of the clause, and a *do* or *does* must be present if there is no auxiliary verb. In Old English, the negative element occurs at the beginning of the contraction, because it typically preceded the auxiliary in sentences. The rules determining the placement of the negative morpheme have changed. Such syntactic changes may take centuries to be fully completed, and there are often intermediate stages.

Another syntactic change in English affected the rules of "comparative" and "superlative" constructions. Today we form the comparative by adding -*er* to the adjective or by inserting *more* before it; the superlative is formed by adding -*est* or by inserting *most*. In Malory's *Tales of King Arthur,* written in 1470, double comparatives and double superlatives occur, which today are ungrammatical: *more gladder, more lower, moost royallest, moost shamefullest.*

When we study a language such as Elizabethan English solely from written records, we see only sentences that are grammatical, unless ungrammatical sentences are used deliberately. Without native speakers of Elizabethan English to query, we can only infer what was ungrammatical. Such inference leads us to

---

[4]From E. C. Traugott. 1972. *The History of English Syntax.* Holt, Rinehart and Winston. New York. *Note:* þ, or "thorn," was pronounced [θ].

believe that expressions like *the Queen of England's crown* were ungrammatical in former versions of English. The title *The Wife's Tale of Bath* (rather than *The Wife of Bath's Tale*) in *The Canterbury Tales* supports this inference. Modern English, on the other hand, allows some rather complex constructions that involve the possessive marker. An English speaker can use possessive constructions such as

> The girl whose sister I'm dating's roommate is pretty.
> The man from Boston's hat fell off.

Older versions of English had to resort to an "*of* construction" to express the same thought *(The hat of the man from Boston fell off)*. It is clear that a syntactic change took place that accounts for the extended use of the possessive morpheme *'s*.

Lexical Change

Curl'd minion, dancer, coiner of sweet words.
Matthew Arnold, "Sohrab and Rustum"

Changes in the lexicon also occur, including the addition of new words, changes in the meanings of words, and the loss of words.

Addition of Words

Chapter 4 discussed ways in which new words can enter the language—for example, by *compounding*, the recombining of old words to form new ones with new meanings. Thousands of common English words have entered the language by this process, including *afternoon, bigmouth, chickenhearted, do in, egghead, force feed, g-string, icecap, jet set, longshoreman, moreover, nursemaid, offshore, pothole, railroad, sailboat, takeover, undergo, water cooler, x-ray,* and *zooecology*.

We also saw that new words may be formed by derivational processes, as in *uglification* or *finalize* (from which we get a "bonus," *finalization*). Other methods for enlarging the vocabulary that were discussed include word coinage, deriving words from names, blends, back-formations, acronyms, and abbreviations or clippings.

Borrowings

Neither a borrower nor a lender be.
Polonius, *Hamlet*

Another important source of new words is borrowing from other languages. Borrowing occurs when one language takes a word or morpheme from another language and adds it to its lexicon. Most languages are borrowers, so the lexicon can be divided into native and nonnative words (often called **loan words**). A *native word* is one whose history (or **etymology**) can be traced back to the earliest known stages of the language.

A language may borrow a word *directly* or *indirectly*. A *direct* borrowing means that the borrowed item is a native word in the language from which it is borrowed. *Feast* was borrowed directly from French and can be traced back to Latin *festa*. On the other hand, the word *algebra* was borrowed from Spanish, which in turn had borrowed it from Arabic. Thus *algebra* was indirectly borrowed from Arabic, with Spanish as an intermediary.

Some languages are heavy borrowers. Albanian has borrowed so heavily that few native words are retained. On the other hand, most native American languages borrowed little from their neighbors.

English has borrowed extensively. Of the 20,000 or so words in common use, about three-fifths are borrowed. Of the 500 most frequently used words, however, only two-sevenths are borrowed, and because these ''common'' words are used over and over again in sentences, the actual frequency of appearance of native words is about 80 percent. Morphemes such as *and, be, have, it, of, the, to, will, you, on, that,* and *is* are all native to English.

The history of the English-speaking peoples can be followed by studying the kinds of loan words in the language and when they entered. Until the Norman Conquest in 1066, England was inhabited chiefly by the Angles, the Saxons, and the Jutes, peoples of Germanic origin who came to England in the fifth century C.E. and eventually became the English. (The word *England* is derived from *Angla-land*.) Originally, they spoke Germanic dialects, from which Old English developed directly. These dialects contained a number of Latin borrowings but were otherwise undiluted by foreign elements. These Germanic tribes had displaced the earlier Celtic inhabitants, whose influence on Old English was confined to a few Celtic place-names. (The modern languages Welsh, Irish, and Scots Gaelic are descended from the Celtic dialects.)

For three centuries after the Norman Conquest, French was the language used for all affairs of state and for most commercial, social, and cultural matters. The West Saxon literary language was abandoned, but regional varieties of English continued to be used in homes, in the churches, and in the marketplace. During these three centuries, vast numbers of French words entered English, of which the following are representative:

government	crown	prince	state	parliament
nation	jury	judge	crime	sue
attorney	property	miracle	charity	court
lechery	virgin	saint	pray	mercy
religion	value	royal	money	society

Until the Norman invasion, when an Englishman slaughtered an ox for food, he ate *ox*. If it was a pig, he ate *pig*. If it was a sheep, he ate *sheep*. However, ''ox'' served at the Norman tables was *beef (boeuf)*, ''pig'' was *pork (porc)*, and ''sheep'' was *mutton (mouton)*. These words were borrowed from French into English, as were the food-preparing words *boil, fry, stew,* and *roast.*

English borrowed many ''learned'' words from foreign sources during the Renaissance. In 1476 the printing press was introduced in England by William Caxton, and by 1640, 55,000 books had been printed in English. The authors of these books used many Greek and Latin words, and as a result, many words of ancient Greek and Latin entered the language.

From Greek came *drama, comedy, tragedy, scene, botany, physics, zoology,* and *atomic.* Greek roots have also provided English with a means for coining new words. *Thermos* ''hot'' plus *metron* ''measure'' give us *thermometer.* From *akros* ''topmost'' and *phobia* ''fear'' we get *acrophobia* ''dread of heights.'' An ingenious cartoonist, Robert Osborn, has ''invented'' some phobias, to each of which he gives an appropriate name:[5]

logizomechanophobia	''fear of reckoning machines'' from Greek *logizomai* ''to reckon or compute'' + *mekhane* ''device'' + *phobia*
ellipsosyllabophobia	''fear of words with a missing syllable'' from Greek *elleipsis* ''a falling short'' + *syllabē* ''syllable'' + *phobia*
pornophobia	''fear of prostitutes'' from Greek *porne* ''harlot'' + *phobia*

Latin loan words in English are numerous. They include:

bonus	scientific	rape	exit
alumnus	quorum	orthography	describe

Latin, like Greek, has also provided prefixes and suffixes that are used productively with both native and nonnative roots. The prefix *ex-* comes from Latin:

ex-husband	ex-wife	ex–sister-in-law

The suffix *-able/-ible* is also Latin, borrowed via French, and can be attached to almost any English verb, as in:

writable	readable	answerable	movable

During the ninth and tenth centuries, the Scandinavians, who first raided and then settled in the British Isles, left their traces in the English language. The pronouns *they, their,* and *them* are loan words from the Scandinavian language Old Norse, from which modern Danish, Norwegian, and Swedish have descended. This

[5]From *An Osborn Festival of Phobias.* Copyright © 1971 by Robert Osborn. Text Copyright © 1971 by Eve Wengler. Reprinted by permission of Liveright Publishers, New York.

period is the only time that English ever borrowed pronouns. Many English words beginning with [sk] are of Scandinavian origin: *scatter, scare, scrape, skirt, skin, sky*.

Bin, flannel, clan, slogan, and *whisky* are all words of Celtic origin, borrowed at various times from Welsh, Scots Gaelic, or Irish.

Dutch was a source of borrowed words, too, many of which are related to shipping: *buoy, freight, leak, pump, yacht*.

From German came *quartz, cobalt*, and—as we might guess—*sauerkraut* and *beer*.

From Italian, many musical terms, including words describing opera houses, have been borrowed: *opera, piano, virtuoso, balcony*, and *mezzanine*.

Words having to do with mathematics and chemistry were borrowed from Arabic, because early Arab scholarship in these fields was quite advanced. *Alcohol, algebra, cipher*, and *zero* are a representative sample. Arabic loan words have also entered English through Spanish, the original borrower.

Spanish has loaned us (directly) *barbecue, cockroach, guitar*, and *ranch*, as well as *California*, literally "hot furnace."

With the settlement of the "New World," the English-speaking colonists borrowed from native American languages as well as from Spanish. Such languages provided us with *pony, hickory*, and *squash*, to mention only a few, and nearly half the state names of the United States are from native American languages.

Hundreds of "place names" in the United States are of non-English origin. We certainly cannot call native American names "foreign," except in the sense that they were foreign to English. Native American place names include:

Connecticut	Potomac	Ohio	Mississippi
Erie	Huron	Michigan	Alleghenies
Appalachians	Ozarks	Massachusetts	Kentucky
Wisconsin	Oregon	Texas	Chattanooga
Chicago	Milwaukee	Omaha	Passaic

Spanish place names include:

Rio Grande	Colorado	Sierra Nevada	Santa Fe
Los Angeles	San Francisco	Santa Barbara	San Jose

Dutch place names include:

Brooklyn	Harlem

The influence of Yiddish on English is interesting; Yiddish words are used by many non-Jews as well as by non-Yiddish-speaking Jews in the United States. There was even a bumper sticker proclaiming: "Marcel Proust is a yenta." *Yenta* is a Yiddish word meaning "gossipy woman" or "shrew." *Lox* "smoked salmon," *bagel* "a hard roll resembling a doughnut," and *matzo* "unleavened cracker" belong to American English, as well as Yiddish expressions like *chutzpah, schmaltz, schlemiel, schmuck, schmo,* and *kibitz.*

Other languages also borrow words, and many of them have borrowed from English. Twi speakers drank palm wine before Europeans arrived in Africa. Now they also drink [bia] "beer," [hwiski] "whisky," and [gɔrdɔn ǰin] "Gordon's gin."

Italian is filled with "strange" words like *snack* (pronounced "znak"), *poster,* and *puzzle* ("pootsle"), and Italian girls use *blushes* and are warned by their mothers against *petting.*

Young Russians have incorporated into their language words like *jazz, rock,* and the *twist,* which they dance in their *blue jeans* to *rock music.* When former President Nixon was considered for impeachment by the Congress, the official Communist Party newspaper *Pravda* used the word *impeechmente* instead of the previously used Russian word *ustraneniye* "removal."

For thousands of years Japanese borrowed heavily from Chinese (to which it is unrelated). Because Japanese uses Chinese characters in its writing system, many native Japanese words coexist with a Chinese loan word. Japanese even has two ways of counting, one using native Japanese words and the other using Chinese loan words for the numbers.

In the past 100 years Japanese has borrowed heavily from European languages, especially American English. The Japanese have a special "syllabary" (similar to our alphabet, but see Chapter 9 on writing systems), which is used primarily to transcribe loan words. Japanese has many thousands of loan words from English, including technical vocabulary, sports terms, and the jargon used in advertising.

Loss of Words

Words also can be *lost* from a language, though an old word's departure is never as striking as a new word's arrival. When a new word comes into vogue, its unusual presence draws attention; but a word is lost through inattention—nobody thinks of it; nobody uses it; and it fades out of the language.

As a reading of Shakespeare's work shows, English has lost many words, such as these taken from *Romeo and Juliet: beseem* "to be suitable," *mammet* "a doll or puppet," *wot* "to know," *gyve* "a fetter," *fain* "gladly," and *wherefore* "why."

Semantic Change

His talk was like a stream which runs
with rapid change from rocks to roses.
It slipped from politics to puns;
It passed from Mahomet to Moses.

Winthrop Mackworth Praed, "The Vicar"

We have seen that a language may gain or lose lexical items. Additionally, the meaning or semantic representation of words may change, becoming broader, narrower, or shifted.

Broadening When the meaning of a word becomes broader, that word means everything it used to mean, and then some. The Middle English word *dogge* meant a specific breed of dog, but it was eventually **broadened** to encompass all members of the species *Canis familiaris*. The word *holiday* originally meant "holy day," a day of religious significance. Today the word signifies any day on which we do not have to work. *Butcher* once meant "slaughterer of goats" (and earlier "of bucks"), but its modern usage is more general. Similarly, *picture* used to mean "painted representation," but today you can take a picture with a camera. A *companion* used to mean a person with whom you shared bread, but today it is a person who accompanies you. *Quarantine* once had the restricted meaning "forty days' isolation," and *bird* once meant "young bird." The invention of steam-powered boats gave the verb *sail* an opportunity to extend its dominion to boats without sails, just as the verb *drive* widened in meaning to encompass self-propelled vehicles.

Narrowing In the King James version of the Bible (1611), God says of the herbs and trees, "to you they shall be for meat" (Genesis 1:29). To a speaker of seventeenth-century English, *meat* meant "food," and *flesh* meant "meat." Since that time, semantic change has **narrowed** the meaning of meat to what it is in Modern English. The word *deer* once meant "beast" or "animal," as its German related word *Tier* still does. The meaning of *deer* has been narrowed to a particular kind of animal. Similarly, the word *hound* used to be the general term for "dog," like the German *Hund*. Today *hound* means a special kind of dog. The Old English word that occurs as modern *starve* once meant "to die." Its meaning has narrowed to become "to die of hunger," and in colloquial language "to be very hungry," as in "I'm starved." *Token* used to have the broad meaning "sign," but long ago was specialized to mean a physical object that is a sign, such as a *love token*. *Liquor* was once synonymous with *liquid, reek* used to mean "smoke," and *girl* once meant "young person of either sex."

Meaning Shifts The third kind of semantic change that a lexical item may undergo is a shift in meaning. The word *bead* originally meant "prayer." During the Middle Ages the custom arose of repeating prayers (that is, *beads*) over and over and counting them by means of little wooden balls on a rosary. The meaning of *bead* shifted from "prayer" to the visible sign of a prayer. The word *knight* once meant "youth" but was elevated in meaning in time for the age of chivalry. *Lust* used to mean simply "pleasure," with no negative or sexual overtones. *Lewd* was merely "ignorant," and *immoral* meant "not customary." *Silly* used to mean "happy" in Old English. By the Middle English period it had come to mean "naive," and only in Modern English does it mean "foolish." The overworked Modern English word *nice* meant "ignorant" a thousand years ago. When Juliet tells Romeo, "I am too *fond*," she is not claiming she likes Romeo too much. She means "I am too *foolish*."

Reconstructing "Dead" Languages

. . . Philologists who chase
A panting syllable through time and space
Start it at home, and hunt it in the dark,
To Gaul, to Greece, and into Noah's Ark.

Cowper, "Retirement"

The branch of linguistics that deals with how languages change, what kinds of changes occur, and why they occurred is called **historical and comparative lin-guistics.** It is *historical* because it deals with the history of particular languages; it is *comparative* because it deals with relations between languages.

The nineteenth-century historical and comparative linguists based their theo-ries on the observations that there is a resemblance between certain languages, and that the *differences* among languages showing such resemblance are *systematic:* in particular, that there are regular sound correspondences. They also assumed that languages displaying systematic differences, no matter how slight in resemblance, had descended from a common source language—that is, were genetically related.

The chief goal of the nineteenth-century historical-comparativists was to de-velop and elucidate the genetic relationships that exist among the world's lan-guages. They aimed to establish the major language families of the world and to define principles for the classification of languages. Their work grew out of earlier research.

In 1786 Sir William Jones (a British scholar who found it best to reside in India because of his sympathy for the rebellious American colonists) delivered a paper in which he observed that Sanskrit bore to Greek and Latin ''a stronger affinity . . . than could possibly have been produced by accident.'' Jones suggested that these three languages had ''sprung from a common source'' and that probably Germanic and Celtic had the same origin. The classical philologists of the time attempted to disprove the idea that there was any genetic relationship among San-skrit, Latin, and Greek, because if such a relationship existed it would make their views on language and language development obsolete. A Scottish philosopher, Dugall Stewart, for example, put forth the hypothesis that Sanskrit and Sanskrit literature were inventions of Brahmans, who used Greek and Latin as models to deceive Europeans. He wrote on this question without knowing a single Sanskrit character, whereas Jones was an eminent Sanskritist.

About thirty years after Jones delivered his important paper, the German linguist Franz Bopp pointed out the relationships among Sanskrit, Latin, Greek, Persian, and Germanic. At the same time, a young Danish scholar named Rasmus Rask corroborated these results, and brought Lithuanian and Armenian into the relationship as well. Rask was the first scholar to describe formally the regularity of certain phonological differences between related languages.

Rask's investigation of these regularities was followed up by the German linguist Jakob Grimm (of fairy-tale fame), who published a four-volume treatise

(1819–1822) that specified the regular sound correspondences among Sanskrit, Greek, Latin, and the Germanic languages. It was not only the similarities that intrigued Grimm and the other linguists, but the systematic nature of the differences. Where Latin has a [p], English often has an [f]; where Latin has a [t], English often has a [θ]; where Latin has a [k], English often has an [h].

Grimm pointed out that certain phonological changes that did not take place in Sanskrit, Greek, or Latin must have occurred early in the history of the Germanic languages. Because the changes were so strikingly regular, they became known as "Grimm's Law," which is illustrated in Figure 8–3.

Earlier stage:[6]	bh	dh	gh	b	d	g	p	t	k
	↓	↓	↓	↓	↓	↓	↓	↓	↓
Later stage:	b	d	g	p	t	k	f	θ	x (or h)

FIGURE 8–3 Grimm's Law (an early Germanic sound shift).

Grimm's Law can be expressed in terms of natural classes of speech sounds: voiced aspirates become deaspirated; voiced stops become voiceless; voiceless stops become fricatives.

By observing **cognates,** words in related languages that developed from the same word (and hence often, but not always, have the same meaning), we can observe sound correspondences and from them deduce sound changes. Thus, from the cognates of Sanskrit, Latin, and English (representing Germanic) shown in Figure 8–4, the regular correspondence *p–p–f* indicates that the languages are genetically related. Indo-European *p is posited as the origin of the *p–p–f* correspondence:[7]

Indo-European	**Sanskrit**	**Latin**	**English**
*p	p	p	f
	pitar-	pater	father
	pad-	pēs	foot
	No cognate	piscis	fish
	pasu	pecu	fee

FIGURE 8–4 Cognates of Indo-European *p.

A more complete chart of correspondences is given in Figure 8–5, where a single representative example of each regular correspondence is presented. In most cases *many cognate sets* exhibit the same correspondence, which leads to the reconstruction of the Indo-European sound shown in the first column.

---

[6]This "earlier stage" is the original parent of Sanskrit, Greek, the Romance and Germanic languages, and other languages—namely, Indo-European. The symbols *bh*, *dh*, and *gh* are "breathy voiced" stop phonemes, often called "voiced aspirates."

[7]The asterisk before a letter indicates a "reconstructed" sound. It does not mean an unacceptable form. This use of the asterisk occurs only in this chapter.

Indo-European	Sanskrit		Latin		English	
*p	p	pitar-	p	pater	f	father
*t	t	trayas	t	trēs	θ	three
*k	ś	śun[8]	k	canis	h	hound
*b	b	No cognate	b	labium	p	lip
*d	d	dva-	d	duo	t	two
*g	j	ajras	g	ager	k	acre
*bh	bh	bhrātar-	f	frāter	b	brother
*dh	dh	dhā	f	fē-ci	d	do
*gh	h	vah-	h	veh-ō	g	wagon

FIGURE 8–5 Some Indo-European sound correspondences.

Sanskrit underwent the fewest consonant changes, while Latin underwent somewhat more, and Germanic (under Grimm's Law) underwent almost a complete restructuring. Still, the fact that it was the phonemes and phonological rules that changed, and not individual words, has resulted in the remarkably regular correspondences that allow us to reconstruct much of the sound system of Indo-European.

Exceptions can be found to these regular correspondences, as Grimm was aware. He stated: "The sound shift is a general tendency; it is not followed in every case." Karl Verner in 1875 explained some of the exceptions to Grimm's Law. He formulated "Verner's Law" to show why Indo-European *p*, *t*, and *k* failed to correspond to *f*, θ, and *x* in certain cases:

> Verner's Law: *When the preceding vowel was unstressed,* **f**, **θ**, *and* **x** *underwent a further change to* **b**, **d**, *and* **g.**

A group of young linguists known as the **Neo-Grammarians** went beyond the idea that such sound shifts represented only a tendency, and claimed that sound laws have no exception. They viewed linguistics as a natural science, and therefore believed that laws of sound change were unexceptionable natural laws. The "laws" they put forth often had exceptions, however, which could not always be explained as dramatically as Verner's Law explained the exceptions to Grimm's Law. Still, the work of these linguists provided important data and insights into language change and why such changes occur.

The linguistic work of the early nineteenth century had some influence on Charles Darwin, and in turn, Darwin's Theory of Evolution had a profound influence on linguistics, and on all areas of science. Some linguists thought that languages had a "life cycle" and developed according to evolutionary laws. In addition, it was believed that each language can be traced to a common ancestor. This theory of biological naturalism, called *Stammbaum* ("family tree") theory, has an element of truth to it; but it is a vast oversimplification of the way languages change and evolve into other languages.

---

[8]ś is a sibilant different from *s*.

The Comparative Method

When the differences among two or more languages are systematic and regular, as exemplified by regular sound correspondences, the languages are likely to be related. Even if the "parent" language no longer exists, by comparing the "daughter" languages we may deduce many facts about the parent language. The method of **reconstruction** of a parent language from a comparison of its daughters is called the **comparative method.**

A brief example will illustrate how the comparative method works. Consider these words in four Romance languages:[9]

French	Italian	Spanish	Portuguese	
cher	**c**aro	**c**aro	**c**aro	"dear"
champ	**c**ampo	**c**ampo	**c**ampo	"field"
chandelle	**c**andela	**c**andela	**c**andeia	"candle"

In French [š] corresponds to [k] in the three other languages. This regular sound correspondence, [š]–[k]–[k]–[k], along with other facts, supports the view that French, Italian, Spanish, and Portuguese descended from a common language. The comparative method leads to the reconstruction of [k] in "dear," "field," and "candle" of the parent language, and shows that [k] underwent a change to [š] in French, but not in Italian, Spanish, or Portuguese, which retained the original [k] of the parent language, Latin.

To use the comparative method, analysts identify regular sound correspondences (not always easy to do) in what they take to be "daughter" languages; and for each correspondence, they reconstruct a sound of the parent language. In this way the entire sound system of the parent may be reconstructed. The various phonological changes that occurred in the development of each "daughter" language as it descended and changed from the parent are then identified. Sometimes the sound that analysts choose in their reconstruction of the parent language will be the sound that appears most frequently in the correspondence. This approach was illustrated above with the four Romance languages.

Other considerations may outweigh the "majority rules" principle. The likelihood of certain phonological changes may persuade the analyst to reconstruct a "minority" sound, or even a sound that does not occur at all in the correspondence. For example, consider data in these four hypothetical languages:

Language A	Language B	Language C	Language D
hono	hono	fono	vono
hari	hari	fari	veli
rahima	rahima	rafima	levima
hor	hor	for	vol

[9]Data from Winfred P. Lehmann. 1973. *Historical Linguistics,* 2nd ed. Holt, Rinehart and Winston. New York. (*Note:* ch = [š]; c = [k].)

Wherever Languages A and B have an *h*, Language C has an *f* and Language D has a *v*. Therefore we have the sound correspondence *h–h–f–v*. We might be tempted by the comparative method to reconstruct *h* in the parent language; but from other data on historical change, and from phonetic research, we know that *h* seldom becomes *f* or *v*. Generally the reverse is the case. Therefore linguists reconstruct an **f* in the parent, and posit the sound change "*f* becomes *h*" in Languages A and B, and "*f* becomes *v*" in Language D. The other correspondences are not problematic insofar as these data are concerned. They are:

o–o–o–o   n–n–n–n   a–a–a–e   r–r–r–l   m–m–m–m

They lead to the reconstructed forms **o, *n, *a, *r, *m* for the parent language, and the sound changes "*a* becomes *e*" and "*r* becomes *l*" in Language D. They are "natural" sound changes often found in the world's languages. Language D, in this example, is the most *innovative* of the three languages, as it has undergone three sound changes.

It is by means of the comparative method that nineteenth-century linguists, beginning with August Schleicher in 1861, were able to initiate the reconstruction of the long-lost parent language so aptly conceived by Jones, Bopp, Rask, and Grimm. This is the language, which we believe flourished about 6000 years ago, that we have been calling **Indo-European.**

Historical Evidence

You know my method. It is founded upon the observance of trifles.
Sir Arthur Conan Doyle, "The Boscombe Valley Mystery," *The Memoirs of Sherlock Holmes*

How do we discover phonological changes? How do we know how Shakespeare or Chaucer or the author of *Beowulf* pronounced their versions of English? We have no phonograph records or tape recordings that give us direct knowledge.

For many languages, historical records go back more than a thousand years. These records are studied to find out how languages were once pronounced. The spelling in early manuscripts tells us a great deal about the sound systems of older forms of modern languages. If certain words are always spelled one way, and other words another way, it is logical to conclude that the two groups of words were pronounced differently, even if the precise pronunciations are not known. For example, a linguist who did not know English but consistently found that the word that meant "deep hole" was written as *pit*, whereas the word for a domesticated animal was written as *pet*, would think it safe to assume that these two words were pronounced differently. Once a number of orthographic contrasts are identified, good guesses can be made as to actual pronunciation. These guesses are supplemented by common words that show up in all stages of the language, allowing their pronunciation to be traced from the present, step by step, into the past.

Another clue to earlier pronunciation is provided by non-English words used in the manuscripts of English. Suppose a French word that scholars know contains the vowel [o:] is borrowed into English. The way the borrowed word is spelled reveals a particular letter–sound correspondence.

Other documents can be examined for evidence. Private letters are an excellent source of data. Linguists prefer letters written by "naive" spellers, who will misspell words according to the way they pronounce them. For instance, at one point in English history all words spelled with *er* in their stems were pronounced as if they were spelled with *ar*, just as in modern British English *clerk* and *derby* are pronounced "clark" and "darby." Some poor speller kept writing *parfect* for *perfect*, which helped linguists to discover the older pronunciation.

Clues are also provided by the writings of the prescriptive grammarians of the period. Between 1550 and 1750 a group of prescriptivists in England known as **orthoepists** attempted to preserve the "purity" of English. In prescribing how people should speak, they told us how people actually spoke. An orthoepist alive in the United States today might write in a manual: "It is incorrect to pronounce *Cuba* with a final *r*." Future scholars would know that there were speakers of English who pronounced it that way.

Some of the best clues to earlier pronunciation are provided by puns and rhymes in literature. Two words rhyme if the vowels and final consonants are the same. When a poet rhymes the verb *found* with the noun *wound*, it strongly suggests that the vowels of these two words were identical:

BENVOLIO: . . . 'Tis in vain to seek him here that means to not be found.
ROMEO: He jests at scars that never felt a wound.

Shakespeare's rhymes are helpful in reconstructing the sound system of Elizabethan English. For example, the rhyming of *convert* with *depart* in Sonnet XI strengthens the conclusion that *er* was pronounced as *ar*.

Dialect differences may provide clues as to what earlier stages of a language were like. There are many dialects of English spoken around the world, including the United States. By comparing the pronunciation of various words in several dialects, we can "reconstruct" earlier forms and see what changes took place in the inventory of sounds and in the phonological rules. When we study different dialects it becomes apparent that all language change is not "hidden." We can actually observe some changes in progress.

For example, since some speakers of English pronounce *Mary, merry,* and *marry* with three different vowels (that is, [meri], [mɛri], and [mæri], respectively), we suspect that at one time all speakers of English did so. (The different spellings are also a clue.) For some dialects, however, only one of these sounds can occur before /r/, namely the sound [ɛ], so we can "see" a change taking place. This same change can also be seen in this "drinking song" of the University of California:

They had to carry Harry to the ferry
And the ferry carried Harry to the shore
And the reason that they had to carry Harry to the ferry
Was that Harry couldn't carry any more.

This song was written by someone who rhymed *Harry, carry,* and *ferry*. It does not sound quite as good to those who do not rhyme *Harry* and *ferry*.

The historical-comparativists working on Indo-European languages, and other languages with written records, had a difficult job, but not nearly as difficult as scholars who are attempting to discover genetic relationships among languages with no written history. Linguists have, however, been able to establish language families and reconstruct the histories of such individual languages. They first study the languages and dialects spoken today and compare the sound systems, the vocabularies, and the syntax, seeing what correspondences exist. By this method, Major John W. Powell, Franz Boas, Edward Sapir, Mary Haas, and others have worked out the complex relationships of native American languages. Other linguists have worked with African languages and have established a number of major and minor language families in Africa, each containing many subgroups. They have established that over a thousand different languages are spoken in Africa.

The Genetic Classification of Languages

The Sanskrit language, whatever be its antiquity, is of a wonderful structure, more perfect than the Greek, more copious than the Latin, and more exquisitely refined than either, yet bearing to both of them a stronger affinity, both in the roots of verbs and in the forms of grammar, than could possibly be produced by accident; so strong, indeed, that no philologer could examine all three, without believing that they have sprung from some common source, which, perhaps, no longer exists. . . .

Sir William Jones, 1786

We have discussed how different languages descend from one language, and how historical and comparative linguists classify languages into families and reconstruct earlier forms of the ancestral language. When we examine the languages of the world, we perceive similarities and differences among them that provide further evidence for the ''genetic'' relatedness we know exists.

Counting to five in English, German, and Vietnamese shows similarities between English and German not shared by Vietnamese.

English	German	Vietnamese
one	ein	mot
two	zwei	hai
three	drei	ba
four	vier	bon
five	funf	nam

This similarity between English and German is pervasive. Sometimes it is extremely obvious *(man/Mann)*, at other times a little less obvious *(child/Kind)*.

Because German and English are human languages, we expect to find certain similarities reflecting the Universal Grammar between them. English and German, however, are not related because they are highly similar. Rather, the particular kinds of similarities are the result of their being related. They are related because at one time in history they were the same language.

Fifth-century Germanic is the parent of Modern English and Modern German, which are its "daughters"; English and German are "sisters." Sisterhood is the fundamental genealogical relationship between languages. Similarly, the Romance languages of French, Spanish, Portuguese, Italian, and Romanian are daughters of Latin and sisters to one another.

Where there are mothers and sisters, there must be "cousins." At one time, well over 2000 years ago, an early form of Germanic and an early form of Latin were sisters. The respective offspring are cousins. The five Romance languages mentioned above are cousins to English and German. The numbers from one to three in English and two Romance languages, compared with the unrelated Japanese, reveal this relationship:

Spanish	French	English	Japanese
uno	un	one	ichi
dos	deux	two	ni
tres	trois	three	san

Norwegian, Yiddish, Danish, Icelandic, and Dutch are all close relatives of English. They, like English, are Germanic. Greek is a somewhat more distant cousin. The Celtic language gave birth to Irish, Scots Gaelic, Welsh, and Breton, all cousins of English. Breton is spoken by the people living in the northwest coastal regions of France, called Brittany. It was brought there by Celts fleeing from Britain in the seventh century and has been preserved as the language of some Celtic descendants in Brittany ever since. Russian is also a distant cousin, as are its sisters, Bulgarian, Serbo-Croatian, Polish, Czech, and Slovak. The Baltic language Lithuanian is related to English, as is its sister language, Latvian. A neighboring language, Estonian, however, is not a relative. Sanskrit, as pointed out by Sir William Jones, though far removed geographically, is nonetheless a relative. Its daughters, Hindi and Bengali, spoken primarily in India and Bangladesh, are distantly related to English. Even the Persian spoken in modern Iran is a distant cousin of English.

All the languages mentioned in the last paragraph, except for Estonian, are related, more or less distantly, because they descended from Indo-European.

Figure 8–6 (on page 323), an abbreviated "family tree" of the Indo-European family of languages, gives a genealogical and historical classification of the languages shown. All the languages of the world may be similarly classified. This diagram is somewhat simplified. For one thing, the "dead ends"—languages that evolved and died, leaving no offspring—are not included.

A language dies when no children learn it. This situation may come about in two ways: either all the speakers of the language are annihilated by some cataclysm, or more commonly, the speakers of the language are absorbed by another culture that speaks a different language. The children, at first bilingual, grow up using the language of the dominant culture. Their children, or their children's children, fail to learn the old language, so it dies. This fate has befallen many native American languages. Cornish, a Celtic language akin to Breton, met a similar fate in England in the seventeenth century. Today, however, there are "revival" movements among some peoples to resurrect their old languages. Hebrew is an example of a nearly extinct language that was brought back to life. For centuries it was used only in religious ceremonies, but today it is the national language of Israel and is spoken natively by a large number of people.

The family tree also fails to show a number of intermediate stages that must have existed in the evolution of modern languages. Languages do not evolve abruptly, which is why comparisons with the genealogical trees of biology have limited usefulness.

Finally, the diagram fails to show a number of Indo-European languages because of lack of space.

Obviously, most of the world's languages do not belong to the Indo-European family. Linguists have also attempted to classify the non–Indo-European languages according to their genetic relationships. The task is to identify the languages that constitute a family and the relationships that exist among them.

The results of this research are often surprising: faraway Punjabi is an Indo-European language, whereas Hungarian, surrounded on all sides by Indo-European languages, is not.

For linguists interested in the nature of human language, the number of languages in the many different language families provides necessary data. Although these languages are diverse in many ways, they are also remarkably similar in many ways. We find that the languages of the "wretched Greenlanders," the Maoris of New Zealand, the Zulus of Africa, and the native peoples of North and South America all have similar sounds, similar phonological and syntactic rules, and similar semantic systems. There is evidence, then, that we need a theory of language that aims at universality as well as specificity.

At the end of this chapter we have included a table of some languages of the world, showing genetic relationships, the principal geographic areas where the language is spoken, and the number of speakers (as nearly as that can be determined).

Why Do Languages Change?

Stability in language is synonymous with rigor mortis.
Ernest Weekley

No one knows exactly how or why languages change. As we have shown, linguistic changes do not happen suddenly. Speakers of English did not wake up one morning and decide to use the word *beef* for "ox meat"; nor do all the children of one particular generation grow up to adopt a new word. Changes are more gradual, particularly changes in the phonological and syntactic system.

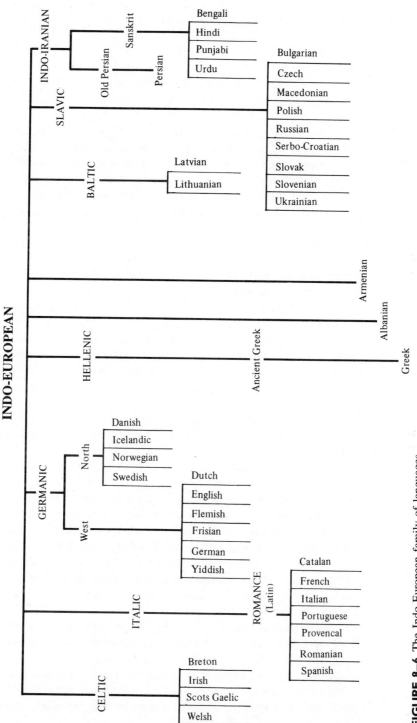

FIGURE 8–6 The Indo-European family of languages.

Of course, certain changes may occur instantaneously for any one speaker. When a new word is acquired by a speaker, it is not "gradually" acquired, although full appreciation for all of its possible uses may come slowly. When a new rule is incorporated into a speaker's grammar, it is either in or not in the grammar. It may at first be an optional rule, so that sometimes it is used and sometimes it is not, possibly determined by social context or other external factors; but the rule is either there and available for use or not. What is gradual about language change is the spread of certain changes over an entire speech community.

A basic cause of change is the way children acquire the language. No one teaches a child the rules of the grammar; each child constructs a personal grammar alone, generalizing rules from the linguistic input received. As will be discussed in Chapter 10, the child's language develops in stages until it approximates the adult grammar. The child's grammar is never exactly like that of the adult community, because children receive diverse linguistic input. Certain rules may be simplified or overgeneralized, and vocabularies may show small differences that accumulate over several generations.

The older generation may be using certain rules optionally. For example, at certain times they may say "It's I" and at other times "It's me." The less formal style is usually used with children, who as the next generation may use only the "me" form of the pronoun in this construction. In such cases, the grammar will have changed.

The reasons for some changes are relatively easy to understand. Before television there was no such word as *television*. It soon became a common lexical item. Borrowed words, too, generally serve a useful purpose and their entry into the language is not mysterious. Other changes are more difficult to explain, such as the Great Vowel Shift in English.

We have some plausible explanations for some of the phonological changes in languages. Some of these changes are due to physiological mechanisms. Some sounds and combinations of sounds are "easier to pronounce" than others. One example is the simplification of geminate [f:] to single [f], which we noted earlier contributed to the phonemicization of [v] to /v/ in English.

Another example: Vowels are frequently nasalized before nasal consonants because it is difficult to time the lowering of the velum to produce nasality with the consonant articulation. As Chapter 3 explained, the effect of one sound on another is called **assimilation;** the vowel **assimilates** to the nasality of the nasal consonant. Once the vowel is nasalized, the contrast that the nasal consonant provided can be equally well provided by the nasalized vowel alone, and the redundant consonant may be deleted. The contrast between oral and nasal vowels that exists in many languages of the world today results from just such a historical sound change.

In French at one time, *bol* "basin," *botte* "high boot," *bog* "a card game," *bock* "Bock beer," and *bon* "good" were pronounced [bɔl], [bɔt], [bɔg], [bɔk], and [bɔ̃n], respectively. Notice that in *bon* there was a final nasal consonant, which *conditioned* the nasalization of the preceding vowel. Due to a sound change that deleted nasal consonants in word-final position, *bon* is pronounced [bɔ̃] in modern French; the nasal vowel maintains the contrast with the other words.

Another example from English illustrates how such assimilative processes can change a language. In English *key*, the /k/ is articulated forward in the mouth in anticipation of the high front "palatal" vowel /i/. In *cot*, the /k/ is pronounced farther back in anticipation of the low back vowel /a/. The /k/ in *key* is slightly "palatalized." In Old English there were a number of words that began with a palatalized /k/, which is written as [kʲ]. When [kʲ] was followed by /i/, it became our modern palatal affricate /č/, as illustrated by the following words:

Old English (*c* = [kʲ])	**Modern English (*ch* = [č])**
ciese	cheese
cinn	chin
cild	child

The same process of palatalization that produced the /č/ in English from an older /k/ is also found in many other languages. In Twi, for example, the word meaning "to hate" was once pronounced [ki]. The [k] became first [kʲ] and then finally [č], so that today "to hate" is pronounced [či].

Such assimilative processes gave rise to a *"theory of least effort"* to explain linguistic change. According to this theory, sound changes are primarily due to an economy of effort. We tend to assimilate one sound to another, to drop out unstressed syllables, and so on.

Another kind of change that can be thought of as "economy of memory" results in a reduction of the number of exceptional or irregular morphemes. This kind of change has been called **internal borrowing**—that is, we "borrow" from one part of the grammar and apply the rule generally. It is also called **analogic change.** It may be by analogy to *foe/foes* and *dog/dogs* that speakers started saying *cows* as the plural of *cow* instead of the earlier plural *kine*. By analogy to *reap/reaped, seem/seemed,* and *ignite/ignited,* children and adults are presently saying *I sweeped the floor* (instead of *swept*), *I dreamed last night* (instead of *dreamt*), and *She lighted the bonfire* (instead of *lit*).

The same kind of analogic change is exemplified by our "regularization" of exceptional plural forms, which is a kind of morphological change. We have borrowed words like *datum/data, agendum/agenda, curriculum/curricula, bandit/banditi, memorandum/memoranda, medium/media, criterion/criteria,* and *virtuoso/virtuosi,* to name just a few. The irregular plurals of these nouns have been replaced by regular plurals among many speakers: *agendas, curriculums, memorandums, criterias, virtuosos.* In some cases the borrowed original plural forms were considered to be the singular (as in *agenda* and *criteria*) and the new plural is therefore a "plural-plural." Also, many speakers now regard *data* and *media* as nouns that do not have plural forms, like *information.* All these changes lessen the number of irregular forms that must be remembered.

The "theory of least effort" does seem to account for some linguistic changes, but it cannot account for others. Simplification and regularization of grammars occur, but so does elaboration or complication. Old English rules of syntax became more complex, imposing a stricter word order on the language, at the same time that case endings were being simplified. A tendency toward simplification is counteracted by the need to limit potential ambiguity. Much of language change is a balance between the two.

Many factors contribute to linguistic change: simplification of grammars, elaboration to maintain intelligibility, borrowing, and lexical additions. Changes are realized by children learning the language, who incorporate them into their grammar. The exact reasons for linguistic change are still elusive, though it is clear that the "imperfect" learning of the adult dialects by children is a contributing factor. Perhaps language changes for the same reason all things change: that it is the nature of things to change. As Heraclitus pointed out thousands of years ago, "All is flux, nothing stays still. Nothing endures but change."

Languages of the World

And the whole earth was of one language, and of one speech.
Genesis 11:1

Let us go down, and there confound their language, that they may not understand one another's speech.
Genesis 11:7

How many people of the world can be brought together so that no one person understands the language spoken by any other person? Considering that there are over five billion inhabitants on the planet (the five-billionth was supposedly born on July 7, 1986), the number of mutually unintelligible languages is relatively small— somewhat over four thousand, according to most estimates. Table 8–1 (on pages 327–329) lists some of these languages. Despite the seemingly large number of languages spoken in the world today, one-half of the world's total population speaks but eight languages. As the figures in the table show, if you speak Mandarin Chinese, English, Hindi, Spanish, and Russian, you can speak with over two billion people.

On the other hand, many languages have few speakers. Despite the fact that our figures show Apache as having under ten speakers, in *The World According to Garp* by John Irving, Garp claims that his mother's popular book has been translated into many foreign languages, including Apache.

TABLE 8–1 Some Languages of the World[10]

		INDO-EUROPEAN FAMILY (see Figure 8–6)		
Subfamily	Language	Principal Geographic Areas Where Spoken	Rank	Number of Speakers
Germanic	Danish	Denmark		5,000,000
	Dutch	Netherlands, Indonesia		14,000,000
	English	North America, Great Britain, Australia, New Zealand	(2)	415,000,000
	Flemish	Belgium		6,000,000
	Frisian	Northern Holland		445,000
	German	Germany, Austria, Switzerland	(10)	118,000,000
	Icelandic	Iceland		218,000
	Norwegian	Norway		5,300,000
	Swedish	Sweden		9,000,000
	Yiddish	(diffuse)		4,000,000
Romance (Latin)	Catalan	Andorra, Spain, France		6,000,000
	French	France, Belgium, Switzerland, Canada	(11)	112,000,000
	Italian	Italy, Switzerland	(16)	63,000,000
	Portuguese	Portugal, Brazil	(8)	161,000,000
	Provençal	Southern France		4,000,000
	Romanian	Rumania		24,000,000
	Spanish	Spain, Latin America	(4)	285,000,000
Celtic	Breton	Brittany (France)		1,100,000
	Irish	Ireland		822,000
	Scots Gaelic	Scotland		78,000
	Welsh	Wales		522,000
Hellenic	Greek	Greece, Cyprus		11,000,000
Baltic	Latvian	Latvia (USSR)		2,000,000
	Lithuanian	Lithuania (USSR)		3,000,000
Slavic	Bulgarian	Bulgaria		9,000,000
	Byelorussian	Western USSR		9,000,000
	Czech	Czechoslovakia		12,000,000
	Macedonian	Southern Yugoslavia		2,000,000
	Polish	Poland	(27)	40,000,000
	Russian	USSR	(5)	282,000,000
	Serbo-Croatian	Yugoslavia		25,000,000
	Slovak	Czechoslovakia		5,000,000
	Slovenian	Yugoslavia		5,000,000
	Ukrainian	Southwest USSR	(26)	42,000,000
Indo-Iranian	Bengali	Bangladesh, India	(7)	166,000,000
	Hindi	Northern India	(3)	287,000,000
	Marathi	Western India	(19)	60,000,000

[10]These data are compiled from the 1986 *World Almanac* and the 1985 edition of the *Encyclopaedia Britannica*. Languages such as Dutch/Flemish (called collectively *Netherlandish*), which are close enough to be considered dialects, are nonetheless listed as separate languages out of political considerations. So are Norwegian/Danish, Hindi/Urdu, Malay/Indonesian, and Thai/Lao.

TABLE 8-1 Some Languages of the World (continued)

INDO-EUROPEAN FAMILY (see Figure 8-6)

Subfamily	Language	Principal Geographic Areas Where Spoken	Rank	Number of Speakers
	Persian	Iran, Afghanistan		30,000,000
	Punjabi	Northern India, Pakistan	(14)	70,000,000
	Urdu	Pakistan	(13)	80,000,000
Armenian	Armenian	Southwest USSR		4,000,000
Albanian	Albanian	Albania		4,000,000

AMERINDIAN LANGUAGES

Subfamily	Language	Principal Geographic Areas Where Spoken	Rank	Number of Speakers
Algonquian	Arapaho	Wyoming		1,000
	Blackfoot	Montana		1,000
	Cheyenne	Montana		4,000
	Cree	Ontario (Canada)		89,000
	Menomini	Wisconsin		2,200
	Ojibwa	Ontario		25,000
Athapaskan	Apache	Oklahoma		Less than 10
	Chipewyan	Alberta (Canada)		4,400
	Navajo	Arizona		137,000
	Sarsi	Alberta		450
Iroquoian	Cherokee	Oklahoma, North Carolina		27,000
	Mohawk	Northern New York		6,700
Mayan	Maya	Guatemala, Mexico		600,000
Quechumaran	Quechua (Incan)	Bolivia, Peru		7,000,000
Uto-Aztecan	Hopi	Northwest Arizona		7,900
	Nahuatl (Aztec)	Southern Mexico		1,200,000
	Pima-Papago	Southern Arizona		25,000
Yuman	Diegueño	Southern California		75
	Mohave	Western Arizona		2,000

OTHER LANGUAGES

Subfamily	Language	Principal Geographic Areas Where Spoken	Rank	Number of Speakers
Afro-Asiatic (includes Semitic languages)	Amharic	Ethiopia		10,000,000
	Arabic	North Africa, Middle East	(6)	171,000,000
	Berber	Morocco		8,000,000
	Oromo (Galla)	Somaliland, Ethiopia		8,000,000
	Hausa	Northern Nigeria		28,000,000
	Hebrew	Israel		3,000,000
	Somali	Somalia		2,000,000
Altaic	Japanese	Japan	(9)	121,000,000
	Korean	Korea	(15)	64,000,000
	Mongolian	Mongolia		2,000,000
	Tartar (Tatar)	Western USSR		7,000,000
	Turkish	Turkey	(22)	50,000,000
	Uzbek	Southwest USSR		10,000,000
Austro-Asiatic	Khmer	Kampuchea		6,000,000
	Vietnamese	Vietnam	(22)	50,000,000
Austro-Tai	Batak	Sumatra		2,000,000
	Chamorro	Mariana Islands (Guam)		63,000

TABLE 8–1 Some Languages of the World (continued)

OTHER LANGUAGES

Family	Language	Principal Geographic Areas Where Spoken	Rank	Number of Speakers
	Fijian	Fiji Islands		270,000
	Hawaiian	Hawaii		250
	Indonesian	Indonesia	(12)	110,000,000
	Javanese	Java	(22)	50,000,000
	Lao	Laos		3,000,000
	Malagasy	Madagascar		10,000,000
	Malay	Malaysia, Singapore		15,000,000
	Maori	New Zealand		100,000
	Samoan	Samoa		200,000
	Tagalog	Philippines		30,000,000
	Tahitian	Tahiti		66,000
	Thai	Thailand	(25)	43,000,000
Caucasian	Avar	Southwest USSR		500,000
	Georgian	Southwest USSR		4,000,000
Dravidian	Kannada	Southwest India	(28)	37,000,000
	Malayalam	Southwest India	(30)	32,000,000
	Tamil	Southeast India, Sri Lanka	(17)	61,000,000
	Telugu	Southeast India	(17)	61,000,000
Niger-Kordofanian*	Efik	Southeast Nigeria		3,000,000
	Ewe	Ghana		3,700,000
	Fulani (Fula)	Northeast Nigeria		10,000,000
	Ibo (Igbo)	Southeast Nigeria		14,000,000
	Luganda	Uganda		3,000,000
	Nupe	Nigeria		1,000,000
	Shona	Zimbabwe		5,000,000
	Swahili	East Africa	(28)	37,000,000
	Twi-Fante (Akan)	Ghana, Ivory Coast		6,000,000
	Yoruba	Nigeria		16,000,000
	Zulu	South Africa		7,000,000
Sino-Tibetan	Burmese	Burma		28,000,000
	Cantonese	South China	(20)	58,000,000
	Hakka	Southeast China		25,000,000
	Mandarin	North China	(1)	771,000,000
	Min	Eastern China, Taiwan		44,000,000
	Tibetan	Tibet		6,000,000
	Wu	East Central China	(21)	56,000,000
Uralic**	Estonian	Estonia (USSR)		1,000,000
	Finnish	Finland		5,000,000
	Hungarian	Hungary		14,000,000
	Lapp	Northern parts of Norway, Finland, Sweden, USSR		35,000

*All languages given belong to the subfamily of Niger-Congo. Swahili, Luganda, Shona, and Zulu are Bantu languages.

**All languages given belong to the subfamily Finno-Ugric. The other Uralic subfamily is Samoyed.

Note: Obviously, we have omitted thousands of languages. These examples are only some of the languages in some of the language families and subfamilies.

Summary

All living languages change regularly through time. Evidence of linguistic change is found in the history of individual languages and in the **regular correspondences** that exist between different languages and dialects. **Genetically related** languages "descend" from a common "parent" language through linguistic change. An early stage in the history of related languages is that they are dialects of the same parent.

All parts of the grammar may change. That is, **phonological, morphological, syntactic, lexical,** and **semantic** changes occur. Words, morphemes, phonemes, and rules of all types may be added, lost, or altered. The meaning of words and morphemes may expand, narrow, or shift.

No one knows all the causes for linguistic change. Basically, change comes about through the restructuring of the grammar by children learning the language. Grammars are both simplified and elaborated; the elaborations may arise to counter the simplifications that could lead to unclarity and ambiguity.

Some sound changes result from physiological, **assimilative** processes. Others, like the Great Vowel Shift, are more difficult to explain. Grammatical changes may be explained, in part, as **analogic** changes, which are simplifications or generalizations. External borrowing from other languages also affects the grammar.

The study of linguistic change is called **historical and comparative linguistics.** By examining the internal structure of languages as well as comparing related languages, linguists are able to reconstruct earlier forms of particular language families. A particularly effective technique for reconstructing "dead" languages is the **comparative method.** By comparing the various "daughter" languages or dialects, the linguistic history of a language family may be partially reconstructed and represented in a "family tree" similar to Figure 8–6.

In spite of the differences between languages, there is a vast number of ways in which languages are alike. That is, there are language universals as well as differences.

References

Anttila, Raimo. 1972. *An Introduction to Historical and Comparative Linguistics*. Macmillan. New York.

Baugh, A. C. 1978. *A History of the English Language*. 3rd ed. Prentice-Hall. Englewood Cliffs, N.J.

Cassidy, Frederic G., ed. 1986. *Dictionary of American Regional English*. The Belknap Press of Harvard University Press. Cambridge, Massachusetts.

Hoenigswald, Henry M. 1960. *Language Change and Linguistic Reconstruction*. University of Chicago Press. Chicago.

Jeffers, Robert J., and Ilse Lehiste. 1979. *Principles and Methods for Historical Linguistics*. M.I.T. Press. Cambridge, Mass.

Lehmann, W. P. 1973. *Historical Linguistics: An Introduction*. 2d ed. Holt, Rinehart and Winston. New York.

Pedersen, H. 1962. *The Discovery of Language*. University of Indiana Press. Bloomington.

Pyles, Thomas. 1982. *The Origins and Development of the English Language*. 3rd ed. Harcourt Brace Jovanovich. New York.

Traugott, E. C. 1972. *A History of English Syntax*. Holt, Rinehart and Winston. New York.

Exercises

1. Many changes in the phonological system have occurred in English since 449 C.E. Below are some Old English words (given in their spelling and phonetic forms), and the same words as we pronounce them today. They are typical of regular sound changes that took place in English. What sound changes have occurred in each case?

   Example: OE hlud [xlu:d] → Mod. Eng. loud
   Changes: (1) The [x] was lost.
   (2) The long vowel [u:] became [aw].

   OE   Mod E
   a. crabbe [krabə] → crab
      Changes:

   b. fisc [fɪsk] → fish
      Changes:

   c. fūl [fu:l] → foul
      Changes:

   d. gāt [ga:t] → goat
      Changes:

   e. lǣfan [læ:van] → leave
      Changes:

   f. tēþ [te:θ] → teeth
      Changes:

2. The Great Vowel Shift in English left its traces in Modern English in such meaning-related pairs as:

   a. serene/serenity [i]/[ɛ]
   b. divine/divinity [aj]/[ɪ]
   c. sane/sanity [e]/[æ]

   List five such meaning-related pairs that relate [i] and [ɛ] as in example *a*, [aj] and [ɪ] as in *b*, and [e] and [æ] as in *c*.

	[i]/[ɛ]	[aj]/[ɪ]	[e]/[æ]
i.			
ii.			
iii.			
iv.			
v.			

3. Below are given some sentences taken from Old English, Middle English, and early Modern English texts, illustrating some changes that have occurred in the syntactic rules of English grammar. (Note: In the sentences, the earlier spelling forms and words have been changed to conform to Modern English. That is, the OE sentence *His suna twegen mon brohte to þæm cynige* would be written as *His sons two one brought to that king,* which in Modern English would be *His two sons were brought to the king.*) Underline the parts of each sentence that differ from Modern English. Rewrite the sentence in Modern English. State, if you can, what changes must have occurred.

> Example: It *not* belongs to you. (Shakespeare, *Henry IV*)
> Mod. Eng.: *It does not belong to you.*
> ᐧ Change: At one time a negative sentence simply had a *not* before the verb. Today, the word *do*, in its proper morphological form, must appear before the *not*.

a. It nothing pleased his master.
    Mod. Eng.:
    Change:

b. He hath said that we would lift them whom that him please.
    Mod. Eng.:
    Change:

c. I have a brother is condemned to die.
    Mod. Eng.:
    Change:

d. I bade them take away you.
    Mod. Eng.:
    Change:

e. I wish you was still more a Tartar.
    Mod. Eng.:
    Change:

f. Christ slept and his apostles.
    Mod. Eng.:
    Change:

g. Me was told.
    Mod. Eng.:
    Change:

4. It is not unusual to find a yearbook or almanac publishing a "new word list." In the 1980s several new words entered the English language, such as *barf* meaning "to throw up." From the computer field, we have new or incipient words such as *byte* and *kludge*. Other words have been expanded in meaning, such as *memory* to refer to the storage part of a computer, *hacker* to refer to someone who uses a computer compulsively, and *O.D.* to mean "overdose," as in "O.D. on chocolate."

    a. Think of five other words or compound words that have entered the language in the last ten years. Describe briefly the source of the word.

        i.

        ii.

        iii.

        iv.

        v.

    b. Think of three words that might be "on the way out." (Hint: Consider *flapper, groovy,* and *slay/slew.* Dictionary entries that say "archaic" are a good source.)

        i.

        ii.

        iii.

5. Here is a table showing, in phonemic form, the Latin ancestors of ten words in modern French:

Latin	French	
kor	kør	"heart"
kantāre	šāte	"to sing"
klārus	kler	"clear"
kervus	sɛrf	"hart" (deer)
karbō	šarbõ	"coal"
kwandō	kã	"when"
kentum	sã	"hundred"
kawsa	šoz	"thing"
kinis	sādrə	"ashes"
kawda } koda	kø	"tail"

Are the following statements true or false?

		True	False
a.	The modern French word for "thing" shows that a [k], which occurred before the vowel [o] in Latin, became an [š] in French.	_____	_____
b.	The French word for "tail" probably derived from the Latin word [koda] rather than from [kawda].	_____	_____
c.	One historical change illustrated by these data is that [s] became an allophone of the phoneme /k/ in French.	_____	_____
d.	If there was a Latin word *kertus*, the modern French word would probably be *sert*. (Consider only the initial consonant.)	_____	_____

6. Here is how to count to five in a dozen languages. Six of these languages are Indo-European and six are not. Circle the Indo-European.

	L1	L2	L3	L4	L5	L6
1	en	jedyn	i	eka	ichi	echad
2	twene	dwaj	liang	dvau	ni	shnayim
3	thria	tři	san	trayas	san	shlosha
4	fiuwar	štyri	ssu	catur	shi	arba?a
5	fif	pjeć	wu	pañca	go	chamishsha

	L7	L8	L9	L10	L11	L12
1	mot	ün	hana	yaw	uno	nigen
2	hai	duos	tul	daw	dos	khoyar
3	ba	trais	set	dree	tres	ghorban
4	bon	quatter	net	tsaloor	cuatro	durben
5	nam	tschinch	tasŏt	pindze	cinco	tabon

7. More than 4000 languages exist in the world today. State one reason why this number might grow larger and one reason why it might grow smaller. Do you think the number of languages will increase or decrease in the next 100 years? Justify your answer.

8. The vocabulary of English consists of "native" words as well as thousands of loan words. Look up the following words in a dictionary that provides the etymologies (histories) of words. Speculate how each word came to be borrowed from the particular language.

a.	size	h.	robot	o.	skunk	v.	pagoda
b.	royal	i.	check	p.	catfish	w.	khaki
c.	aquatic	j.	banana	q.	hoodlum	x.	shampoo
d.	heavenly	k.	keel	r.	filibuster	y.	kangaroo
e.	skill	l.	fact	s.	astronaut	z.	bulldoze
f.	ranch	m.	potato	t.	emerald		
g.	blouse	n.	muskrat	u.	sugar		

9. Consider the "Peanuts" cartoon below:

PEANUTS   **Schulz**

© 1982 United Feature Syndicate, Inc.

  a. Use a dictionary to find the source of this "phobia." (Hint: It has nothing to do with spiders.)

  b. Using Latin or Greek loan words that you know or look up, make up three of your own phobias.

10. **Analogic change** and **internal borrowing** refer to a tendency to generalize the rules of language, a major cause of language change. We mentioned two instances, the generalization of the plural rule (*cow/kine* becoming *cow/cows*) and the generalization of the past-tense formation rule (*light/lit* becoming *light/lighted*). Think of at least three other instances of "nonstandard" usage that are analogic; they are indicators of possible future changes in the language. (Hint: Consider fairly general rules and see if you know of dialects or styles that overgeneralize them, for example, comparative formation by adding *-er*.)

11. Below is a passage from Shakespeare's *Hamlet*, Act IV, scene iii:

HAMLET: A man may fish with the worm that hath eat of a king, and eat of the fish that hath fed of that worm.

KING: What dost thou mean by this?

HAMLET: Nothing but to show you how a king may go a progress through the guts of a beggar.

KING: Where is Polonius?

HAMLET: In heaven. Send thither to see. If your messenger find him not there, seek him i' the other place yourself. But indeed, if you find him not within this month, you shall nose him as you go up the stairs into the lobby.

Study these lines and identify every difference in expression between Elizabethan and Modern English that is evident. (For example, in line 3, *thou* is now *you*.)

12. Consider these data from two American Indian languages:

Yerington Paviotso = YP	Northfork Monachi = NM	Gloss
mupi	mupi	"nose"
tama	tawa	"tooth"
piwɨ	piwɨ	"heart"
sawaʔpono	sawaʔpono	"a feminine name"
nɨmɨ	nɨwɨ	"liver"
tamano	tawano	"springtime"
pahwa	pahwa	"aunt"
kuma	kuwa	"husband"
wowaʔa	wowaʔa	"Indians living to the west"
mɨhɨ	mɨhɨ	"porcupine"
noto	noto	"throat"
tapa	tape	"sun"
ʔatapɨ	ʔatapɨ	"jaw"
papiʔi	papiʔi	"older brother"
patɨ	petɨ	"daughter"
nana	nana	"man"
ʔatɨ	ʔetɨ	"bow," "gun"

A.   Identify each sound correspondence. (Hint: There are ten different correspondences of consonants and six different correspondences of vowels: for example, *p–p*, *m–w*, *a–a*, and *a–e*.)

B.   a.   For each correspondence you identified in A not containing an *m* or *w*, reconstruct a proto-sound. (For example, for *h–h*, *h; *o–o*, *o.)

    b.   If the proto-sound underwent a change, indicate what the change is and in which language it took place.

C.   a.   Whenever a *w* appears in YP, what appears in the corresponding position in NM?

    b.   Whenever an *m* occurs in YP, what two sounds may correspond to it in NM?

    c.   On the basis of the position of *m* in YP words, can you predict which sound it will correspond to in NM words? How?

D.   a.   For the three correspondences you discovered in A involving *m* and *w*, should you reconstruct two or three proto-sounds?

    b.   If you chose three proto-sounds, what are they and what did they become in the two "daughter" languages, YP and NM?

    c.   If you chose two proto-sounds, what are they and what did they become in the "daughter" languages? What further statement do you need to make about the sound changes? (Hint: One proto-sound will become two different pairs, depending on its phonetic environment. It is an example of a **conditioned** sound change.)

E. Based on the above, reconstruct all the words given in the common ancestor from which both YP and NM descended. (For example, "porcupine" is reconstructed as *mɨhɨ.)

C H A P T E R

9

Writing: The ABCs of Language

The Moving Finger writes; and, having writ,
Moves on: nor all thy Piety nor Wit
*   Shall lure it back to cancel half a Line,*
Nor all thy Tears wash out a Word of it.

Omar Khayyám, *Rubáiyát*

The palest ink is better than the sharpest memory.

Chinese proverb

PEANUTS   **Charles Schulz**

© 1986 United Feature Syndicate, Inc.

Previous chapters have discussed language in its spoken form, and Chapter 2 presented a phonetic alphabet for transcribing the sounds of human language into a written form. Of course, most people who learn to read and write do not learn the phonetic alphabet; they learn the writing system of their language. (There are new writing systems of formerly unwritten languages that have adopted some phonetic

338

symbols such as ŋ as part of their alphabet.) By "writing" we mean any of the many visual systems for representing language, including handwriting, printing, and electronic displays of these written forms. In this chapter we shall examine the history, nature, and use of writing systems.

The development of writing was one of the great human inventions. It is difficult for many people to imagine language without writing; the spoken word seems intricately tied to the written word. Nevertheless children speak before they learn to write, and millions of people in the world speak languages with no written form. Among these people oral literature abounds, and crucial knowledge is memorized and passed between generations. However, human memory is short-lived, and the brain's storage capacity is limited. Writing overcame such problems and allowed communication across the miles and through the centuries. Writing permits a society to record permanently its poetry, its history, and its technology.

It might be argued that today we have electronic means of recording sound and cameras to produce films and television, so writing is becoming obsolete. If writing became extinct, there would be no knowledge of electronics for TV technicians to study; there would be, in fact, little technology in years to come. There would be no film or TV scripts, no literature, no books, no mail, no newspapers. There would be some advantages—no bad novels, junk mail, poison-pen letters, or "fine print"; but the losses would far outweigh the gains.

The History of Writing

One picture is worth a thousand words.
Chinese proverb

There are almost as many legends and stories about the invention of writing as there are about the origin of language. Greek legend has it that Cadmus, Prince of Phoenicia and founder of the city of Thebes, invented the alphabet and brought it with him to Greece. (He later was banished to Illyria and changed into a snake.) In one Chinese fable, the four-eyed dragon-god Cang Jie invented writing, but in another, writing first appeared to humans in the form of markings on a turtle shell. In an Icelandic saga, Odin was the inventor of the runic script. In other myths, the Babylonian god Nebo and the Egyptian god Thoth gave humans writing as well as speech. The Talmudic scholar Rabbi Akiba believed that the alphabet existed before humans were created; and according to Islamic teaching, the alphabet was created by Allah himself, who presented it to humans but not to the angels.

Although these stories are delightful, it is evident that before a single word was written, uncountable billions were spoken; it is highly unlikely that a particularly gifted ancestor awoke one morning and decided, "Today I'll invent a writing system."

Pictograms and Ideograms

By permission of Johnny Hart and North American Syndicate, Inc.

The seeds out of which writing developed were probably the early drawings made by ancient humans. Cave drawings such as those found in the Altamira cave in northern Spain, drawn by humans living over 20,000 years ago, can be "read" today. They are literal portrayals of aspects of life at that time. We have no way of knowing why they were produced; they may well be aesthetic expressions rather than pictorial communications. Later drawings, however, are clearly "picture writings," or **pictograms.** Unlike modern writing systems, each picture or pictogram is a direct image of the object it represents. There is a **nonarbitrary** relationship between the form and meaning of the symbol. Comic strips minus captions are pictographic—literal representations of the ideas to be communicated. This early form of "writing" did not have any direct relation to the language spoken, because the pictures represented objects in the world, rather than the linguistic names given to these objects; they did not represent the sounds of spoken language.

Pictographic "writing" has been found among peoples throughout the world, ancient and modern: among African tribes, native Americans, Alaskan Eskimos, the Incas of Peru, the Yukagirians of Siberia, and the people of Oceania. Pictograms are used today in international road signs and in other places where the native language of the region might not be adequate. The advantage of such symbols is that they can be understood by anyone, because they do not depend on the words of any language. To understand the signs used by the National Park Service, for example, a visitor does not need to know English (Figure 9–1).

FIGURE 9–1 Six of seventy-seven symbols developed by the National Park Service for use as signs to indicate activities and facilities in parks and recreation areas. These symbols denote: environmental study area; grocery store; men's restroom; women's restroom; fishing; amphitheater. Certain symbols are available with a "prohibiting slash"—a diagonal red bar across the symbol that means the activity is forbidden. (National Park Service, U.S. Department of the Interior)

Once a pictogram was accepted as the representation of an object, its meaning was extended to attributes of that object, or concepts associated with it. Thus, a picture of the sun could represent "warmth," "heat," "light," "daytime," and so on. Pictograms thus began to represent *ideas* rather than objects. Such pictograms are called **ideograms** ("idea pictures" or "idea writing").

Later pictograms and ideograms became stylized, possibly because of the ambiguities that could result from "poor artists" or creative "abstractionists" of the time. The simplifying conventions that developed so distorted the literal representations that it was no longer easy to interpret symbols without learning the system. The ideograms became *linguistic* symbols as they came to stand for the *sounds* that represented the ideas—that is, for the words of the language. This stage represented a revolutionary step in the development of writing systems.

Cuneiform Writing

Much of our information on the development of writing stems from the records left by the Sumerians, an ancient people of unknown origin who built a civilization in southern Mesopotamia over 5000 years ago. They left innumerable clay tablets containing business documents, epics, prayers, poems, proverbs, and so on. So copious are these written records that scholars studying the Sumerians are publishing a seventeen-volume dictionary of their written language. The first of these volumes appeared in 1984.

The writing system of the Sumerians is the oldest one known. They were a commercially oriented people, and as their business deals became increasingly complex, the need for permanent records arose. An elaborate pictography was developed along with a system of "tallies." Some examples are shown here:

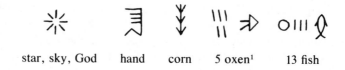

star, sky, God   hand   corn   5 oxen[1]   13 fish

Over the centuries their pictography was simplified and conventionalized. The characters or symbols were produced by using a wedge-shaped stylus that was pressed into soft clay tablets, made from the clay found on the land between the Tigris and Euphrates rivers. This form of writing is called **cuneiform**—literally, "wedge-shaped" (from Latin *cuneus* "wedge"). Here is an illustration of how Sumerian pictograms evolved to cuneiform:

became   became   star

became   hand

became   fish

The cuneiform "words" do little to remind us of the meaning represented. As cuneiform evolved, its users began to think of the symbols more in terms of the *name* of the thing represented than of the actual thing itself. Ultimately cuneiform script came to represent words of the language, and hence became a **word-writing system.** In this kind of writing system the symbol stands for both the sounds used to

---

[1]The pictograph for "ox" evolved, much later, into our letter A.

pronounce the word and for the concept, which it may still resemble, however abstractly.

The cuneiform writing system was borrowed by the Assyrians (or Babylonians) when they conquered the Sumerians, and later by the Persians. In adopting cuneiform to their own languages, the borrowers used them to represent the *sounds* of the *syllables* in their words. In this way cuneiform evolved into a **syllabic writing system.**

In a syllabic writing system, each syllable in the language is represented by its own symbol, and words are written syllable by syllable. Cuneiform writing was never purely syllabic; there was always a large residue of symbols that stood for whole words. The Assyrians retained a large number of word symbols, even though every word in their language could be written out syllabically if it were desired. Thus they could write <symbol> *mātu* ''country'' as:

| ma | + | a | + | tu |

The Persians (ca. 600–400 B.C.E.) devised a greatly simplified syllabic alphabet for their language, which had little recourse to word symbols. By the reign of Darius I (522–468 B.C.E.) this writing system was in wide use. It is illustrated by the following characters:

<symbol>   da

<symbol>   di

<symbol>   fa

<symbol>   ma

<symbol>   tu

The Rebus Principle

When a graphic sign no longer has any visual relationship to the word it represents, it becomes a symbol for the sounds that represent the word. A single sign can then be used to represent all words with the same sounds—the homophones of the language. If, for example, the symbol ☉ stood for *sun* in English, it could then be used in a sentence like *My* ⊙ *is a doctor*. This sentence is an example of **the rebus principle.**

A rebus is a representation of words or syllables by pictures of objects whose names *sound like* the intended syllables. Thus ◁◉▷ might represent *eye* or the pronoun *I*. The sounds of the two monosyllabic words are identical, even though the meanings are not. In the same way, 🐝🍃 could represent *belief* (*be* + *lief* = *bee* + *leaf* = /bi/ + /lif/), and 🐝🍃🍃 could be the verb form, *believes*.

Similarly, 2 👄 —/tu/ + /lɪp/—could represent *tulip*. Proper names can also be "written" in such a way. If the symbol ❘ is used to represent *rod* and the symbol 🔱 represents *man*, then ❘ 🔱 could represent *Rodman*, although the name is unrelated to either rods or men, at least at this point in history. Such combinations often become stylized or shortened so as to be more easily written. *Rodman*, for example, might be "written" in such a system as ❘☆ or even ⋌.

This system is not an efficient one, because the words of many languages do not lend themselves to subdivision into sequences of sounds that represent independent meaning. It would be difficult, for example, to represent the word *English* (/iŋ/ + /glɪš/) in English according to the rebus principle. *Eng* by itself does not "mean" anything, nor does *glish*. In some languages, however, a rebus system of writing may lead to a syllabic writing system, which has many advantages over word writing; such a change occurred in the Semitic languages spoken many thousands of years ago in what is now the Middle East.

From Hieroglyphs to the Alphabet

At the time that Sumerian pictography was flourishing (around 4000 B.C.E.), a similar system was being used by the Egyptians, which the Greeks later called **hieroglyphics** (*hiero* "sacred" + *glyphikos* "carvings"). That the early "sacred carvings" were originally pictography is shown by the following hieroglyphics:

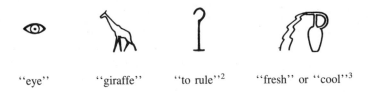

"eye"   "giraffe"   "to rule"[2]   "fresh" or "cool"[3]

Like the Sumerian pictograms, the hieroglyphs began to represent the sounds of the words they symbolized. This **phoneticization** of the pictography made hieroglyphics a word-writing system, paralleling the Sumerian cuneiform development. Possibly influenced by the Sumerians, the Egyptian system also became, in part, a syllabic writing system.

---

[2]The symbol portrays the Pharaoh's staff. [3]Water trickling out of a vase.

In this advanced "syllabic" stage, hieroglyphics were borrowed by many people, including the Phoenicians, a Semitic people who lived on the eastern shores of the Mediterranean. By 1500 B.C.E. a system of twenty-two syllabic characters, the West Semitic Syllabary, was in use, in which a single symbol represented both a consonant and a following vowel (CV).

This syllabic system, first borrowed by the Greeks in the tenth century B.C.E., proved to be inefficient because Greek has a complex syllable structure. The simpler syllabic structure of Semitic languages, together with the fact that the vowel within a syllable is often grammatically predictable, made syllable writing more feasible for these languages than for others.

The ancient Greeks nevertheless borrowed the Phoenician writing system, using the symbols to represent the individual vowels and consonants of their language rather than syllables. The Phoenicians had taken the first step in this direction by using certain symbols to represent consonants alone. The language spoken by the Phoenicians, however, had more consonants than Greek, so when the Greeks borrowed the system they used the extra symbols to represent vowel sounds. The result was an **alphabetic writing system.** (The word *alphabet* is derived from *alpha* and *beta*, the first two letters of the Greek alphabet.)

Alphabetic systems are those in which each symbol typically represents one sound unit. Such systems are primarily *phonemic* rather than *phonetic*, as is illustrated by the fact that the *p* in both *pit* and *spit* in the English alphabet system is one rather than two "letters," even though the sounds are phonetically distinct.

There are arguments as to whether this event—the development of an alphabetic writing system—occurred more than once in history. Most scholars believe that all alphabetic systems in use today derive from the Greek system. This alphabet became known to the pre-Latin people of Italy, the Etruscans, who in turn passed it on to the Romans. The Roman Empire spread it throughout the world.

According to one view, the alphabet was not invented; it was *discovered*.[4] If language did not include discrete individual sounds, no one could have invented alphabetic letters to represent such sounds. When humans started to use one symbol for one phoneme, they had merely brought their intuitive knowledge of the language sound system to consciousness; they discovered what they already "knew." Furthermore, children (and adults) can learn an alphabetic system only if each separate sound has some psychological reality.

Modern Writing Systems

. . . but their manner of writing is very peculiar, being neither from the left to the right, like the Europeans; nor from the right to the left, like the Arabians; nor from up to down, like the Chinese; nor from down to up, like the Cascagians, but aslant from one corner of the paper to the other, like ladies in England.

Jonathan Swift, *Gulliver's Travels*

---

[4]Dr. Sven Ohman, Professor of Phonetics at the University of Uppsala, Sweden; paper presented at the International Speech Symposium, Kyoto, Japan, 1969.

We have already mentioned the three types of writing systems used in the world: *word writing, syllable writing,* and *alphabetic writing.*

Of the world's major languages, only Chinese and Japanese lack an alphabetic writing system. Both languages, however, use alphabetic transcription systems, which are sometimes learned in schools and which can be used by foreigners. There is some question as to whether the writing systems of Semitic languages such as Hebrew or Arabic are truly alphabetic. These languages can be written using only consonants, because the vowels are fairly predictable from context. Thus a consonant symbol in effect stands for the consonant plus the appropriate vowel, which gives the writing system a syllabic flavor. There are, however, many words in Hebrew or Arabic with the same consonants but different vowels. Semitic writing systems and others derived from them, such as some Austro-Tai languages, are not fully syllabic.

Word Writing

PEANUTS   **Charles Schulz**

Reprinted by permission: © 1964 United Feature Syndicate.

In a word-writing system the written symbol represents a whole word. The awkwardness of such a system is obvious. For example, the editors of *Webster's Third New International Dictionary* claim more than 450,000 entries. All these words are written using only twenty-six alphabetic symbols, a dot, a hyphen, an apostrophe, and a space. It is understandable why, historically, word writing gave way to alphabetic systems in most places in the world.

The major exceptions are the writing systems used in China and Japan. The Chinese system has an uninterrupted history that goes back more than 3500 years. For the most part it is a word-writing system, each character representing an individual word or morpheme. Longer words may be formed by combining two words or morphemes, as shown by the word meaning "business," *măimai,* which is formed by combining the words meaning "buy" and "sell." This system, which could create serious problems if used for English and other Indo-European languages, works for Chinese because *spoken* Chinese has little affixation of bound morphemes (such as the *un-* in *unhappy* or the *-fy* in *beautify*).

Chinese writing utilizes a system of **characters,** each of which represents the "meaning" of a word. Chinese dictionaries and rhyme books contain tens of thousands of these characters, but a person "only" needs to know about 5000 to read a newspaper. In 1956 the Chinese government moved to simplify the characters. This process had started in 213 B.C.E., when Li Si published an official list of over 3000 characters, which eliminated the different characters representing the same words; but successive generations kept adding new characters and changing and complicating the characters. The character simplification efforts that have been under way in the last thirty years are therefore of major importance. An example of the simplifications is given below:[5]

Original	Simplified	Pronunciation	Meaning
餐	歺	cān	"meal"
酒	氿	jiǔ	"wine"
漆	汢	qī	"paint"
稻	籾	dào	"rice crops"
副	付	fù	"deputy"
賽	寈	sài	"to compete"

The Chinese government has adopted a spelling system using the Roman alphabet, called **Pinyin,** which is now used for certain purposes along with the regular system of characters. Many city street signs are printed in both systems, which is helpful to foreign tourists. It is not their intent, however, to replace the traditional writing, which is viewed as an integral part of Chinese culture. In addition, writing is an art—**calligraphy**—and thousands of years of poetry, literature, and history are preserved in the old system.

An additional reason for keeping the traditional system is that it permits all literate Chinese to communicate even though their spoken languages are mutually unintelligible. Thus writing has served as a unifying factor throughout Chinese history, in an area where hundreds of languages and different dialects of what we call "Chinese" exist. For example, in one county in the Fujian province, three major and over ten minor dialects are spoken. It is said that "people separated by a blade of grass cannot understand each other"; but all the dialects use the one writing system, and a common sight in a city like Hong Kong is for two people to be talking and at the same time drawing characters in the air with their forefingers to overcome their spoken linguistic differences.

This use of written Chinese characters is parallel to the use of Arabic numerals, which mean the same in all European countries. Though the spoken word for "eight" is different in English, Greek, and Finnish, the written *8* can be understood

---

[5]W. P. Lehmann (ed). 1975. *Language and Linguistics in the People's Republic of China.* University of Texas Press. Austin, Texas.

by all. Similarly, the spoken word for "rice" is different in the various Chinese languages, but the written character is the same. If the writing system in China were to become alphabetic, each language would be as different in writing as in speaking, and written communication would no longer be possible among the various language communities.

Every writing system has some traces of word writing. In addition to numerals in which a single symbol represents a whole word, other symbols, such as $, %, &, +, −, and =, are ideograms or word symbols.

Syllable Writing

Syllabic writing systems are more efficient than word-writing systems, and they are certainly less taxing on the memory. However, languages with a rich structure of syllables containing many consonant "clusters" (such as *tr* or *spl*) cannot be efficiently written with a syllabary. To see this difficulty, consider the syllable structures of English.

I	/ay/	V	*an*	/æn/	VC
key	/ki/	CV	*ant*	/ænt/	VCC
ski	/ski/	CCV	*ants*	/ænts/	VCCC
spree	/spri/	CCV	*pant*	/pænt/	CVCC
seek	/sik/	CVC	*pants*	/pænts/	CVCCC
speak	/spik/	CCVC	*splints*	/splɪnts/	CCCVCCC
scram	/skræm/	CCCVC	*stamp*	/stæmp/	CCVCC
striped	/straypt/	CCCVCC			

Together with more than thirty consonants and over twelve vowels, the number of different possible syllables is immense, which is why English, and Indo-European languages in general, are unsuitable for syllabic writing systems.

The Japanese language, on the other hand, is more suited for syllabic writing, because all words in Japanese can be phonologically represented by about 100 syllables, mostly of the consonant-vowel (CV) type, and there are no consonant clusters. To write these syllables the Japanese have two **syllabaries,** each containing forty-six characters, called *kana*. Together with several diacritical markers,[6] the entire Japanese language can be written using kana. One syllabary, *katakana*, is used for loan words and for special effects similar to italics in European writing. The other syllabary, *hiragana,* is used for native words and may occur with Chinese characters, which the Japanese call *kanji*. Thus Japanese writing is part word writing, part syllable writing.

During the first millennium, the Japanese tried to use Chinese characters to write their language. However, the Japanese language is unrelated to Chinese, and a word-writing system alone was not suitable. Japanese is a highly inflected language; verbs may occur in thirty or more different forms. Using modified Chinese charac-

---

[6]Diacritical markers are small symbols added to a letter that alter its pronunciation, such as the two dots over the *ü* in German writing that shows it is to be pronounced as a high *front* rounded vowel [y].

ters, the syllabaries were devised to represent the inflectional endings and other grammatical morphemes. Thus, in Japanese writing, Chinese characters will commonly be used for the verb roots, and hiragana symbols for the inflectional markings.

For example, 行 is the character meaning ''go,'' pronounced [i]. The word for ''went'' in formal speech is *ikimashita*, written as 行きました, where the hiragana symbols きました represent the syllables *ki, ma, shi, ta*. Nouns, on the other hand, are not inflected in Japanese, and they can generally be written using Chinese characters alone.

In theory all of Japanese could be written in hiragana. There are many homophones in Japanese, however, and the use of word characters disambiguates a word that would be ambiguous if written syllabically. Also, like Chinese, Japanese kanji writing is an integral part of Japanese culture, and it is unlikely to be abandoned.

In 1821, Sequoyah, often called the ''Cherokee Cadmus,'' invented a syllabic writing system for his native language Cherokee. Sequoyah's script, which survives today essentially unchanged, proved useful to the Cherokee people and is justifiably a point of great pride for them. The syllabary contains eighty-five symbols, many of them derived from Latin characters, which efficiently transcribes spoken Cherokee. A few symbols are shown here:

J	gu
∩	hu
℮℮	we
W	ta
H	mi

An alphabetic character can be used to represent a syllable in some languages. In words such as OK and bar-b-q, the single letters represent syllables (*b* for [bi] or [bə], *q* for [kju]).

Alphabetic Writing

Alphabetic writing systems are easy to learn, convenient to use, and maximally efficient for transcribing any human language.

The term **sound writing** is sometimes used in place of alphabetic writing, but it does not truly represent the principle involved in the use of alphabets. One-sound–one-letter is inefficient, because we do not need to represent the [pʰ] in *pit* and the [p] in *spit* by two different letters. It would also be confusing, because the

THE FAR SIDE   **Gary Larson**

"All right! All right! If you want the truth, off and on
I've been seeing *all* the vowels—a, e, i, o, u. ...
Oh, yes! And *sometimes* y!"

nonphonemic differences between sounds are seldom perceptible to speakers. Except for the phonetic alphabets, whose function is to record the sounds of all languages for descriptive purposes, most, if not all, alphabets have been devised on the **phonemic principle.**

In the twelfth century, an Icelandic scholar developed an orthography derived from the Latin alphabet for the writing of the Icelandic language of his day. Other scholars in this period were also interested in orthographic reform, but the Icelander, who came to be known as "the First Grammarian" (because his anonymous paper was the first entry in a collection of grammatical essays), was the only one of the time who left a record of his principles. The orthography he developed was clearly based on the phonemic principle. He used minimal pairs to show the distinctive contrasts; he did not suggest different symbols for voiced and unvoiced [θ] and [ð], nor for [f] or [v], nor for velar [k] and palatal [č], because these pairs, according to him, represented allophones of the phonemes /θ/, /f/, and /k/, respectively. He did not use these modern technical terms, but the letters of his alphabet represent the distinctive phonemes of Icelandic of that century.

King Seijong of Korea (1417–1450) realized that the same principles held true for Korean when he designed a phonemic alphabet. The king was an avid reader, and he realized that the more than 30,000 Chinese characters that were being used to write the Korean language discouraged literacy among the people.

The alphabet was not reinvented by Seijong. Rather, the alphabetic principle was borrowed from the Hindu grammarians through Indian scholars who had visited Korea. Still, the Korean alphabet, called *hankul*, was conceived with remarkable insight. Originally hankul had eleven vowels and seventeen consonants (it is down to fourteen consonants and ten vowels at present). The characters representing consonants were drawn according to the place and manner of articulation. For example, 人   is meant to represent the teeth, and it is a part of each consonant character in which the tongue is placed behind the teeth (that is, alveolar or alveopalatal sounds). Thus 人 alone stands for /s/ (with allophones [s] and [š]). When crossed, 人 represents /ts/ (an alveolar affricate) with allophones [ts] and [tš] (=[č]). A bar above the character means aspiration, so 人 represents /ts^h/. Hundreds of years later, Francis Lodwick, Cave Beck, and Henry Sweet used a similar principle to design their phonetic alphabets.

King Seijong constructed each of eleven vowel characters by using one or more of three "atomic" characters: ○, |, and ▁; for example, | is /i/, ▁ is /u/, and ○ is /a/. The "strokes" used in drawing the vowels and consonants were also used in drawing the Chinese characters familiar to most Koreans.

Although Korean has the sounds [l] and [r], Seijong represented them by a single "letter" because they are allophonic variants of the same phoneme.[7] The same is true for the sounds [s] and [š], and [ts] and [tš]. Seijong knew that a narrow phonetic alphabet would be confusing to a Korean speaker.

Seijong's contribution to the Korean people has been recorded in a delightful legend. It is said that after he designed the alphabet he was afraid it would not be accepted, so he concocted a scheme to convince the people that it was a gift from heaven. He wrote each one of the new letters in honey on individual leaves that had fallen from a tree in the palace garden. When the king walked with his soothsayer in the garden the next day, the insects had eaten the honey and the leaf fiber underneath, just as he had hoped, and the leaves were etched with the alphabetic letters. The soothsayer and the Korean people were convinced that these letters represented a message from the gods. It is essentially this alphabet that is used in Korea today.

In North Korea the alphabet is used exclusively. In South Korea it is mixed with Chinese characters. The alphabet is often used for inflectional affixes, whereas the Chinese characters represent the root. This mixture is similar to the way Japanese use kanji for roots and hiragana for affixing. In Korean the alphabetic characters are not always written linearly, but are grouped in squarish shapes according to

[7]See Exercise 1 of Chapter 3 (p. 116).

the syllable structure. So Korean has a tinge of syllabic writing, and the unique style of Korean writing is unlike that of the Europeans, the Arabians, the Chinese, the Cascagians, or even "ladies in England."

Many languages have their own alphabet, and each has developed certain conventions for converting strings of alphabetic characters into sequences of sound (reading), and converting sequences of sounds into strings of alphabetic characters (writing). As we have illustrated with English, Icelandic, and Korean, the rules governing the sound system of the language play an important role in the relation between sound and character.

Most European alphabets make use of Latin (Roman) characters or letters, making minor adjustments to accommodate individual characteristics of a particular language. For instance, Spanish uses /ñ/ (an /n/ with a "tilde") to represent the palatalized nasal of *señor*, and German has added an "umlaut" for certain of its vowel sounds that did not exist in Latin (for example, in *über*). Such "extra" marks are called **diacritics.** Some languages use two letters together—called a digraph— to represent a single sound for which there is no corresponding single letter. English includes **digraphs** such as *sh* /š/, *ch* /č/, *ng* /ŋ/, and so on.

As mentioned above, some languages that have more recently developed a writing system use some of the IPA phonetic symbols in their alphabet. Twi, for example, uses ŋ, ɔ, and ɛ.

Besides the European languages, such languages as Turkish, Indonesian, Swahili, and Vietnamese have adopted the Latin alphabet.

The **Cyrillic** alphabet, named for St. Cyril, who brought Christianity to the Slavs, is used by many Slavic languages, including Russian. It is derived directly from the Greek alphabet without Latin mediation.

The contemporary Semitic alphabets, and those used for Persian and Urdu writing, are derived from the West Semitic Syllabary.

Figure 9–2 shows a greatly abbreviated "family tree" of alphabetic writing systems.

Writing and Speech

. . . *Ther is so great diversite*
In English, and in wryting of oure tonge,
So prey I god that non myswrite thee. . . .
Geoffrey Chaucer

The development of writing freed us from the limitations of time and geography, but spoken language still has primacy. Writing systems, however, are of interest for their own sake.

The written language reflects, to a certain extent, the elements and rules that together constitute the grammar of the language. The system of phonemes is repre- sented by the letters of the alphabet, although not necessarily in a direct way. The

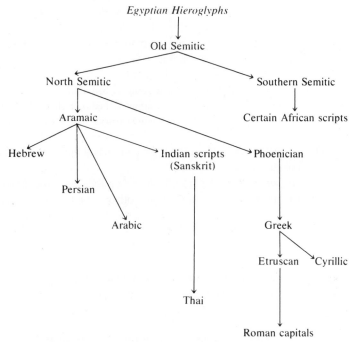

FIGURE 9–2 Family tree of alphabetic writing systems. (Adapted from Ernst Doblhofer. 1961. *Voices in Stone.* Viking. New York.)

independence of words is revealed by the spaces in the written string; but in languages where words are composed of more than one morpheme, the writing usually does not show the individual morphemes, even though speakers "know" what they are. In fact, many languages such as Japanese or Thai do not space between words, although speakers and writers are aware of the individual words. The sentences of some languages are indicated in the written form by capitals at the beginning and periods at the end. Other punctuation, such as question marks, italics, commas, and exclamation marks, is used to reveal syntactic structure, and to some extent intonation, stress, and contrast; but the written forms of other languages do not use such punctuation.

The possible ambiguity in the meanings of some sentences can be prevented by the use of commas:

    (1) The Greeks, who were philosophers, loved to talk a lot.
    (2) The Greeks who were philosophers loved to talk a lot.

Sentence 1, with the commas, means:

    (1) The Greeks were philosophers, and they loved to talk a lot.

The meaning of the second sentence, without the commas, can be paraphrased as:

(2) Among the Greeks it was the philosophers who loved to talk a lot.

Similarly, by using an exclamation point or a question mark, the intention of the writer can be made clearer.

(3) The children are going to bed at eight o'clock. *(simple statement)*
(4) The children are going to bed at eight o'clock! *(an order)*
(5) The children are going to bed at eight o'clock? *(a question)*

These punctuation marks reflect the pauses and the intonations that would be used in the spoken language.

In sentence 6 *he* can refer to either John or someone else, but in sentence 7 the pronoun must refer to someone other than John:

(6) John said he's going.
(7) John said, "He's going."

The apostrophe used in contractions and possessives also provides syntactic information not always available in the spoken utterance.

(8) My cousin's friends *(one cousin)*
(9) My cousins' friends *(two or more cousins)*

Writing, then, somewhat reflects the spoken language, and punctuation may even distinguish between two meanings not revealed in the spoken forms, as shown in sentences 8 and 9.

In the normal written version of sentence 10,

(10) John whispered the message to Bill and then he whispered it to Mary.

he can refer to either John or Bill. In the spoken sentence, if *he* receives extra stress (called **contrastive stress**), it must refer to Bill; if *he* receives normal stress, it refers to John.

A speaker can usually emphasize any word in a sentence by using contrastive stress. Writers sometimes attempt to show emphasis by using all capital letters or underlining the emphasized word:

(11) *John* kissed Bill's wife. (Bill didn't)
(12) John *kissed* Bill's wife. (rather than hugging her)
(13) John kissed *Bill's* wife. (not Dick's or his own)
(14) John kissed Bill's *wife*. (not Bill's mother)

Although such "visual" devices can help in English, it is not clear that they can be used in a language such as Chinese. In Japanese, however, this kind of emphasis can be achieved by writing a word in katakana.

The written language is also more conservative than the spoken language.

When we write something—particularly in formal writing—we are more apt to obey the ''prescriptive rules'' taught in school, or to use a more formal style, than we are to use the rules of our ''everyday'' grammar. ''Dangling participles'' (for example, *While studying in the library, the fire alarm rang*) and ''sentences ending with a preposition'' (for example, *I know what to end a sentence with*) abound in spoken language, but may be ''corrected'' by copy editors, diligent English teachers, and careful writers. A linguist wishing to describe the language that people regularly use therefore cannot depend on written records alone.

Spelling

"Do you spell it with a 'v' or a 'w'?" inquired the judge.
  "That depends upon the taste and fancy of the speller, my Lord," replied Sam.

Charles Dickens, *The Pickwick Papers*

B.C.   **Johnny Hart**

By permission of Johnny Hart and North America Syndicate, Inc.

If writing represented the spoken language perfectly, spelling reformers would never have arisen. In Chapter 2 we discussed some of the problems in the English orthographic (spelling) system. These problems prompted George Bernard Shaw to write:

> . . . It was as a reading and writing animal that Man achieved his human eminence above those who are called beasts. Well, it is I and my like who have to do the writing. I have done it professionally for the last sixty years as well as it can be done with a hopelessly inadequate alphabet devised centuries before the English language existed to record another and very different language. Even this alphabet is reduced to absurdity by a foolish orthography based on the notion that the business of spelling is to represent the origin and history of a word instead of its sound and meaning. Thus an intelligent child who is bidden to spell *debt*, and very properly spells it *d-e-t*, is caned for not spelling it with a *b* because Julius Caesar spelt the Latin word for it with a *b*.[8]

[8]George Bernard Shaw, Preface to R. A. Wilson. 1948. *The Miraculous Birth of Language*. Philosophical Library. New York.

The irregularities between **graphemes** (letters) and phonemes have been cited as one reason "why Johnny can't read." Different spellings for the same sound, the same spellings for different sounds, "silent letters," and "missing letters"—all provide fuel for the flames of spelling-reform movements. Here are examples:

Same Sound, Different Spelling	Different Sound, Same Spelling		Silent Letters	Missing Letters
/aj/	thought	[θ]	listen	use /yuz/
	though	[ð]	debt	fuse /fyuz/
aye	Thomas	[t]	gnosis	
buy			know	
by	ate	[e]	psychology	
die	at	[æ]	right	
hi	father	[a]	mnemonic	
Thai	many	[ɛ]	arctic	
height			balm	
guide			honest	
			sword	
			bomb	
			clue	
			Wednesday	

Chapters 2 and 8 have discussed some of the reasons for the nonphonemic aspects of our spelling system. "Spelling is the written trace of a word. Pronunciation is its linguistic form."[9] The spelling of most of the words in English today is based on the Late Middle English pronunciation (that used by Chaucer) and on the early forms of Modern English (used by Shakespeare). The many changes that have occurred in the sound system of English, like the Great Vowel Shift, were not always reflected in changes in the spelling of the words that were affected.

When the printing press was introduced in the fifteenth century, not only were archaic pronunciations "frozen," but the spelling did not always represent even those pronunciations, because many of the early printers were Dutch and were unsure of English pronunciation.

During the Renaissance, in the fifteenth and sixteenth centuries, many scholars who revered Classical Greek and Latin became "spelling reformers." Unlike the later reformers who wished to change the spelling to conform to pronunciation, these scholars changed the spelling of English words to conform to their etymologies—the "original" Latin, or Greek, or French spellings. Where the Latin had a *b*, they added a *b* even if it was not pronounced; and where the original spelling had a *c* or *p* or *h*, these letters were added, as is shown by these few examples:

[9]D. Bolinger. 1968. *Aspects of Language*. Harcourt Brace Jovanovich. New York.

Middle English Spelling		"Reformed" Spelling
indite	→	indi**c**t
dette	→	de**b**t
receit	→	recei**p**t
oure	→	**h**our

Such spelling habits inspired Robert N. Feinstein to compose the following poem, entitled *Gnormal Pspelling*:[10]

Gnus and gnomes and gnats and such—
Gnouns with just one G too much.
Pseudonym and psychedelic—
P becomes a psurplus relic.
Knit and knack and knife and knocked—
Kneedless Ks are overstocked.
Rhubarb, rhetoric and rhyme
Should lose an H from thyme to time.

For these reasons, modern English orthography does not always represent what we know about the phonology of the language. The disadvantage is partially offset by the fact that the writing system allows us to read and understand what people wrote hundreds of years ago without the need for translations. If there were a one-to-one correspondence between our spelling and the sounds of our language, we would have difficulty reading the Constitution or the Declaration of Independence.

Today's language is no more static than was yesterday's; it would be impossible to maintain a perfect correspondence between pronunciation and spelling. We do not mean to say that certain reforms would not be helpful. Some "respelling" is already taking place; advertisers often spell *though* as *tho*, *through* as *thru*, and *night* as *nite*. For a period of time the Chicago *Tribune* used such spellings, but it gave up the practice in 1975. Spelling habits are hard to change.

In the case of homophones, it is helpful at times to have different spellings for the same sounds, as in the following pair:

The book was red.   The book was read.

Lewis Carroll once more makes the point with humor:

"And how many hours a day did you do lessons?" said Alice.
"Ten hours the first day," said the Mock Turtle, "nine the next, and so on."
"What a curious plan!" exclaimed Alice.
"That's the reason they're called *lessons*," the Gryphon remarked, "because they *lessen* from day to day."

[10]Reprinted with permission from *National Forum: The Phi Kappa Phi Journal,* Summer 1986.

There are also reasons for using the same spelling for different pronunciations. In Chapter 4 it was shown that a morpheme may be pronounced differently when it occurs in different contexts, and that in most cases the pronunciation is "regular"; that is, it is determined by rules that apply throughout the language. The identical spelling reflects the fact that the different pronunciations represent the same morpheme.

Similarly, the phonetic realizations of the vowels in the following forms are "regular":

ay/ɪ	ɪ/ɛ	e/æ
divine/divinity	*serene/serenity*	*sane/sanity*
sublime/sublimate	*obscene/obscenity*	*profane/profanity*
sign/signature	*hygiene/hygienic*	*humane/humanity*

The spelling of such pairs thus reflects our knowledge of the sound pattern of the language and the semantic-morphological relations between the words.

Other examples provide further evidence. The *b* in *"debt"* may remind us of the related word *debit*, in which the *b* is pronounced. The same principle is true of pairs such as *sign/signal, knowledge/acknowledge, bomb/bombardier,* and *gnosis/prognosis/agnostic.*

It is doubtful that anyone would suggest that the plural morpheme should be spelled *s* in *cats* and *z* in *dogs*. The sound of the morpheme is determined by rules, in this case as in other cases.

There are also different spellings that represent the different pronunciations of a morpheme when confusion would arise from using the same spelling. For example, there is a rule in English phonology that changes a /t/ to an /s/ in certain cases: *democrat → democracy*. The different spellings are due in part to the fact that this rule does not apply to all morphemes, so that *art + y* is *arty*, not **arcy*. Regular phoneme-to-grapheme rules determine in many cases when a morpheme is to be spelled identically and when it is to be changed.

Other subregularities are apparent. A *c* always represents the /s/ sound when it is followed by a *y, i,* or *e,* as in *cynic, citizen,* and *censure*. Because it is always pronounced [k] when it is the final letter in a word or when it is followed by any other vowel (*coat, cat, cut,* and so on), no confusion results. The *th* spelling is usually pronounced voiced as [ð] between vowels (the result of an historical intervocalic voicing rule).

Such rules of orthography could be taught to children learning to read, which would lessen the difficulties they have with the spelling system. For example, by pointing out the alternate pronunciations of morphemes such as the [o] in *melodious* or the [g] in *signal*, teachers could make it easier for students to remember how to spell the related words *melody* or *sign*.

There is another important reason why spelling should not always be tied to the phonetic pronunciation of words. Different dialects of English have divergent pronunciations. Cockneys drop their "haitches" and Bostonians and Southerners drop their "*r*'s"; *neither* is pronounced [niðər] and [niðə] by Americans, [nayðə]

by the British, and [neðər] by the Irish; some Scots pronounce *night* as [nɪxt];
people say "Chicago" and "Chicawgo," "hog" and "hawg," "bird" and
"boyd"; *four* is pronounced [fɔ:] by the British, [fɔr] in the Midwest, and [foə] in
the South; *orange* is pronounced in at least two ways in the United States: [arənǰ]
and [ɔrənǰ].

While dialectal pronunciations differ, the common spellings represent the fact
that we understand each other. It is necessary for the written language to transcend
local dialects. With a uniform spelling system, a native of Atlanta and a native of
Glasgow can communicate through writing. If each dialect were spelled according
to its own pronunciation, written communication among the English-speaking peoples of the world would suffer more than the spoken communication does today.

Spelling Pronunciations

*For pronunciation, the best general rule is to consider those as the most elegant speakers who
deviate least from written words.*
Samuel Johnson, 1755

Despite the primacy of the spoken over the written language, the written word is
often regarded with excessive reverence. The stability, permanency, and graphic
nature of writing cause some people to favor it over ephemeral and elusive speech.
Humpty Dumpty expressed a rather typical attitude: "I'd rather see that done on
paper."

Writing has affected speech only marginally, however, most notably in the
phenomenon of **spelling pronunciation.** Since the sixteenth century, we find that
spelling has to some extent influenced standard pronunciation. The most important
of such changes stem from the eighteenth century under the influence and "de-
crees" of the dictionary-makers and the schoolteachers. The struggle between those
who demanded that words be pronounced according to the spelling and those who
demanded that words be spelled according to their pronunciation generated great
heat in that century. The "preferred" pronunciations were given in the many dictionaries printed in the eighteenth century, and the "supreme authority" of the
dictionaries influenced pronunciation in this way.

Spelling also has influenced pronunciation in words that are infrequently used
in normal daily speech. Many words that were spelled with an initial *h* were not
pronounced with any /h/ sound as late as the eighteenth century. Thus, at that time
no /h/ was pronounced in *honest, hour, habit, heretic, hotel, hospital, herb.* Frequently used words like *honest* and *hour* continued to be pronounced without the
/h/, despite the spelling; but all those other words were given a "spelling pronunciation." Because people did not hear them often, when they saw them written they
concluded that they must begin with an /h/. *Herb* is currently undergoing this
change; in Standard British English the *h* is pronounced, whereas in Standard American English it is not.

Similarly, many words now spelled with a *th* were once pronounced /t/ as in

Thomas; later most of these words underwent a change in pronunciation from /t/ to /θ/, as in *anthem, author, theater*. "Nicknames" often reflect the earlier pronunciations: "Ka*t*e" for "Ca*t*herine," "Be*tt*y" for "Eliza*b*e*th*," "Ar*t*" for "Ar*t*hur." The words *often* and *soften*, which are usually pronounced without a /t/ sound, are pronounced with the /t/ by some people because of the spelling.

The clear influence of spelling on pronunciation is observable in the way place-names are pronounced. *Berkeley* is pronounced [bʌrkli] in California, although it stems from the British [baːkli]; *Worcester* [wʊstər] or [wʊstə] in Massachusetts is often pronounced [wʊrčɛstər] in other parts of the country; *Magdalen* is pronounced [mɔdlɪn] in England and [mægdələn] in the United States.

Although the written language has some influence on the spoken, it does not change the basic system—the grammar—of the language. The writing system, conversely, reflects, in a more or less direct way, the grammar that every speaker knows.

Summary

Writing is one of the basic tools of civilization. Without it, the world as we know it could not exist.

The first writing was "picture writing," which used **pictograms** to represent objects directly. Pictograms became stylized, and people came to associate them with the *sounds* that represented the object in their language. The Sumerians first developed a pictographic writing system to keep track of commercial transactions. It was later expanded for other uses and eventually evolved into the highly stylized (and stylus-ized) **cuneiform** writing. Cuneiform was borrowed by several nations and was adapted for use in syllabic writing systems by application of the **rebus principle,** which used the symbol of one word to represent any word or syllable with the same sounds.

The Egyptians also developed a pictographic system, which became known as **hieroglyphics.** This system was borrowed by many peoples, including the Phoenicians, who improved on it, using it as a **syllabary.** In a syllabic writing system, one symbol is used for each syllable. The Greeks borrowed the Phoenician system, and in adapting it to their own language they used the symbols to represent individual sound segments, thus inventing the first **alphabet.**

There are three types of writing systems still being used in the world: **word writing,** where every symbol or character represents a word or morpheme (as in Chinese); **syllable writing,** where each symbol represents a syllable (as in Japanese); and **alphabetic writing,** where each symbol represents (for the most part) one phoneme (as in English).

Many of the world's languages do not have a written form, but this fact does not mean the languages are any less developed. We learn to speak before we learn to write, and historically tens of thousands of years went by during which language was spoken before there was any writing.

The writing system may have some small effect on the spoken language. Languages change in time, but writing systems tend to be more conservative. Thus spelling no longer accurately reflects pronunciation. Also, when the spoken and written forms of the language become divergent, some words may be pronounced as they are spelled, sometimes due to the efforts of "pronunciation reformers."

There are advantages to a conservative spelling system. A common spelling permits speakers whose dialects have diverged to communicate through writing, as is best exemplified in China, where the "dialects" are mutually unintelligible. We are also able to read and understand the language as it was written centuries ago. In addition, despite some gross lack of correspondences between sound and spelling, the spelling often reflects speakers' morphological and phonological knowledge.

References

Diringer, D. 1962. *Writing*. Holt, Rinehart and Winston. New York.

Doblhofer, E. 1961. *Voices in Stone: The Decipherment of Ancient Scripts and Writings*. Viking Press. New York.

Gelb, I. J. 1952. *A Study of Writing*. University of Chicago Press. Chicago.

Robertson, S., and F. G. Cassidy. 1954. *The Development of Modern English*. Prentice-Hall. Englewood Cliffs, N.J. Pp. 353–374 (on spelling and spelling reform).

Wang, William S-Y. 1973. "The Chinese Language." *Scientific American* 228 (2): 50–63.

Wang, William S-Y. 1981. "Language Structure and Optimal Orthography." In *Perception of Print: Reading Research in Experimental Psychology*, O. J. L. Tzeng and H. Singer, eds. Erlbaum. Hillsdale, N.J.

Exercises

1. A. "Write" the following words and phrases, using pictograms that you invent:

    a. eye
    b. a boy
    c. two boys
    d. library
    e. tree
    f. forest
    g. war
    h. honesty
    i. ugly
    j. run
    k. Scotch tape
    l. smoke

    B. Which words are most difficult to symbolize in this way? Why?
    C. How does the following sentence reveal the problems in pictographic writing? "A grammar represents the unconscious, internalized linguistic competence of a native speaker."

2. A *rebus* is a written representation of words or syllables using pictures of objects whose names resemble the sounds of the intended words or syllables. For example, might be the symbol for "eye" or "I" or the first syllable in "idea."

    A. Using the rebus principle, "write" the following words:

    a. tearing
    b. icicle
    c. bareback
    d. cookies

    B. Why would such a system be a difficult system in which to represent all words in English? Illustrate with an example.

3. A. Construct non-Roman alphabetic letters to replace the letters used to represent the following sounds in English:

    t   r   s   k   w   č   i   ae   f   n

    B. Use these symbols plus the regular alphabet symbols for the other sounds to write the following words in your "new orthography."

    a. character
    b. guest
    c. cough
    d. photo

     e. cheat
     f. rang
     g. psychotic
     h. tree

4. Suppose the English writing system were a *syllabic* system instead of an *alphabetic* system. Use capital letters to symbolize the necessary syllabic units for the words below, and list your "syllabary." Example: Given the words *mate, inmate, intake,* and *elfin,* you might use: A = mate, B = in, C = take, and D = elf. In addition, write the words using your syllabary. Example: *inmate*—BA; *elfin*—DB; *intake*—BC; *mate*—A. (Do not use any more syllable symbols than you absolutely need.)

     a. childishness
     b. childlike
     c. Jesuit
     d. lifelessness
     e. likely
     f. zoo
     g. witness
     h. lethal
     i. jealous
     j. witless
     k. lesson

5. In the following pairs of English words the boldfaced portions are pronounced the same but spelled differently. Can you think of any reason why the spelling should remain distinct? (Hint: **reel** and **real** are pronounced the same, but *reality* shows the presence of a phonemic /ae/ in *real*.)

	A	B	Reason
a.	I **am**	i**amb**	
b.	g**oose**	pr**oduce**	
c.	fa**sh**ion	compli**c**ation	
d.	New**ton**	org**an**	
e.	**no**	**kn**ow	
f.	hy**mn**	**hi**m	

6. In the following pairs of words the boldfaced portions are spelled the same but pronounced differently. Try to state some reasons why the spelling of the words in column B should not be changed.

	A	B	Reason
a.	mi**ng**le	lo**ng**	The **g** is pronounced in *longer*.
b.	l**i**ne	ch**i**ldren	

c. sonar   resound
d. cent   mystic
e. crumble   bomb
f. cats   dogs
g. stagnant   design
h. serene   obscenity

7. Each of the following sentences is ambiguous in the written form. How can these sentences be made unambiguous when they are spoken?

> *Example:* John hugged Bill and then he kissed him.
>
> For the meaning ''John hugged and kissed Bill,'' use normal stress (*kissed* receives stress). For the meaning ''Bill kissed John,'' contrastive stress is needed on both *he* and *him*.

a. What are we having for dinner, Mother?
b. She's a German language teacher.
c. They formed a student grievance committee.
d. Charles kissed his wife and George kissed his wife too.

8. In the written form, the following sentences are not ambiguous, but they would be if spoken. State the devices used in writing that make the meanings explicit.

a. They're my brothers' keepers.
b. He said, ''He will take the garbage out.''
c. The red book was read.
d. The flower was on the table.

9. Below are ten samples of writing from the ten languages listed. Match the writing to the language. There are enough ''hints'' in this chapter to get most of them. (The source of these examples, and many others, is *Languages of the World* by Kenneth Katzner. Funk & Wagnalls: New York. 1975.)

a. _____Cherokee

1. 仮に勝手に変えるようなことをすれば,

b. _____Chinese

2. Κι ὁ νοῦς του ἀγκάλιασε πονετικὰ τὴν Κρήτη.

c. _____German (Gothic style)

3. «Что это? я падаю? у меня ноги подкашиваются»,

d. _____Greek

4. וְהָיָ֣ה ׀ בְּאַחֲרִ֣ית הַיָּמִ֗ים נָכ֨וֹן יִהְיֶ֤ה הַר

e. _____Hebrew

5. Saá sàre yi bèŋ atskyé bí â mpɔ̀tɔrɔ áhyé

f. _____Icelandic

6. 既然必须和新的群众的时代相结合.

g. _____Japanese

7. ᏣᎳᎩ ᎠᏂ ᎤᎾᏓᏤᎵ ᏣᎳᎩ ᏍᏆᏯ.

h. _____Korean

8. Þótt þú langförull legðir sérhvert land undir fót,

i. _____Russian

9. Pharao's Anblick war wunderbar.

j. _____Twi

10. 스위스는 독특한 체제

Biological Aspects of Language

The functional asymmetry of the human brain is unequivocal, and so is its anatomical asymmetry. The structural differences between the left and the right hemispheres are visible not only under the microscope but to the naked eye. The most striking asymmetries occur in language-related cortices. It is tempting to assume that such anatomical differences are an index of the neurobiological underpinnings of language.

Antonio and Hanna Damasio

[The brain is] the messenger to the understanding [and the organ whereby] in an especial manner we acquire wisdom and knowledge.

Hippocratic treatise "On the Sacred Disease," c. 377 B.C.E.

Language Acquisition

The acquisition of language "is doubtless the greatest intellectual feat any one of us is ever required to perform."
Leonard Bloomfield, *Language* (1933)

Every aspect of language is extremely complex; yet very young children—before the age of 5—already know most of the intricate system we have been calling the grammar of a language. Before they can add 2 + 2, children are conjoining sentences, asking questions, selecting appropriate pronouns, negating sentences, forming relative clauses, and using the syntactic, phonological, morphological, and semantic rules of the grammar.

A normal human being can go through life without learning to read or write. Millions of people in the world today prove it. These same millions all speak and understand and can discuss complex and abstract ideas as well as literate speakers can. Therefore, learning a language and learning to read and write are somehow different. Similarly, millions of humans grow to maturity and never learn algebra or chemistry or how to use a typewriter. They must be taught these skills or systems, but they do not have to be taught to walk or to talk.

The study of the nature of human language itself has revealed a great deal about language acquisition, about what the child does and does not do when learning or acquiring a language.

1. Children do not learn a language by storing all the words and all the sentences in some giant mental dictionary. The list of words is finite, but no dictionary can hold all the sentences, which are infinite in number.
2. Children learn to construct sentences, most of which they have never produced before.
3. Children learn to understand sentences they have never heard before. They cannot do so by matching the "heard utterance" with some stored sentence.

367

4. Children must therefore construct the "rules" that permit them to use language creatively.
5. No one teaches them these rules. Their parents are no more aware of the phonological, syntactic, and semantic rules than are the children.

Even if you remember your early years, you will not remember anyone telling you to form a sentence by adding a verb phrase to a noun phrase, or to add [s] or [z] to form plurals. Children, then, seem to act like efficient linguists equipped with a perfect theory of language, who use this theory to construct the grammar of the language they hear.

In addition to acquiring the complex rules of the grammar (that is, linguistic competence), children must also learn the complex rules of the appropriate social use of language, what certain scholars have called communicative competence. These rules include, for example, the greetings that are to be used, the "taboo" words, the polite forms of address, the various styles that are appropriate to different situations, and so forth.

Stages in Language Acquisition

. . . for I was no longer a speechless infant; but a speaking boy. This I remember; and have since observed how I learned to speak. It was not that my elders taught me words . . . in any set method; but I . . . did myself . . . practice the sounds in my memory. . . . And thus by constantly hearing words, as they occurred in various sentences . . . I thereby gave utterance to my will.

St. Augustine, *Confessions* (circa 400 C.E.)

Children do not wake up one morning with a fully formed grammar in their heads or with all the "rules" of social and communicative intercourse. Linguistic knowledge develops by stages, and, it is suggested, each successive stage more closely approximates the grammar of the adult language. Observations of children in different language areas of the world reveal that the stages are similar, possibly universal. Some of the stages last for a short time; others remain longer. Some stages may overlap for a short period, though the transition between stages is often sudden.

The earliest studies of child language acquisition come from diaries kept by parents. More recent studies include the use of tape recordings, videotapes, and controlled experiments. Spontaneous utterances of children are recorded, and in addition various elicitation techniques have been developed so that the child's production and comprehension can be scientifically studied.

The First Sounds

An infant crying in the night:
An infant crying for the light:
And with no language but a cry.

Alfred Lord Tennyson, "In Memoriam H.H.S."

The stages of language acquisition can be divided into prelinguistic and linguistic stages. Most scholars agree that the earliest cries, whimpers, and cooing noises of the newborn, or neonate, cannot be considered early language. Such noises are completely stimulus-controlled; they are the child's involuntary responses to hunger, discomfort, the desire to be cuddled, or the feeling of well-being. A major difference between human language and the communication systems of other species is that human language is creative, as discussed earlier, in the sense of being free from either external or internal stimuli. The child's first noises are, however, simply responses to stimuli.

During the earliest period, the noises produced by infants in all language communities sound the same. Children who are born deaf also produce these same sounds, even though they receive no auditory stimuli.

The early view that the neonate is born with a mind that is like a blank slate is countered by the evidence showing that infants are highly sensitive to certain subtle distinctions in their environment and not to others. That is, the mind appears to be "prewired" to receive only certain kinds of information.

By using a specially designed nipple with a pressure-sensitive device that records sucking rate, it has been found that infants will increase their sucking rate when stimuli (visual or auditory) presented to them are varied, but will decrease the sucking rate when the same stimuli are presented over and over again. Experiments have shown that infants will respond to visual depth and distance distinctions, to differences between rigid versus flexible physical properties of objects, and to human faces rather than to other visual stimuli.

Similarly, newborn infants respond to phonetic contrasts found in some human languages even when these differences are not phonemic in the language spoken in the baby's home. A baby hearing a human voice over a loudspeaker saying [pa] [pa] [pa] will slowly decrease her rate of sucking; if the sound changes to [ba] or even [pʰa], the sucking rate increases dramatically. There will be no response to sound signals that are intermediate between, say, [pa] and [pʰa], differences that never signal phonemic contrasts in any human language. The infants could not have learned to make these phonetic distinctions; they seem to be born with the ability to perceive just those sounds that are phonemic in some language. Thus, children have the sensory and motor abilities to produce and comprehend speech, even in the period of life before language acquisition occurs.

Babbling

From this golden egg a man, Prajapati, was born. . . . A year having passed, he wanted to speak. He said bhur and the earth was created. He said bhuvar and the space of the air was created. He said suvar and the sky was created. That is why a child wants to speak after a year. . . . When Prajapati spoke for the first time, he uttered one or two syllables. That is why a child utters one or two syllables when he speaks for the first time.

Hindu myth

In the first few months, usually around the sixth month, the infant begins to babble.

The sounds produced in this period (apart from the continuing stimulus-controlled cries and gurgles) seem to include a large variety of sounds, many of which do not occur in the language of the household. Deaf children also babble, and their babbling, like their earliest cries and coos, seems similar to that of normal children. Hearing children born of nonspeaking deaf parents also babble. Thus, babbling does not depend on the presence of acoustic, auditory input.

One view suggests that it is during this period that children are learning to distinguish between the sounds of their language and the sounds that are not part of the language. During the babbling period children learn to maintain the "right" sounds and suppress the "wrong" ones.

During the babbling stage the pitches, or intonation contours, of infants' utterances begin to resemble the intonation contours of sentences spoken by adults. The semantically different intonation contours are among the first linguistic contrasts that children perceive and produce. Babbling does not seem to be a prerequisite for language acquisition. Infants who are unable to produce any sounds at this early stage due to physical motor problems begin to talk properly once the disability has been corrected. This fact supports the idea that the babbling stage is a prelinguistic stage.

First Words

DOONESBURY   **Garry Trudeau**

Sometime after one year (it varies from child to child and has nothing to do with how intelligent the child is), children begin to use the same string of sounds repeatedly to "mean" the same thing. They have learned that sounds are related to meanings, and they are producing their first "words." Most children seem to go through the "one word = one sentence" stage. These one-word "sentences" are called **holophrastic** sentences (from *holo* ''complete'' or ''undivided'' plus *phrase* ''phrase'' or ''sentence'').

One child, J.P., illustrates how much the young child has learned even before the age of two years. J.P.'s words of April 1977, at the age of 16 months, were as follows:[1]

[ʔaw]	''not'' ''no'' ''don't''	[s:]	''aerosol spray''
[bʌʔ]/[mʌʔ]	''up''		
[da]	''dog''	[sʲu:]	''shoe''
[iʔo]/[siʔo]	''Cheerios''	[haj]	''hi''
[sa]	''sock''	[sr]	''shirt''
[aj]/[ʌj]	''light''		''sweater''
[ma]	''mommy''	[sæ:]/[əsæ:]	''what's that?''
[baw]/[daw]	''down''		''hey, look!''
[dæ]	''daddy''		

J.P.'s mother reports that before April he also had used the words [bʊ] for ''book,'' [ki] for ''kitty,'' and [tsi] for ''tree'' but seemed to have ''lost'' them.

What is more interesting than merely the list of J.P.'s vocabulary is the way he used these words. ''Up'' was originally restricted to mean ''Get me up'' when he was either on the floor or in his high chair, but later was used to mean ''Get up!'' to his mother as well. J.P. used his word for ''sock'' not only for socks but also for other undergarments that go over the feet, which illustrates how a child may extend the meaning of a word from a particular referent to encompass a larger class.

When J.P. first began to use these words, the stimulus had to be visible; but soon, it was no longer necessary. *Dog*, for example, was first only used when pointing to a real dog but later was used for pictures of dogs in various books. A new word that entered J.P.'s vocabulary at seventeen months was *uh-oh*, which he would say after he had an accident like spilling juice, or when he deliberately poured his yogurt over the side of his high chair. His use of this word shows his developing use of language for social purposes. At this time he also added two new words meaning ''no,'' [do:] and [no]. He used these words frequently when anyone attempted to take something from him that he wanted or tried to make him do something he did not want to do. He used this negative either imperatively (for example, ''Don't do that!'') or assertively (for example, ''I don't want to do that.''). Even in his early holophrastic stage, J.P. was using words to convey a variety of ideas, feelings, and social awareness.

According to some child-language researchers, the words in the holophrastic stage serve three major functions: they either are linked with a child's own action or desire for action (as when J.P. would say ''up'' to express his wish to be picked up), or are used to convey emotion (J.P.'s ''no''), or serve a naming function (J.P.'s ''Cheerios,'' ''shoes,'' ''dog,'' and so on).

---

[1]We give special thanks to John Peregrine Munro for providing us with such rich data, and to Drs. Pamela and Allen Munro, J.P.'s parents, for their painstaking efforts in recording these data.

At this stage the child uses only one word to express concepts or predictions that will later be expressed by complex phrases and sentences.

Phonologically, J.P.'s first words, like the words of most children at this stage of learning English and other languages, were generally monosyllabic with a CV (consonant-vowel) form; the vowel part may be diphthongal, depending on the language being acquired. His phonemic or phonetic inventory (at this stage they are equivalent) is much smaller than is found in the adult language. It was suggested by the linguist Roman Jakobson[2] that children first will acquire the sounds found in all languages of the world, no matter what language they are exposed to, and in later stages will acquire the "more difficult" sounds. For example, most languages have the sounds [p] and [s], but [θ] is a rare sound. J.P. was no exception. His phonological inventory at an early stage included the consonants [b, m, d, k], which are frequently occurring sounds in the world's languages.

Many studies have shown that children in the holophrastic stage can perceive or comprehend many more phonological contrasts than they can produce themselves. Therefore, even at this stage, it is not possible to determine the extent of the grammar of the child simply by observing speech production.

The Two-Word Stage

Children begin to produce two-word utterances around the time of their second birthday. At first these utterances appear to be strings of two of the child's earlier holophrastic utterances, each word with its own single-pitch contour. Soon after this juxtaposition, children begin to form actual two-word sentences with clear syntactic and semantic relations. The intonation contour of the two words extends over the whole utterance rather than being separated by a pause between the two words. The following "sentences" illustrate the kinds of patterns that are found in children's utterances at this stage.[3]

allgone sock	hi Mommy
byebye boat	allgone sticky
more wet	beepbeep bang
it ball	Katherine sock
dirty sock	here pretty

During the two-word utterance stage there are no syntactic or morphological markers—that is, no inflections for number, person, tense, and so on. Pronouns are rare, although many children use *me* to refer to themselves, and some children use other pronouns as well. Bloom has noted that in noun + noun sentences such as *Mommy sock*, the two words can express a number of different grammatical rela-

---

[2]R. Jakobson. 1941. *Kindersprache, Aphasie, und Allgemeine.* Almqvist and Wiksell. Uppsala, Sweden. (English translation by A. Keiler. 1968. *Child Language, Aphasia, and Phonological Universals.* Mouton. The Hague.)

[3]All the examples given in this chapter are taken from utterances produced by children actually observed by the authors or reported in the literature. The various sources are listed in the reference section at the end of the chapter.

tions that will later be expressed by other syntactic devices.[4] Bloom's conclusions were reached by observing the situations in which the two-word sentence was uttered. Thus, for example, *Mommy sock* can be used to show a subject + object relation in the situation when the mother is putting the sock on the child, or a possessive relation when the child is pointing to Mommy's sock. Two nouns can also be used to show a subject–locative relation, as in *sweater chair* to mean "The sweater is on the chair," or to show conjunction, to mean "sweater and chair."

From Telegraph to Infinity

There does not seem to be any "three-word" sentence stage. When a child starts stringing more than two words together, the utterances may be two, three, four, or five words or longer. By studying the increasing lengths of the utterances that children use, however, a comparison across children as to stage of language acquisition can be made by the **mean length of utterances** (MLU) rather than by chronological age. That is, children producing utterances that average 2.3 to 3.5 morphemes in length seem to be at the same stage of grammar acquisition.

The first utterances of children longer than two words have a special characteristic. The small "function" words such as *to, the, can, is*, and so on, are missing; only the words that carry the main message—the "content" words—occur. Children often sound as if they are reading a Western Union message, which is why such utterances are sometimes called **telegraphic speech:**

> Cat stand up table
> What that?
> He play little tune
> Andrew want that
> Cathy build house
> No sit there

JP's early sentences were similar:

Age in Months

25 months	[dan ʔiʔ tˢɪʔ]	"don't eat (the) chip"
	[bʷaʔ tat]	"(the) block (is on) top"
26 months	[mamis tu hæs]	"Mommy's two hands"
	[mo bʌs go]	"where's another bus?"
	[dædi go]	"where's Daddy?"
27 months	[ʔaj gat tu dʲus]	"I got two (glasses of) juice"
	[do bajʔ mi]	"don't bite (kiss) me"
	[kʌdər sʌni ber]	"Sonny color(ed a) bear"
28 months	[ʔaj gat pwe dɪs]	"I('m) play(ing with) this"
	[mamis tak mɛns]	"Mommy talk(ed to the) men"

[4]L. M. Bloom. 1972. *Language Development: Form and Function in Emerging Grammar*. M.I.T. Press. Cambridge, Mass.

Apart from lacking grammatical morphemes, these utterances appear to be "sentence-like"; they have hierarchical, constituent structures similar to the syntactic structures found in the sentences produced by the adult grammar.

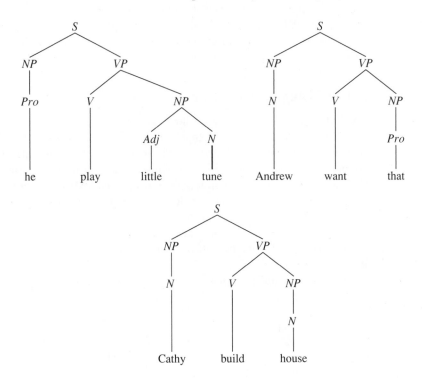

Children's utterances are not simply words that are randomly strung together, but from a very early stage reveal their grasp of the principles of sentence formation.

Though the utterances are described as "telegraphic," the child does not deliberately leave out the noncontent words as does an adult sending a telegram.

As children produce sentences that more and more closely approximate the adult grammar, they begin to use syntactic or grammatical function words and also to acquire the inflectional and derivational morphemes of the language. Brown and his associates at Harvard studied the spontaneous utterances of three children— Adam, Sarah, and Eve—over a long period of time, noting the appearance of grammatical morphemes, free and bound.[5] They found that the sequences of acquisition of the morphemes were the same for all three children, and this finding has been replicated by others. *-ing*, the ending that represents the present progressive form of the verb, as in *Me going*, was found to be among the earliest inflectional morphemes acquired. The prepositions *in* and *on* next entered the speech of the the children studied, and then the regular plural ending, as in "two doggies" /tu dɔgiz/. It is interesting that the third person singular marker (as in *Johnny comes*) and the

[5]R. O. Brown. 1973. *A First Language: The Early Stages*. Harvard University Press. Cambridge, Mass.

possessive morpheme (as in *Daddy's hat*), which have the same phonological shape as the plural /s/, entered the children's speech between six months and a year later, showing that acquisition of these morphemes is syntax-dependent.

Eventually all the other inflections were added, along with the syntactic rules, and finally the child's utterances sounded like those spoken by adults.

This feat is incredible, because the syntactic rules of all languages are complex; moreover, the child must "figure out" what these rules are from very "noisy" data. The child hears sentence fragments, false starts, speech errors, and interruptions; no one tells the child "this is a grammatical utterance and this is not." Somehow the adult grammar is acquired. A basic question is how the child accomplishes this task.

Theories of Child Language Acquisition

Do Children Learn by Imitation?

CHILD: *My teacher holded the baby rabbits and we patted them.*
ADULT: *Did you say your teacher held the baby rabbits?*
CHILD: *Yes.*
ADULT: *What did you say she did?*
CHILD: *She holded the baby rabbits and we patted them.*
ADULT: *Did you say she held them tightly?*
CHILD: *No, she holded them loosely.*

Courtney Cazden[6]

Various theories have been proposed to explain how children manage to acquire the adult language. There are those who think that children merely imitate what they hear. Imitation is involved to some extent, of course, but the sentences produced by children show that children are not imitating adult speech. From whom would children hear *Cat stand up table* or any of the utterances they produce?

a my pencil	other one pants
two foot	Mommy get it my ladder
what the boy hit?	cowboy did fighting me

Even when children are deliberately trying to imitate what they hear, they are unable to produce sentences that cannot be generated by their grammar.

ADULT: He's going out.	CHILD: He go out.
ADULT: That's an old-time train.	CHILD: Old-time train.
ADULT: Adam, say what I say:	CHILD: Where I can
Where can I put them?	put them?

---

[6]C. Cazden. 1972. *Child Language and Education*, Holt, Rinehart and Winston. New York. P. 92.

Neither can the "imitation" theory account for another important phenomenon. There are children who are unable to speak for neurological or physiological reasons; yet these children learn the language spoken to them and understand what is said. When they overcome their speech impairment they immediately use the language for speaking.

Do Children Learn by Reinforcement?

> CHILD: Nobody don't like me.
> MOTHER: No, say "Nobody likes me."
> CHILD: Nobody don't like me.
>
> *(dialogue repeated eight times)*
>
> MOTHER: Now, listen carefully, say *"Nobody likes me."*
> CHILD: Oh, nobody don't likes me.

Another theory of language acquisition suggests that children learn to produce "correct" sentences because they are positively reinforced when they say something right and negatively reinforced when they say something wrong. This view assumes that children are being constantly corrected for using "bad grammar" and rewarded when they use "good grammar." Brown and his colleagues[7] report from their studies that reinforcement seldom occurs, and when it does, it is usually incorrect pronunciation or incorrect reporting of facts that is corrected. They report, for example, that the ungrammatical sentence *Her curl my hair* was not corrected because Eve's mother was in fact curling her hair. However, when the syntactically correct sentence *Walt Disney comes on on Tuesday* was produced, her mother corrected Eve because the program on television was shown on Wednesday. They conclude that it is "truth value rather than syntactic well-formedness that chiefly governs explicit verbal reinforcement by parents—which renders mildly paradoxical the fact that the usual product of such a training schedule is an adult whose speech is highly grammatical but not notably truthful" (p. 330).

Even if syntactic correction occurred more often, it would not explain how or what children learn from such adult responses or how children discover and construct the correct rules.

In fact, attempts to "correct" a child's language seem to be doomed to failure. Children do not know what they are doing wrong and are unable to make corrections even when they are pointed out, as shown by the example above and the following one:

> CHILD: Want other one spoon, Daddy.
> FATHER: You mean, you want *"the other spoon."*
> CHILD: Yes, I want other one spoon, please, Daddy.
> FATHER: Can you say "the other spoon"?

[7]Ibid.

CHILD: Other . . . one . . . spoon.
FATHER: Say . . . "other."
CHILD: Other.
FATHER: Spoon.
CHILD: Spoon.
FATHER: Other . . . spoon.
CHILD: Other . . . spoon. Now give me other one spoon?

As already noted, such conversations between parents and children do not occur often. The above conversation was between a linguist studying child language and his child. Mothers and fathers are usually delighted that their young children are talking at all and consider every utterance to be a gem. The "mistakes" children make are "cute" and repeated endlessly to anyone who will listen.

Children Form Rules and Construct a Grammar

THE BORN LOSER   **Art Sansom**

Reprinted by permission of Newspaper Enterprise Association, Inc.

The "reinforcement" theory fails along with the "imitation" theory. Neither of these views accounts for the nonrandom mistakes children make, the speed with which the basic rules of grammar are acquired, the ability to learn language *without any formal instruction,* and the regularity of the acquisition process across diverse languages and environmental circumstances. Between the ages of five and seven, children from diverse backgrounds reach the same stage of grammar acquisition irrespective of whether their parents talk to them constantly or whether they are brought up to be seen and not heard and are seldom spoken to.

It appears that the child is equipped from birth with the neural prerequisites for language and language use, just as birds are biologically "prewired" to learn the songs of their species. Our linguistic ability permits us to acquire any human language to which we are exposed. Thus, children born of Zulu parents and raised in an English-speaking environment will learn English, and vice versa.

Different phrase structure rules (and later transformational rules) govern the construction of sentences as the grammar is learned. Consider, for example, the increasing complexity of one child's negative sentences. At first the child simply added a *no* (or some negative morpheme) at the beginning or at the end of a sentence:

> no heavy
> no singing song
> no want stand head
> no Fraser drink all tea
> no the sun shining

Fraser did not hear such sentences. He used a simple way to form a negative, but it is not the way negative sentences are constructed in English. At some point he began to insert a *no* or *can't* or *don't* inside the sentence.

> He no bite you
> I no taste them
> That no fish school
> I can't catch you

The child progressed from simple rules to more complex rules, as is shown below:

Declarative:	I want some food.	
Negative 1:	No want some food.	(*no* added to beginning of sentence)
Negative 2:	I no/don't want some food.	(negative element inserted; no other change)
Negative 3:	I don't want no food.	(negative element inserted: negation "spread"—*some* becomes *no*)
Negative 4:	I don't want any food.	(negative element inserted correctly; *some* changed to *any*)

All children do not show exactly the same development as the child described above, but they all show similar regular changes. One child studied by Carol Lord first differentiated affirmative from negative sentences by pitch; her negative sentences were all produced with a much higher pitch. When she began to use a negative morpheme, the pitch remained high, but then the intonation became normal as the negative syntactic markers "took over."

Similar changes in the grammar are found in the acquisition of questions. One child first formed a question by using a "question intonation" (a rise of pitch at the end of the sentence):

> Fraser water?
> I ride train?
> Sit chair?

At the next stage the child merely "tacked on" a question word in front of the sentence; he did not change the word order or insert *do*.

> What he wants?
> What he can ride in?
> Where I should put it?
> Where Ann pencil?
> Why you smiling?

Such sentences are perfectly regular. They are not "mistakes" in the child's language; they reflect the grammar at a certain stage of development.

Errors or Rules?

A final word about the theory of errors. Here it is that the causes are complex and multiple. . . .
Henri Poincaré (1854–1912)

Give me fruitful error any time, full of seeds, bursting with its own corrections.
Vilfredo Pareto (1848–1923)

Children seem to form the simplest and most general rule they can from the language input they receive, and to be so "pleased" with their "theory" that they use the rule wherever they can.

Inflectional Errors This "overgeneralization" of constructed rules is clearly revealed when children treat irregular verbs and nouns as if they were regular. We have probably all heard children say *bringed, goed, doed, singed,* or *foots, mouses, sheeps, childs.*

These mistakes tell us more about how children learn language than the "correct" forms they use. The child could not be imitating; children use such forms in families where the parents would never utter such "bad English." In fact, children may say *brought* or *broke* before they begin to use the incorrect forms. At the earlier stage they never use any regular past-tense forms like *kissed, walked,* or *helped.* They probably do not know that *brought* is a "past" at all. When they begin to say *played* and *hugged* and *helped* as well as *play, hug,* and *help,* they have "figured out" how to form a past tense—they have constructed the rule. At that point they form all past tenses by this rule—they overgeneralize—and they no longer say *brought* but *bring* and *bringed.* The acquisition of the rule overrides previously learned words and is unaffected by "practice" reinforcement. At a later time, children will learn that there are "exceptions" to the rule, and only then will they once more say *brought.* Children look for general patterns, for systematic occurrences.

Semantic Overgeneralizations Such overgeneralizations have also been observed in children's acquisition of the semantic system. They may learn a word such as *papa* or *daddy*, which they first use only for their own father. This word may then be extended to apply to all men. As they acquire new words, the "overgeneralized" meaning becomes narrowed down until once more it has its usual referent. The linguist Eve Clark has found this process to be true of many other words and semantic features. She has observed that children make overgeneralizations which are based on shape, size, sound, taste, and texture. One child's word for "moon" /mo:i/ became the name for cakes, round marks on windows, writing on a window, round shapes in books, tooling on leather book covers, round postmarks, and the letter O. Similarly, the word for "watch," *tick tock*, was used for all objects shaped like a watch: clocks, gas meters, a fire hose wound on a spool, and a bath scale. The word for "fly" /flai/ was used for other small-sized objects, like specks of dirt, dust, all small insects, the child's own toes, and crumbs; and /dani/ was first used for the sound of a bell, and then for a clock, a telephone, and a doorbell. As more words were added and semantic features became more specified, the meaning of these words became narrowed.

Phonological and Morphological Rule Acquisition The child's ability to generalize patterns and construct rules is also shown in phonological development. In early language, children may not distinguish between voiced and voiceless consonants, for example. When they first begin to contrast one set—that is, when they learn that /p/ and /b/ are distinct phonemes—they also begin to distinguish between /t/ and /d/, /s/ and /z/, and so on. The generalizations refer, as we would expect, to natural classes of speech sounds.

The child's phonological and morphological rules emerge quite early. In 1958, Berko-Gleason[8] conducted a study that has now become a classic in our understanding of child language acquisition. She worked with preschool children and with children in the first, second, and third grades. She showed each child a drawing of a nonsense animal like the funny creature below and gave the "animal" a nonsense name. She would then say to the child, pointing to the picture, "This is a wug."

Then she would show the child a picture of two of the animals and say, "Now here is another one. There are two of them. There are two ____?"

The child's "task" was to give the plural form, "wugs" [wʌgz]. Another little make-believe animal was called a "bik," and when the child was shown two biks, he or she again was to say the plural form [bɪks]. Berko-Gleason found that the

[8]J. Berko. 1958. "The Child's Learning of English Morphology." *Word* 14: 150–177.

children applied the regular plural-formation rule to words never heard before. Because the children had never seen a "wug" or a "bik" and had not heard these "words," their ability to add a [z] when the animal's name ended with a voiced sound and an [s] when there was a final voiceless consonant showed that the children were using rules based on an understanding of natural classes of phonological segments, and not simply imitating words they had previously heard.

Such regular stages and patterns support the notion that language acquisition is grammar construction.

The Acquisition of Syntax

Children eventually acquire all the phonological, syntactic, and semantic rules of the grammar. This task is most difficult, and, in fact, seems to be an impossible one; yet not only is the child more successful than the most brilliant linguist, but the grammars of children, at each stage of their acquisition, are highly similar, and deviate from the adult grammar in highly specific constrained ways.

To account for the ability of children to construct the complex syntactic rules of their grammar, it has been suggested that the child's "grammar" is semantically based. This view holds that the child's early language does not make reference to syntactic categories and relations (Noun, Noun Phrase, Verb, Verb Phrase, subject, object, and so on) but rather solely to semantic roles (like agent or theme). Nina Hyams,[9] however, studying the language of Italian-speaking children of about two years old, shows clearly that their utterances can only be explained by reference to syntactic categories and relations.

This point is easier to see in Italian where there is subject–verb agreement than in English. The Italian verb is inflected for person and number to agree with the subject, as shown in the following utterances produced by an Italian child:

(1) Tu legg*i* il libro   "you read (2nd person singular) the book"
(2) Io vad*o* fuori   "I go (1st person singular) outside"
(3) Gir*a* il pallone   "Turns the balloon (3rd person singular)"
(4) Dorm*e* miao   "Sleeps (3rd person singular) the cat"

Subject–verb agreement cannot be semantically based, because the subject is an agent in utterances 1 and 2 but not in 3 and 4. Instead, agreement must be based on whatever noun phrase is the subject, a syntactic relationship.

Hyams upholds this position by reference to other kinds of agreement as well, providing further support for the view that each stage of a child's early grammar is qualitatively similar to the adult grammar in that it includes both a syntactic and a semantic component.

Thus, just as human adult languages are governed by universal characteristics, the child's grammar, while differing from the adult grammar in specific ways,

[9]N. Hyams. 1985. "Semantically-Based Child Grammars: Some Empirical Inadequacies." *Papers and Reports on Child Language* No. 23. Stanford University. Stanford, Calif.

also follows universal principles. This fact shows that language acquisition must be biologically based, which will be further discussed in the next section and also in Chapter 11.

The Biological Foundations of Language Acquisition

Just as birds have wings, man has language.
George Henry Lewes (1817–1878)

The ability of children to form complex rules and construct the grammars of the languages used around them in a relatively short time is indeed phenomenal. The similarity of the language acquisition stages across diverse peoples and languages supports the view that children seem to be equipped with special abilities to know what generalizations to look for and what to ignore, and how to discover the regularities of language. Children learn language the way they learn to walk. They are not taught to walk, but all normal children begin to do so at around the same age. ''Learning to walk'' or ''learning language'' is different than ''learning to read'' or ''learning to ride a bicycle.'' Many people never learn to read because they are not taught to do so, and there are large groups of people in many parts of the world that do not have any written language. However, they all have language.

The "Innateness Hypothesis"

Chomsky explains the ability to acquire language in the following way:

> It seems plain that language acquisition is based on the child's discovery of what from a formal point of view is a deep and abstract theory—a generative grammar of his language. . . . A consideration of the character of the grammar that is acquired, the degenerate quality and narrowly limited extent of the available data, the striking uniformity of the resulting grammars, and their independence of intelligence, motivation, and emotional state, over wide ranges of variation, leave little hope that much of the structure of the language can be learned by an organism initially uninformed as to its general character. . . . It may well be that the general features of language structure reflect, not so much the course of one's experience, but rather the general character of one's capacity to acquire knowledge.[10]

It is this human capacity to acquire language that has led to ''the innateness hypothesis'' of child language acquisition, which posits that not only is the human species genetically ''prewired'' to acquire language, but that the kind of language is also determined. The principles that determine the class of human languages that can be acquired unconsciously, without instruction, in the early years of life has

---

[10]Noam Chomsky. 1965. *Aspects of the Theory of Syntax*. M.I.T. Press. Cambridge, Mass.

been referred to as the Universal Grammar (or the UG). This Universal Grammar underlies the specific grammars of all languages. We are still far from understanding the nature of our genetic ''prewiring,'' or the specific details of the language-learning device or Universal Grammar with which the human animal appears to be born; but there seems to be little doubt that the human brain is specially equipped for language acquisition. Chapter 11 will consider some aspects of the organization of the brain that appear to underlie our language abilities.

Sign Languages: Evidence for the Biology of Language

People talking without speaking,
People hearing without listening
Paul Simon, "The Sounds of Silence"[11]

It is not the want of organs that [prevents animals from making] . . . known their thoughts . . . for it is evident that magpies and parrots are able to utter words just like ourselves, and yet they cannot speak as we do, that is, so as to give evidence that they think of what they say. On the other hand, men who, being born deaf and mute . . . are destitute of the organs which serve the others for talking, are in the habit of themselves inventing certain signs by which they make themselves understood.
René Descartes, *Discourse on Method*

Deaf children, who are unable to hear the sounds of spoken language, do not acquire spoken languages as hearing children do. However, deaf children of deaf parents who are exposed to sign language learn sign language in stages parallel to language acquisition by hearing children learning oral languages. These sign languages are human languages that do not utilize sounds to express meanings. Instead, hand and body gestures are the forms used to represent morphemes or words. Sign languages are fully developed languages, and those who know sign language are capable of creating and comprehending unlimited numbers of new sentences, just like speakers of spoken languages.

Current research on sign languages has been crucial in the attempt to understand the biological underpinnings of human language acquisition and use. Some discussion on sign languages is therefore essential.

About one in a thousand babies is born deaf, or with a severe hearing deficiency. One major effect is the difficulty the deaf have in learning a spoken language. It is nearly impossible for those unable to hear language to learn to speak naturally. Normal speech depends to a great extent on constant auditory feedback. Hence a deaf child will not learn to speak without extensive training in special schools or programs designed especially for the deaf.

Although deaf persons can be taught to speak a language intelligibly, they can never understand speech as well as a hearing person. Seventy-five percent of the words spoken cannot be read on the lips with any degree of accuracy. The ability of

---

[11]Paul Simon. "The Sounds of Silence." Copyright 1974, 1965. Used by permission.

many deaf individuals to comprehend spoken language is therefore remarkable; they combine lip reading with knowledge of the structure of the language and the semantic redundancies.

If, however, human language is universal in the sense that all members of the human species have the ability to learn a language, it is not surprising that nonspoken languages have developed as a substitute for spoken languages among nonhearing individuals. The more we learn about the human linguistic ability, the more it is clear that language acquisition and use are not dependent on the ability to produce and hear sounds, but on a much more abstract cognitive ability, biologically determined, which therefore accounts for the similarities between spoken and sign languages.

American Sign Language (ASL)   The major language used by the deaf in the United States is American Sign Language (or AMESLAN or ASL). ASL is an independent, fully developed language that historically is an outgrowth of the sign language used in France and brought to the United States in 1817 by the great educator Thomas Hopkins Gallaudet. Gallaudet was hired to establish a school for the deaf, and after studying the language and methods used in the Paris school founded by the Abbé de l'Épée in 1775, he returned to the United States with Laurent Clerc, a young deaf instructor, establishing the basis for ASL. Like all living languages, ASL continues to change; only 60 percent of the present ASL vocabulary is of French origin. Not only have new signs entered the language, but the forms of the signs have changed, in ways similar to the historical changes in the phonological structure of words in spoken language. For example, many signs that were originally formed at waist or chest level are now produced at a higher level near the neck or upper chest.

ASL has its own morphological, syntactic, and semantic systems. Its formal units, corresponding to the phonological elements of spoken language, were originally called **cheremes**[12] (to correspond to the term phoneme) and are now more often referred to as **primes.** The signs of the language that correspond to morphemes or words of spoken language can be specified by primes of three different sets: hand configuration, the motion of the hand(s) toward or away from the body, and the place of articulation or the locus of the sign's movement.

Figure 10–1 illustrates the hand configuration primes.

There are minimal pairs in sign languages just as there are in spoken languages. Figure 10–2[13] shows minimal contrasts involving hand configuration, place of articulation, and movement.

The sign meaning "arm" can be described as a flat hand, moving to touch the upper arm. Thus it has three prime features: flat hand, motion toward, upper arm.

Just as spoken language has sequences of sounds that are not permitted in the

---

[12]W. C. Stokoe, Jr., D. Casterline, and C. Croneberg. 1965. *A Dictionary of American Sign Language on Linguistic Principles.* Gallaudet College Press. Washington, D.C.

[13]Figures 10–1 and 10–2 are from E. S. Klima and U. Bellugi. 1979. *The Signs of Language.* Harvard University Press. Cambridge, Mass. Pp. 46 and 42.

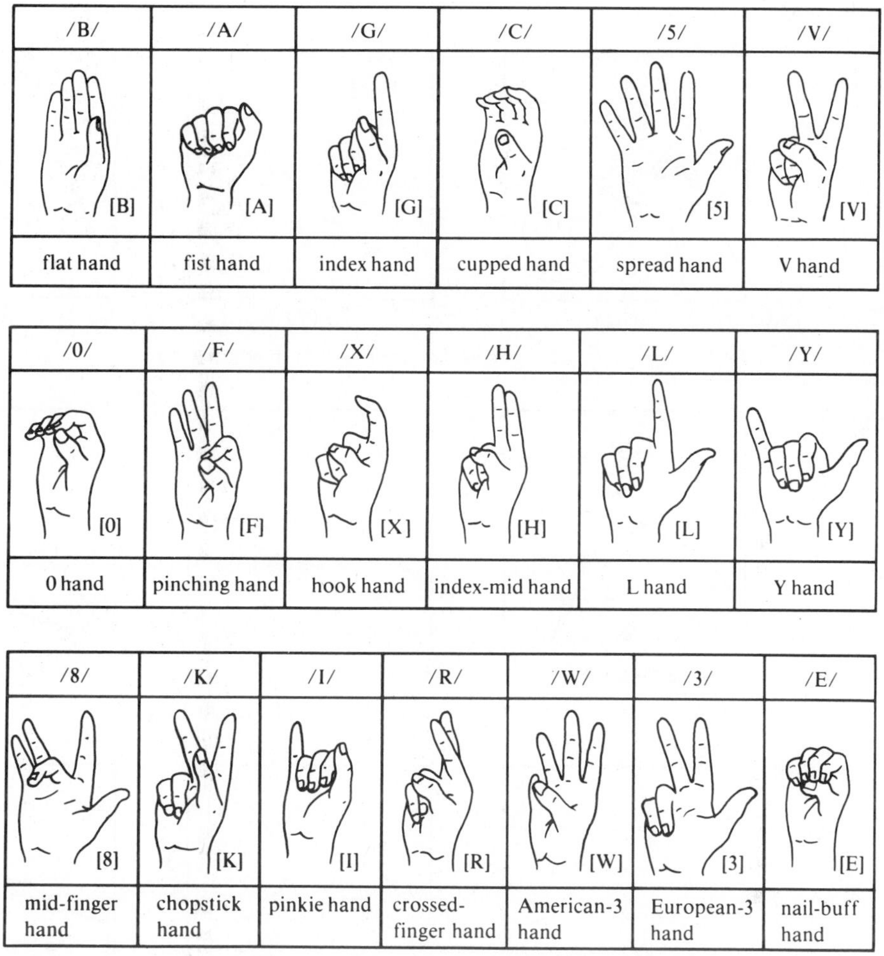

/B/	/A/	/G/	/C/	/5/	/V/
[B]	[A]	[G]	[C]	[5]	[V]
flat hand	fist hand	index hand	cupped hand	spread hand	V hand

/0/	/F/	/X/	/H/	/L/	/Y/
[0]	[F]	[X]	[H]	[L]	[Y]
0 hand	pinching hand	hook hand	index-mid hand	L hand	Y hand

/8/	/K/	/I/	/R/	/W/	/3/	/E/
[8]	[K]	[I]	[R]	[W]	[3]	[E]
mid-finger hand	chopstick hand	pinkie hand	crossed-finger hand	American-3 hand	European-3 hand	nail-buff hand

Copyright © 1979 by Harvard University Press. Reproduced by permission of Harvard University Press.

FIGURE 10–1 Hand configuration primes arranged in order of frequency (with descriptive phrases used to refer to them).

language, so sign languages have forbidden combinations of features. They differ from one sign language to another, just as the constraints on sounds and sound sequences differ from one spoken language to another. A permissible sign in a Chinese sign language may not be a permissible sign in ASL, and vice versa.

The linguistic study of ASL also reveals a complex system of morphological and syntactic rules that parallel those found in spoken languages.[14]

The other sign language used in the United States is called Signed English (or

---

[14]T. Supalla and E. Newport. 1978. "How Many Seats in a Chair? The Derivation of Nouns and Verbs in American Sign Language." In P. Siple, ed., *Understanding Language Through Sign Language Research*. Academic Press. New York. Pp. 91–132.

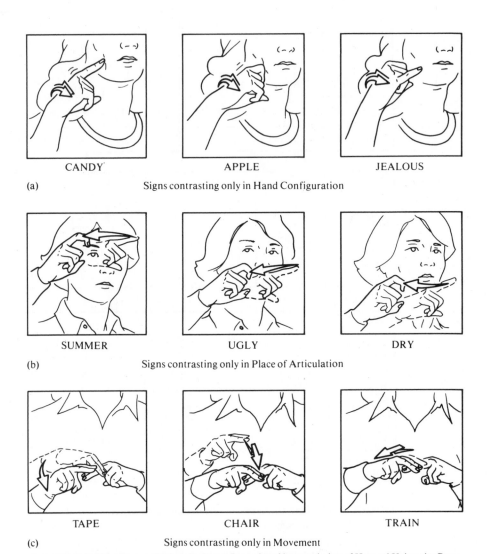

CANDY   APPLE   JEALOUS

(a)   Signs contrasting only in Hand Configuration

SUMMER   UGLY   DRY

(b)   Signs contrasting only in Place of Articulation

TAPE   CHAIR   TRAIN

(c)   Signs contrasting only in Movement

Copyright © 1979 by Harvard University Press. Reproduced by permission of Harvard University Press.

FIGURE 10–2 Minimal contrasts illustrating major formational parameters.

Siglish). Essentially, it consists in the replacement of each spoken English word (and morpheme) by a sign. The syntax and semantics of Signed English are thus approximately the same as those of ordinary English. It is thus a rather unnatural language similar to speaking French by translating every English word or morpheme into its French counterpart. Of course, there is not always a corresponding morpheme, and that would create problems just as it does in signing English.

If there is no sign in ASL, signers utilize another mechanism, the system of finger spelling. This method is also used to add new proper nouns or technical vocabulary. Sign interpreters of spoken English often finger spell such words. A manual alphabet consisting of various finger configurations, hand positions, and movements gives visible symbols for the alphabet and ampersand.

Signs, however, are produced differently than are finger-spelled words. "The sign DECIDE cannot be analyzed as a sequence of distinct, separable configurations of the hand. Like all other lexical signs in ASL, but unlike the individual finger-spelled letters in D-E-C-I-D-E taken separately, the ASL sign DECIDE does have an essential movement [but] [t]he handshape occurs simultaneously with the movement. In appearance, the sign is a continuous whole."[15] This sign is shown in Figure 10–3.

transition a.   sign b.   transition c.

FIGURE 10–3 The ASL sign DECIDE. (a) and (c) show transitions from the sign; (b) illustrates the single downward movement of the sign.

An accomplished signer can "speak" at a normal rate, even when there is a lot of finger spelling. Television stations sometimes have programs that are interpreted in sign for the deaf in a corner of the TV screen. If you have ever seen such a program, you were probably amazed at how well the interpreter kept pace with the spoken sentences.

Language arts are not lost to the deaf. Poetry is composed in sign language, and stage plays such as Sheridan's *The Critic* have been translated into sign language and acted by the National Theatre of the Deaf (NTD). Sign language was so highly thought of by the anthropologist Margaret Mead that, in an article discussing the possibilities of a universal second language, she suggests using some of the basic ideas that sign languages incorporate.

The Acquisition of ASL   Given the universal aspects of sign and spoken languages, it is not surprising that deaf children of deaf signing parents parallel the stages of spoken language acquisition. They start with single signs similar to the single words in the holophrastic stage and then begin to combine signs. There is also a telegraphic stage in which the "grammatical" signs are omitted. Grammatical or function signs appear at around the same age for deaf children as function words in spoken languages.

---

[15]Klima and Bellugi, pp. 38 and 62.

Bellugi and Klima[16] point out that deaf children's acquisition of the negative morphemes in American Sign Language (ASL) shows much the same pattern as in spoken language. NO and NEG (a headshake) are frequently used signs in adult ASL, with different restrictions on their use. The children acquiring ASL use them interchangeably in initial position of a signed sentence, like hearing children starting negative sentences with *no* but unlike the ways in which negative signs are used in adult ASL. We see that the acquisition of ASL cannot be simple imitation any more than spoken language is acquired simply by imitation.

Hearing children of deaf parents acquire both sign language and spoken language when exposed to both, although studies have shown that the child's first signs emerge a few months before the first spoken words. It is interesting that deaf children appear to begin producing signs earlier than hearing children produce spoken words. It has been suggested that this timing may be because control of hand muscles develops earlier than the control of oral and laryngeal muscles.

Deaf children of hearing parents who are not exposed to manual sign language from birth suffer from a great handicap in acquiring language; yet language learning ability seems so strong in humans that even they begin to develop their own manual gestures to express their thoughts and desires. A study of six such children revealed that they not only developed individual signs but joined pairs and formed sentences (up to thirteen "words") with definite syntactic order and systematic constraints.

This fact, of course, should not be surprising; sign languages are as grammatical and systematic as are spoken languages. We saw in Chapter 1 that the signs are conventional or arbitrary and not imitative. Furthermore, because all languages change in time, just as there are many different spoken languages, there are many different sign languages, all of which (spoken and sign) reveal the same linguistic universals. Deaf children often sign themselves to sleep just as hearing children talk themselves to sleep; deaf children report that they dream in sign language as French-speaking children dream in French and Hopi children dream in Hopi. Deaf children sign to their dolls and stuffed animals; slips of the hand occur similar to slips of the tongue; finger fumblers amuse signers as tongue twisters amuse speakers. We see that sign languages resemble spoken languages in all major aspects, showing that there truly are universals of language despite differences in the modality in which the language is performed. This universality is predictable because it is language, not speech, that is biologically based.

Learning a Second (or Third or . . .) Language

He that understands grammar in one language, understands it in another as far as the essential properties of Grammar are concerned. The fact that he can't speak, nor comprehend, another language is due to the diversity of words and their various forms, but these are the accidental properties of grammar.

Roger Bacon (1214–1294)

[16]U. Bellugi and E. S. Klima. 1976. "The Roots of Language in the Sign Talk of the Deaf." *Psychology Today* 6:60–64.

DENNIS THE MENACE Hank Ketcham

"Gina is by lingal . . . that means she can say the same thing twice, but you can only understand it once."

DENNIS THE MENACE® used by permission of Hank Ketcham and © by North America Syndicate.

Anyone who has attempted to learn a second language in school or when visiting a foreign country knows that it is different from learning our first, native language. Even "talented language learners" require some instruction, or at least find a dictionary and "grammar" useful. Some of us are total failures at second language learning. We may be extremely fluent in our native language, we may get all As in composition and write beautiful poetry, but still find we are unable to learn another language.

The younger you are, the easier it seems to be to learn a language. Language is unique in that no other complex system of knowledge is more easily acquired at the age of two or three than at the age of thirteen or twenty.

Young children who are exposed to more than one language before the age of puberty seem to acquire all the languages equally well. Many bilingual and multilingual speakers acquired their languages early in life. Sometimes one language is the first learned, but if the child is exposed to additional languages at an early age they will also be learned.

It has been suggested that there is a "critical age" for language acquisition, or at least for language acquisition without special teaching and without the need for special learning. We will review some neurological views of this special period in Chapter 11.

Learning a second language (often referred to in the literature as L2) differs qualitatively from learning a first language (L1). To see why, various factors—psychological, physical, and sociological—must be considered in addition to the linguistic structure of L2 and how it differs from the native language. Individuals who are self-conscious about making mistakes often find learning L2 difficult, which is not a problem for children, who are unconcerned or unaware that they are making mistakes.

On the other hand, due to the universal characteristics of human language, adults who know one language already "know" much about the underlying structure of every language. This fact is shown by the stages in second language acquisition, which are similar to those in first language acquisition. For example, Carol Chomsky[17] found that in the earliest years, children learning English natively interpret sentences like *John is easy to see* as *It is easy for John to see*. French speakers learning English seem to go through a similar stage; yet this difficulty cannot be due to any "interference" from French grammar, because in this sense, French is similar to English. The acquisition of grammatical morphemes (both bound and free) in learning English as a second language proceeds in similar order as in children's acquisition, no matter what the system is in the native language of the learner.

However, *interference* from native phonology, morphology, and syntax can create difficulties that persist as a foreign "accent" in phonology and in the use of nonnative syntactic structures.

Second Language Teaching Methods

Many approaches to foreign language instruction have developed over the years. In one method, **grammar-translation,** the student memorizes words, inflected words, and syntactic rules and uses them to translate from English to L2 and vice versa. The **direct method** abandons memorization and translation; the native language is never used in the classroom, and the structure of the L2 language or how it differs from the native language is not discussed. The direct method attempts to simulate learning a language as if the students found themselves in a foreign country without anyone except natives to speak to. In other words, the direct method assumes that adults can learn a foreign language in the way they learned their native language as children. Practically, it is difficult to duplicate the social, psychological, or physical environment of the child, or even the number of hours that the learner is exposed to the language to be learned, even if there is no "critical age" factor.

An **audio-lingual** language teaching method is based on the assumption that language is acquired mainly through imitation, repetition, and reinforcement. Be-

[17]C. Chomsky. 1969. *The Acquisition of Syntax in Children from Five to Ten*. M.I.T. Press. Cambridge, Mass.

cause language use is creative and is not a form of habitual behavior, it is unfortunate that this method is still quite widely used.

Most specific methods have serious limitations; and probably a combination of many methods is required, as well as motivation on the part of the student, intensive and extensive exposure, native or near-native speaking teachers who can serve as models, and instruction and instructional material that is based on linguistic analysis of all aspects of the language.

Acquiring Versus Learning?

Stephen Krashen has proposed a distinction between acquisition—the process by which children unconsciously acquire their native language—and learning, which he defines as "conscious knowledge of a second language, knowing the rules, being aware of them, and being able to talk about them."[18]

It is clear that children *acquire* their first language without explicit learning. A second language is usually *learned* but to some degree may also be acquired or "picked up," depending on the environmental setting and the input received by the second language learner.

Can Chimps Learn Human Language?

. . . It is a great baboon, but so much like man in most things. . . . I do believe it already understands much English; and I am of the mind it might be taught to speak or make signs.
Entry in Samuel Pepys' *Diary*, August 1661

In this chapter, the discussion has centered on the biologically determined *human* language acquisition ability. Recently, much effort has been expended to determine whether nonhuman primates (chimpanzees, monkeys, gorillas, and so on) can learn human language. In their natural habitat, primates communicate with each other in systems that include visual, auditory, olfactory, and tactile signals. Many of these signals seem to have meaning associated with the animals' immediate environment or emotional state. They can signal "danger" and can communicate aggressiveness and subordination. Females of some species emit a specific call indicating that they are anestrous (sexually quiescent), which inhibits attempts by males to copulate. However, the natural sounds and gestures produced by all nonhuman primates show their signals to be highly stereotyped and limited in the type and number of messages they convey. Their basic "vocabularies" occur primarily as emotional responses to particular situations. They have no way of expressing the anger they felt yesterday or the anticipation of tomorrow.

Despite these characteristics of nonhuman primate *natural* systems of communication, there has been an interest in whether these animals may have a capacity

---

[18]Stephen D. Krashen. 1982. *Principles and Practice in Second Language Acquisition*. Pergamon Press. Oxford, England.

for acquiring more complex linguistic systems that are similar to human language.

In the 1930s, Winthrop and Luella Kellogg raised their infant son with an infant chimpanzee named Gua to determine whether a chimpanzee raised in a human environment and given language instruction could learn a human language. Gua understood about 100 words at sixteen months, more words than their son at that age; but she never went beyond that. Moreover, comprehension of language involves more than understanding the meanings of isolated words. When their son could understand the difference between *I say what I mean* and *I mean what I say,* Gua could not understand either sentence.

A chimpanzee named Viki was raised by Keith and Cathy Hayes, and she too learned a number of individual words, even learning to "articulate" with great difficulty the words *mama, papa, cup,* and *up.* That was the extent of her language production.

Psychologists Allen and Beatrice Gardner recognized that one disadvantage suffered by the primates was their physical inability to pronounce many different sounds. Without a sufficient number of phonemic contrasts, spoken human language is impossible. Many species of primates are manually dextrous, and this fact inspired the Gardners to attempt to teach American Sign Language to a chimpanzee whom they named Washoe, after the Nevada county in which they lived. Washoe was brought up in much the same way as a human child in a deaf community, constantly in the presence of people who used ASL. She was deliberately taught to sign, whereas children raised by deaf signers acquire sign language without explicit teaching, as hearing children learn spoken language.

By the time Washoe was four years old (June 1969), she had acquired 85 signs with such meanings as "more," "eat," "listen," "gimme," "key," "dog," "you," "me," "Washoe," and "hurry." According to the Gardners, Washoe was also able to produce sign combinations such as "baby mine," "you drink," "hug hurry," "gimme flower," and "more fruit."

At about the same time that Washoe was growing up, psychologist David Premack attempted to teach a chimpanzee named Sarah an artificial language designed to resemble human languages in some aspects. The "words" of Sarah's "language" were differently shaped and colored plastic chips that were metal-backed. Sarah and her trainers "talked" to each other by arranging these symbols on a magnetic board. Sarah was taught to associate particular symbols with particular meanings. The form–meaning relationship of these "morphemes" or "words" was arbitrary; a small red square meant "banana" and a small blue rectangle meant "apricot," while the color red was represented by a gray chip and the color yellow by a black chip. Sarah learned a number of "nouns," "adjectives," and "verbs," symbols for abstract concepts like "same as" and "different from," "negation," and "question."

There were drawbacks to the Sarah experiment. She was not allowed to "talk" spontaneously, but only in response to her trainers. There was the possibility that her trainers unwittingly provided cues, which Sarah responded to rather than the plastic chips.

To avoid these and other problems, Duane and Sue Rumbaugh and their associates at the Yerkes Regional Primate Research Center began in 1973 to teach a different kind of artificial language, called Yerkish, to three chimpanzees, Lana, Sherman, and Austin. Instead of plastic chips, the words, called lexigrams, were geometric symbols displayed on a computer keyboard. The computer recorded every button that was pressed; certain fixed orders of these lexigrams constitute grammatical sentences in Yerkish. The researchers, however, are particularly interested in the ability of primates to communicate using functional symbols.

Another experiment aimed at teaching sign language to primates involved a gorilla named Koko, who was taught by her trainer, Francine "Penny" Patterson. Patterson claims that Koko learned several hundred signs, is able to put signs together to make "sentences," and is capable of making linguistic jokes and puns, composing rhymes such as BEAR HAIR (which is a rhyme in spoken language but not ASL), and inventing metaphors such as FINGER BRACELET for ring.

In a project specifically designed to test the linguistic claims that emerged from these primate experiments, another chimpanzee, named Nim Chimpsky, who was taught ASL by an experienced teacher, was studied by the psychologist H. S. Terrace and his associates.[19] Under carefully controlled experimental conditions that included thorough record keeping and many hours of videotaping, Nim's teachers hoped to show beyond a reasonable doubt that chimpanzees had a humanlike linguistic capacity, in contradiction to the view put forth by Noam Chomsky (after whom Nim was ironically named) that human language is species-specific. In the nearly four years of study, Nim learned about 125 signs, and during the last two years Nim's teachers recorded more than 20,000 "utterances" including two or more signs. Nim produced his first ASL sign (DRINK) after just four months, which greatly encouraged the research team at the start of the study. Their enthusiasm soon diminished when he never seemed to go much beyond the two-word stage. Terrace concluded that "his three-sign combinations do not . . . provide new information. . . . Nim's most frequent two- and three-sign combinations [were] PLAY ME and PLAY ME NIM. Adding NIM to PLAY ME is simply redundant" writes Terrace. This kind of redundancy is illustrated by a sixteen-sign utterance of Nim's: GIVE ORANGE ME GIVE EAT ORANGE ME EAT ORANGE GIVE ME EAT ORANGE GIVE ME YOU. This utterance does not sound much like the early sentences of children cited above.

Nim rarely signed spontaneously as do children when they begin to use language (talk or sign). Only 12 percent of his utterances were spontaneous. Most of Nim's signing occurred only in response to prompting by his trainers and was related to eating, drinking, and playing; that is, it was "stimulus-controlled." As much as 40 percent of his output was simply repetitions of signs made by the trainer. Children initiate conversations more and more frequently as they grow older, and their utterances repeat less and less of the adult's prior utterance. Some children hardly ever imitate in conversation. Children become increasingly more

---

[19]Collaborating with Terrace were Laura Pettito, Richard Sanders, and Thomas Bever. The results of Project Nim are reported in H. S. Terrace, 1979. *Nim: A Chimpanzee Who Learned Sign Language.* Knopf. New York.

creative in their language use, but Nim showed almost no tendency toward such creativity. Furthermore, children's utterances increase in length and complexity as time progresses, finally mirroring the adult grammar, whereas Nim's "language" did not.

The lack of spontaneity and the excessive "noncreative" imitative nature of Nim's signing led to the conclusion that Nim's acquisition and use of language is qualitatively different from a child's. After examining the films of Washoe, Koko, and others, Terrace drew similar conclusions regarding the signing of the other primates.

Signing chimpanzees are also unlike humans in that when several of them are together they do not sign to each other as freely as humans would under similar circumstances. There is also no evidence to date that a signing chimp (or one communicating with plastic chips or computer symbols) will teach another chimp language, or that its offspring will acquire language from their parents.

Premack and the Rumbaughs, like Terrace, suggest that the sign language studies are too uncontrolled and that the reported results were thus too anecdotal to support the view that primates are capable of acquiring a human language. They also question whether each of the others' studies, and all those attempting to teach sign language to primates, suffer from what has come to be called the Clever Hans phenomenon.

Clever Hans, a horse owned by von Osten at the turn of the century, became famous because of his apparent ability to do arithmetic, read and spell, and even solve problems of musical harmony. He answered the questions posed by his interrogators by stamping out numbers with his hoof. It turned out, not surprisingly, that Hans did not know that $2 + 2 = 4$, but he was clever enough to pick up subtle cues conveyed unconsciously by his trainer as to when he should stop tapping his foot.

Sarah, like Clever Hans, took prompts from her trainers and her environment to produce the plastic chip sentences. In responding to the string of chips standing for

SARAH INSERT APPLE PAIL BANANA DISH

all Sarah had to figure out was to place certain fruits in certain containers, and she could decide which by merely seeing that the apple symbol was next to the pail symbol, and the banana symbol was next to the dish symbol. There is no conclusive evidence that Sarah actually grouped strings of words into constituents. There is also no indication that Sarah would understand a *new* compound sentence of this type; the creative ability so much a part of human language is not demonstrated by this act.

Problems also exist in Lana's "acquisition" of Yerkish. The LANA project was studied by Thompson and Church,[20] who were able to simulate Lana's behavior by a computer model. They concluded that the chimp's "linguistic" behavior can

[20]Claudia R. Thompson and Russell M. Church. 1980. "An Explanation of the Language of a Chimpanzee." *Science* 208:313–314.

all be accounted for by her learning to associate or pair lexigrams with objects, persons, or events, and to produce one of several ''stock sentences'' depending on situational cues (like Clever Hans).

There is another difference between the way Sarah and Lana learned whatever they learned and the way children learn language. In the case of the chimpanzees, each new ''rule'' or sentence form was introduced in a deliberate, highly constrained way. As we noted earlier, when parents speak to children they do not confine themselves to a few words in a particular order for months, rewarding the child with a chocolate bar or a banana each time the child correctly responds to a command. Nor do they wait until the child has mastered one rule of grammar before going on to a different structure. Young children require no special training.

As often happens in science, the search for the answers to one kind of question leads to answers to other questions not originally asked. The linguistic experiments with primates have led to many advances in our understanding of primate cognitive ability. Premack has gone on to investigate other capacities of the chimp mind, such as causality; the Rumbaughs are continuing to study the ability of chimpanzees to use symbols. These studies also point out how remarkable it is that human children, by the age of three or four, without explicit teaching, without overt reinforcement, create new and complex sentences never spoken and never heard before.

Summary

When children learn a language, they learn the grammar of that language—the phonological, morphological, syntactic, and semantic rules—as well as the words or vocabulary. No one teaches them these rules; children just ''pick them up.''

Before infants begin to produce ''words,'' they produce sounds, some of which will remain if they occur in the language being acquired, and others that will disappear. This babbling stage is thus a prelinguistic period.

A child does not learn the language ''all at once.'' The grammar is acquired by stages. Children's first utterances are one-word ''sentences'' (the **holophrastic stage**). After a few months, the two-word stage arises, in which the child puts two words together. These two-word sentences are not random combinations of words; the words have definite patterns and express both grammatical and semantic relationships. Later, but still in the very early years, in what has been called the **telegraphic stage,** longer sentences appear, composed primarily of content words and lacking function or grammatical morphemes. The child's early grammar lacks many of the rules of the adult grammar but is not qualitatively different, and eventually it mirrors the language used in the community.

A number of theories have been suggested to explain the acquisition process. Neither the imitation theory, which claims that children learn their language by imitating adult speech, nor the reinforcement theory, which hypothesizes that children are conditioned into speaking correctly by being negatively reinforced for "errors" and positively reinforced for "correct" usage, is supported by observational and experimental studies. Neither can explain how children form the rules that they then use to produce new sentences.

Deaf children exposed to **sign language** show the same stages of language acquisition as do hearing children exposed to spoken languages. Sign languages, including the major language of the deaf in the United States, called **American Sign Language** (or **AMESLAN** or **ASL**), are fully developed, complete languages with grammars comparable to those of spoken languages. The signs, representing the morphemes and words, are constructed from a finite set of primes—hand configurations, movements of the hands, and places of articulation—that permit the generation of an infinite set of sentences. The grammars of sign languages include, in addition to their lexicons, rules of sign formation, morphology, semantics, and syntax.

The acquisition of a second or third language parallels the acquisition of a first native language. If a second language is learned early in life, it is usually acquired with no difficulty. The difficulties encountered in attempting to learn languages after puberty have given rise to a **critical age hypothesis** that refers to a biological period in which language can be acquired without overt teaching. A number of second-language teaching methods have been proposed, reflecting different theories of the nature of language and language acquisition. These methods, however, do not explain the apparent differences between first and second language acquisition.

Questions as to whether language is unique to the human species have led researchers to attempt to teach nonhuman primates systems of communication that purportedly resemble human language. Chimpanzees like Sarah and Lana have been taught to manipulate symbols to gain rewards, and other chimpanzees like Washoe and Nim Chimpsky have been taught a number of ASL signs. A careful examination of the "utterances" in ASL by these chimps shows that unlike children, their language exhibits little spontaneity, is highly imitative (echoic), and reveals little syntactic structure.

The universality of the human language-acquisition process, of the stages of development, and of the relatively short period in which the child constructs such a complex grammatical system without overt teaching, and the limited results of the chimpanzee experiments, suggest that the human species is "innately" endowed with special language-acquisition abilities, that language is biologically and genetically part of the human neurological system. Biology may also account for the differences in learning a first language as a child and a "foreign" language as a teenager or an adult.

All normal children everywhere learn language. This ability is not dependent on race, social class, geography, or even intelligence (within a normal range). This ability is uniquely human.

References

Bloom, L. M. 1972. *Language Development: Form and Function in Emerging Grammar.* M.I.T. Press. Cambridge, Mass.

Bowerman, M. 1973. *Early Syntactic Development*. M.I.T. Press. Cambridge, Mass.

Brown, R. O. 1973. *A First Language: The Early Stages*. Harvard University Press. Cambridge, Mass.

Clark, H. H., and E. V. Clark. 1977. *Psychology and Language*. Harcourt Brace Jovanovich. New York.

de Villiers, Peter A., and Jill G. de Villiers. 1978. *Language Acquisition*. Harvard University Press. Cambridge, Mass.

Ellis, R. 1985. *Understanding Second Language Acquisition*. Oxford University Press. Oxford, England.

Feldman, H., S. Goldin-Meadow, and L. Gleitman. 1978. ''Beyond Herodotus: The Creation of Language by Linguistically Deprived Deaf Children.'' In *Action, Symbol, and Gesture: The Emergence of Language*. A. Lock, ed. Academic Press. New York. Pp. 351–413.

Gleitman, H., and L. R. Gleitman. 1981. *Psychology*. W. W. Norton. New York. Ch. 10.

Hyams, Nina. 1986. *Language Acquisition and the Theory of Parameters*. Reidel Publishers. Dordrecht, The Netherlands.

Klima, E., and U. Bellugi. 1979. *The Signs of Language*. Harvard University Press. Cambridge, Mass.

Krashen, Stephen D. 1982. *Principles and Practice in Second Language Acquisition*. Pergamon Press. Oxford, England.

Premack, Ann J., and D. Premack. 1972. ''Teaching Language to an Ape.'' *Scientific American* (October), 92–99.

Rumbaugh, D. M. 1977. *Acquisition of Linguistic Skills by a Chimpanzee*. Academic Press. New York.

Sebeok, T. A., and Jean Umiker-Sebeok. 1980. *Speaking of Apes: A Critical Anthology of Two-Way Communication with Man*. Plenum Press. New York.

Sebeok, Thomas A., and Robert Rosenthal, eds. 1981. ''The Clever Hans Phenomenon: Communication with Horses, Whales, Apes, and People.'' *Annals of the New York Academy of Sciences* 364.

Terrace, Herbert S. 1979. *Nim: A Chimpanzee Who Learned Sign Language*. Knopf. New York.

Exercises

1. "Baby talk" is a term used to label the word-forms that many adults use when speaking to children. Examples in English are *choo-choo* for "train" and *bow-wow* for "dog." Baby talk seems to exist in every language and culture. At least two things seem to be universal about baby talk: the words that have baby-talk forms fall into certain semantic categories (for example, food and animals) and the words are "phonetically simpler" than the adult forms (for example, *tummy* /tʌmi/ for "stomach" /stʌmək/). List all the baby-talk words you can think of in your native language; then (1) separate them into semantic categories, and (2) try to state general rules for the kinds of phonological "reductions" or "simplifications" that occur.

2. In this chapter the way a child learns "negation" of sentences and "question formation" was discussed. Can they be considered examples of a process of overgeneralization in syntax acquisition? If so, for each stage indicate *what* is being overgeneralized.

3. Find a child between two and four years old and play with the child for about thirty minutes. Keep a list of all words and/or "sentences" that are used inappropriately. Describe what the child's meanings for these words probably are. Describe the syntactic or morphological errors (including omissions). If the child is producing multi-word sentences, write a grammar that could account for the data you have collected.

4. Chomsky has been quoted as saying:

   > It's about as likely that an ape will prove to have a language ability as that there is an island somewhere with a species of flightless birds waiting for human beings to teach them to fly.

   In the light of evidence presented in this chapter, comment on Chomsky's remark. Do you agree or disagree, or do you think the evidence is inconclusive?

Brain, Mind, and Language

The nervous systems of all animals have a number of basic func-
tions in common, most notably the control of movement and the
analysis of sensation. What distinguishes the human brain is the
variety of more specialized activities it is capable of learning. The
preeminent example is language. . . .

Norman Geschwind, 1979

Even if we completely understood the language-acquisition process and the production and perception of speech, it would not tell us how the human animal is able to
accomplish these feats. Why are we the only species that learns and uses language
without being taught? What aspects of the human neurological makeup explain this
ability? How did these brain mechanisms develop?

The attempts to understand the complexities of human cognitive abilities are
as old and as continuous as the attempts to understand language. The view that the
brain is the source of human language and cognition goes back over 2000 years. The
Assyrian and Babylonian cuneiform tablets mention disorders of intelligence that
may develop "when man's brain holds fire." Egyptian doctors noted on their papy-
rus records that "the breath of an outside god" had entered their patients who
became "silent in sadness." In one of the Hippocratic treatises dealing with epilepsy, the brain is referred to as "the messenger to the understanding" and the
organ by which "in an especial manner we acquire wisdom and knowledge."

Because of the recognition of the relationship between brain and cognition,
one way of investigating mental abilities and processes has been through an investigation of language. Research on the brain in humans and nonhuman primates,
anatomically, psychologically, and behaviorally, is, for similar reasons, helping to
answer the questions posed above. The study concerned with the biological foundations of language and the brain mechanisms underlying its acquisition and use is
called **neurolinguistics.**

Although neurolinguistics is still in its infancy, our understanding has progressed a great deal since the day in September 1848 when a foreman of a road construction gang named Phineas Gage became a famous figure in medical history. He achieved his "immortality" when a four-foot-long iron rod was blown through his head. Despite the gaping tunnel in his brain, Gage maintained the ability to speak and understand and retained whatever intellectual abilities he had prior to the injury, although he suffered major changes in his personality (he became "cranky" and "inconsiderate"), in his sexual behavior, and in his ability to control his emotions or make plans. Both Gage and science benefited from this explosion. Phineas gained monetarily by becoming a one-man touring circus; he traveled all over the country charging money to those curious enough to see him and the iron rod. Nevertheless, he died penniless in an institution twelve years after the accident. Science benefited because brain researchers were stimulated to learn why his intelligence remained intact.

Since that time we have learned a great deal about the brain—the most complicated organ of the body. It lies under the skull and consists of approximately 10 billion nerve cells (**neurons**) and billions of fibers that interconnect these cells according to specific and highly selective patterns. (Not every neuron connects to every other neuron but only to a few other neurons.) The neurons or gray matter form the surface of the brain, which is called the **cortex.** Under the cortex is the white matter, which consists primarily of the connecting fibers, as well as a variety of subcortical gray matter centers, such as the basal ganglia and the thalamus, which can be viewed as computational units. The **cerebral cortex** is the decision-making organ of the body. It receives messages from all the sensory organs, and it initiates all voluntary actions. It is "the seat of all which is exclusively human in the mind." It is the storehouse of "memory" as well. Somewhere in this gray matter the grammar that represents our knowledge of language resides.

The brain or **cerebrum** is divided into two parts (called **cerebral hemispheres**), one on the right and one on the left. These hemispheres are connected like Siamese twins right down the middle by the **corpus callosum,** consisting of about two million nerve fibers interconnecting selected cortical regions across the midline, permitting the "two brains" to communicate with each other.

In general, the left hemisphere controls voluntary movements of the right hand and foot and the right hemisphere the movements of the left side. If you point with your right hand, it is the left hemisphere that has "directed" your action.

The **cerebellum,** also divided into two hemispheres, is located underneath the cerebral hemispheres. It is also involved in motor function—motor learning, guidance of fine movements, and control of balance. At the bottom of the brain is the **brain stem,** which connects the brain to the spinal cord. It contains a variety of lower-order controls for visceral functions (cardiac, respiratory, and so on) as well as the cranial nerve nuclei associated with the movements for phonation in speech.

The Two Sides of the Brain

It only takes one hemisphere to have a mind.
A. W. Wigan, 1844

THE FAR SIDE   **Gary Larson**

Brain aerobics

Since the middle of the nineteenth century, there has been a basic assumption that it is possible to find a direct relation between language and the brain, and a continuous effort to discover direct centers where language capacities (competence and performance) may be localized.

In the early part of the nineteenth century F. Gall and G. Spurzheim put forth theories of **localization,** holding that different human abilities and behaviors are traceable to specific parts of the brain. The bases for some of their theories are amusing when looked at from our present state of knowledge. Gall, for example, suggested that the frontal lobes of the brain were the locations of language because when he was young he had noticed that the most articulate and intelligent of his fellow students had protruding eyes, which he believed reflected overdeveloped brain material. This notion actually served as a stimulus to the scientists interested in brain function in the mid-nineteenth century, and it gave birth to ''phrenology,'' a ''theory'' put forth by Spurzheim. He based his theory on the idea that personality traits and intellectual abilities could be determined by an examination of the ''bumps'' on the skull.

Although phrenology—except for a few remaining adherents—has long been discarded as a scientific theory, Gall's view that the brain is not a uniform mass and that some linguistic capacities are functions of localized brain areas has been upheld.

It was not until 1861 that language was specifically related to the left side of the brain. At a scientific meeting in Paris, Paul Broca[1] stated that we speak with the left hemisphere in his report that damage to the anterior part of the left hemisphere resulted in loss of speech, whereas damage to the right side did not. Language, then, is said to be **lateralized. Lateralization** is the term used to refer to any cognitive functions that are primarily localized to one side of the brain or the other.

Today, patients with such damage or lesions are said to have **Broca's aphasia. Aphasia** is the neurological term used to refer to any acquired (as opposed to developmental) language disorder that follows a focal (localized) brain lesion caused by a stroke, a tumor, a gunshot wound, or an infection.

The speech output of Broca's aphasia patients is minimal at the outset of the condition, and they may even be mute for hours or days. Gradually some effortful speech emerges, characterized by word-finding pauses, loss of ''function'' words (grammatical morphemes), and, quite often, disturbed word order. Auditory comprehension for colloquial conversation gives the impression of being generally good, although controlled testing reveals considerable impairments. The term **agrammatism,** used in linguistic studies of aphasia, is almost synonymous with Broca's aphasia, although some Broca's patients are not agrammatic and some agrammatics would hardly classify as Broca's.

In 1873, Carl Wernicke presented a paper that described another variety of aphasia. Unlike Broca's patients, Wernicke's spoke fluently with good intonation and pronunciation, but with numerous instances of lexical errors (word substitutions) and often with phonological errors. They also had difficulty in comprehending speech. Wernicke's patients had lesions in the posterior or back portion of the left temporal lobe. The area of the brain that when damaged seems to lead to these symptoms is now, not surprisingly, known as **Wernicke's area,** and the patients are said to suffer from **Wernicke's aphasia.** For similar reasons we refer to **Broca's area** and **Broca's aphasia.**

In the 1930s the surgeon Wilder Penfield and his colleagues at the Montreal Neurological Institute had the opportunity to stimulate different parts of the cortex of patients who were undergoing brain surgery for the treatment of epileptic seizures. This research was yet another way in which parts of the human cortex were ''mapped,'' revealing areas responsible for motor activities of different parts of the body, sensations of touch, visual perception, and so on. Figure 11–1 shows some of these areas of the left side of the brain.

There is now a consensus that the so-called higher functions are greatly lateralized. Research, some of which will be discussed below, shows that though the nervous system is generally symmetrical—what exists on the left exists on the right and vice versa—the two sides of the brain form an exception. During development, the two sides of the brain become specialized for different functions; lateralization (one-sidedness) takes place. Until recently it was believed that this brain asymmetry

---

[1] In 1836, in a paper unknown to Broca, Mark Dax had made a similar claim, but little attention has been paid to it.

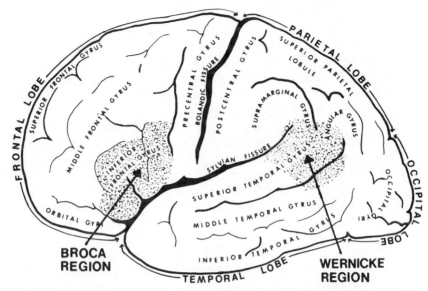

FIGURE 11-1 Lateral (external) view of the human left hemisphere. Note the position of Broca and Wernicke regions—two key areas of the cortex related to language processing.

was found only in humans. New evidence, however, shows that other species display lateralization both anatomically and functionally—for example, canaries and zebra finches.

Evidence for Brain Lateralization

PEANUTS   **Charles Schulz**

Aphasia Studies

Aphasia studies provide unequivocal evidence that language is predominantly and most frequently a left-hemisphere function.[2] In the great majority of cases, lesions to the left hemisphere result in aphasia but injuries to the right do not (although such lesions result in perceptual difficulties, defects in pattern recognition, and other cognitive deficits). If both hemispheres were equally involved with language, this finding should not be the case.

The language impairments suffered by aphasics are not due to any general cognitive or intellectual impairments. Nor are they due to loss of motor or sensory controls of the nerves and muscles of the speech organs or hearing apparatus. Aphasics can produce sounds and hear sounds. Whatever loss they suffer has to do with the production or comprehension of language (or of parts of the grammar). This connection is dramatically shown by the fact that deaf signers with damage to the left hemisphere show aphasia for sign language similar to the language breakdown in hearing aphasics. Bellugi and her colleagues at the Salk Institute have found that deaf patients with lesions in Broca's area show language deficits similar to those found in hearing patients—severe dysfluent, agrammatic sign production with relatively preserved sign comprehension. Although deaf aphasic patients show marked sign language deficits, they have no difficulty in processing nonlanguage visual-spatial relationships, just as hearing aphasics have no problem with processing nonlinguistic auditory stimuli. Therefore the left hemisphere is not lateralized for hearing or speech per se, but rather language.

As shown by the different symptoms of Broca's and Wernicke's aphasias, many aphasics do not show total language loss. Rather, different aspects of language are impaired. Broca's aphasics reveal a breakdown in phonological planning and implementation, a word-finding problem, and problems with syntax. A sample of speech from an agrammatic patient[3] illustrates these difficulties. The patient was asked what brought him back to the hospital. He answered:

> Yes . . . ah . . . Monday . . . ah . . . Dad . . . and Dad . . . ah . . . Hospital . . . and ah . . . Wednesday . . . Wednesday . . . nine o'clock and ah Thursday . . . ten o'clock ah doctors . . . two . . . two . . . an doctors and . . . ah . . . teeth . . . yah. And a doctor . . . an girl . . . and gums, and I.

Wernicke's aphasics, on the other hand, produce fluent but often unintelligible speech, have serious comprehension problems, and show difficulty in lexical selection. One patient replied to a question about his health with:

> I felt worse because I can no longer keep in mind from the mind of the minds to keep me from mind and up to the ear which can be to find among ourselves.

Patients suffering from **anomia** reveal defects in the ability to name objects

---

[2]For some people—about a third of all left-handers—there is still lateralization, but it is the right side that is specialized for language. In other words, the special functions are switched, but asymmetry still exists.

[3]Harold Goodglass. 1973. "Studies on the Grammar of Aphasics." In *Psycholinguistics and Aphasia*. H. Goodglass and S. Blumstein, eds. Johns Hopkins University Press. Baltimore.

that are presented to them (auditorially or visually). As of now, there is no evidence for any specific site of the brain damage giving rise to anomia.

Some aphasics produce **semantic jargon.** One patient, for example, described a fork as "a need for a schedule"; another, when asked about his poor vision, said "My wires don't hire right." A patient might call a chair an *engine* or a *California* with the substituted words bearing little semantic relation to the intended word. Other **semantic verbal paraphasias** are more like normal speech errors, with the two words semantically related; for example, the substitution of *table* for *chair* or *boy* for *girl*.

Paraphasia has been defined as the mispronunciation of words, or the production of inappropriate words. One type of paraphasia, called **phonemic jargon,** results from the substitution of phonemic segments. Thus *table* might be pronounced as *sable*. The substituted segments often share most of the distinctive features of the intended phonemes.

An extreme variety of phonemic jargon, **neologistic jargon,** results in the production of **neologisms**—nonoccurring but possible words. One patient, a physician prior to his aphasia, when asked if he was a doctor, replied:

> Me? yes sir. I'm a male demaploze on my own. I still know my tubaboys what for I have that's gone hell and some of them go.

Other kinds of language disorder following lesions to the left side of the brain have led to further breakdown of aphasia types and to an increased understanding of their anatomical correlates. The Damasios and their colleagues have described the occurrence of aphasia following focal damage to the basal ganglia and thalamus on the left side, indicating that the complex linguistic processes of the cortex are assisted by the deep gray masses under it. Hanna Damasio has also shown that **global aphasia**— a combination of Broca's and Wernicke's aphasia—can occur as a result of separate lesions.

The different kinds of language impairments found in aphasia patients provide information on the nature of the grammar. The aphasic patients that produce long strings of "jargon," which sound like well-formed grammatical language but which are uninterpretable, show that the phonological and phonetic systems of language are separate components of language. The substitution of semantically related words reveals the reality of semantic features. The substitution of phonologically similar words (*pool* for *tool* or *crucial* for *crucible*) provides information on the organization of the lexicon. Words in the lexicon seem to be connected to other words by phonology and semantics.

The difference between syntactic classes of words is revealed in aphasia cases by the omission of grammatical morphemes in the speech of Broca's aphasics.

Most of us have experienced some anomia or word-finding difficulties, as did Alice:

> "And now, who am I? I will remember, if I can. I'm determined to do it!" But being determined didn't help her much, and all she could say, after a great deal of puzzling, was "L, I know it begins with L."

This "tip-of-the-tongue" phenomenon is not uncommon, but if you never could find the word you wanted, you can imagine how serious a problem you would have.

Such paraphasias may appear in the spontaneous speech of some patients, in the attempt to name an object (presented visually or described auditorially), or in reading (**acquired dyslexia**) and/or writing (**agraphia**). Not only are the components of the grammar differentially affected by lesions to different brain areas, but different performance modalities may be independently affected.

There is much evidence from aphasia studies to support the distinction that has been made between linguistic competence and linguistic performance. Production or comprehension errors may occur one day and not another. Patients who cannot produce the word *chair* or their own names on one occasion will do so spontaneously on another. The linguistic knowledge must still exist in the mental grammar of these patients, although their ability to access it reveals performance difficulties.

The interest in aphasia goes back to long before Broca. In the New Testament, St. Luke reports that Zacharias could not speak but could write. Likewise in 30 c.e. the Roman writer Valerius Maximus describes an Athenian who was unable to remember his ''letters'' (sounds) after being hit in the head with a stone. It is, however, primarily in the last few decades that controlled scientific studies of aphasia have been conducted. They are revealing a great deal both about language and about the brain.

Split Brains

"It's finally happening, Helen. The hemispheres of my brain are drifting apart."

Drawing by Lorenz; © 1980 The New Yorker Magazine, Inc.

Aphasia studies provide good evidence that language is primarily processed in the left hemisphere. Other evidence is provided by patients who have one of the hemispheres removed. If the right hemisphere is cut out, language remains intact, although other cognitive losses may result. Because language is such an important aspect of our daily life, surgical removal of the left hemisphere was only performed in dire cases of malignant brain tumor and is no longer practiced.

"Split-brain" patients provide important evidence for language lateralization and for understanding brain functions. In recent years it was found that persons suffering from serious epilepsy could be treated by cutting the corpus callosum. This "freeway" between the two brain halves consists of two million fibers connecting the cells of the left and right hemispheres. The corpus callosum is shown in the three pictures in Figure 11–2. When this pathway is split there is no "communication" between the "two brains." (The two hemispheres are also linked by a smaller "corpus callosum," that may or may not be severed in split-brain operation.) The psychologist Michael Gazzaniga states:[4]

> With [the corpus callosum] intact, the two halves of the body have no secrets from one another. With it sectioned, the two halves become two different conscious mental spheres, each with its own experienced base and control system for behavioral operations. . . . Unbelievable as this may seem, this is the flavor of a long series of experimental studies first carried out in the cat and monkey.

When the brain is split surgically, certain information from the left side of the body is received only by the right side of the brain and vice versa (because of the "criss-cross" phenomenon discussed above). For example, suppose a monkey is trained to respond with its hands to a certain visual stimulus, such as a flashing

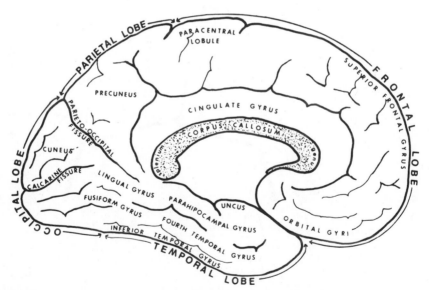

FIGURE 11–2 Internal view of the human left hemisphere. Note the position of the corpus callosum, which joins the structures of the left and right hemispheres across the midline.

[4]Michael Gazzaniga. 1970. *The Bisected Brain*. Appleton-Century-Crofts. New York.

light. If the brain is split after the training period, and the stimulus is shown only to the left visual field (the right brain), the monkey will perform only with the left hand, and vice versa. Many such experiments have been done on animals. They all show the independence of the two sides of the brain.

Persons with split brains have been tested by psychologists, showing that, like the monkey brain, the two human hemispheres are distinct. However, these tests showed that messages sent to the two sides of the brain result in different responses, depending on which hemisphere "receives" the message. If an apple is put in the left hand of a split-brain human whose vision is cut off, the person can use it appropriately but cannot name it. The right brain senses the apple and distinguishes it from other objects, but the information cannot be relayed to the left brain for linguistic naming. By contrast, if a banana is placed in the right hand, the subject is immediately able to name it as well as describe it. (See Figure 11–3.)

Various experiments of this sort have been performed, all providing information on the different capabilities of the "two brains." The right brain does better

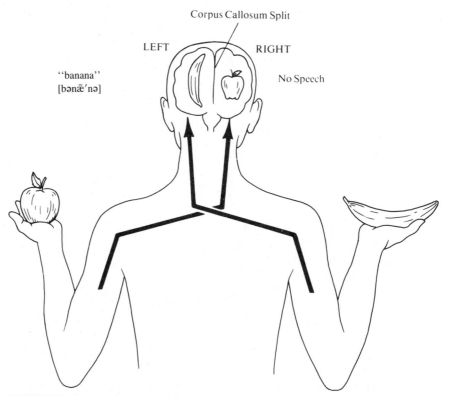

FIGURE 11–3 Sensory information is received in the *contralateral* (opposite) side of the brain from the side of the body from which it is sent. In a split-brain patient, the information in the right hemisphere cannot get across to the left hemisphere, so this patient does not produce the word "apple."

than the left in pattern-matching tasks, in recognizing faces, and in spatial orientation. The left hemisphere is superior for language, for rhythmic perception, for temporal-order judgments, and for mathematical thinking. According to Gazzaniga, "the right hemisphere as well as the left hemisphere can emote and while the left can tell you why, the right cannot."

Studies of human split-brain patients have shown that when the interhemispheric visual connections are severed, visual information from the right and left visual fields becomes confined to the left and right hemispheres respectively. Because of the crucial endowment of the left hemisphere for language, written material delivered to the right hemisphere can not be read if the brain is split, because the information can not be transferred to the left hemisphere.

An image or picture—say, of a cube—that is flashed to the right visual field of a split-brain patient (and is therefore processed by the left hemisphere) can be named. However, when the picture is flashed in the left visual field and lands in the right hemisphere, it cannot be named.

A new technique using a movable contact lens permits complex experiments testing different hemispheric abilities. Results show that a picture of a cube can be copied more accurately by the left hand (right hemisphere) than by the right hand. The left hemisphere, however, is shown to be better at analytic tasks such as deciding or analogizing how paired figures are similar to each other. It has also been shown that the right hemisphere may have some limited language abilities, primarily related to single words, but that syntactic processing is a left-hemisphere function.[5]

More Lateralization Evidence

Aphasia studies and split-brain research all involve "nonnormal" human subjects (in one way or another). Other experimental techniques that can be used with all human subjects have been developed to explore the specialized capabilities of the two hemispheres.

One such method, called **dichotic listening,** uses auditory signals. Subjects hear two different sound signals simultaneously through earphones. For example, a subject may hear "boy" in one ear and "girl" in the other, or "crocodile" in one ear and "alligator" in the other; or the subject may hear a horn tooting in one ear and rushing water in the other. When asked to state what they heard in each ear, subjects are more frequently correct in reporting linguistic stimuli (words, nonsense syllables, and so on) delivered directly to the right ear but are more frequently correct in reporting nonverbal stimuli (musical chords, environmental sounds, and so on) delivered to the left ear. That is, if subjects hear "boy" in the right ear and "girl" in the left ear, they are more likely to report the word heard in the right ear correctly. If they hear coughing in the right ear and laughing in the left, they are more apt to report the laughing stimulus correctly. The same acoustic signal may be

[5]E. Zaidel. 1975. "A Technique for Presenting Lateralized Visual Input with Prolonged Exposure." *Vision Research* 15: 283–289.

processed in one hemisphere or the other depending on whether the subjects perceive it as part of their language system or not. Thai speakers show a right ear advantage (left hemisphere) in distinguishing between CV syllables that contrast in tone (pitch contours); English subjects do not show the right ear advantage when they hear the same stimuli, because English is not a tone language.

Both hemispheres receive signals from both ears, but the "crossed" contralateral stimuli (right to left and vice versa) compete successfully with the "same side" ipsilateral stimuli, either because they are received earlier, or because they are not weakened by having to cross the corpus callosum. The fact that the left hemisphere has an edge in linguistic processing and the right hemisphere is better at nonverbal material determines the accuracy with which subjects report on what they have heard.

This lateralized "ear advantage" for different kinds of stimuli has also been shown in Japanese monkeys in discriminating between an acoustic feature that plays a relevant role in their communication system ("peak") and one that does not ("pitch"). The animals were more proficient in discriminating the peak feature when stimuli were presented to the right ear (left hemisphere) but showed a left-ear processing advantage or no ear advantage for pitch features.

These experiments are important in that they show that the left hemisphere is not superior for processing all sounds, but only for those that are linguistic in nature. That is, the left side of the brain is specialized for language, not sounds.

Other experimental techniques are also being used to map the brain and to investigate the independence of different aspects of language and the extent of the independence of language from other cognitive systems.

The advent of **emission tomography** has finally given researchers the means of detecting changes in brain activity in extremely small areas of the cerebrum or cerebellum, and relating these changes not only to focal brain damage but also to cognitive tasks controlled in a laboratory setting. The techniques depend on the introduction of a radioisotope into the brain circulation (for example, xenon 133), on the ability to measure the marked substance, and on well-designed experiments that control specific cognitive processes (linguistic or visual nonverbal or motor). Two methods are in use—PET (an acronym for Positron Emission Tomography) and SPET (Single Photon Emission Tomography). The technical terms or techniques are not important for our purposes, but this new technology is contributing in important ways to the understanding of the **modularity**—independence—of brain activity underlying distinct cognitive systems.

Even before these spectacular new technologies were introduced in the 1970s, researchers were taping electrodes to different areas of the skull and investigating the electrical activity of the brain by comparing the signals emitted from these electrodes. In such experiments the electrical signals emitted from the brain in response to different kinds of stimuli (called evoked potentials or event-related potentials or erps) are measured. For example, electrical differences may result when the subject hears speech sounds and nonspeech sounds. These experiments show that neuronal activity in different locations varies with different stimuli and different tasks, and provide further support for the views on lateralization presented above.

The results of these studies, using different techniques and diverse subjects, both normal and brain-damaged, are converging to provide the information we seek on the relationship between the brain and various language and nonlanguage cognitive systems.

The Critical Age Hypothesis

In Chapter 10 we mentioned that there appears to be a period during which language learning can proceed easily, swiftly, and without external intervention or teaching. The development of lateralization in the brain may be connected to the language-learning abilities of children, in that the "critical age" for first-language acquisition coincides with the period when lateralization is taking place and ends when it is complete. The earliest hypothesis placed the end of lateralization at puberty, which appeared to be a crucial limit for ease of acquisition. More recently, however, it has been suggested that lateralization may be complete by the age of five. Perhaps this is why so much of the grammar has already been acquired by the child at that age.

It was once assumed that at birth the two sides of the brain are nonspecialized and equipotential, so that if damage occurs in the left hemisphere of an infant the right hemisphere can equally well acquire and use language. This assumption is now questioned; children with left hemispheres removed because of tumors or other problems do develop language, but their language may differ syntactically from normal language development.

Language learning and lateralization may go hand in hand, but the relationship between the two is not clearly understood. We are not certain whether language is a prerequisite for the development of lateralization or whether lateralization precedes language acquisition.

In the attempt to understand the role of lateralization as it relates to the critical age hypothesis, it is interesting to look at the development of bird songs and calls. Some bird species do not "learn" at all; the cuckoo will sing a fully developed song even if it never hears another cuckoo sing. These communicative messages are clearly innate. For other species, songs appear to be completely learned; the bullfinch, for example, will learn any song it is exposed to, even that of another species, however "unbullfinchlike" it may be. There do not appear to be any "bullfinch universals."

The chaffinch represents a different acquisition pattern. Certain calls and songs of this species will vary depending on the geographical "dialect" area that the bird inhabits. The message is the same, but the "pronunciation" or form is different. Usually a young bird will exhibit a basic version of the song shortly after hatching, and later on will undergo further learning in acquiring its final, "dialect" version of the song. Because birds from the same brood will acquire different dialects depending on the area in which they finally settle, part of the song must be learned. Because a fledgling chaffinch will sing the song of its species in a simple, degraded form, even if it has never heard it sung, some aspect of its "language" is biologically determined; that is, it is innate.

The chaffinch acquires its fully developed song in several stages, just as human children appear to acquire language in several stages. Furthermore, the chaffinch brain may also be lateralized, with the left half more dominant for song production than the right.

A critical age in the song learning of chaffinches, white-crowned sparrows, zebra finches, and other species has been described. If these birds are not exposed to the songs of their species during certain fixed periods after their birth (the period differs from species to species) song acquisition does not occur. The chaffinch is unable to learn new song elements after ten months of age. If it is isolated from other birds before attaining the full "grammar" and then reexposed after ten months, its song will not develop further. If white-crowns are deafened during a critical period *after* they have learned to sing, they produce a song that differs from other white-crowns; they need to hear themselves sing to produce particular whistles and other song features. If, however, the deafening occurs after the critical period, the songs are normal.

From the point of view of human language research, the relationship between the innate and learned aspects of bird songs is significant. Apparently, the basic nature of the song of some species is biologically determined, but the details are learned, and can only be learned if exposure to the songs of their species occurs within a critical period. Similarly, it appears that the basic nature of human language is biologically determined, whereas the details of languages that make them different from each other are learned, and that the learning must occur within a critical period.

In the Beginning: The Origin of Language

Nothing, no doubt, would be more interesting than to know from historical documents the exact process by which the first man began to lisp his first words, and thus to be rid for ever of all the theories on the origin of speech.
M. Müller, 1871

If the human brain is uniquely suited to the acquisition and use of language, how and when did this development occur? Two scholarly societies, the American Anthropological Association and the New York Academy of Sciences, held forums in 1974 and 1976 to review recent research on this question. It is not a new question, however; it seems to have originated with the origin of the species.

All religions and mythologies contain stories of language origin. Philosophers through the ages have argued the question. Scholarly works have been written on the subject. Prizes have been awarded for the "best answer" to this eternally perplexing problem. Theories of divine origin, evolutionary development, and language as a human invention have all been suggested. Such widespread speculation is not surprising. Humanity's curiosity about itself led to curiosity about language. Many of the early theories on the origin of language resulted from an interest in human origins and human nature. Because language appeared so uniquely human, it was believed that if we knew how, when, and where language arose, perhaps we would know how, when, and where the human species arose.

The difficulties inherent in answering these questions about language are immense. Anthropologists think that the species has existed for at least one million years, and perhaps for as long as five or six million years. However, the earliest deciphered written records are barely 6000 years old, dating from the writings of the Sumerians of 4000 B.C.E. These records appear so late in the history of the development of language that they provide no clue to the origin of language.

For these reasons, scholars in the latter part of the nineteenth century, who were only interested in "hard science," ridiculed, ignored, and even banned discussions of language origin. In 1886, the Linguistic Society of Paris passed a resolution "outlawing" any papers concerned with this subject, a view that Lord Monboddo, a Scottish anthropologist in the eighteenth century, would have strongly disagreed with. In his book, *Of the Origin and Progress of Language,* published in 1774, he wrote:

> The origin of an art so admirable and so useful as language . . . must be allowed to be a subject, not only of great curiosity, but likewise very important and interesting, if we consider, that it is necessarily connected with an inquiry into the original nature of man, and that primitive state in which he was, before language was invented.

Despite the difficulty of finding scientific evidence, speculations on language origin have provided valuable insights into the nature and development of language, which prompted the learned scholar Otto Jespersen to state that "linguistic science cannot refrain forever from asking about the whence (and about the whither) of linguistic evolution." A brief look at some of these speculative notions will reveal this.

God's Gift to Humanity?

And out of the ground the Lord God formed every beast of the field, and every fowl of the air, and brought them unto Adam to see what he would call them: and whatsoever Adam called every living creature, that was the name thereof.

Genesis 2:19

According to Judeo-Christian beliefs, God gave Adam the power to name all things. Similar beliefs are found throughout the world. According to the Egyptians, the creator of speech was the god Thoth. Babylonians believed the language giver was the god Nabu, and the Hindus attributed our unique language ability to a goddess; Brahma was the creator of the universe, but language was given to us by his wife, Sarasvati.

The belief in the divine origin of language has continued through the ages. Cotton Mather wrote his master's thesis at Harvard on the question, providing a detailed defense of this theory.

Belief in the divine origin of language is closely intertwined with the magical properties that have been associated with language and the spoken word. Children in all cultures utter "magic" words like *abracadabra* to ward off evil or bring good luck. Despite the childish jingle "Sticks and stones may break my bones, but names will never hurt me," name-calling is insulting, cause for legal punishment, and feared. In some cultures, when certain words are used, listeners are required to counter them by "knocking on wood." Language is used to bring down the curses of the gods. People offer prayers and converse with their gods in language. According to the Bible, only the true God would respond when called upon; the false idols did not know the "word of God."

We find taboo words all over the world. In western societies it is forbidden to "take the Lord's name in vain." In folk tales, forbidden names such as *Rumpelstiltskin* can break spells if discovered. Personal names also carry special properties— a Jewish child is not to be named after a living person, and in some cultures it is forbidden to utter the name of someone who has died. In ancient Egypt every person was given two names, one of which was secret. If the secret name was discovered, the discoverer had power over the person.

In many religions only special languages may be used in prayers and rituals. The Hindu priests of the fifth century B.C.E. believed that the original pronunciations of Vedic Sanskrit had to be used. This belief led to important linguistic study, because their language had already changed greatly since the hymns of the Vedas had been written. The first linguist known to us is Pāṇini, who in the fourth century B.C.E. wrote a detailed grammar of Sanskrit in which the phonological rules revealed the earlier pronunciation for use in religious worship. Until recently, only Latin could be used in the Catholic Mass. Among Moslems, the Koran was not to be translated and could be read only in Arabic; and Hebrew continues to be the one language used in the prayers of orthodox Jews throughout the world.

These myths and customs and superstitions do not tell us much about language. They do tell us about the importance ascribed to language and in some cases provide insights into its nature.

An example of such insights is found in a paper delivered before the Prussian Academy in 1756 by a statistician-clergyman, Johann Peter Suessmilch. He reasoned that humans could not have invented language without thought, and that thought depends on the prior existence of language. The only escape from the paradox is to presume that God must have given language to humanity. Suessmilch, unlike other philosophers of his time, did not view primitive languages as "less developed" or "imperfect." He suggested just the opposite—that all languages are "perfect" and thus the reflection of God's perfection. He cites examples from the European languages, from Semitic languages, and from languages of "primitive" peoples to prove the perfection of all human language. To oppose the idea that there are primitive languages, he noted that the great and abstract ideas of Christianity can be discussed even by the "wretched Greenlanders."

Suessmilch made other sophisticated observations. He pointed out that any child is able to learn perfectly "the language of the Hottentots" although adults cannot, revealing his awareness of the difference between acquisition of first and second languages, and anticipating the "critical age hypothesis." He also pointed out that all languages have grammars that are highly regular, for otherwise children would be unable to learn them.

There is no way to "prove" or "disprove" the divine origin of language, just as no one can argue scientifically for or against the existence of God.

The First Language

Imagine the Lord talking French! Aside from a few odd words in Hebrew, I took it completely for granted that God had never spoken anything but the most dignified English.
Clarence Day, *Life with Father*

Among the proponents of the divine origin theory a great interest arose in the language used by God, Adam, and Eve. For millennia, "scientific" experiments have reportedly been devised to verify particular theories of language origin. In the fifth century B.C.E. the Greek historian Herodotus reported that the Egyptian Pharaoh Psammetichus (664–610 B.C.E.) sought to determine the most primitive "natural" language by experimental methods. The monarch was said to have placed two infants in an isolated mountain hut, to be cared for by a mute servant. The Pharaoh believed that without any linguistic input the children would develop their own language and would thus reveal the original tongue of man. Patiently the Egyptian waited for the children to become old enough to talk. According to the story, the first word uttered was *bekos*. Scholars were consulted, and it was discovered that *bekos* was the word for "bread" in Phrygian, the language spoken in the province of Phrygia (the northwest corner of modern Turkey). This ancient language, which has long since died out, was thought, on the basis of this "experiment," to be the original language.

Whether James IV of Scotland (1473–1513) had read the works of Herodotus is not known. According to reports he attempted a replication of the isolation experiment, but his attempt yielded different results. The Scottish children matured and "spak very guid Ebrew," providing "scientific evidence" that Hebrew was the language used in the Garden of Eden.

History is replete with other proposals. J. G. Becanus in the sixteenth century argued that German must have been the primeval language, because God would have used the most perfect language. In 1830 the lexicographer Noah Webster asserted that the "proto-language" must have been Chaldee (Aramaic), the language spoken in Jerusalem during the time of Jesus. In 1887, Joseph Elkins maintained that "there is no other language which can be more reasonably assumed to be the speech first used in the world's gray morning than can Chinese."

The belief that all languages originated from a single source—the **monogenetic theory** of language origin—is not only found in the Tower of Babel story in Genesis, but also in a similar legend of the Toltecs, early inhabitants of Mexico, and in the myths of other peoples as well.

We are no further along today in discovering the original language (or languages) than was Psammetichus when he attempted to use "experimental methods" to answer this question. Any such experiment is bound to fail. For obvious reasons, linguists would not attempt to duplicate such tests—although we may applaud the

Pharaoh's motivation we must condemn his lack of humanity. However, the misfortunes of life can be as cruel as a Pharaoh. There have been a number of cases of children reared in environments of extreme social isolation. Such reported cases go back at least to the eighteenth century. In 1758, Carl Linneaus first included Homo ferus (wild or feral man) as a subdivision of Homo sapiens. According to Linnaeus, a defining characteristic of Homo ferus was lack of speech or observable language of any kind. All the cases in the literature support his view.

The most dramatic cases of children raised in isolation are those described as "wild" or "feral" children, who have reportedly been reared with wild animals or have lived alone in the wilderness. In 1920 two feral children, Amala and Kamala, were found in India, supposedly having been reared with wolves. The most celebrated case, documented in François Truffaut's film *The Wild Child,* is that of Victor, "the wild boy of Aveyron," who was found in 1798. It was ascertained that he had been left in the woods when a very young child and had somehow survived. There are other cases of children whose isolation resulted from deliberate efforts to keep them from normal social intercourse. As recently as 1970 a child, called Genie in the scientific reports, was discovered who had been confined to a small room under conditions of physical restraint, and who had received only minimal human contact from the age of eighteen months until almost fourteen years. None of these children, regardless of the cause of isolation, was able to speak or knew any language at the time of reintroduction to society. Genie, however, did begin to acquire some language; but although she was able to learn a large vocabulary, her syntax never fully developed, providing additional support to the critical age hypothesis.

Human Invention or the Cries of Nature?

Language was born in the courting days of mankind; the first utterances of speech I fancy to myself like something between the nightly love lyrics of puss upon the tiles and the melodious love songs of the nightingale.

Otto Jespersen, *Language, Its Nature, Development and Origin*

The Greeks speculated about everything in the universe, including language. The earliest surviving linguistic treatise that deals with the origin and nature of language is Plato's *Cratylus.* A commonly held view among the classical Greeks, expressed by Socrates in this dialogue, was that at some ancient time there was a "legislator" who gave the correct, natural name to everything.

The question of language origin was closely tied to the debate among the Greeks as to whether there is a truth or correctness in "names" regardless of the language, as opposed to the view that words or names for things are arbitrary, resulting merely from an agreement—a convention—among speakers. This debate between the **naturalists** and the **conventionalists** was one of the first major linguistic arguments. History and linguistic research have decided in favor of the conventionalists.

Despite all the contrary evidence, the idea that the earliest form of language was imitative, or "echoic," was proposed up to the twentieth century. According to this view, a dog, which emits a noise that (supposedly) sounds like "bow-wow," would be designated by the word *bow-wow*.

A parallel view states that languages at first consisted of emotional ejaculations of pain, fear, surprise, pleasure, anger, and so on. This proposal—that the earliest manifestations of language were "cries of nature" that humans shared with animals—was the view proposed by Jean Jacques Rousseau, in the middle of the eighteenth century, in his two treatises dealing with the origin of language. According to him, humans used both emotive cries and gestures at first, but gestures proved to be too inefficient for communicating, so they invented language. It was out of the natural cries that they "constructed" words.

Almost two hundred years later, Sir Richard Paget, in *Human Speech* (published in 1930), argued for an "oral gesture theory." He suggested that human speech arose out of a generalized unconscious pantomimic gesture language made by the limbs and features as a whole (including the tongue and lips), which became specialized in gestures of the organs of articulation, owing to the human hands (and eyes) becoming continuously occupied with the use of tools.

Another hypothesis concerning the development of human language suggests that language arose out of the rhythmical grunts of people working together. One of the more charming views on language origin was suggested by Otto Jespersen, who proposed that language derived from song as an expressive rather than a communicative need, with love being the greatest stimulus for language development.

Just like the beliefs in a divine origin of language, many of these proposals that language was invented or that it arose in the course of human development are unprovable. The debate is unsettled, and it continues.

The Biological Basis of Language Origin

But language just happened. It happened because language is the most natural outcome in a world of people where babies babble, and mothers babble back—and where the baby also has the potential for metaphor.

Louis Carini

In 1769, thirteen years after Suessmilch's defense of the divine origin of language, the Prussian Academy reopened the discussion. They offered a prize for the best paper on the same question. Johann Herder, the German philosopher and poet, won the prize with an essay that opposed both views. Herder argued against Rousseau's view that language developed out of the "cries of nature" that humans shared with animals by citing the fundamental differences between human language and the instinctive cries of animals. Herder believed that language and thought are inseparable, and that humans must be born with a capacity for both:

> Parents never teach their children language, without the latter at the same time inventing it themselves. The former only direct their children's attention to the difference between things, by certain verbal signs, and thus do not supply these, but by means of language only facilitate and accelerate for the children the use of reason.

These insightful remarks foreshadowed what we know today about how children acquire language.

Herder's main point was that language ability is innate. We cannot talk of human existence before language. Language is part of our essential human nature and was therefore neither invented nor handed down as a gift. Herder drew on the universality of all human languages as an argument to justify a monogenetic theory of origin. According to him, we have all descended from the same parents, and all languages therefore have descended from one language. He put forth this theory to explain why languages, despite their diversity, have universal common properties. Even though the monogenetic theory is not widely accepted today, the universality of human language is, and can be plausibly explained by Herder's argument that people everywhere are endowed with biologically determined linguistic ability, which can be called the Universal Grammar. Herder accepted the Cartesian **rationalist** position that human languages and animal cries are as different from each other as human thought and animal instinct.

The Evolution of Language

As the voice was used more and more, the vocal organs would have been strengthened and perfected through the principle of the inherited effects of use; and this would have reacted on the power of speech. But the relation between the continued use of language and the development of the brain has no doubt been far more important. The mental powers in some early progenitor of man must have been more highly developed than in any existing ape, before even the most imperfect form of speech could have come into use. . . .
Charles Darwin, *The Descent of Man*

Scholars are now concerned with how the development of language is related to the evolutionary development of the human species. There are those who view language ability as a difference in degree between humans and other primates, and those who see the onset of language ability as a qualitative leap. Those who support the "discontinuity" view believe that language is species-specific. Some scholars further believe that the brain mechanisms that underlie this language ability are specific to language, rather than being a mere offshoot of more highly developed cognitive abilities. This latter view holds that all humans are innately or genetically equipped with a unique language learning ability or with genetically determined, specifically linguistic, neurological mechanisms. Such linguists agree with the earlier views of Herder.

In trying to understand the development of language, scholars past and present have debated the role played by the vocal tract and the ear. For example, it has been suggested that speech could not have developed in nonhuman primates because their vocal tracts were anatomically incapable of producing a large enough inventory of speech sounds. According to this hypothesis, the development of language is linked to the evolutionary development of the speech production and perception apparatus. This development, of course, would be accompanied by changes in the brain and the nervous system toward greater complexity. Such a view implies that the languages of our human ancestors of millions of years ago may have been syntactically and phonologically simpler than any language known to us today. "Simpler," however, is left undefined. One suggestion is that this primeval language had a smaller phonetic inventory.

One evolutionary step must have resulted in the development of a vocal tract capable of producing the wide variety of sounds utilized by human language, as well as the mechanism for perceiving and distinguishing them. That this step is insufficient to explain the origin of language is evidenced by the existence of mynah birds and parrots, which have the ability to imitate human speech, but not the ability to acquire language.

We also know that the ability to hear speech sounds is not a necessary condition for the acquisition and use of language, because humans who are born deaf learn the sign languages that are used around them.

The complexity of language argues against the notion that it could have been caused by a single event or one mutation in the evolution of the species. It is more likely that the language faculty originated from a convergence of a number of evolutionary developments.

The major step in the development of language most probably relates to evolutionary changes in the brain. It is not yet clear what role, if any, hemispheric lateralization played in its development. Lateralization certainly makes greater specialization possible, but we have seen from the research conducted with birds and monkeys that lateralization is not unique to the human brain. It may constitute a necessary step in the evolution of language, but it is not a sufficient one.

The new technology for studying the brain, behavior, and cognition may provide new answers to this age-old question. Whatever the origin, language and humanity are intricately connected.

Summary

The attempt to understand what makes language acquisition and use possible has led to research on brain mechanisms and the relationship between the brain and language. The study of this relationship is called **neurolinguistics.**

The brain is the most complicated organ of the body, controlling motor and sensory activities and thought processes. Research conducted for over a century reveals that different parts of the brain control different body functions. The nerve cells that form the surface of the brain are called the **cortex,** which serves as the intellectual decision-maker, receives messages from the sensory organs, and initiates all voluntary actions. The brain or **cerebrum** of all higher animals is divided into two parts called the **cerebral hemispheres,** which are connected by the **corpus callosum,** a pathway that permits the left and right hemispheres to communicate with each other. The **cerebellum** is also divided into two hemispheres and is located under the cerebrum.

Although each hemisphere appears to be a mirror image of the other, the control of movements and sensation is accomplished **contralaterally,** or in a crossed fashion. That is, the left hemisphere controls the right hand, leg, visual field, and so on, and the right brain controls the left side of the body. Despite this seeming symmetry, there is much evidence that the left and right hemispheres may be specialized for different functions. Evidence from **aphasia** (language dysfunction as a result of brain injuries), surgical removal of parts of the brain, electrical stimulation studies, emission tomography results, dichotic listening, and experiments measuring brain electrical activity all show a lack of symmetry of function of the two hemispheres. These results are further supported by studies of split-brain patients, who, for medical reasons, have had the corpus callosum severed. For normal right-handers and many left-handers, the left side of the brain appears to be specialized for language. This **lateralization** of functions develops from birth and, according to some neurologists, neuropsychologists, and neurolinguists, is closely related to a **critical period,** during which language acquisition occurs naturally.

Aphasia studies, and the other experiments mentioned, also show differential language impairment. Different parts of the grammar can be lost or become inaccessible. Thus, patients with **Broca's aphasia** reveal impaired phonological and syntactic systems or impaired ability to access them, whereas **Wernicke's aphasia** patients are fluent speakers but have difficulty in comprehension and produce semantically empty utterances. **Anomia** is a form of aphasia in which the patient has word-finding difficulties. **Jargon aphasia** patients may substitute words unrelated semantically to their intended messages; others produce phonemic substitution errors, or **neologisms** (nonsense), making their utterances uninterpretable.

There appears to be a **critical age** during which a child may acquire its native language, which may be related to the development of brain lateralization. Some songbirds also appear to have a critical period for the acquisition of their calls and songs; there is also evidence to support the view that in many species the songs that are produced are innately determined.

The evolution of the human brain is related to the development of language in the human species. Interest in this question historically led to conflicting notions about language origin. There is no way at present to "prove" or "disprove" these hypotheses, but they are of interest for the light they shed on the nature of human language.

The idea that language was God's gift to humankind is found in religions throughout the world. The continuing belief in the miraculous powers of language is tied to this notion. The assumption of the divine origin of language stimulated interest in discovering the first primeval language. There are legendary "experiments" in which children were isolated in the belief that their first words would reveal the original language. Children will learn the language spoken to them; if they hear no language they will speak none. Actual cases of socially isolated children show that language develops only when there is sufficient linguistic input.

Opposing views suggest that language is a human invention. The Greeks believed that an ancient "legislator" gave the true names to all things. Others have suggested that language developed from "cries of nature," or "early gestures," or onomatopoeic words, or even from songs to express love.

A renewed interest in language origin has arisen. Various evolutionary theories oppose both the divine origin and the invention theory. Rather, it is suggested that in the course of evolution both the human species and language developed.

Some scholars suggest that they developed simultaneously, and that from the start the human animal was innately equipped to learn language. Studies of the evolutionary development of the brain provide some evidence for physiological, anatomic, and "mental" preconditions for language development.

References

Bogen, J. E. 1969. "The Other Side of the Brain: An Appositional Mind." *Bulletin of the Los Angeles Neurological Societies* 34: 135–162.

Caplan, D., ed. 1980. *Biological Studies of Mental Processes*. M.I.T. Press. Cambridge, Mass.

Damasio, A., and N. Geschwind. 1984. "The Neural Basis of Language." *Annual Review of Neuroscience* 7:127–147.

Damasio, H. 1981. "Cerebral Localization of the Aphasias." In *Acquired Aphasia*. M. Taylor Sarno, ed. Academic Press. New York. Pp. 27–65.

Gazzaniga, M. S. 1970. *The Bisected Brain*. Appleton-Century-Crofts. New York.

Geschwind, N. 1979. "Specializations of the Human Brain." *Scientific American* 206 (September): 180–199.

Herder, J. G. 1969. "Essay on the Origin of Language." In *Plato to Von Humboldt*. P. E. Salus, ed. Holt, Rinehart and Winston. New York.

Krashen, S. 1973. "Lateralization, Language Learning, and the Critical Period: Some New Evidence." *Language Learning* 23: 63–74.

Lenneberg, Eric H. 1967. *Biological Foundations of Language*. Wiley. New York.

Lesser, R. 1978. *Linguistic Investigation of Aphasia*. Elsevier. New York.

Lieberman, P. 1975. *On the Origins of Language*. Macmillan. New York.

Newcombe, F., and J. C. Marshall. 1972. "Word Retrieval in Aphasia." *International Journal of Mental Health* 1:38–45.

Nottebohm, F. 1975. "Vocal Behavior in Birds." In *Avian Biology,* V. D. S. Farner, ed. Academic Press. New York.

Petersen, M. R., M. D. Beecher, S. R. Zoloth, D. B. Moody, and W. E. Stebbins. 1978. "Neural Lateralization of Species-Specific Vocalizations by Japanese Macaques (Macaca fuscata)." *Science* 202: 324–326.

Rousseau, J. J. 1969. "Discourse on the Origin and Foundations of Inequality among Men" (1755) and "Essay on the Origin of Languages" (published posthumously, 1822). In *Plato to Von Humboldt*. P. E. Salus, ed. Holt, Rinehart and Winston. New York.

Segalowitz, S. J., ed. 1983. *Language Functions and Brain Organization*. Academic Press. New York.

Springer, S. P., and G. Deutsch. 1981. *Left Brain, Right Brain*. W. H. Freeman. San Francisco.

Stam, J. 1976. *Inquiries into the Origin of Language: The Fate of a Question*. Harper & Row. New York.

Exercises

1. The Nobel Prize laureate Roger Sperry has argued that split-brain patients have two minds:

    > Everything we have seen so far indicates that the surgery has left these people with two separate minds, that is, two separate spheres of consciousness. What is experienced in the right hemisphere seems to lie entirely outside the realm of experience of the left hemisphere.

    Another Nobel Prize winner in physiology, Sir John Eccles, disagrees. He does not think the right hemisphere can think; he distinguishes between ''mere consciousness,'' which animals possess as well as humans, and language, thought, and other purely human cognitive abilities. In fact, according to him, the human aspect of human nature is all in the left hemisphere.

    Write a short essay discussing these two opposing points of view, stating your own opinion on how to define ''the mind.''

2. A. Some aphasic patients, when asked to read a list of words, substitute other words for those printed. In many cases there are similarities between the printed words and the substituted words. The data given below are from actual aphasic patients. In each case state what the two words have in common and how they differ:

Printed Word	Word Spoken by Aphasic
a. liberty	freedom
canary	parrot
abroad	overseas
large	long
short	small
tall	long
b. decide	decision
conceal	concealment
portray	portrait
bathe	bath
speak	discussion
remember	memory

    B. What do the words in groups a and b reveal about how words are likely to be stored in the brain?

3. The following are some sentences spoken by aphasic patients, collected and analyzed by Dr. Harry Whitaker of the University of Maryland. In each case state how the sentence deviates from normal nonaphasic language.

    a. There is under a horse a new sidesaddle.
    b. In girls we see many happy days.

c. I'll challenge a new bike.
d. I surprise no new glamor.
e. Is there three chairs in this room?
f. Mike and Peter is happy.
g. Bill and John likes hot dogs.
h. Proliferate is a complete time about a word that is correct.
i. Went came in better than it did before.

4. A young patient at the Division of Neuropsychology of the Radcliffe Infirmary, Oxford, England, following a head injury, appears to have lost the spelling-to-pronunciation and phonetic-to-spelling rules that most of us can use to read and write new words or nonsense strings. He also is unable to get to the phonemic representation of words in his lexicon. Consider the following examples of his reading pronunciation and his writing from dictation.

	Reading Pronunciation	**Writing from Dictation**
fame	/fæmi/	FAM
café	/sæfi/	KAFA
time	/tajmi/	TIM
note	/noti/ or /nɔti/	NOT
praise	/pra-aj-si/	PRAZ
treat	/tri-æt/	TRET
goes	/go-ɛs/	GOZ
float	/flɔ-æt/	FLOT

His reading and writing errors are not random, but rule-governed. See if you can figure out the rules he uses to relate his (spelling) orthography to his pronunciation.

5. Compare the ideas of Rousseau, Herder, and Suessmilch on the origin of language. Note the similarities and the differences. Argue in favor of one of these theories or argue for another point of view refuting all three positions.

6. Invent your own theory of language origin and argue plausibly in favor of it.

Language Processing: Human and Machine

Human Processing of Language: Linguistic Performance

> *No doubt a reasonable model of language use will incorporate, as a basic component, the generative grammar that expresses the speaker-hearer's knowledge of the language; but this generative grammar does not, in itself, prescribe the character or functioning of a perceptual model or a model of speech production.*
>
> Noam Chomsky, *Aspects of a Theory of Syntax*

The area of linguistics that is concerned with linguistic performance—how we use our knowledge of language in speech production and comprehension and how a child acquires that knowledge—is called **psycholinguistics.** How we acquire and process knowledge depends to a great extent on the nature of that knowledge. If, for example, language were not "open-ended" but consisted of a finite store of fixed phrases and sentences, then speaking might simply be finding a sentence that expresses a thought and producing it. Comprehension would be the reverse—matching the sounds we hear to a stored string of words that gives their meanings. We know this method is not possible because of the creativity of language. In Chapter 10, we saw that children do not learn language by imitating and storing sentences but by constructing a grammar. When we speak, we **access** this grammar to find the words, construct novel sentences, and produce the sounds that express the message we wish to convey. When we listen to someone speaking, we also access the grammar to process the utterances in order to assign a meaning to the sounds we hear.

The grammar contains the units and rules of the language that make speech production and comprehension possible; but the grammar does not describe the psychological processes that are used in producing and understanding utterances. When we speak we do not "generate" a sentence by starting with a symbol S and applying rules consecutively until the final output is a string of phonetic symbols, which then must be "translated" into neuromuscular commands to the articulators to produce speech. Rather, we use grammatical knowledge together with other cognitive structures and capabilities to produce utterances. A theory of linguistic performance describes the relationship between the mental grammar and the psychological processes by means of which this grammar is accessed to permit speech and comprehension. This chapter will discuss these processes of speech communication.

Comprehension

"I quite agree with you," said the Duchess; "and the moral of that is—'Be what you would seem to be'—or, if you'd like it put more simply—'Never imagine yourself not to be otherwise than what it might appear to others that what you were or might have been was not otherwise than what you had been would have appeared to them to be otherwise.'"

"I think I should understand that better," Alice said very politely, "if I had it written down: but I can't quite follow it as you say it."

Lewis Carroll, *Alice's Adventures in Wonderland*

The difficulty Alice had in understanding this complex grammatical English sentence is not surprising. What is surprising is that we usually do understand what is said to us, although to understand even a simple sentence like *John is an idiot* is a complex task.

The Speech Signal

Be a craftsman in speech that you may be strong, for the strength of one is the tongue, and speech is mightier than all fighting.

Ptahhotep, *Maxims* (c. 3400 B.C.E.)

Speech was given to the ordinary sort of men whereby to communicate their mind; but to wise men, whereby to conceal it.

Robert South, *Sermon* (1676)

The first stage in the comprehension process is the perception of the speech signal, an **acoustic signal** produced by the speaker. In Chapter 2 speech sounds were described according to the ways in which they are produced—the position of the tongue, the lips, and the velum, the state of the vocal cords, the airstream mechanisms, whether the articulators obstruct the free flow of air, and so on. All of these articulatory characteristics are reflected in the physical characteristics of the sounds produced.

Speech sounds can also be described in physical or **acoustic** terms. Physically, a sound is produced whenever there is a disturbance in the position of air molecules. The question asked by ancient philosophers as to whether a sound is produced if a tree falls in the middle of the forest with no one to "hear" it has been answered by the science of acoustics. Objectively, a sound is produced; subjectively, there is no sound. In fact, there are sounds we cannot hear because our ears are not sensitive to all changes in air pressure (which result from the movement of air molecules). Acoustic phonetics is concerned only with speech sounds, all of which can be heard by the normal human ear.

When we push air out of the lungs through the glottis, it causes the vocal cords to vibrate; this vibration in turn produces pulses of air, which escape through the mouth (and sometimes also the nose). These pulses are actually small variations in the air pressure, due to the wavelike motion of the air molecules.

The sounds we produce can be described in terms of how fast the variations of the air pressure occur, which determines the **fundamental frequency** of the sounds and is perceived by the hearer as **pitch.** We can also describe the magnitude or **intensity** of the variations, which determines the **loudness** of the sound. The **quality** of the sound is determined by the shape of the vibrations, or **wave form,** which is determined by the shape of the vocal tract when the air is flowing through it.

An important tool in acoustic research is a machine called a **sound spectrograph.** When you speak into a microphone connected to this machine (or when a tape recording is plugged in), a "picture" is made of the speech signal. The patterns produced are called **spectrograms** or, more vividly, "visible speech." More recently these pictures have been referred to as **voiceprints.** A spectrogram of the words *heed, head, had,* and *who'd* is shown in Figure 12–1.

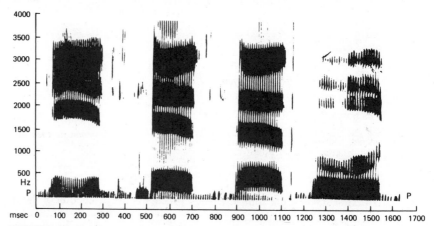

FIGURE 12–1 A spectrogram of the words *heed, head, had,* and *who'd,* as spoken in a British accent (speaker: Peter Ladefoged, February 16, 1973).

Time in milliseconds moves horizontally from left to right; vertically, the "graph" represents pitch (or, more technically, frequency). Notice that for each vowel there are a number of dark bands that differ in their placement according to their pitch. They represent the **overtones** produced by the shape of the vocal tract and are called the **formants** of the vowels. Because the tongue is in a different position for each vowel, the formant frequencies, or overtone pitches, differ for each vowel. It is the different frequencies of these formants that account for the different vowel qualities you hear. The pitch of the entire utterance (intonation contour) is shown by the "voicing bar" marked P on the spectrogram. When the striations are far apart, the vocal cords are vibrating slowly and the pitch is low; when the striations are close together, the vocal cords are vibrating rapidly and the pitch is high.

By studying spectrograms of all speech sounds and many different utterances, acoustic phoneticians have learned a great deal about the basic acoustic components that reflect the articulatory features of speech sounds.

Speech Perception

PEANUTS   **Charles Schulz**

Reprinted by permission of United Feature Syndicate, Inc.

If you hear a car backfire, you may wonder whether the sound represented a gunshot or a backfiring. Your **perception** of the particular acoustic signal and your knowledge of what creates different sounds result in your assigning some "meaning" to the sounds you heard. Similarly, when you hear the sounds represented by the phonetic transcription

$$[\text{j u a r ə̃ n ɪ d i j ə t}]$$

you assign the meaning "You are an idiot" to the sound signal. The acoustic signal, however, does not reach our ears in phonemic segment-sized chunks; it is a semicontinuous signal. In order for us to process it as speech, it must be segmented into phonemes, words, phrases, and sentences. Speech perception is a process by which we segment the continuous signal and, in so doing, may "mischunk" or misperceive the speaker's intended utterance. One reason for this error is illustrated in Figure 12–2, a spectrogram of the phrase *an idiot*.

The [n] can be distinguished from the vowels that surround it, but it is not possible to determine from the signal whether the nasal segment "belongs with" the preceding vowel or the following one. Without knowledge that *nidiot* is not a word in English or that *idiot* is, you could make the same mistake that Sally made in the "Peanuts" cartoon; the acoustic signal does not show word boundaries. The cartoon also shows that Sally knows that *a* is the phonological form of the indefinite article before a noun that begins with a consonant, and *an* the form before vowel-initial nouns, which is why she concluded that *ucklehead* is an English word. It is interesting that the ambiguity of the acoustic signal that confused Sally also caused an historical change. The original form of the word *apron* was *napron,* which was misperceived by hearers in the way Sally misperceived *idiot* and *knucklehead*.

The difficulties inherent in speech perception are compounded by the fact, noted in Chapter 2, that the speech signal for the "same" utterance varies greatly from speaker to speaker and from one time to the next by the same speaker. Nevertheless the brain is able to analyze these different signals, conclude that they are the same linguistically, segment the utterance into a phonetic/phonological string of words, "look up" the meaning of these words in the mental dictionary, analyze the linear string of words into a hierarchical syntactic structure, and, most of the time, end up with the intended meaning. All this work is done so quickly we are unaware that it is going on at all.

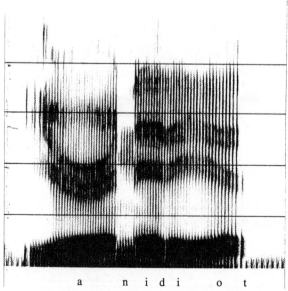

a   n   i   d   i   o   t

FIGURE 12–2 A spectrogram of the phrase *an idiot* as spoken by UCLA student Derek Collins.

Despite the variation between speakers and occurrences, there must be certain invariant features of speech sounds that permit us to perceive a /d/ or an /a/ produced by one speaker as identical **phonologically** with a /d/ and /a/ produced by another. The relations between the formants of the vowels of one speaker are similar to those of another speaker of the same language, even though the absolute frequencies may differ. When a stop consonant is produced, the signal is interrupted slightly, and the frequency of the "explosion" that occurs at the release of the articulators in producing stop consonants differs from one consonant to another. The transitions between consonants and vowels provide important information as to the identity of the consonants. After voiceless consonants, the onset of vowel formants starts at higher frequencies than after voiced consonants. Different places of articulation influence the starting frequencies of formant onsets. There are many such acoustic cues that, together with our knowledge of the language we are listening to, permit us to perform a "phonetic analysis" on the incoming acoustic signal. Confusions may also be disambiguated by lexical, syntactic, and semantic cues, which will be discussed below.

Speech communication often occurs in a noisy environment, but we can still pick out of the sound signal those aspects that pertain to speech. We are thus able to ignore large parts of the acoustic signal in the process of speech perception, which has led to the view that the human auditory system—perhaps in the course of evolution—has developed a special ability to detect and process speech cues.

Understanding Sentences

. . . To understand an utterance we must, in some fashion, retrieve information about the words in that utterance, discover the structural relationship and semantic properties of those words, and interpret these in the light of the various pragmatic and discourse constraints operating at the time. Further, all of this takes place at a remarkably rapid pace. . . .
David Swinney[1]

Analyzing the speech signal in speech perception is a necessary but not sufficient step in understanding a sentence or utterance. Suppose you heard someone say:

A sniggle blick is procking a slar.

and were able to perceive the sounds as

/ə snɪgəl blɪk ɪz prakɪŋ ə slar/

You would still be unable to assign a meaning to the sounds, because the meaning of a sentence depends on the meanings of its words, and the only English lexical items in this string are the morphemes *a, is,* and *-ing.* The sentence lacks any English content words.

---

[1]David A. Swinney. 1982. Chapter 8 in *Perspectives on Mental Representation*. J. Mehler, E. C. T. Walker, and M. Garrett, eds. Lawrence Erlbaum Associates. Hillsdale, N.J.

You can only know that the sentence has no meaning by attempting a **lexical lookup** of the phonological strings you construct; finding no entries for *sniggle, blick, prock,* or *slar* in your mental dictionary tells you that the sentence is composed of nonsense strings.

If instead you heard someone say *The cat chased the rat,* through a lexical lookup process you would conclude that an event concerning a cat, a rat, and the activity of chasing had occurred. Who chased whom is determined by syntactic processing. That is, processing speech to get at the meaning of what is said requires syntactic analysis as well as knowledge of lexical semantics.

Stress and intonation provide some cues to syntactic structure. We know, for example, from Chapter 3, that the different meanings of the sentences *He lives in the white house* and *He lives in the White House* can be signaled by differences in their stress patterns. Relative loudness, pitch, and duration of syllables thus provide important information in the comprehension process.

Experimental Studies

I have experimented and experimented until now I know that [water] never does run uphill, except in the dark. I know it does in the dark, because the pool never goes dry; which it would, of course, if the water didn't come back in the night. It is best to prove things by experiment; then you know; whereas if you depend on guessing and supposing and conjecturing, you will never get educated.

Mark Twain, *Eve's Diary*

In this laboratory the only one who is always right is the cat.

Motto in laboratory of Arturo Rosenblueth

The psychological stages and processes that a listener goes through in comprehending the meaning of an utterance are complex. Psycholinguists have found that speech perception and comprehension involves **top down (deductive** or **predictive)** processing as well as **bottom up (inductive)** processing. In other words, in speech understanding, we use stored semantic, lexical, and syntactic information as well as the sensory information in the signal itself. Evidence is provided by a number of experiments. For example, subjects make fewer errors identifying words when the words occur in sentences than when they are presented in isolation. This finding is true even when the stimuli are presented in the presence of noise. They also do better if the words occur in grammatical meaningful sentences as opposed to grammatical anomalous sentences; identification of words in ungrammatical sentences produces the most errors. This outcome supports the idea that lexical and syntactic information are used in comprehension.

Top down processing is also shown by the fact that when subjects hear recorded sentences in which some part of the signal is removed and a cough substituted, they "hear" the sentence without a missing phoneme and, in fact, are unable to say which phonemic segment the cough replaced. Context plays a major role in determining what sounds the subjects replace. Thus, "[cough] eel" is heard as *wheel, heel, peel,* or *meal* depending on whether the sentence in which the distorted word occurs refers to an axle, shoe, orange, or food, respectively.

In a shadowing task (where subjects are asked to repeat as rapidly as possible what they hear), they "correct" speech errors or mispronunciations unconsciously. Even when they are told the speech they are to shadow includes errors and they should repeat the errors, they are unable to do so, again showing that speech perception does not occur solely by processing the incoming signal.

Another technique used in psycholinguistic experiments involves **response** or **reaction time** measurements. The assumption is that complex tasks require more processing, hence more time, than simpler ones. Using such measurements, it has been found that ambiguous sentences take longer to process than nonambiguous sentences. It appears that even if subjects are not aware of the multiple meanings of an ambiguous sentence, both meanings are evoked and interfere with each other.

Reaction time is also measured in experiments using a **priming** technique. It has been found, for example, that if subjects hear a word such as *nurse*—the prime—their response to *doctor* will be faster than to a semantically unrelated word such as *flower*. This speed may be due to the fact that semantically related words are located in the same part of the lexicon; once the "path" to that section has been taken, it is easier to travel that way a second time. It may also be due to the fact that other words are "triggered" when we "look up" a semantically related word.

In priming experiments, the response required may be a **lexical decision.** That is, the subject is presented with a prime and then another stimulus, which may be a word or a nonsense string, and must respond by pressing a button if the second stimulus is an actual word. An interesting finding in such experiments is that a lexically ambiguous word can be primed by a word referring to either meaning, even if the context of the ambiguous word disambiguates it. For example, either *harbor* or *wine* will prime the word *port* (result in faster response time) in the sentence

> The ship is in port.

This finding shows that as we listen to speech, all the meanings represented by a phonological form in our mental lexicon will be "triggered."

The frequency of words—how often they are used in ordinary speech or writing—also affects response time, showing that comprehension involves both linguistic and nonlinguistic factors.

The ability to comprehend what is said to us is a complex psychological process involving the internal grammar, motivation, frequency factors, memory, and both linguistic and nonlinguistic context.

Speech Production

And has the reader never asked himself what kind of a mental fact is his intention of saying a thing before he has said it? . . . How much of it consists of definite sensorial images, either

of words or of things? Hardly anything! Linger, and the words and things come to mind. . . . The intention welcomes them.
William James, 1890

The speech chain starts with a speaker who, through some complicated set of neuromuscular processes, produces an acoustic signal that represents a thought, idea, or "message" to be conveyed to a listener, who must then **decode** the signal to arrive at a similar message. It is more difficult to devise experiments that provide information on how the speaker proceeds than to do so from the listener's side of the process. The best information has come from observing and analyzing spontaneous speech.

Planning Units We might suppose that the thoughts of the speaker are simply "translated" into words one after the other through a semantic mapping process. Grammatical morphemes would be added as demanded by the syntactic rules of the language. The phonetic representation of each word in turn would then be mapped onto the neuromuscular commands to the articulators to produce the acoustic signal representing it.

We know, however, that this supposition is not a true picture of speech production. Although when we speak, the sounds we produce and the words we use are linearly ordered, speech errors show that the prearticulation stages involve units larger than the single phonemic segment or even the word. Phrases and even whole sentences are constructed prior to the production of a single sound. Errors show that features, segments, and words can be **anticipated,** that is, produced earlier than intended, or reversed (as in typical Spoonerisms), so the later words or phrases in which they occur must already be conceptualized. This point is illustrated in the following examples. (The intended utterance is to the left of the arrow; the actual utterance including the error is to the right of the arrow.)

1. The *h*iring of minority *f*aculty. → The *f*iring of minority faculty.
   (The intended *h* is replaced by the *f* of *faculty,* which occurs later in the intended utterance.)
2. *a*d h*o*c → *o*dd h*a*ck
   (The vowels /æ/ of the first word and /a/ of the second are exchanged or reversed.)
3. *b*ig and *f*at → *p*ig and *v*at
   (The values of a single feature are switched: [+voiced] becomes [−voiced] in *big* and [−voiced] becomes [+voiced] in *fat*.)
4. There are many ministers in our church. → There are many churches in our minister.
   (The stem morphemes *minister* and *church* are exchanged; the grammatical plural morpheme remains in its intended place in the phrase structure.)
5. Seymour sliced the salami with a knife. → Seymour sliced a knife with the salami.
   (The entire noun phrases—article + noun—were exchanged.)

In these errors, the intonation contour (primary stressed syllables and variations in pitch) remained the same as in the intended utterances, even when the words were disordered. In the intended utterance of 5, the highest pitch would be on *knife*. In the disordered sentence the highest pitch occurred on the second syllable of *salami*. The pitch rise and increased loudness, determined by the syntactic structure of the sentence, must be constructed prior to articulation and be independent of the individual words. Thus syntactic structures also are units in linguistic performance.

Such errors show that speech production involves different kinds of units—features, segments, morphemes, words, phrases, the very units that exist in the grammar. They also show that when we speak, smaller units are structured into larger ones that are stored in a kind of "buffer" memory before segments or features or words are inadvertently disordered. This storage must occur prior to the articulatory stage. Thus, we do not select one word from our mental dictionary and say it, then select another word and say it. We organize an entire phrase and in many cases an entire sentence.

Lexical Selection

. . . Humpty Dumpty's theory, of two meanings packed into one word like a portmanteau, seems to me the right explanation for all. For instance, take the two words "fuming" and "furious." Make up your mind that you will say both words but leave it unsettled which you will say first. Now open your mouth and speak. If . . . you have that rarest of gifts, a perfectly balanced mind, you will say "frumious."

Lewis Carroll, Preface to *The Hunting of the Snark*

In Chapter 6, word substitution errors were used to illustrate the semantic properties of words. Such substitutions are seldom random; they show that in speaking, in our attempt to express our thoughts through words in the lexicon, we may make an incorrect lexical selection based on partial similarity or relatedness of meanings.

Blends, in which we produce part of one word and part of another, further illustrate the lexical selection process in speech production; we may select two or more words to express our thoughts and instead of deciding between them, produce them as "portmanteaus," as Humpty Dumpty calls them. Such blends are illustrated in the following errors:

1. splinters/blisters   →   splisters
2. edited/annotated   →   editated
3. a swinging/hip chick   →   a swip chick
4. frown/scowl   →   frowl

Application and Misapplication of Rules

I thought . . . four rules would be enough, provided that I made a firm and constant resolution not to fail even once in the observance of them.

René Descartes (1596–1650)

Spontaneous errors show that the rules of morphology and syntax, discussed in earlier chapters as part of competence, may also be applied (or misapplied) when we speak. It is hard to see this process in normal error-free speech, but when someone says *groupment* instead of *grouping, ambigual* instead of *ambiguous,* or *bloodent* instead of *bloody,* it shows that regular rules are applied to morphemes to form possible but nonexistent words.

Inflectional rules also surface. The UCLA professor who said *We swimmed in the pool knows that the past tense of *swim* is *swam* but mistakenly applied the regular rule to an irregular form.

Morphophonemic rules also appear to be performance rules as well as rules of competence. Consider the *a/an* alternation rule in English. Errors such as *an istem* for the intended *a system* or *a burly bird* for the intended *an early bird* show that when segmental disordering changes a noun beginning with a consonant to a noun beginning with a vowel, or vice versa, the indefinite article is also changed so that it conforms to the grammatical rule.

Such utterances also reveal that in speech production, internal "editing" or monitoring attempts to prevent errors. When an error slips by the editor, such as the disordering of phonemes, the editor prevents a compounding of errors. Thus, when the /b/ of "bird" was anticipated and added to the beginning of "early" the result was not *an burly bird. The editor applied (or reapplied) the *a/an* rule to produce *a burly bird.*

An examination of such data also tells us something about the stages in the production of an utterance. Disordering of phonemes must occur before the indefinite article is given its phonological form or the morphological rule must reapply after the initial error has occurred. An error such as *bin beg* for the intended *Big Ben* shows that phonemes are disordered before phonetic allophones are determined. That is, the intended *Big Ben* phonetically is [bɪg bɛ̃n] with an oral [ɪ] before the [g] and a nasal [ɛ̃] before the [n]. In the utterance that was produced, however, the [ɪ̃] is nasalized because it now occurs before the disordered [n], whereas the [ɛ] is oral before the disordered [g]. If the disordering occurred after the phonemes had been replaced by phonetic allophones, the result would have been the phonetic utterance [bɪn bɛ̃g].

Nonlinguistic Influences   The discussion on speech comprehension suggested that nonlinguistic factors are involved in and sometimes interfere with linguistic processing. They also affect speech production. The individual who said *He made hairlines* instead of *He made headlines* was referring to a barber. The fact that the two compound nouns both start with the same sound, are composed of two syllables, have the same stress pattern, and contain the identical second morphemes undoubtedly played a role in producing the error; but the relationship between hairlines and barbers may also have been a contributing factor.

Other errors show that thoughts unrelated structurally to the intended utterance may have an influence on what is said. One speaker said "I've never heard of classes *on April 9*" instead of the intended *on Good Friday.* Good Friday fell on April 9 that year. The two phrases are not similar phonologically or morphologically; yet the nonlinguistic association seems to have influenced what was said. This influence is a further example of the distinction between linguistic competence and performance.

Modeling the Production Process

When we say that we have succeeded in understanding a group of natural processes, we invariably mean that a constructive theory or model has been found which covers the processes in question.

Albert Einstein

Speech production is as complex as speech comprehension. The two processes are not mirror images of each other; each aspect of linguistic performance depends on its own set of psychological mechanisms. The grammar connects the two sides of the communication chain because it underlies both production and comprehension. Ignoring for simplicity's sake the role of nonlinguistic interference, stages in the speech production process can be outlined as follows:

Stages in the Production of an Utterance

(1) Thought generated.

"Big Ben"
"London"

(2) Syntactic structure planned.
Grammatical morphemes inserted.

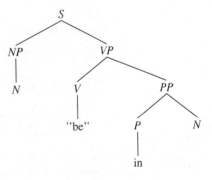

(3) Sentence stress and intonation assigned on basis of syntactic structure.

Sentence primary stress assigned to stressed syllable on final noun.

(4) Lexical selection based on ideation in stage 1.	*Big Ben London* /bɪg bɛn/ /lʌndʌn/
(5) Disordering of phonemes during or after lexical selection.	/bɪn bɛg/
(6) Application of morphophonemic rules.	"be" → /ɪz/
(7) Nasalization of vowel before nasal.	[bĩn bɛg] [ɪz] [ĩn] [lʌ̃ndʌ̃n]
(8) Neuromuscular commands to articulators to produce sounds corresponding to phonetic string.	*Bin Beg is in London.*

This "model" is of course a highly oversimplified version of the speech production process. It does, however, give some idea of the complexity involved.

Computer Processing of Language

The fact is, that civilization requires slaves. The Greeks were quite right there. Unless there are slaves to do the ugly, horrible, uninteresting work, culture and contemplation become almost impossible. Human slavery is wrong, insecure, and demoralizing. On mechanical slavery, on the slavery of the machine, the future of the world depends.
Oscar Wilde

Throughout history, only human beings have had the capability to process language. This ability is now being shared with the computer. **Computational linguistics** is the subfield of linguistics and computer science that is concerned with computer processing of human language, which includes automatic machine translation of one language into another, the analysis of texts, the use of human language in person–computer interactions, artificial intelligence, and computer modeling of human linguistic competence and performance.

Machine Translation

Egad, I think the interpreter is the hardest to be understood of the two!
R. B. Sheridan, *The Critic*

. . . There exist extremely simple sentences in English—and . . . for any other natural language—which would be uniquely . . . and unambiguously translated into any other language by anyone with a sufficient knowledge of the two languages involved, though I know of no program that would enable a machine to come up with this unique rendering. . . .
Yeshua Bar-Hillel

The first use of computers for natural language processing began in the 1940s with the attempt to develop **Automatic Machine Translation.** During World War II, United States scientists without the assistance of computers deciphered coded Japanese military communications and proved their skill in coping with difficult language problems. The idea of using deciphering techniques to translate from one language into another was expressed in a letter written to Norbert Wiener by Warren Weaver, a pioneer in the field of computational linguistics: ''When I look at any article in Russian, I say: 'This is really written in English, but it has been coded in some strange symbols. I will now proceed to decode.' ''[2]

The aim in automatic translation is to ''feed'' into the computer a written passage in the **source language** (the input) and to receive a grammatical passage of equivalent meaning in the **target language** (the output). In the early days of machine translation, it was believed that this task could be accomplished by entering into the memory of a computer a dictionary of a source language and a dictionary with the corresponding morphemes and words of a target language. The ''translation'' decoding program consisted of ''matching'' the morphemes of the input sentence with those of the target language. Unfortunately, what often happened was a process called by early machine translators ''language in, garbage out.''

Translation is more than word-for-word replacement. Often there is no equivalent word in the target language, and the order of words may differ, as in translating from a Subject-Verb-Object (SVO) language like English to a Subject-Object-Verb (SOV) language like Japanese. There is also difficulty in translating idioms, metaphors, jargon, and so on.

These problems are dealt with by human translators because they know the grammars of the two languages and draw on general knowledge of the subject matter and the world to arrive at the intended meaning. Machine translation is often impeded by lexical and syntactic ambiguities, structural disparities between the two languages, morphological complexities, and other cross-linguistic differences. It is often difficult to get good translations even when humans do the translating, as is illustrated by some of the ''garbage'' printed on signs in non-English-speaking countries as ''aids'' to tourists:

> Utmost of chicken with smashed pot (restaurant in Greece)
> Nervous meatballs (restaurant in Bulgaria)
> The nuns harbor all diseases and have no respect for religion (Swiss
>   nunnery hospital)
> All the water has been passed by the manager (German hotel)
> Certified midwife: entrance sideways (Jerusalem)

Such ''translations'' represent the difficulties of just finding the ''equivalent'' words; but word choice is a minor problem in automatic translation. The syntactic problems are more complex.

---

[2]W. N. Locke and A. D. Boothe, eds. 1955. *Machine Translation of Languages*. Wiley. New York.

The greater recognition of the role of syntax and the application of linguistic principles over the past 40 years have made it possible to use computers to translate "simple" texts grammatically and accurately between well-studied languages such as English and Russian. More complex texts require human intervention if the translation is to be grammatical and semantically faithful. The use of computers to aid the human translator can improve efficiency by a factor of ten or more, but the day when travelers can whip out a "pocket translator," hold it up to the mouth of a native speaker, and receive a translation in their own language is as yet beyond the horizon.

Text Processing

[The professor had written] all the words of their language in their several moods, tenses and declensions [on tiny blocks of wood, and had] emptied the whole vocabulary into his frame, and made the strictest computation of the general proportion there is in books between the numbers of particles, nouns, and verbs, and other parts of speech.

Jonathan Swift, *Gulliver's Travels*

Jonathan Swift prophesied one way computers would be put to work in linguistics— in the statistical analysis of language. Computers can be programmed to reveal such properties of language as the distribution of sounds, allowable word orders, permitted combinations of morphemes, relative frequencies of words and morphemes (that is, their "general proportion"), and so on.

Such analyses can be conducted on existing texts (such as the works of Shakespeare or the Bible) or on a collection of utterances gathered from spoken or written sources, called a **corpus.** One such corpus, compiled at Brown University, consists of over one million words from fifteen sources of written American English, including passages from daily newspapers, magazines, and literary material.[3] Because this corpus is available in computer-readable form, many scholars are able to use it in their research.

A corpus of *spoken* American English, similar in size to the Brown corpus, was also collected.[4] A computer analysis of this corpus was conducted and the result was compared with the Brown corpus, which provided a contrast between written and spoken American English. Not surprisingly, the pronoun *I* occurs ten times more frequently in the spoken corpus. Profane and taboo words are, as expected, more frequent in spoken language; *shit* occurs 128 times in the spoken corpus, but only four times in the written one. All of the prepositions except *to* occur more frequently in written than in spoken English, suggesting that different syntactic structures are used in written English than in spoken English.

A computer can also be used to produce a **concordance** of a literary text, which gives the frequency of every word in a text and the line and page number of

---

[3]H. Kučera and W. N. Francis. 1967. *Computational Analysis of Present-Day American English.* Brown University Press. Providence.
[4]H. Dahl. 1979. *Word Frequencies of Spoken American English.* Verbatim. Essex, CT.

each occurrence. Such analyses, once carried out painstakingly over many years, were only produced for the most eminent of texts (such as the Bible). Now a concordance can be accomplished in a short time on any text that has been entered into a computer. The use of concordances on *The Federalist Papers* helped ascribe the authorship of a disputed paper to James Madison rather than to Alexander Hamilton, by comparing the concordance of the paper in question with those of known works by the two writers.

A concordance of *sounds* by computer may reveal patterns in poetry that would be nearly impossible for a human to detect. Such an analysis on the *Iliad* showed that many of the lines with an unusual number of etas (/i/) related to youth and lovemaking; the line with the most alphas (/a/) was interpreted as being an imitation of stamping feet.

Poetic and prosaic features such as assonance, alliteration, meter, and rhythm have always been studied by literary scholars. Today, computers can do the tedious mechanical work of such analyses, leaving the human more time to contemplate new ideas.

Computer Communication

The first generations of computers had received their inputs through glorified typewriter key-boards, and had replied through high-speed printers and visual displays. Hal could do this when necessary, but most of his communication with his shipmates was by means of the spoken word. Poole and Bowman could talk to Hal as if he were a human being, and he would reply in the perfect idiomatic English he had learned during the fleeting weeks of his electronic childhood.

Arthur C. Clarke, 2001, A Space Odyssey

The ideal computer is multilingual; it should "speak" computer languages such as FORTRAN and human languages such as English. For many purposes it would be helpful if we could communicate with computers as we communicate with other humans, through our native language; but the computers portrayed in films and on television as capable of speaking and understanding human language do not yet exist.

Computers are at present severely limited in their ability to comprehend and produce spoken language, and programming them to do so is one of the most difficult and challenging goals of computational linguistics. Properly programmed, a computer can "understand" language fragments with vocabularies of 100 to 1000 words in an extremely narrow context (simple syntax and a limited semantic field). (The vocabulary can be larger for written language.) Computers can produce synthetic speech that imitates the human voice fairly well, but humans must program them to do it and tell them what to say.

Just as human speech production and comprehension differ in the psychological mechanisms involved (although they access the same mental grammar), comprehension and production of speech by computers require entirely different programs. In some cases the attempt is to model the human processor; in others, the goal is to get the computer to speak and understand, rather than to shed light on human performance.

Computer comprehension consists of **speech recognition,** the perception of sounds and words, and **speech understanding,** the interpretation of the words recognized. Some comprehension programs bypass speech recognition by processing written text. Visual scanners are able to "read" printed texts.

Speech production consists of **language generation**—deciding what to say—and **speech synthesis,** the actual creation of speech sounds. As in attempts at computer comprehension, different research groups concentrate on one aspect or another of speech production, and with different purposes.

Talking Machines (Speech Synthesis)

Machines which, with more or less success, imitate human speech, are the most difficult to construct, so many are the agencies engaged in uttering even a single word—so many are the inflections and variations of tone and articulation, that the mechanician finds his ingenuity taxed to the utmost to imitate them.

Scientific American, January 14, 1871

DOONESBURY   **Garry Trudeau**

Early efforts toward building "talking machines" were more concerned with machines that could produce sounds that imitated human speech than with machines that could figure out what to say. In 1779, Christian Gottlieb Kratzenstein won a prize for building such a machine ("an instrument constructed like the *vox humana* pipes of an organ which . . . accurately express the sounds of the vowels") and for answering a question posed by the Imperial Academy of St. Petersburg: "What is the nature and character of the sounds of the vowels *a, e, i, o, u* [which make them] different from one another?" Kratzenstein constructed a set of "acoustic resonators" similar to the shapes of the mouth when these vowels are articulated and set them resonating by a vibrating reed that produced pulses of air similar to those coming from the lungs through the vibrating vocal cords.

Twelve years later, Wolfgang von Kempelen of Vienna constructed a more elaborate machine with bellows to produce a stream of air such as is produced by the lungs, and with other mechanical devices to "simulate" the different parts of the vocal tract. Von Kempelen's machine so impressed the young Alexander Graham Bell, who saw a replica of the machine in Edinburgh in 1850, that he, together with his brother Melville, attempted to construct a "talking head," making a cast from a human skull. They used various materials to form the velum, palate, teeth, lips, tongue, cheeks, and so on, and installed a metal larynx with vocal cords made by stretching a slotted piece of rubber. They used a keyboard control system to manipulate all the parts with an intricate set of levers. This ingenious machine produced vowel sounds and some nasal sounds and even a few short combinations of sounds.

With the advances in the acoustic theory of speech production and the technological developments in electronics, machine production of speech sounds has made great progress. We no longer have to build actual physical models of the speech-producing mechanism; we can now imitate the process by producing the physical signals electronically.

Research on speech has shown that all speech sounds can be reduced to a small number of acoustic components. One way to produce artificial or **synthetic** speech is to mix these important parts together in the proper proportions, depending on the speech sounds to be imitated. It is rather like following a recipe for making soup, which might read: "Take two quarts of water, add one onion, three carrots, a potato, a teaspoon of salt, a pinch of pepper, and stir it all together."

This method of producing synthetic speech would include a "recipe" that might read:

1. Start with a tone at the same frequency as vibrating vocal cords (higher if a woman's or child's voice is being synthesized, lower for a man's).
2. Add overtones corresponding to the formants required for a particular vowel quality.
3. Add hissing or buzzing for fricatives.
4. Add nasal resonances for any nasal sounds.
5. Temporarily cut off sound to produce stops and affricates.
6. and so on . . .

All these "ingredients" are blended together electronically, using computers to produce highly intelligible, more or less natural-sounding speech.

Most synthetic speech still has a machinelike quality or "accent," due to small inaccuracies in simulation and because suprasegmental factors such as changing intonation and stress patterns are not yet fully understood. Still, speech synthesizers today are no harder to understand than a person speaking with a slight "accent."

Of course, the machine used to produce synthetic speech does not "know" what it is saying. It may be reading a text, a useful function for persons unable to read for some reason, but this employs no linguistic knowledge of syntax or semantics. Speech synthesis in the future can be highly beneficial to mute patients with laryngectomies, advanced multiple sclerosis, or other medical conditions that prevent normal speech production.

Those concerned with automatic *language generation* attempt to give the computer bits of knowledge in computer-digestible form (for example, the day's baseball scores), and then program the computer to state that knowledge in fluent, grammatically and semantically correct human language (for example, a report of the baseball scores on the news). This program requires adherence to the rules of syntax and semantics, as well as morphology and phonetics. In some sense the machine "knows" what it is saying, because if you changed the bits of knowledge fed to it, the statement of that knowledge would change too, providing the computer were correctly programmed.

Machines for Understanding Speech

By permission of Johnny Hart and North America Syndicate, Inc.

A computer understands a subset of English if it accepts input sentences which are members of this subset, and answers questions based on information contained in the input.
Daniel Bobrow

Understanding is a relative concept. We often complain that our parents or mates or children "don't understand" what we say, and we are probably at least partially right: 100 percent understanding is an ideal goal toward which we strive in communication, including communication with machines.

Machine understanding of spoken language is generally programmed as a two-stage process: *speech recognition,* or the recognition of sounds and/or words; and *speech understanding,* the comprehension of those words as they occur in phrases and sentences. As stated above, in machine understanding these two stages are more or less independent of each other, depending on how the system is designed. In human processing of language these two stages blend together in a continual interplay of recognizing individual words and the meaning they convey, and apprehending the meaning and from that figuring out the words actually spoken.

Speech Recognition   Speech recognition is far more difficult than speech synthesis. It is comparable to trying to transcribe a spectrogram with only phonetic knowledge of the language spoken. (It is a difficult task even when you know in advance what was said.) As we discussed in the section on human speech perception, the speech signal is not physically divided into discrete sounds. Human ability to "segment" the signal arises from knowledge of the grammar, which tells us how to pair certain sounds with certain meanings, what sounds or words may be "deleted" or "pushed together," and when two different speech signals are linguistically "the same" and when two similar signals are linguistically "different." The difficulty of programming a computer to have and use such linguistic knowledge in recognizing speech is enormous.

There are two kinds of speech recognizers. One recognizes speech at the word level, the other at the phoneme level. A word-level recognizer keeps the acoustic patterns of its vocabulary in its "memory." When it "hears" something, it matches the acoustic pattern of the input signal with all of its prestored acoustic patterns. The best match is chosen as the word or words recognized.

A phoneme-level recognizer operates in a similar manner, prestoring acoustic patterns of the sounds of the language and attempting to match them to incoming sound patterns. Phoneme-level recognition is more error-prone than word-level recognition because individual sounds are more confusable than individual words. That is, the machine is more likely to confuse the sound [b] with the sound [d] than it is to confuse the word *boy* with the word *dog;* words contain more redundant information than sounds, which helps to resolve confusions and ambiguities. In fact, human speech perception functions similarly, as was pointed out in discussing some of the psycholinguistic experiments on human processing.

To ease the difficulties of recognition in some speech recognizer systems, the user must insert a short pause of about 1/3 second after each word spoken. (The pause between words must exceed the pause that occurs within words during stop and affricate articulation.) This pause shifts the burden of word boundary detection to the human speaker and makes the machine recognition process more accurate, but it is inconvenient to speak in this manner and reveals that the computer is not capable of "perceiving" in the way a human perceives.

Other speech recognizers accept continuously spoken speech, providing the speaker articulates carefully and clearly. In this case the speaker may not apply certain optional rules such as vowel reduction to schwa, vowel and/or consonant deletion, consonant assimilation at word boundaries, and so on; so *did you* is pronounced [dɪd ju], not [dɪjə]. Natural, rapidly spoken continuous speech—the kind that humans usually use—is not yet machine recognizable with a useful degree of accuracy.

Parsing In natural speech comprehension, because the semantics of an utterance is at least partially dependent on the syntax, humans must assign structure to utterances. Machines must also do so, and much computational linguistics research has been devoted to the development of **parsers,** which are computer programs that assign phrase structure to strings of words. Parsers may use a phrase structure grammar and lexicon similar to those discussed in Chapter 5 to assign structure.

B.C.   **Johnny Hart**

By permission of Johnny Hart and North America Syndicate, Inc.

Another type of parser uses **transition networks,** which represent the grammar as a complex of **nodes** (circles) and **arcs** (arrows). A network that is the equivalent of the phrase structure rule S → NP VP may be illustrated as:

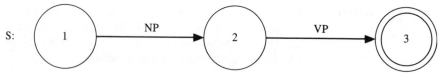

Transition Network for S → NP VP

The nodes are numbered to distinguish them; the double circle is the "final" node.

The parser would start at node 1, examine an input string of words, and if the string began with a noun phrase, "move" to node 2. (If it did not find a noun phrase, it would decide that the input string was not a sentence, unless there were other S networks in the grammar to try.) The parser would then look for a verb phrase, and if one were found the VP arc could be traversed to node 3. Because node 3 is a final node, the parser would indicate that the input string was a sentence consisting of a noun phrase and a verb phrase. The program would, of course, also have to specify what string of words constitutes an NP, VP, and so on.

Augmented Transition Networks (ATN) are transition networks in which each arrow not only indicates a syntactic category, but may carry other information essential to accurate parsing as well. For example, an ATN extension to the above example might carry a condition on the VP arc to ensure "agreement," as shown below:

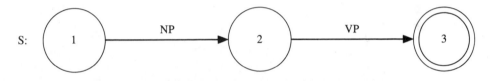

S:

Condition: If subject is third person
singular, Verb has an −s
ending.

Augmented Transition Network for S → NP VP

Semantic Processing Once a sentence is parsed, the machine can try to find the meaning or semantic representation. This task requires a dictionary with the meaning of each word, and rules for combining meanings, as discussed in Chapter 6. The question of how to represent meaning is one that has been debated for thousands of years, and it continues to engender much research in linguistics, philosophy, psychology, and computer science.

One approach common to several semantic processing methods first locates the verb of the sentence—based on the sentence parse—and then identifies its "arguments," that is, the logical subject, logical object, any complements, and so on. Semantic representation based on mathematical logic might express the sentence *Zachary loves sushi* as

LOVE(ZACHARY, SUSHI)

where *LOVE* is a "two-place predicate" with arguments *ZACHARY* and *SUSHI*. A rule of semantic interpretation indicates that Zachary is the one loving, and sushi is the object loved.

Semantic networks are also used to represent meaning. They are similar to ATNs in appearance, consisting of nodes and arcs, but they function differently. *Zachary loves sushi* might be represented in either of two ways using semantic networks:

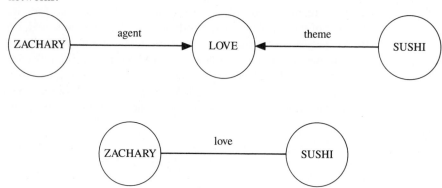

Both logical expressions and semantic networks are convenient for *machine* representation of meaning because they are easily programmed and because the meanings thus represented can be used linguistically. For example, if the computer is asked ''Who loves sushi?'' it can search through its ''knowledge base'' for a node labeled *love,* look to see if an arc labeled ''theme'' is connected to *sushi,* and if so, find the answer by looking for an arc labeled ''agent.''

Computer Models of Grammars

I am never content until I have constructed a . . . model of the subject I am studying. If I succeed in making one, I understand; otherwise I do not.

William Thomson (Lord Kelvin), *Molecular Dynamics and the Wave Theory of Light*

A theory has only the alternative of being right or wrong. A model has a third possibility: it may be right, but irrelevant.

Manfred Eigen, *The Physicist's Conception of Nature*

The grammars used by computers for parsing are not the same as the grammars linguists construct for human languages, which are models of linguistic competence; nor are they similar, for the most part, to models of linguistic performance. Computers are different than people, and they achieve similar ends differently. Just as an efficient flying machine is not a replica of any bird, efficient grammars for computers do not resemble human language grammars in every detail.

Computers are often used to model physical or biological systems, which allows researchers to study those systems safely and sometimes even cheaply. For example, the performance of a new aircraft can be simulated and the test pilot informed as to safe limits in advance of actual flight.

Computers can also be programmed to model the grammar of a language. An accurate grammar—one that is a true model of a speaker's mental grammar— should be able to generate *all* and *only* the sentences of the language. Failure to generate a grammatical sentence means a "bug" in the grammar, because the human mental grammar has the capacity to generate all possible grammatical sentences—an infinite set. In addition, if the grammar produces a string that speakers consider to be ungrammatical, that too indicates a defect in the grammar; although in actual speech performance we often produce ungrammatical strings—sentence fragments, slips of the tongue, word substitutions and blends, and so on—we will judge them to be ill-formed if we notice them. Our grammars cannot generate these strings.

One computer model of a grammar was developed by Joyce Friedman to test a generative grammar of English produced at U.C.L.A. in the late 1960s. This model was primarily concerned with syntax. Several projects in the 1970s attempted to model human memory and semantic processing ability; many valuable insights resulted from these projects, but no computer program has even approximated human linguistic performance abilities. It is just because human linguistic knowledge and behavior are so complex that we look to computers to help in testing theories of competence and performance for accuracy and completeness.

Language and Artificial Intelligence

Man is not a machine. . . . Although man most certainly processes information, he does not necessarily process it in the way computers do. Computers and men are not species of the same genus. . . . However much intelligence computers may attain, now or in the future, theirs must always be an intelligence alien to genuine human problems and concerns.

Joseph Weizenbaum

I propose to consider the question, "Can machines think?"

A. M. Turing, "The Imitation Game"

In answer to the above question, Turing proposed that if a machine could impersonate a human being, apart from physical attributes, under any conceivable cross-examination, then the machine was thinking. The "Turing test" includes a command of human language such that a conversation between the machine and the human would be indistinguishable from a conversation between two humans.

Similarly, a computer may be said to have **artificial intelligence (AI)** when it exhibits intelligence ordinarily associated with human behavior—reasoning, learning, use of language, and so on. There are opposing philosophical viewpoints and research strategies in the field of AI as to whether computers should be programmed to imitate the way the human mind works, or whether computers should simply simulate human behavior in any way practical, whether or not that is the way people think. In linguistic terms the debate boils down to whether the grammars that machines use to communicate should be actual grammars of the language, or any kind of grammatical system that gives acceptable results.

All computer activity results from programs, usually written by humans, but sometimes written by the computer itself. A question of interest is how an AI program differs from a non-AI program. It is not always easy to distinguish between them, but computer scientists generally agree that an AI program is designed to process **knowledge** and that such processing includes **inferencing**—the ability to derive additional knowledge from the original knowledge base.

Most computer programs designed for natural language communication exploit AI techniques. In speech understanding, for example, knowledge may be stored in the form of acoustic patterns for recognizing sounds, grammatical rules for determining sentence structure, and semantic rules for determining meaning.

Inferencing capabilities are required, for example, to fulfill the task of determining phonemes from variable sounds or allophones. The phoneme underlying an alveolar stop whose voicing in the input signal is indeterminate—a /t/ or a /d/—can be inferred; if the sound occurs at the beginning of a word whose other segments are [ɪ] and [g], it must be a /d/ since *tig* is not a word but *dig* is. Similarly, an intelligent parser, faced with the sequence *the /si/ was* . . . would choose the noun *sea* rather than the verb *see,* because the presence of the article reveals that a noun must follow.

Semantic inferencing has been widely researched since the 1960s. Suppose there is a knowledge base—information stored in the computer memory— that includes such facts as "Tweety is a canary," "a canary is a bird," "a bird is an animal," and "most birds can fly," which might be represented by the following semantic net:

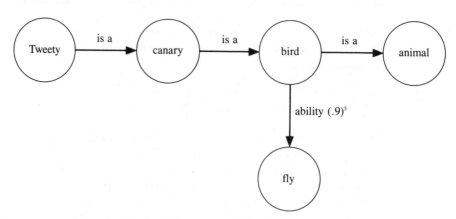

An intelligent computer program will use inferencing to deduce the further facts that Tweety is a bird, Tweety is an animal, and it is likely that Tweety can fly, none of which facts are directly represented in the original knowledge base.

If "intelligent computers" are ever developed, if artificial intelligence ever approaches human intelligence, it is clear that linguistics will play a major role in

---

[5]The .9 on the "ability" arc shows the degree to which this ability occurs; it quantifies the concept "most" because not all birds fly.

these developments, because human linguistic ability is the single most prolific manifestation of intelligence.

Summary

Psycholinguistics is concerned with linguistic **performance** or **processing,** the use of linguistic knowledge (competence) in speech production and perception.

To comprehend what is said, the hearer receives as input speech sounds in the form of a semicontinuous **acoustic signal.** Physically speech sounds may be specified by a number of acoustic properties: *fundamental frequency* or *pitch; intensity* or *loudness;* the shape of the sound wave; the presence or absence of *voicing vibrations;* the presence or absence of *hiss* or *fricative noise;* and vowel *formants,* the overtones that occur at different frequencies. Information on the acoustics of speech is obtained through the use of an instrument called a **sound spectrograph,** which produces a visual display of the physical acoustic signal called a **spectrogram.**

Because the acoustic signal does not consist of discrete phonemes or words, **speech perception** requires that we segment the continuous sound. In addition, we unconsciously and automatically perform a phonemic analysis, which is necessary because of the variations within and across speakers. The resulting phonological representation of the input signal can then be matched with a stored morpheme or word in our mental dictionary. This matching involves **lexical lookup** to find the meaning of the phonological string, similar to looking up a word in a dictionary to find out what it means.

Comprehension involves more than speech perception; understanding an utterance also requires our ability to **parse** the string into syntactic structures, which together with the lexical meanings are needed to arrive at the intended meaning of the speaker.

Psycholinguistic experimental studies show that comprehension involves **top down** processing—the use of grammatical and contextual information—as well as **bottom up** processing—the use of the sensory information of the signal. This fact explains why it is easier to identify sounds when they are presented in words, and words when they occur in sentences, than when these units are presented in isolation. Top down processing is also shown by the fact that listeners ''restore'' deleted sounds without being aware of the ''gap'' in the words, and fail to detect errors.

A number of experiments that use psycholinguistic **priming** and measure **response times** to different psycholinguistic tasks show that it takes longer to comprehend ambiguous utterances. Other experiments reveal that we **access** the mental grammar and also use nonlinguistic clues in comprehension.

The units and stages in **speech production** have been studied by analyzing spontaneously produced speech errors. **Anticipation** errors, in which a sound is produced earlier than in the intended utterance, and **Spoonerisms,** in which sounds or words are exchanged or reversed, show that we do not produce one sound or one word or even one phrase at a time but construct and store larger units with their syntactic structures specified prior to mapping these linguistic structures onto neuro-muscular commands to the articulators. In producing speech, we select words from the mental lexicon whose meanings partially express thoughts we wish to convey. Word **substitutions** and **blends** may occur, showing that words are connected to other words phonologically and semantically.

Computers, too, can process language. They can be programmed to translate from a **source language** into another **target language,** and they can aid scholars examining a literary text as well as a **corpus** of linguistic data.

Speech synthesis is accomplished by programming computers to imitate the human voice electronically. **Speech understanding** is a far more difficult task, because the physical speech signal alone is insufficient for understanding a spoken message; much linguistic knowledge is required. Machine comprehension of speech begins with **speech recognition,** which attempts to identify phonemes and words from the raw acoustic signal. To understand a string of recognized words, the machine must first **parse** the string (that is, determine its syntactic structure), and then analyze the string semantically, using **logical representations, semantic networks,** or other devices to represent meaning.

Computers may be programmed to model a grammar of a human language and thus rapidly and thoroughly test that grammar.

Artificial intelligence is the endowing of machines with humanlike intellectual capabilities. The use of language by machines to communicate with humans is one of the most important manifestations of artificial intelligence.

References

Barr, A., and E. A. Feigenbaum, eds. 1981. *The Handbook of Artificial Intelligence,* I. William Kaufmann. Los Altos, CA.

Carroll, D. W. 1986. *Psychology of Language.* Brooks/Cole. Monterey, CA.

Fodor, J. A., Garrett, M., and T. G. Bever. 1974. *The Psychology of Language.* McGraw-Hill. New York.

Foss, D. J., and E. T. Hakes. 1978. *Psycholinguistics: An Introduction to the Psychology of Language.* Prentice-Hall. Englewood Cliffs, NJ.

Fromkin, V. A., ed. 1973. *Speech Errors as Linguistic Evidence.* Mouton. The Hague.

Fromkin, V. A., ed. 1980. *Errors in Linguistic Performance.* Academic Press. New York.

Hockey, S. 1980. *A Guide to Computer Applications in the Humanities.* Duckworth. London.

Ladefoged, P. 1981. *Elements of Acoustic Phonetics.* 2d ed. University of Chicago Press. Chicago.

Lea, W. A. 1980. *Trends in Speech Recognition.* Prentice-Hall. Englewood Cliffs, NJ.

Slocum, J. 1985. ''A Survey of Machine Translation: Its History, Current Status, and Future Prospects.'' *Computational Linguistics* 11 (1).

Weizenbaum, J. 1976. *Computer Power and Human Reason.* W. H. Freeman. San Francisco.

Winograd, T. 1983. *Language as a Cognitive Process.* Addison-Wesley. Reading, Mass.

Witten, I. H. 1986. *Making Computers Talk.* Prentice-Hall. Englewood Cliffs, NJ.

Exercises

1. a. What aspects of linguistic performance (speech production and perception) are dependent on linguistic competence (the mental grammar)?
    b. What are the characteristics of linguistic performance that distinguish it from competence?

2. A simplified model of speech production is presented in the chapter, listing the possible stages a speaker goes through in the production of the utterance *Big Ben is in London*. Construct a similar model for the comprehension of this utterance (ignoring the speech error in the example in the text).

3. The use of spectrograms or ''voiceprints'' for speaker identification is based on the fact that no two speakers have exactly the same speech characteristics. List some of the differences you have noticed in the speech of several individuals. Can you think of any possible reasons why such differences exist?

4. What similarities and differences might there be between looking up a word in a dictionary and the process called *lexical lookup* in speech production and comprehension? Consider the reasons for the two processes.

5. Using a bilingual dictionary of any language, attempt to translate the following English sentences by looking up each word.

    The children will eat the fish.

    Send the professor a letter from your new school.

    The fish will be eaten by the children.

    Who is the person that is hugging that dog?

    The spirit is willing, but the flesh is weak.

    A. What difficulties did you encounter in carrying out this task? Briefly mention five of them:

        a.

        b.

        c.

        d.

        e.

B. If you can, have a person who knows the "target" language translate your translation back into English. What problems come to light? Are they related to any of the difficulties you mentioned in Part A?

6. Suppose you were given a manuscript of a play and were told that it is either by Christopher Marlowe or William Shakespeare (both born in 1564). Suppose further that this work, and all of the works of Marlowe and Shakespeare, were in a computer. Describe how you would use the computer to help determine the true authorship of the mysterious play.

7. Speech synthesis is useful because it allows computers to convey information without requiring the user to be sighted. Think of five other uses for speech synthesis in our society.

   a.

   b.

   c.

   d.

   e.

8. Some advantages of speech recognition are similar to those of speech synthesis. A computer that understands speech does not require a person to use hands or eyes in order to convey information to the computer. Think of five other possible uses for speech recognition in our society.

   a.

   b.

   c.

   d.

   e.

9. Here are some sentences along with a possible representation in predicate logic notation.
   i. Birds fly. FLY(BIRDS)
   ii. The student understands the question. UNDERSTANDS(THE STUDENT, THE QUESTION)
   iii. Penguins do not fly. NOT(FLY(PENGUINS))
   iv. The wind is in the willows. IN(THE WIND, THE WILLOWS)
   v. Kathy loves her cat. LOVES(KATHY, (POSS(KATHY, CAT)))

A. Based on the examples in the text, and those in part B of this exercise, give a possible semantic network representation for each of these examples.

i.

ii.

iii.

iv.

v.

B. Here are five more sentences and a possible semantic network representation for each. Give a representation of each of them using the predicate logic notation. (*Hint:* Review Chapter 6 for the meanings of *agent, theme, patient, goal,* and so on.)

i. Seals swim swiftly.

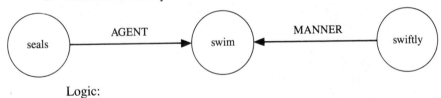

Logic:

ii. The student doesn't understand the question.

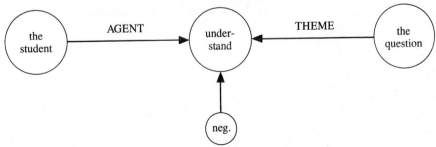

Logic:

iii. The pen is on the table.

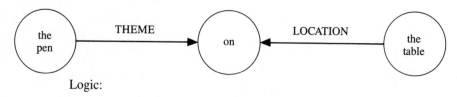

    Logic:

iv. My dog eats bones.

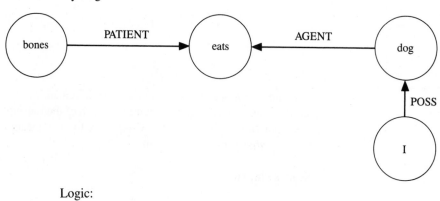

    Logic:

v. Emily gives money to charity. (*Hint: Give* is a three-place predicate.)

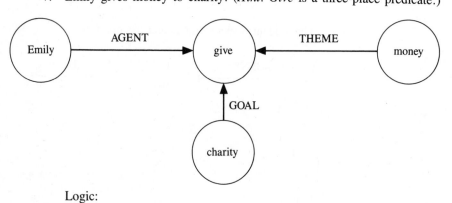

    Logic:

Index